She Sleeps Well

The Extraordinary Life and Murder of Dr. Helene Elise Hermine Knabe

by
Nicole R. Kobrowski, MS Adult Ed.

Unseenpress.com, Inc.
Westfield, Indiana

No part of this book may be reproduced, transmitted in any form or by any means, known or unknown, electronic or mechanical, including photocopying, recording, or by an information storage and retrieval system-except by a reviewer who may quote brief passages in a review to be printed in a magazine, newspaper or on the Web- without permission in writing from the publisher.

For information or copies contact:
Unseenpress.com, Inc.
PO Box 687
Westfield, IN 46074

Library of Congress Cataloging-in-Publication Data

Kobrowski, Nicole
     She Sleeps Well: The Extraordinary Life and Murder of Dr. Helene Elise Hermine Knabe/Nicole Kobrowski
       1. Physicians Indiana; 2. Feminism; 3. Women; 4. Indiana History; 5. Indiana Travel. I. Title

Library of Congress Control Number: 2016907487
Includes bibliographical references and index.
ISBN-13: 978-0-9774130-5-8
ISBN-0-9774130-5-5

Printed in the United States of America

Published by
Forgotten History
an imprint of Unseenpress.com, Inc.
PO Box 687
Westfield, IN 46074

Although the authors and publisher have made every effort to ensure the accuracy and completeness of information contained in this book, we assume no responsibility for errors, inaccuracies, omissions or any inconsistency herein. We also disclaim any liability in connection with the use of this book. The publishers and author do not condone, advise, or recommend visiting sites mentioned in this book without obtaining permission.

Any slights of people, places or organizations are unintentional.

The Unseenpress.com, Inc. website is
http://www.unseenpress.com/

Cover design by Unseenpress.com, Inc.
Text layout and design by Unseenpress.com, Inc.

TABLE OF CONTENTS

DEDICATION	7
ACKNOWLEDGEMENTS	9
FOREWARD	11
EARLY LIFE AND FAMILY	15
BECOMING A DOCTOR	33
IMMERSING HERSELF IN HER PROFESSION	49
MURDER INVESTIGATION	95
HEADS OF THE MURDER INVESTIGATION	147
THE DETECTIVES AND INVESTIGATORS	148
INDICTMENTS AND TRIAL	165
THE ACCUSED	168
THE PLAYERS	185
JUDGE AND STATE PROSECUTION	186

DR. CRAIG'S DEFENSE TEAM	**187**
WHERE ARE THEY NOW?	**225**
ABOUT THE AUTHOR	**247**
AUTHOR'S NOTES	**249**
CHAPTER NOTES	**261**
PHOTOGRAPH CREDITS	**289**
BIBLIOGRAPHY	**293**
INDEX	**329**

DEDICATION

This book is dedicated to:

- My husband, Michael, who is on this journey with me. He values a strong woman, which makes him my forever friend.
- My children, Brittany and Christopher, who have listened to me jabber about Dr. Knabe for years. I've tried to teach them that life is too short to be anything but strong and you have to be true to who and what you are.
- Anyone who has been marginalized or minimized for any reason. We are all human and should be celebrated as such.

Acknowledgements

I wish to thank the following people and organizations (in no particular order). Without their help, this book would not have been as thoroughly researched.

- Bruce Aldridge, for his amazing article in the Indianapolis Magazine, which was the single most informative article about Dr. Helene Knabe and was the springboard for my obsession.
- Dr. Charles Bonsett, for his fair research on Dr. Knabe and his willingness to answer questions.
- Michael Kobrowski, for being my partner in this crime (as so many others). Thank you for the scans, the time, the food, the water, the tea and putting up with my muse soundtracks.
- Jerzy Bukalowski, Darlowko/Darlowo: The kindness of Jerzy and his family in Poland was overwhelming and lovely. Często myślimy o Tobie, zwłaszcza gdy przyrządzamy bigos.
- Allison DePrey Singleton and Phyllis Miller Fleming: These genealogists/researchers were relentless in their search for my materials. Allison is a whiz at anything Marion County related and Phyllis is the go-to person for Shelby County. If they don't find it, it is either so lost no one will find it or it just doesn't exist. Each email I received from them was like a present.
- The staff of the Ruth Lilly Archives for their unfailing help and knowledge of their holdings and their help in where to find anything medical related.
- Lieutenant Roger L. Spurgeon, Indianapolis Marion County Police Department: Thank you for answering my questions so many years ago. You gave me some good avenues to pursue.
- William Rouse, thank you for answering my desperate case file questions. Although your answers were not what I hoped, I feel much better knowing I followed up through you.
- Patrick Pearsey, Indianapolis Marion County Police Department: Thank you for helping me track down pictures of the policemen involved in the case. It is always good to connect with people who enjoy history.
- The staff of the Indiana State Library, and especially Justin Davis, Librarian.

The staff never ceases to amaze me with their knowledge and the types of collections they have. Justin provided beautiful newspaper scans that cleared up a few picture mysteries.
- Kelley L. Walker Perry, who provided me additional information around Shelbyville and the trial. Thank you for answering all my questions, providing copies and resources.
- Dale Steenbarger for taking an interest and providing photocopies to me. The Shelbyville Republican article with the trial players was invaluable.
- Alan January, Michael Vetman and the staff of the Indiana State Archives for their exceptional archive of information. Quality pictures of the police would not have been possible without you.
- Madison County Historical Society (Anderson, Indiana): Thanks to all, especially Nancy Lawler, for providing such good information about Dr. Etta Charles.
- Frances Lee Watson, Clinical Professor of Law, Indiana University Robert H. McKinney School of Law: Thank you for the clarification on the trial. Your input and suggestions made this section so much better.
- Dr. Richard T. Miyamoto, Professor Emeritus, Department of Otolaryngology- Head and Neck Surgery: Thank you for your input on Dr. Knabe's wounds.
- Crown Hill Cemetery, especially Tom Davis and Nikki Schofield. Thank you for providing copies of burial and death records.
- The staff of the IUPUI library. Thank you for allowing Michael Kobrowski so many hours at your microfilm machine.
- Leah Orr, thank you for your starting point with your research on the Delaware Flats.
- The Fort Wayne Public Library: Its obituary collections are amazing.
- Stout's Shoes, especially Stephanie Stout: Thank you for allowing us to photograph your facility and answering my questions. (Your shoes are amazing and comfortable!) We're up for tours of any of your historic buildings anytime.
- My muses: A-ha, Asia, Brad Gillis, Jefferson Starship, Night Ranger, Peter Gregson, REO Speedwagon, and many others.

Foreward

An easy, delicious, tortuous obsession is what I've called this journey. Since I found the account of Dr. Knabe in an unsolved murder article in an Indianapolis Star article by Harold Sabin from 1968 I've been consumed with learning more about Dr. Helene Elise Hermine Knabe. Her death seems to overshadow her life because of its gruesome and mysterious nature, however her life is just as captivating. From her mysterious family life to her groundbreaking travels, education, research and work, Dr. Knabe conquered everything she set out to do until her death.

When I found out about her, I immediately looked through all the available newspaper accounts of the day. Luckily over the last 10 years or so, more resources have become available online. However back in the day, Michael and I had to sit at microfilm machines- one armed bandits, I called them for all the quarters we put into them- at the Indiana State Library and at IUPUI. One of the most useful was the tantalizing article was from Bruce Aldridge's "Scribbling Gourmand" in Indianapolis Magazine. Bruce was the head of the business section for the Indianapolis Marion County Public Library. His article about "Who Killed Dr. Knabe" was a treasure trove full of clues and information.

From the newspapers and J.P. Dunn's book, *Greater Indianapolis: The History, the Industries, the Institutions, and the People of a City of Homes, Volume 1 and 2,* I began piecing together Dr. Knabe's life and the trail she made from Rügenwaldermünde, Germany (now Darlowo/Darlowko, Poland due to the shifting of country lines after WWII). In 2007 I had the opportunity to travel to her hometown and research her life further. On first pass, much of what I was looking for seemed to be gone. The records of her area, including birth, baptism, death and burial records were supposed to be largely thrown into the Baltic Sea when the Russians advanced during WWII. Family members whose burial markers would have been in church plots were long since gone. In Germany and in many European countries, if one doesn't have a perpetual endowment for the plot, after so many years, a body is either exhumed or put into a place where old bones are kept ("bone house", Knochenhaus, in German). During WWII and the years after, many of the burial markers were used for drainage and for repairing roads.

Vital records for this area of Poland/Germany are hard to find. Some records are in the hands of private individuals and time has claimed others. Others have been lost to time. Still others are in the hands of private collectors. What is contained in this book is a mix of vital records, her own words and triangulation of information from a variety of other sources. In the Berlin archives and many others, we were told the records didn't exist, that they didn't have them, didn't know where the records were and so on.

    I will be the first to admit I am not the most patient person, as my husband can attest. I was disappointed and didn't quite believe the full story. While I don't believe anyone was intentionally leading me down the wrong path, I've been told nothing exists before and years later, I find exactly what I am looking for or someone provides me what I need. In this case, Ancestry.com was a great help. Years after my trip, I found baptism records for some of her family members. I believe down the line, I will find the rest of what I am looking for, but for the purposes of this book, many questions remain unanswered.

    More than anything, I wanted this book to exist. Not for me or the small monetary reward that comes with dedicating uncalculated hours, time and money and a self-published (i.e. designed, marketed and distributed by me) book. I wanted this book for Dr. Knabe. Without her extraordinary life, it wouldn't exist. Her life is a testament to her medical and teaching professions, feminism, basic human rights and equality, and her progressive outlook on life and overcoming adversity, which is something we can all relate to. Finally, so much is left unanswered because of the reasons I stated above, so I wanted what was left to exist in one place. I wanted her story, as incomplete as it is, to *be*.

    Women have been marginalized since the beginning of time and she was marginalized and used for notoriety and personal gain by her professional colleagues and the officials of Indianapolis. It is important that she stop being misused and starts becoming celebrated. Dr. Knabe dedicated her professional life to caring for the sick, to being a lifelong teacher and learner, to becoming the best person she could be despite circumstances of the her life. Who is more deserving of remembrance than a selfless person? She is truly a heroine, not because she possessed superhuman powers and not because she chose to live her life well, but because she was brave and courageous, given her life circumstances, she had the strength of her convictions and was not afraid to go for it, and she achieved so much in the short time she was on this earth. The number of times outside of her death that she was mentioned in the newspaper for her good work in her profession was staggering.

    Dankeschön, Frau Doktor. Ruhe sanft.

Nicole Kobrowski
(On writing sabbatical- Orlando, FL February 3, 2016)

EARLY LIFE AND FAMILY

Helene Elise Hermine Knabe began life in Rügenwaldermünde, Germany, Prussia (now Darlowko/Darlowo, Poland) on December 22, 1875. Rügenwalder/Darlowo was the village furthest from the sea and Rügenwaldermünde/Darlowko was the village that was closest to the sea. When she was born, Germany was in a state of flux, especially with regard to Prussia. Prussia had come out of the Franco-Prussian war in 1871 a somewhat dubious winner and awarded the Alsace-Lorraine area (*Reichland Elsaß-Lothringen*) as part of the Treaty of Frankfurt. Service to King Wilhelm II and Prussia was everything.

This area, on the edge of the Baltic Sea, was a mix of tourist and fishing industries. Rügenwaldermünde[1] has a very short high tourist season and a very short warm season. Even in May the weather is unpredictable and chilly due to the weather patterns coming off the Baltic Sea. The small town has quaint streets, seaside resorts and sandy, undeveloped beaches. It was known in the late 1800s for its delicious smoked goose breast and tea sausages.[2] The beaches were and are largely unspoiled, making them perfect for beach activities. Today, it is still a small village, much as it was in Helene's time.

Parents

Helene Knabe's mother and father were out of her life early, through death for her mother and possibly abandonment and/or divorce for her father. Little is known about either parent.[3] German records are difficult to locate. They have weathered time and numerous wars, which have shifted the boundaries of the county. The *Standesamt*, or city hall recording system was not in place until after 1874 in Prussia, so one must rely on parish records, if indeed the people attended church or were baptized there.[4]

Helene's father, Otto Windschild[5], was born on July 27, 1846 in Magdeburg near Berlin to Carl August Windschild and Luise Auguste (Unger) Windschild. In 1871 he was conscripted to the German army during the Franco-Prussian War. It is unclear if he was discharged from the military or if he was serving his community service portion of his military service[6], but in 1873 Otto passed his engineering tests and started working for the German government as a civil engineer and government architect. His main focus was building bridges and mechanical structures at seaports.

Otto's family worked in "commerce and industrial affairs[7]," which could mean anything from mercantile work or banking to heavy industry such as logging or shipbuilding. His father, Carl August Windschild had been a *Privatier*, which is a man of independent means.[8]

On April 8, 1896 Otto married Louise Amanda Alma Lindemann in the evangelic church. Louise's father, Ernst Ludwig Lindemann, was a master tailor and married to Luise Auguste (Ruske) Lindemann.

On November 25, 1911, Otto Windschild was still employed by the German government. He had worked himself up in his position from a civil engineer to a waterway engineer[9] for King Wilhelm II. For his loyal service in 1911, Otto received a fourth level Order of the Red Eagle[10] for his long service with the government, which by law made him a knight.

Helene Knabe's mother is a different matter. Her name is believed to be Augusta (Krolow)[11] Knabe, just like Dr. Knabe's cousin, Augusta B. Knabe. It is believed "Knabe" was Helene's mother's name at the time Helene was born, but this cannot be verified. The other mystery is how Augusta Krolow became Knabe. Did she get married or remarry after Helene was born? And what happened to the stepfather, if there was one? There are no records at this time that can verify a marriage with Windschild or a Knabe. There are also no records of Augusta Krolow. This thickens the fog surrounding Helene's mother.

Augusta Krolow Knabe's family is described as being more religious and military in nature. Three specific people are mentioned, although no connection to Helene Knabe has yet been made.

The first was Major von Tiede of which nothing is known.

The second relative is described as Reverend Heine[13]. This could possibly be the famous German missionary, Reverend Johannes W.C. Heine, who immigrated from Germany in March 1843 to New Zealand. He was a Lutheran pastor who lived in the Upper Moutere area, near Nelson by 1850. He lived there with his family and built a church in 1864, naming the area Sarau after the northern German village. Big and Little Sarau, Germany were close to the Baltic, as Helene's village was.

The third was Lieutenant-General Krolow and his younger brother Emanuel Krolow. Although not much is known about either of these men, Emanuel Krolow owned a large parcel of land. Because he was benevolent to the people of the area, despite his death at an unknown time, the people still held a remembrance day on November 2 in Dr. Knabe's hometown and in another town close by called Thorn, now Toruń, Poland[14].

Helene's cousin, Augusta B. Knabe, stated that their grandmother on Augusta's father's side/ Dr. Knabe's mother's side belonged to the nobility of southern Germany. This statement was refuted by many people. Who Dr. Knabe's grandmother was, or

Top: View of the Rügenwalder/Darlowo town square.
Bottom: View of the women's beach ca. early 1900s. Women sometimes had a separate place to enjoy the beach where they could relax without disturbances and without men ogling them.

18   *She Sleeps Well*

Top: View of the women's beach ca. early 1900s. Notice the early women's swimsuits. Bottom: A view of the town at the top, the woods and the beach.

what her title was, is unknown and no proof that Dr. Knabe's grandmother was nobility is known to exist.

Daniel Friedrich Wilhelm Ehmke

After Helene's mother died of some unknown malady, her uncle Daniel Ehmke raised her. How he fits into the Knabe family as an Ehmke is still a mystery. Nevertheless, Daniel Ehmke had a very interesting life. Daniel was a diver who repaired boats and cleaned barnacles and other matter off ships. His wife's name is unknown, if she existed, but he had a daughter Clara Ehmke, who was a teacher, of which much is also not known. Clara lived with him as late as 1896.

Daniel must have also cared very much about Dr. Knabe and her mother to have raised Helene as his own daughter especially since he had no known wife living with him during Helene and Clara's growing up years. Raising two girls on a diver's pay may have been difficult. Helene did help financially by becoming a master seamstress. It is unclear if Helene's teenage years and young adulthood were normal or if there were complications due to her home situation, such as bullying, depression over her absent mother and father, or issues with her uncle. Helene was a very detail oriented and dedicated person in her personal, and later her professional, life. She seems to have doted on her uncle. Her uncle was reported in the Indianapolis newspapers as being everything to her, from personal and financial support levels.[15] One fact is very clear. Helene Knabe had all the intelligence, drive and support to be as successful as her father.

Augusta B. Knabe, Cousin

Augusta B. Knabe had moved to Indiana in 1894 [16]. Her stepfather, Franz (Frank) F. W. Kropp immigrated[17] in 1879 with Karoline C. Kropp. It is unclear from genealogy documents available if Karoline was Augusta's mother or stepmother. Franz was a bricklayer when he immigrated and became a worker in a chair factory when he arrived in 1879. He could neither read nor write[18]. Karoline died in 1896 of nephritis[19]. When Augusta moved to America, she lived with Franz until his death. She was a German teacher at School No. 33 Whittier in Indianapolis, among others.

Helene's Childhood and Move to America

In Helene's childhood, men were expected to provide for and take care of the family. Women in Germany were expected to keep to their roles of service to family, husband and children. They were struggling with the same thing as women of different countries. Equality and birth control were hot topics. However, in the small fishing

Top: View of the Darlowo from afar. The tall building in the background is St. Mary's Church.

Top: *A contemporary view of the beach, left much as it was in Helene's time.*

Top: An inviting sandy path leads into the woods near the beach. Helene enjoyed rambling through the woods in her youth.

Top: The many trees near the Darlowko/Darlowo coastline are bent with the force of the wind coming from the Baltic Sea.

village where Helene grew up, her childhood seems to have been a hybrid of these roles and beliefs.

Despite the chilly temperatures, Helene Knabe loved her town and its beauty. With government maintained forests and the sandy beaches within walking distance, Helene enjoyed all sorts of outdoor activities, including walking in and exploring the forest, and swimming. A true water baby, she stated, "One who has spent his youth near a large body of water will always love the water most of all, and I am no exception to the rule. There is also an indefinable charm to the woods even in their most tempestuous moods and this nothing can surpass."

However unusual it may have been for such activities, Helene described her childhood of that of many middle class German children. It was filled with books, including German literature and sewing, especially fancy work and dress making[20]. The latter is believed to have helped her supplement her income in later years and helped when she lived with Daniel Ehmke. Helene also pointed to her ability to draw, which may have assisted with her income after she became a doctor.

Education was also important to Helene. Early on she was educated at public institutions. Later, she had private tutors because her mother wanted her to be close to her and schooled her from home. It is unclear why her mother wanted Helene so close. Could it have been a plot to steal her by Otto Windschild's family? We don't know. Perhaps Helene was schooled from home because she had a somewhat unhappy childhood. It just isn't known. However, the outcome is clear. Helene became a very well educated, intelligent woman.

While it cannot be denied that these activities would be enjoyable, her rambles in the woods and beach may also point to the fact that she was highly intelligent and introspective about her surroundings and her life. She may have also been somewhat introverted. Sadly, it seems she may have been lacking in friends in Germany. In none of the evidence, personal papers, or in any of the numerous newspaper articles written about her, has there ever been proof that she kept in touch with specific friends in Germany or that indeed there were any.

Helene Knabe always wanted to be a doctor[21] and in 1891 when she was 16, she heard someone talking about how women could become doctors in America. In June 1895 when her cousin, Augusta Knabe, visited her, Helene found out that Augusta would continue to make her home in America. She decided that the opportunity had presented itself and on October 31, 1896, Helene made her way to America on the SS Virginia from Stettin, Germany[22]. Records indicate she was a steerage passenger.

She arrived on November 16, 1896 in New York and a day later in Indianapolis. Helene lived with her cousin, Augusta and step-uncle, Franz Kropp, at 1151 (later renumbered to 1205) Bates Street in Indianapolis. In 1900 she was listed as a boarder who worked as a nurse. Helene worked as a domestic, cooking, cleaning, sewing, and serving so that she could save money and learn proper English from the best class of people. She would most definitely need these skills in the future.

Top: The Baltic Sea and Darlowko/Darlowo in the background. The cement barriers in the foreground are to prevent erosion in this beautiful, peaceful spot.

Top: *Rügenwalder from one of the waterways.*

Top: Rügenwaldermünde mole in a storm. Ostseebad was a name given to the town for the type of activities available. For example, Indiana has dunes, French Lick (Indiana) has curative water. Rügenwaldermünde was called "Baltic Sea Beach" (direct translation) as it had excellent beaches and water.

Top: Contemporary view of Darlowko and its main waterway in the town. Notice in the picture above and the historic picture on the next page that the same building still exists today. The drawbridge in the background appears in both photos, although the one on the next page has been replaced by what is seen in this photograph.

Top: Historic Rügenwaldermünde and its main waterway in the town. Notice in the picture above and the historic picture on the previous page that the same building still exists today. The drawbridge in the background, although replaced by the contemporary version in the picture to the left, is still used.

Top: The southeast-southwest port of entrance to Rügenwaldermünde.

Top: A contemporary view of the southeast-southwest port of entrance.

32 *She Sleeps Well*

Top: Contemporary view of Darlowko and its main waterway in the town. The drawbridge opens to let ships and sailboats into the waterway.

BECOMING A DOCTOR

Eighteen hundred and ninety four marked the beginning of coeducational medical schools in the US, but the struggles for women were far from over. Many schools still refused to admit women. Even in 1910, six years after Helene Knabe graduated, 20% of all women were still in women's medical colleges in the United States. It wasn't until World War I when the need for doctors jumped that women were fully taken into traditionally male medical schools [23].

Helene was up for the task. The motto she heard most often growing up was "You cannot be a master in anything unless you know every detail of the work[24]." No one applied this maxim more than Helene. Just to get into medical school, she had to get a certificate of good moral character from two people living in Indiana. She blew this requirement out of the water by securing one from Dr. Henry Jameson, Dean[25] and a professor of medicine at the Medical College of Indiana and Dr. John H. Oliver[26], the treasurer of the medical school and a professor of surgery there. Two people from her village in Germany also wrote recommendations for her, Heinrica Burske and Wilhelm Glose[27].

Top: Drs. Henry Jameson and J. H. Oliver wrote medical school recommendations for Helene Knabe. It is unknown how she knew them, however, it may have been through her domestic work.

Helene also had to prove her intelligence. First, she had to prove preliminary education- either a diploma from a high school or college. She had to prove she had good knowledge of English grammar, rhetoric and composition, history of the United States and general history (mostly Greek, Roman and English), algebra, geometry, physics, biology or botany and zoology, chemistry, and Latin. This may have been why she took classes at Butler College[28] (now University, at the time in Irvington) and Indiana Business College (on the north east corner or North and Delaware Streets), although it is not believed she graduated with a degree [29]. Helene also had to take a state medical school exam and score at least 75% on it.

On September 22, 1900 Helene started medical school at the Medical College of Indiana, which would later become the IU School of Medicine[30]. During her time at school, Helene was required to attend 80% of each course, or she could be released from school. She also had to maintain at least a 75% in all her classes.

The school also required order and adherence to rules. If she or any other student were in the habit of drinking, (the school discouraged the behavior) they could be dismissed from the school immediately.

Medical school was not cheap by 1904 standards. Students had to pay the following fees.

Item	Fee	Yearly Cost
Dissecting materials, each part	$5	$5 for each body part
Hospital fees (for sophomore, junior, seniors)	$6 per year for City Hospital and St. Vincent	$6 x 4 years; more if they attended other hospitals
Graduation fee	$25	$25 x 1
Breakage fees	$3	$3
Didactic and clinical lectures	Free	Free
Tuition	$75	$75
Matriculation	$5	$5
Supplies		Varied
Books	(total 110)	Approx. $30
	TOTAL	Approx. $149 +/-
GRAND TOTAL	$149 x 4 years	**$596 + $5 for every body part= $1096 +/-**

Dissections and books were the most expensive items. Books that were required included no fewer than 110 titles over 4 years. Books of the time cost more than $2.50 each. If Helene bought all the books, the cost of the books alone would be almost as much as her tuition!

Helene Knabe had a great resource in her college professors. The Medical College of Indiana was above the curve on the type of education it offered. Far earlier than the 1910 Flexnor Report, created by Abraham Flexnor, which advocated (among other things) for clinical hands on teaching instead of recitation and Socratic methodology, the Medical College of Indiana employed this and more in 1900. Additionally, lantern illustrations were used as part of the newest methodology of teaching. The school boasted thousands of these slides for use by faculty and students. In 1901 the school added a laboratory specifically dedicated to the Röntgen Ray[31]- the beginning of modern X-Rays. Also in 1901 students began to attend clinical instruction at Central State Hospital for the Insane, and the Maternity Hospital.

Medical education at the college was rigorous. Today, students go almost year round and have internships throughout the year. During Dr. Knabe's time, she went to school from late September to Christmas and then from after New Year's Day to late April. This is about seven months of classes. During that time, in addition to classwork, Helene would also work at Bobb's Free Dispensary and be mentored by a faculty

Left: Dr. James Batey Kirkpatrick was Dr. Knabe's first faculty mentor. He eventually set up practice in Kokomo. He died in 1932 and is buried in Crown Point Cemetery, Kokomo, Indiana.

member. Classes ran from Monday to Saturday from 9:00 a.m. till 7:30 p.m.. Students were also expected to participate in a student medical society to prepare them for their profession and teach them the ability to debate, write papers and take part in all areas of what they would expect in their practice. They were encouraged to join the Young Men's Christian Association and use the Medical Department at the Indianapolis Public Library. Finals were held in December and in April. If students failed to obtain the needed scores, they could be "conditioned," meaning reexamined before the beginning of the next session. If students failed, they were dismissed from the school.

Freshman year: Preceptor- Dr. James Batey Kirkpatrick[32]

Branches	Didactic	Recitations	Practical Work	Yearly total hours
Physiology	2	2		104
Physics	1	1		52
Histology		1	3	104
Osteology and Syndesmology	3	2		130
Chemistry	1	1	2	104
Materia medica	1	2		78
Medical Botany	1			26
Bandaging and surgical dressing	In sections of 6	In sections of 6	2	12 each student
Minor surgery	1			26
Latin		3		78
Anatomy	1	2	10	180
Pharmacy	1			26
				970 hours total

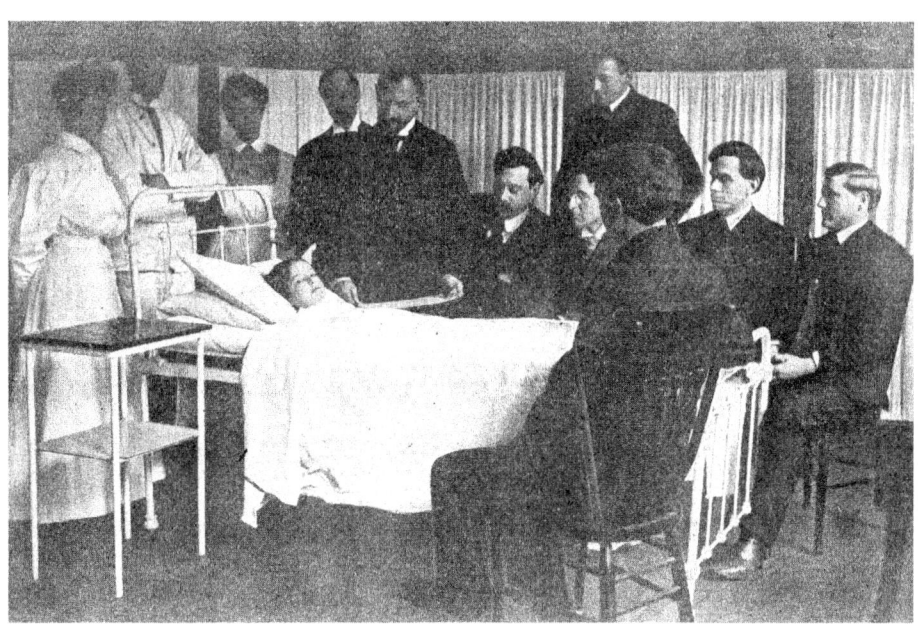

Top: Dr. Schaefer's Clinic at City Hospital.
Bottom: Eye, ear, nose and throat clinic at an unknown location. Notice the African-American child being treated.

Sophomore year: Preceptor- Faculty

Branches	Didactic	Recitations	Practical Work	Clinics	Yearly total
Anatomy		1	10		292
Pathology	2		4		168
Physiology	2	1	2		140
Chemistry	1		4		140
Principles of Medicine	2				56
Surgical Pathology	2	1			84
Medicine				4	112
Surgery				5	140
Disease of Women	1				28
Therapeutics and Pharmacy	3	1			112
Bacteriology			4		112
					1384 hours total

Top left: A candid shot of a clinical laboratory day with students.
Middle right: Students at work in the pathological museum Helene Knabe headed.
Bottom: Books were important in medical school- and expensive. This is a notice for students indicating they'd kept their books a little too long!

Junior year: Preceptor- Faculty

Hour	M	T	W	Th	Friday	Saturday
9-10	Visc Anatomy	Surgery	Syphilogy	Anat nervous system	Gastro-Intes and Rectal	Medicine
10-11	Therapeutics	Obstetrics	Therapeutics	Children's diseases	Surgery	Bacteriology
11-12	Women's diseases	Children's diseases	Rec. Thera.	Med Diagnosis	Surgical anatomy	Therapeutics
2-3	Genito Urinary	Hospital for Insane	City Hospital	Medicine	St Vincent Hospital Clinic	City Hospital Clinic
3-4	Dermatology			Hygiene		
4-5	Dental Surgery			Physical Diagnosis		
5-6	Medical Diagnosis					
7-7:30	Practical anatomy	Practical anatomy	Practical anatomy	Practical anatomy	Practical anatomy	
7:30-9:30	Dissections					Sydenham Society

She Sleeps Well 41

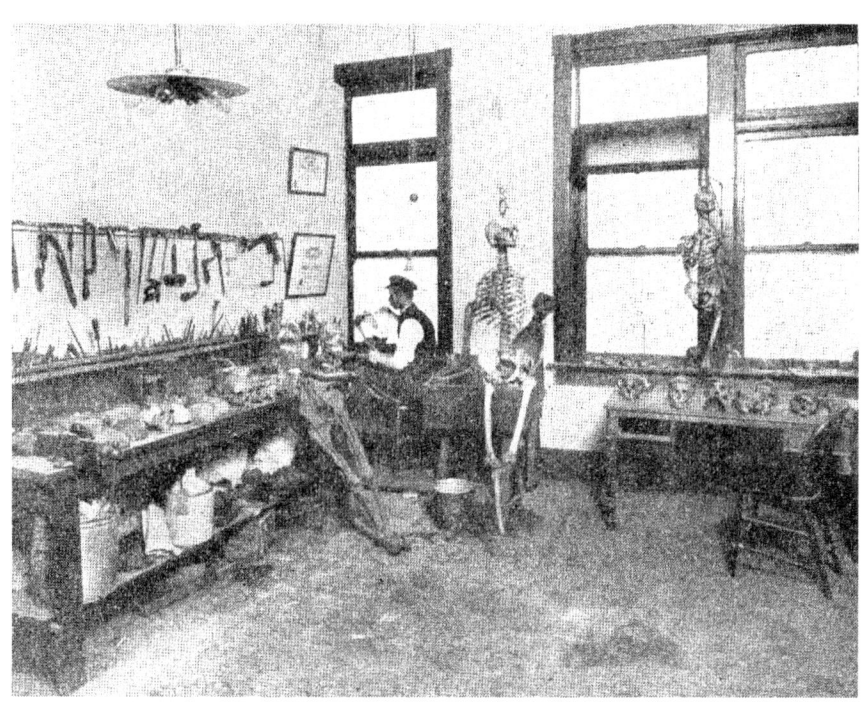

Top: Anatomical workshop of Otto von Tesmar. He was a pharmacist and taxidermist in Indianapolis. He truly enjoyed his work with animals and skeletons.

Bottom right: Dr. Sluss' Surgical Clinic

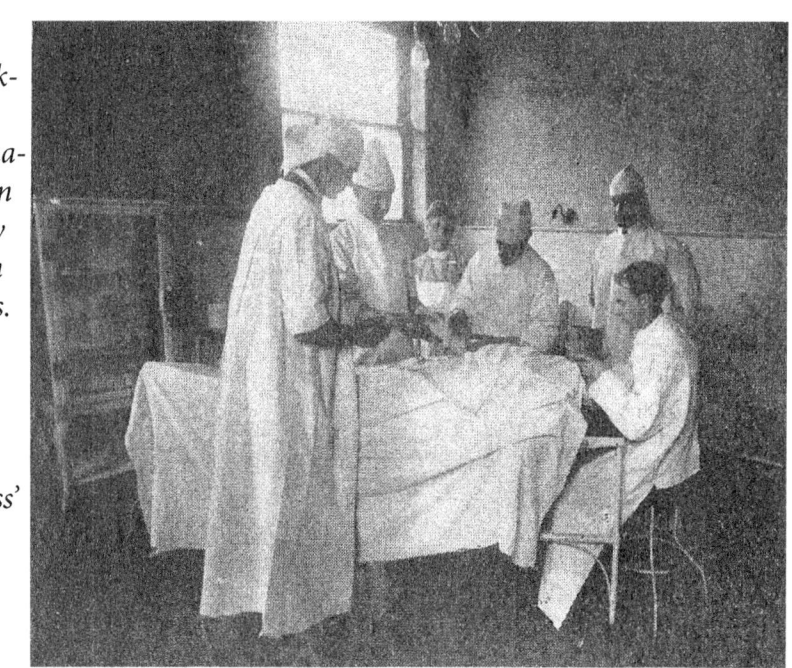

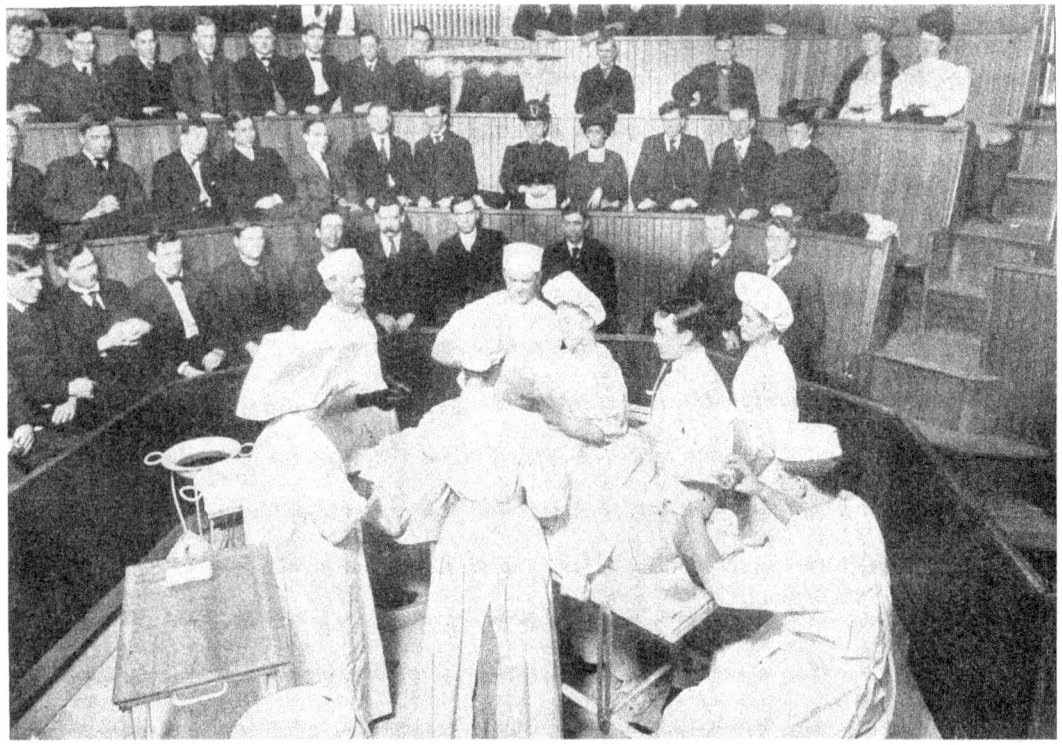

Top: Dr. Oliver's Clinic at St. Vincent Hospital. Bottom: Bobb's Free Dispensary Drug Room.

Senior year: Preceptor- Dr. Frank B. Wynn (he was no one else's preceptor)

Hour	M	T	W	Th	F	S
8:30-9	CLINICS					
9-10						
10-11	Surgery	Disease of the eye	Obstetrics	Children's disease	Dermatology	Obstetrics
11-12	Surgery recitation	surgery	Women's diseases	Practice of Medicine recitation	Disease of nervous system	Obstetrics recitation
2-3	Nose, throat and ear	Hospital for Insane	City Hospital	Clinical Pathology	St Vincent Hospital Clinic	City Hospital Clinic
3-4	Dietetics			Genito-urinary disease		
4-5	Practical Medicine			Practice of medicine		
5-6	Gastro-intestinal and Rectal Disease			Lectures		
7-7:30	Practical anatomy recitation					
7:30-9:30	Dissections					Sydenham Society
7-7:30	Practical anatomy					
7:30-9:30	Dissections					

Classroom lectures were held at the Medical College of Indiana at *Das Deutsche Haus*[33] and at their building on Senate Ave. Additionally, Helene would have attended clinical teachings at Bobb's Free Dispensary and City Dispensary, where outpatient work was done, as well as with doctors in their practices at hospitals around the city, including, Indianapolis City Hospital, St. Vincent Hospital, the Eleanor Hospital for Sick Children[34], Maternity Hospital[35], and Methodist Episcopal Hospital. Helene also attended lectures at Central State Hospital's newly established Pathological Department Building.

Appointments to the hospitals and dispensaries were done on a competitive basis. They were based on an examination by a committee of physicians who were not part of the faculty. The winning students received clinical instruction from the best physicians at the City Hospital (6 students), City Dispensary (5 students) St. Vincent's Hospital (2 students), Protestant Deaconess (2 students) and the College (Bobb's) Dispensary (2 students). Considering she was placed at Bobb's her entire school career and only 17 students out of the whole student body were chosen, Dr. Knabe was already esteemed before she graduated. The second best part of this for the students? These were paid positions. This must have helped Helene immensely in being able to not work so much as a seamstress and domestic and be able to really

Top: The Medical College on Indiana at Senate Avenue (razed).

immerse herself in the work of becoming a doctor.

At Bobb's Free Dispensary, Helene had the opportunity from 8:30-9:30 a.m. to attend clinics including the following areas: laboratory, general medicine, surgery, eyes, nose, throat and ear, gynecology, genito-urinary and venereal, disease of children, disease of the nervous system, skin and gastro-intestinal and rectal diseases. She was assigned a monthly schedule for rotating from the dispensary to City Hospital and St. Vincent, which taught not just the competitive examination recipients but also the rest of the students in groups.

Between classes, Helene had the extra benefit of having a new library with many books at her disposal in the Bobb's Memorial Hall and Library, which may have defrayed some of the hefty book costs she undoubtedly had!

Students also had to compete in a way for preceptors. A preceptor was a practicing doctor who took upperclassmen on as mentees and showed them how to work with patients and work in the area of medicine which most appealed to them. In Helene Knabe's case, it was pathology. Each doctor took one or two students to mentor. Many students ended up settling for doctors that were employed at the hospitals they were taught at. This meant the students competed with the doctors and patients for mentoring time.

Helene was brilliant. During her freshman year, Dr. Kirkpatrick from the medical college was her preceptor. Furthering her school career, by her sophomore year, Dr. Knabe had selected pathology as her specialty. Much to the chagrin of many of her male peers, in her senior year, she'd been selected by Dr. Frank B. Wynn as her preceptor[36].

Dr. Wynn treated Helene just like any other student, despite her gender. He encouraged her in her studies and she helped him complete much of his work in his office at the school- even during her summer break. About a year after Helene began studying with him, he appointed her the curator of the pathological museum at the college in her junior year. She held this position until graduating on April 22, 1904 .

During medical school, despite continuing to work as a seamstress while studying, Helene did find time to do more than study. She networked. Helene was quite busy at the school with not only Dr. Wynn's lab, especially as summer employment, she also worked as a secretary for her freshman, sophomore class and was a member of, and a secretary for, the Sydenham Society her junior year. This organization was formed to allow students to discuss scientific medicine as is done in medical societies to prepare them for such work. Helene did fall ill at one point during her junior year, but bounced back in about a week. The school also listed her as being a member of the Church of German E.A. (*Evangelische Allianz*, translated Evangelical Alliance).

Helene's activities helped her to become a student teacher of pathology under Dr. Wynn's guidance two years before she graduated. This was not the norm and was a highly coveted honor. In 1904 before she graduated, she was able to publish a paper with Dr. Wynn[37] for the American Medical Association.

On October 31, 1903 the Purdue Special, traveling with the football team, coaches, fans, parents and professors, collided with coal cars. The crew of the coal train was not aware that the two special trains were on their way. The coal train was placed on the track as they thought it should be. When the engineer of the first special train saw the coal cars, he threw the train into reverse, and jumped out of the engine, but the train hit the coal cars head on. The first car with the football team and coaches was torn in half, causing many fatalities. Within days, over 16 people lost their lives. More than 50 people were seriously injured with dozens more sustaining minor injuries. The uninjured passengers began an assembly line of caring for the injured and removing the dead. A few of the passengers ran down the track to stop the second train from crashing into the accident, preventing even greater loss of life[38]. Members of the Medical College of Indiana came to the aid of victims and Helene may have been among them.

To graduate, Helene had to maintain her good moral character, be 21 years of age, and prove she'd studied four years at school and/or worked with a physician

Bottom: Dr. Frank Barbour Wynn, Helene Knabe's senior year preceptor and friend.

Top: Artistic heading from The Medical Student during Helene Knabe's senior year.

for four years. She also had to file her paperwork and pass an oral exam. Helene had to maintain the records of her attendance in her courses and prove that they were maintained at 80%. Her college bill had to be paid in full. She also had to prove she'd attended dissections and dissected every part of the human body.

This last part was no easy feat. In the early 1900s, autopsies were not common and the idea of donating a body to science was still considered somewhat barbaric. Schools were not overly concerned about where these cadavers came from, and grave robbing was a very real thing.

In fact, by 1902, a large gang of grave robbers, called the Ghouls, was disbanded and the leader arrested. In the early 1890s, grave robbing became quite lucrative all over the United States. In Indianapolis, the "King of the Ghouls," Rufus Cantrell, delighted in telling all about his grave robbing escapades and about other grave robbers. In fact, after he was arrested and convicted, he decided to write a book about his experiences. He declared, while serving as a cook in the Marion County Jail, that people "flocked" to him like "bees around the queen" when they knew who he was and what he did [39,40]. He later went into local politics!

The thirty-fourth annual commencement of the Medical College of Indiana[41] was held at the English Opera House[42] at 8:00 p.m. on Friday, April 22, 1904. The graduating class and faculty were seated on the stage which was bursting with floral decorations, giving it the look of a conservatory. The college color of royal purple with silk banners streamed throughout the hall. One of Helene's classmates, Clifford Orestes Burroughs[43,44] who died from a fever on April 17th, was honored by having his empty seat draped in black crepe. Family, friends and alumni were also present.

Dr. Winfred Ernest Garrison, Ph.D., president of Butler College gave the address "Opportunity of the Educated Man" in which he urged the students to understand that "the educated man" was someone who valued education, continued to be a lifelong learner, and met the demands of his profession and culture by being moral and ethical.

48 *She Sleeps Well*

    Throughout the program, Dr. Henry Jameson announced the agenda of the evening: invocation conducted by Reverend Albert Hurlstone, pastor of Roberts Park Methodist Episcopal Church, songs and recital selections, the addresses, conferring of degrees by Hon. Addison C. Harris, president of the University of Indianapolis, and Dr. George J. Cook, Secretary of the Faculty at the Medical College of Indiana, called the 82 graduates who rose and remained standing during the roll call, and benediction.

    By the end of the evening, Helene was well on her way to the goals she'd set for herself in Germany. She was no longer simply Helene Knabe. She was *Frau Doktor Helene Elise Hermine Knabe*.

Top: Dr. Helene Elise Hermine Knabe's 1904 medical college graduation picture.

Immersing Herself in Her Profession

Dr. Knabe immersed herself in her profession[45]. The first year following her graduation was busy. She worked with Dr. Charles E. Ferguson as an assistant. They worked with the Indianapolis Water Company to assess the sanitary conditions of the drinking water. For 52 days, from August 26, 1904 to January 4, 1905 they worked to complete their assessment. Dr. Ferguson's bill was $1,750. G.W. Fuller, who did the work on the side of the water company, charged $3,375. Dr. Knabe's bill, submitted alongside Dr. Ferguson's, was $50. It became tied up in a battle between the State Board of Health, who believed the water company should pay it. The water company wasn't sure who should pay it. A meeting was set up to get it settled[46].

State Board of Health

Also during this very busy time, Dr. Knabe began work at the State Board of Health offices, first as a Health Officer in August 1905, ensuring education and proper health practices were enforced in Indiana. She was the first woman to ever hold this office.

As Health Officer, at the request of the Secretary of the State Board of Health Dr. John N. Hurty, Dr. Knabe was sent around Indianapolis and Indiana inspecting water, investigating schools for sanitary and other hazards, making healthful recommendations to schools, doctors, and families. She also generally supported the pet projects Dr. Hurty decided to champion in any given year. While the deputy health officer, she was quoted in the newspaper as saying, "How can a city be made beautiful

Right: Dr. John N. Hurty, Secretary of the State Board of Health. Dr. Knabe worked for him at the State Board of Health and she provided medical illustrations for his book, Life With Health. He appointed her acting superintendent of the State Laboratory of Hygiene with false promises and lies.

unless first of all, it is made clean ?[47]" She wanted to see cleaner, and therefore healthier, cities above all. She also stressed the importance of free lectures that taught people how to keep themselves healthier through cleanliness and other means.

During one of her cases as a health officer on August 14, 1905 Dr. Knabe visited the Indiana National Soldiers Home (National Home for Disabled Volunteer Soldiers) in Marion, Indiana. She studied water and bacteria samples using the Widal test for typhoid. Out of 62 samples, 50 tested positive. By conducting this test, she was able to stop a greater outbreak. Dr. Knabe also believed longer term measures were necessary to stop future outbreaks. She made a report to Dr. Hurty, who brought it to the attention of Commandant Richard M. Smock, head of the institution. He rebutted Dr. Knabe's findings, but didn't deny improvements were needed. Smock simply stated lack of funds and not derelict institution officers, was the reason for the conditions[48]. Dr. Hurty did meet with the Board of Trustees for the hospital and some recommendations were adopted [49], what they were, or if they were implemented is not known.

On October 1, 1905 Dr. Knabe became the assistant pathologist for the Indiana State Laboratory of Hygiene. She was the first person and first woman to ever hold this position. *The Medical Student*, which was a publication for the Medical College of Indiana students and alum, stated "We believe we are safe in saying that the profession of Indiana is much pleased with this appointment because of her unquestionable character and unsurpassed ability ." During the first three months of her work, she had no proper place to do her work- so she did it in the Secretary of the State Board of Health's office, Dr. Hurty . She had a two foot by three foot table with a staining case for slides and microscope. Under these conditions she was able to process 150 specimens, especially diphtheria specimens.

Two days after she became assistant pathologist, Dr. Knabe visited Liberty, Indiana to investigate typhoid fever[50], one of many cases she investigated[51]. She found 41 cases of typhoid started by infection brought to Indiana by William Reilly from his old home in Missouri when he came to stay with his son Robert Beck on July 10, 1905. By the end of July, William had been ill and, Robert and his brothers were also ill. However, Dr. Knabe found that only a report for Robert and his 13-year-old child had been made. Nothing had been reported for William or for Robert's four year old son. Additionally, around the same time, Charles Beck, Robert's brother also became ill. The disease went into the general population and in 17 known houses. This was in part to the "filthy practices indulged at the patient's home" as well as 12 men who drank water from the now-infected well. People who had assisted the sick also became ill[52].

In the case of the farm rented by Charles Beck, the house was on a hill and

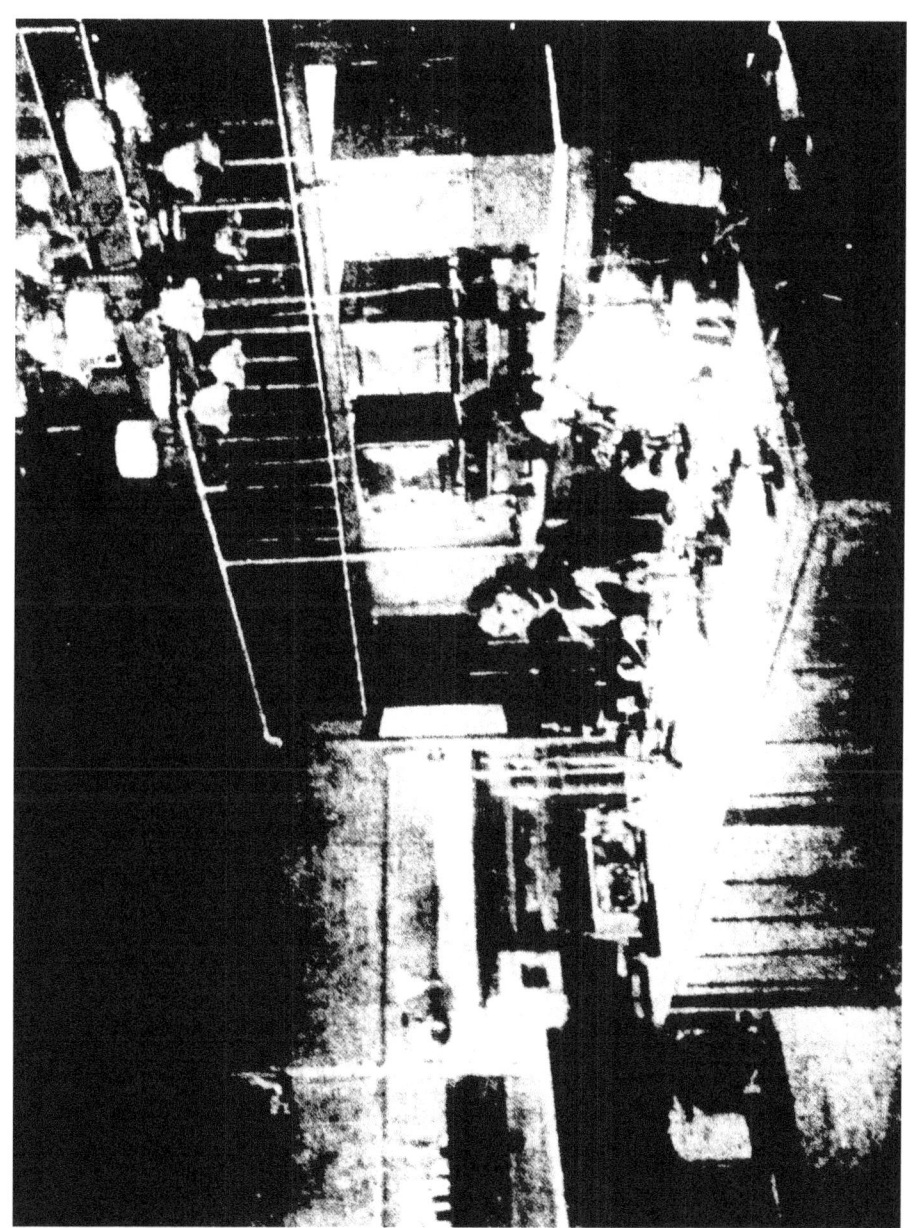

Top: Dr. Knabe and Dr. T. Victor Keene in the second State Board of Health Laboratory of Hygiene. The first office consisted of a table on which Dr. Knabe processed samples. After three months of getting the lab up and running, Dr. Hurty hired Dr. Keene to run it.

badly kept. Five feet from the house was the cistern and a little farther away, the well, covered by dirty boards. Close by was a shed where vegetables were kept. It was full of flies brought by the decaying vegetables that weren't removed. The shed roof was used to dry vegetables in the sun. The apples drying there were so full of flies one could not see the apples. On top of these issues, there were three wells- a Sulphur well, and one spring well, which had a springhouse built over it for storage of milk, butter and other dairy products. Fifteen feet from this and a little higher on a hill was the well that helped spread the infection, and the toilet, which had not been cleaned or disinfected. Usually the family just threw the excrement and urine around the grass on top of the well. Additionally, sour cream was found in an open separator with flies covering it. Boiled water had been provided for the farm workers but the lid had been left off and a dozen flies fell to their deaths in the water.

Dr. Knabe told them not to use the cream, the apples, or the water with flies. Even that only made a small dent in eradicating the disease. From July to December the disease ran its course. Dr. Knabe could not stay the entire time so the record keeping and procedure were left to local doctors. In the case of the Beck family in Liberty, she met with the physician in charge and they created an action plan.

Other farms she visited were similar. Wells with dirty boards over them, wells dug next to manure piles, so wet with urine and feces it was no wonder the family was sick. Some farm owners refused to clean up the issues, which vexed Dr. Knabe and made her job even harder.

During this time, all testing was done at the state level. Doctors had to send samples to the state. There Dr. Knabe or her counterparts in other areas examined or tested them, and interpreted the results. They then sent wires, calls, and/or letters back to the doctors with the results. These tests could take up to fourteen days, and in some cases longer. In the case of Liberty, Dr. Knabe had a very hard time getting these samples shipped but she was firm in her assessment and actions. "Whenever I expressed a desire to ship samples of the water to the State Laboratory, there was opposition, the owner or resident contending that nothing could be the matter with his water. Investigation here at the laboratory has shown, however, that the large majority of the waters sent in are not fit for use. These will be reported to the local health officer, Dr. J.S. Kell and he will condemn the wells."[53]

Dr. Knabe conducted Widal tests[54] and sent water for analysis in Indianapolis. She noted that if the town of Liberty became infected, because of the close homes, shallow wells close to privies which didn't drain properly, it would be very difficult to stop the spread of typhoid.

She noted that nurses were not used. The reports that should have been promptly sent to the State Board of Health were over two weeks late and incomplete. Disinfectants were rarely used and when used were so poor a quantity and quality, that they might as well have used plain water.

In the end, she said, "The families affected are not so poor they cannot afford better things. But they were too miserly about a few extra dollars that might have been used in bettering conditions around them. Again, they would not call a physician until patients actually dropped down, so that by the time medical aid was called all the family had been infected. Even the physicians failed to report the cases, and the result was a general spread of the disease.[55]"

Again, in November 1905 two deaths in Cambridge City, Indiana prompted her to go there and diagnose the disease. A month later, Dr. Knabe was well prepared to give the talk "The Laboratory View on Infectious Disease" at the Indiana Health Officers School for Town Health Officers[56].

By the end of 1905, the State of Indiana appropriated $5,000 for equipment and $10,000 annually for maintenance of the State Board of Health laboratories. Two areas, Chemical and Bacteriological, were formed. Immediately, Dr. Knabe was hired Assistant Bacteriologist and Dr. T. Victor Keene was hired three months later[57].

Dr. Knabe truly did help save lives. A young man had gone west when diagnosed with tuberculosis (TB). A friend of this man told him to go the State Board of Health to see if it really was TB. Dr. Hurty did the physical exam and Dr. Knabe reviewed the sputum. When it was confirmed that the man did have TB, they were able to tell him how to take treatment to save his life, as he was in the first stage of the disease. The State Board of Health did these examinations for free[58].

Within one month of the actual opening of the lab, Dr. Knabe conducted 212 examinations for disease, mostly TB. Of those over 76% contained TB germs. In one case, she was asked to examine a handkerchief for TB germs. Dr. Knabe stated, "If I had $1 for every tubercular germ on that bit of handkerchief, I could build and equip a hospital for consumptives in Indiana[59]."

The new lab did mostly cultures to diagnose disease and to find the existence of germs in specimens. However, Dr. Knabe did participate in the occasional autopsy to determine cause of death, as in the case of a Whiteland man suspected of dying from the "sleeping disease," or hookworm. The unfortunate man had been in the West Indies and contracted it there. In 1906 hookworm was called a "tropical disease" and was thought to be a microbe that lodged in the stomach. Today we know it to be a disease of the tropics, but also of developing nations. The disease is contracted from coming into contact with parasitic roundworm eggs and larvae found in dirt contaminated by feces. The larvae enter the skin or through your windpipe and are carried to your intestines. They can live there for a year or more before being passed out through feces[60,61].

Sometime between 1906 and 1908[62], Dr. Knabe began making examinations of rabid dogs, which later lead to a lucrative private practice[63]. She examined animals of every kind, including many dogs, horses and cows.

In 1906 Dr. Knabe went to Johns Hopkins and studied under Dr. Anna Wessels Williams. While there, she learned the method of rapid diagnosis methodology to prove the existence of rabies in Indiana through scientific methods. Dr. Knabe traveled to New York at her own expense and learned the method directly from Dr. Williams at the New York Research Laboratory.

Dr. Knabe first used this knowledge at the State Board of Health in the diagnosis of rabies using dog heads. When she left the laboratory, no one had been cross trained in the method and Dr. Knabe used this knowledge to earn a fairly good living at her other teaching jobs and at her practice. She also effectively diagnosed rabies. It wouldn't be until 1911 that Indiana enacted legislation to create a state funded laboratory to diagnose rabies. In HB 57, 1911, it stated that the dog tax fund would reimburse farmers for the loss of sheep due to rabies. Additionally from this fund, any nursing, care, lodging or clothing required by the farmers during their treatment with the antirabic virus in Indianapolis would be gratis. In 1935 the law was changed so that the treatment was given at the local physician's office.

Rabies is a savage disease which attacks the brain. It can cause severe agitation, convulsions and paralysis. The victims drift from terror to sleep and can communicate pain and other conditions to their caregivers. They have the inability to swallow liquid, hence rabies' first name, "hydrophobia." What is even worse is that it does not necessarily appear immediately and it can take from one week to over a year in rare cases for the infection to truly present[64]. When it does, death comes usually within a week.

While today there is an immunization against rabies that can be taken shortly after one may have been infected with the disease, during Dr. Knabe's time, there were two treatments. Madstones, calcifications found in the stomach of cud-chewing animals, were thought to draw the poisons out. The treatment preferred by doctors was excising and cauterizing the affected tissue with a hot iron or acid as quickly as possible after the bite or attack took place. It was thought if the tissue was excised, the rabies germs would not travel through the body and thus would spare the patient's life. Otherwise, the best one could do was diagnose it after the fact. This meant looking at

She Sleeps Well 55

DR. KNABE INOCULATING A GUINEA PIG.

Top: Dr. Knabe inoculates a guinea pig with germs in order to determine their effect on it. This picture was taken prior to 1909 when Dr. Knabe was working for the State Board of Health. Her ring finger seems to be sporting a ring of some sort.

the brain. Dr. Knabe was well known for examining dog brains. She even examined the brain of a small boy, something very unusual in the early 1900s.

By July 1908 Indianapolis was fighting a huge war with rabies. Dr. Knabe had examined over 60 specimens in the first six months with more backlogged[65]. When a specimen arrived, she would remove the brain from the head, and perform tests on its fluid, including injecting rabbits and guinea pigs with fluid. If they died in a few days, it was proof that the animal from which the specimen came had rabies[66]. In Spencer, Indiana no fewer than 30 dogs[67] were bitten by one rabid dog. Covington, Indiana had a calf that may have had rabies[68].

One of the largest outbreaks was at Evansville, Indiana. A dog bit eight people and was at large. Dr. Knabe traveled to Evansville to deal with the situation[69]. Another large problem was a water spaniel in Scottsburg that bit at least 20 other dogs[70]. In this case, Dr. Knabe diagnosed rabies. The men of the town were like volunteer militia in formation looking for the infected dogs through the streets[71].

One of the most interesting cases was a woman, Mrs. Alberta Wolff, who worked at the Humane Society. She was asked to resign because it was suspected she poisoned some of the dogs. Be that as it may, after her resignation, she kept many homeless dogs in her home. One of them bit her, her husband, and a neighbor, Henry Aug, who arrived on business, as well as the other three dogs in the home. All the dogs contracted hydrophobia, also known as rabies. It appears the humans were lucky and did not[72].

Promotion and Resignation

In On October 7, 1907, Dr. Knabe was promoted to Acting Superintendent of the State Laboratory of Hygiene. She was only 32 years old. In that year alone, she processed 5,420 pathological specimens including sputum, blood, diphtheria cultures, cancers, tumors, urine, feces, and pathological fluids. The work done in the lab was called "The Life Saving Station." One of the fights she championed was how the specimens were sent to the state laboratory. There were federal guidelines for what could be sent through the mail. The laboratory had its own standards too. Many times, for example, the laboratory would receive a piece of cotton in a tin, which was wholly against best practices. Dr. Knabe tried to raise awareness for doctors and health officers all over Indiana by sending a pamphlet outlining how to send the State Board of Health samples, but it seemed to do no good. A newspaper quipped, "If the germs look too ferocious do you not examine them?" To which she replied that whether specimens were examined or not depended on conditions[73]. What she meant was sometimes the doctors sent specimens without any data, such as the name of the patient, the date it was taken, or any other conditions about the specimen. Many times in the case of diphtheria specimens were sent in single containers, without a solution that was to be included and without the second container to put the specimen in. Often there was no physician name included with samples. For the clerk, Mrs. Florence Carper, to handle these was somewhat dangerous [74].

Dr. Knabe did have a slight brush with the law in 1907. A dog's head came in for rabies diagnosis. It belonged the Arthur F. Greenham. The dog showed signs of rabies, and had scratched the man's child with its paws. Later that day, Greenham and another man killed and buried the dog. Then the family began to think perhaps the dog had licked its paws before attacking the child and it was decided to send the head to the State Board of Health. The sixth culture Dr. Knabe made tested positive for rabies.

Greenham decided to take his child to the Chicago Pasteur Institute[75] and wanted to take the head with them. Dr. H.R. Allen said that treatment had to be done within five days for it to be effective, so time was important. Dr. Allen and Greenham tried to find Dr. Knabe to no avail on Tuesday, which was Christmas Eve. They found her on Christmas Day. Dr. Allen and Greenham said she would not give them the dog's head. The men consulted with an attorney who created a writ of replevin in order to force her to give the head to them. The writ of replevin returns seized goods back to the original owner. The attorney said to start with Dr. Knabe and threaten her with a legal suit before any legal action was taken. When presented with this, Dr. Knabe surrendered a portion of the brain to them. It was taken to Chicago the day after Christmas. Dr. Knabe stated it was all a misunderstanding. First, she worked multiple hours on the specimen on Christmas Eve evening, Christmas Day, and other times she was not busy with other work. Second, it was against the law for her to give specimens to anyone outside the Indiana State Board of Health. Third, Dr. Knabe maintained that she was never properly informed what they wanted it for. Had they done so in their initial request, she would have gladly given them what they asked for from the beginning[76]. She believed the dog had hydrophobia. At the time she gave a portion of the brain away, she had inoculated a guinea pig with a sample from the dog, and was awaiting final results.

West Newton, Indiana also had a rabies outbreak. Two pig heads were sent to the State Board of Health and more pigs, several cows, horses and disreputable dogs were in question. But more important that month was testing the water from the Puro Water Company distilled water supplied in all the drinking units in the State House. Officials began to complain about the water. Dr. Knabe found that it contained streptococci. While this proved the existence of the bacteria, it didn't mean that it was unfit to drink unless it was in certain amounts. Although no official word was given, it is likely that Dr. Knabe gave a recommendation. Whether it was followed is not known. W.P. Lake, secretary-treasurer of Puro, said he'd heard no complaints and that the water was bottled once it was distilled and had no idea how the bacteria would have gotten into the bottles[78].

In addition to rabies, the war was on with tuberculosis. Dr. Hurty and Dr. Knabe traveled to Scottsburg and gave a lecture at the Christian Church with the help of the Scott County Medical Society[77]. They also brought along a mobile diagnosis unit with microscopes and examination equipment. The people who attended had the opportunity to be diagnosed and a treatment plan put in place right away.

Dr. Knabe also worked with other diseases. Diphtheria made another appearance in Indiana and she was dispatched to a town in north central Indiana to contain the spread [79].

Yet in December 1907 Dr. Knabe went to Bridgeport at the local school checking for diphtheria. Dr. Knabe was very kind about explaining the process to the children ahead of time at a level they could understand. She also gave them and the school pamphlets for the parents. Dr. Knabe took 37 swabs and found three that contained diphtheria. The school closed early for Christmas so it could be disinfected. The shopkeepers were asked to disinfect their shops and keep loitering to a minimum. While she was there, a peddler walked into a quarantined house, despite being asked to stay away. With this slight exception, Dr. Knabe believed Bridgeport to be safe from infection as long as the quarantine was enforced. She received quite a bit of help from the doctors and their assistants and wrote a kind word for them in her report[80].

Dr. Knabe was not all work. In the heat of July 1908, she and 150 other state officials enjoyed a watermelon feast in the basement of the State House. It was provided by ex-Governor Durbin and Samuel T. Shut, State House engineer. Dr. Knabe and Dr. Hurty left a meeting about getting an emergency hospital started in Indianapolis to attend[81]. She also was on the entertainment committee for the families of State employees. The event consisted of a baseball game, horseshoes and a basket supper in addition to the entertainment[82].

Again, in by October 1908 a diphtheria epidemic threatened Indiana. Dr. Knabe was sent to Mulberry, Indiana in Clinton County where several deaths occurred. She was sent with culture supplies to test the bacteria and to get it under control[83] - which was successful.

Not so lucky was Plainfield. After two specimens that were sent to the State in

October were found to contain Klebs-Loeeffler bacilli, Dr. Knabe went to Plainfield to see the patients. One was a man who worked at the Indiana School for Boys. The other was a local boy of seven years old. Dr. Knabe couldn't ascertain where the man had contracted his illness, but the boy said he'd been in the company of a "colored boy" who had been ill. She believed that was where he could have contracted the illness. Within a few more days, several children at the boy's school were sick with diphtheria.[84, 85]

While attending a meeting of the Physicians' Protective Association (composed of area physicians from Plainfield, Coatesville, Belleville and other towns) other doctors reported diphtheria cases, one being a small child. The "little patient" was sick for more than six weeks which was puzzling because of the incubation time of the disease. The rest of the physicians promised to send specimens for testing.

Quarantine was put into place, however, people ignored it. Dr. Knabe said this was in part due to people not realizing the danger and in part to doctors believing the "old idea" that diphtheria must always be accompanied by pseudo membrane, and that the patient is well and safe to be around as soon as the inflammatory symptoms were gone.

Dr. Knabe went to the child's school to take samples. Of 45 samples, half came back positive. She quarantined the children despite objections. Some received an antitoxin if they were in early stages. She was "impressed" by the fact children with severe sore throats with their tonsils touching the uvula and full of "cheesy material" were allowed to go to school. Dr. Knabe stated that if left as is the children would develop "adenoid face." Additionally several patients developed conjunctivitis. By December the danger was over.

As Acting Superintendent of the State Laboratory of Hygiene, Dr. Knabe was promised more pay because of her hours and her immense expertise. However, this was not to be the case.

Dr. Knabe was the first bacteriologist for the state. She began the department with Dr. Hurty. Three months into her employment, Dr. T. Victor Keene was hired to be the head of the department. When Keene left in 1906, Dr. Rucker[86] came in December 1906[87]. Still she stayed. When he left, Dr. Knabe was promoted to acting head and was paid $1,400 [88]. She was told by Dr. Hurty that she would receive $1,800 or $2,000 (depending on Dr. Hurty's story of the day). She was told several times over the course of a year that she would receive a raise- the first at three months. When the money didn't materialize, Dr. Knabe brought the matter to Dr. Hurty's attention and was always put off. In the meantime, the work nearly doubled and Dr. Knabe began to have trouble with her eyes. She didn't take time out for herself and gave up her vacations.

Eventually, Dr. Knabe was told that there was no more money. Even though she was considered the state rabies expert, Dr. Hurty also told her that because she was a woman, she couldn't command the amount of money the position should pay[89].

This may have been Dr. Hurty's excuse to Dr. Knabe, but this was far from the exact truth. From the time she was promoted, Dr. Hurty had been on the hunt for a new Superintendent, searching for what he considered, "a real capable man.[90]" When his search was complete, he found a man that according to official records, he paid $2,500 per year, although in all other non-official accounts, he stated that Dr. J.P. Simmonds of St. Louis was paid $2,000 per year[90,91] (Dr. T. Victor Keene was paid $1,800 in 1905). In correspondence, Dr. Hurty said he would pay $2,000 the first year and $3,000 in the second[93]. Even Dr. Harry Barnard, the head of the chemistry division at the State Board of Health had his money issues where Dr. Hurty was concerned. His wife wrote in correspondence that he worked long hours and that when lab work came in to Dr. Hurty, many times it was passed to Dr. Barnard. Hurty sent out the reports and collected the cash, and paid Dr. Barnard "what he pleases.[94]" Additionally, Dr.

Left: Dr. T. Victor Keene. He was a professor at the Medical College of Indiana and the head of the State Laboratory of Hygiene for part of the time Dr. Knabe worked there. He later married Marion Craig.

Barnard's wife did not care for Hurty, saying there was "something sly about him .[95]" Apparently, he had treated Dr. Barnard and his wife "abominably .[96]"

Dr. Knabe cut her losses and tendered her resignation, citing discrimination and broken promises. She stated she would open a private practice, take a vacation, get her eyes seen to and take a post graduate course at Johns Hopkins over the winter months.

As of December 1, 1908, she left the state's employ. Dr. Hurty immediately announced Dr. J.P. Simmonds would replace her. Dr. Hurty had been in talks with Dr. Simmonds since at least October 1908 and even stated that if he accepted the position, he would need to be available and in Indianapolis by December 1, 1908. Dr. Hurty stated that he would be required to obtain a professorship at the Indiana University School of Medicine. Dr. Hurty also said the position had nothing to do with politics.

Dr. Hurty's shady dealing and dishonesty may have helped force Dr. Knabe out of her position at the state, but even he could not take away the processes she put in place for diagnosing disease and rabies. Her legacy lived on despite gender discrimination.

Teaching

In addition to her work at the state, right after Dr. Knabe's graduation from medical school, she was appointed Associate in Clinical Diagnosis, and the superintendent of the Medical College of Indiana's laboratories, including heading Bobb's Free Dispensary, where she'd learned her profession.

Prior to Fall of 1905, Dr. Knabe taught at Purdue University's short lived "Indiana Medical College" in the old school's location at 102 N. Senate Avenue. The third and fourth floors of the college were filled with 100 beds, a move that was made because while Purdue had its school, it contracted with the City Hospital in Indianapolis for exclusive rights to access patients. This left Indiana University without access to large quantities of patients in a hospital setting. From 1905-1911 she was an associate in clinical diagnosis for the Medical College of Indiana (later the Indiana University School of Medicine) located at 210-214 N. Senate Avenue.

Dr. Knabe performed clinical education[97] to upperclassmen outside this area at Bobb's Free Dispensary[98]. Much like she had to do as a student, for four hours a week, her classes applied knowledge from their general laboratory work to diagnose patients and samples including blood, urine, sputum, gastric-contents, feces and pathological exudates and transudates. They were also required to make chemical and microscopical examination of cases assigned to them by their instructors. Dr. Knabe was not paid for the clinical teaching, which was tied her superintendent position, as she was not a professor. This education was considered something that she would do to further herself, her profession and give back to it.

In 1906 the school moved into the 210-214 Senate Avenue building (the former Central College of Physicians and Surgeons building) which adjoined the Protestant Deaconess Hospital. The first floor offered a dispensary for outpatient care and a laboratory. On the second floor was a specimen museum and the third and fourth floor housed the hospital.

In Purdue's former building, the first floor contained a dispensary for out-patient diagnosis and an amphitheater known as "the bullpen." The second floor contained the specimen museum, classrooms and offices. The third floor contained a library, a smaller lecture hall and dissection rooms. The top floor had labs for Pathology, Surgery and Pharmacology.

From 1909, Dr. Knabe also taught for the Indiana Veterinary College (804-814 E. Market Street, at the north east corner of Market and Division Streets), becoming the Chair of Parasitology according to some sources[99], which was the first time a woman in North America had held a position of authority in any veterinary institution. In 1910, she also gave an address to the graduating class at the institution[100].

Additionally, she headed community outreach teaching on her own and through the YWCA and the Flanner Guild[101]. At the time of her death, she was also teaching and attending classes in the North American Gymnastic Association.

Presentations

Presenting was a large part of Dr. Knabe's profession. Whether it was presenting papers, classes or information regarding health, Dr. Knabe did what she could to further her medical profession. She often presented with Dr. Hurty at meetings. In 1908 she presented with him at the Indiana Association of Nurses about the importance of sanitation in work.

Throughout her tenure at the state and beyond, Dr. Knabe published and presented but also found time to continue her education, not just through her jobs, but also by attending American Medical Association conferences and joining organizations.
- ISMA (Indiana State Medical Association)
    - 1906-1907 Member
    - June 7-9, 1905 West Baden ISMA meeting Knabe attended
    - May 22-34, 1907 Attended

- o June 18-19th, 1908 French Lick attended
- AMA (American Medical Association)
  - o 1905, 1908 Member[102]
  - o Attended Portland, Oregon session, registered for Pathology and Physiology (one of 18 members who registered for this new field)[103]
  - o June 2, 1908 she attended the AMA Chicago Session, where she said the men and women had an equal sharing of ideas and planning of the session. Over 300 women attending including at least seven from Indiana: Dr. Mary Spink, Dr. Hannah Graham, Dr. Sarah Stockton, Dr. Gertrude Wolfmann, Dr. Alice Hobbs, Dr. Martha Smith, Dr. Helene

Left: Dr. Knabe had her office in the Board of Trade Building (razed).

Knabe, Dr. Mary Wickens and Dr. Mary Ritter. Dr. Knabe believed that from this showing that an organization of women in medicine would result and she was very much in favor of that.[104]
- September 1911 Indianapolis Sessions of the Indiana State Medical Society held at *Das Deutsche Haus*. Dr. Knabe was a delegate.[105]
- September 1908 State Nurses Association: Dr. Knabe presented "Pathological Specimens of Interest to Nurses [106]" This presentation included what indications of the body show different diseases as well as best practices for cultivating bacteria for study [107].

As much as Dr. Knabe was immersed in her profession, she found that for monetary remuneration and experience, she needed change. She wanted and needed ways to balance what was expected of her by giving back to her profession and being able to make a living at what she loved- the practice of medicine.

Private Practice and Continued Rabies Focus

After Dr. Knabe left her post with the State of Indiana, she opened her own practice in the Board of Trade building[109] at the south east corner of Meridian and Ohio Streets in room 25. She continued to perform rabies diagnosis as well as other pathology work.

Between 1910 and 1911 Dr. Knabe moved her practice to the Delaware Flats building where she saw patients, conducted laboratory work, and lived. She continued diagnosing rabies, however, by that time, many other doctors had taken the rabies work she'd done and also capitalized on it. At the time, Dr. Knabe made $75 per rabies diagnosis. In 1910 the State of Indiana had established the Indiana Pasteur Institute (headed by Dr. T Victor Keene[111]) which promised to diagnose rabies for $50 per case.

The bulk of her medical practice work is lost to time. The location of her patient records are not known. What is known is that she treated anyone who asked her to be treated. After her death, men, woman, and children of many ethnicities and races attended her funeral. Her method of payment was simple. Cash, barter or leave something as collateral.

Dr. Knabe used cash in everyday life to pay her bills and sent the bulk of her money to her Uncle Daniel Ehmke[112] in Germany. Bartering meant providing a service or good for her medical skills. At the time of her death, Dr. Knabe had acquired a piano and lessons to go with them by bartering. She had also engaged Katherine McPherson as her assistant in exchange for treatment for a "nervous disorder." Collateral was also

Top: Dr. Knabe lived where this vacant lot is from 1896-1906

accepted in Dr. Knabe's practice. Among Dr. Knabe's possessions was also a diamond ring, which was later discovered to be the property of a patient who had given it to her until her bill could be paid off[113].

A lifelong learner, dedicated to her profession, Dr. Knabe held other offices to broaden her knowledge and networking ability, although unpaid:

- State Secretary for the Indiana Public Health Educational Committee[114] (non-paid) She was appointed on or after July 29, 1909. Her duties included working largely with women delivering addresses on sanitary matters to the women's clubs around the state. She coordinated efforts and gave free workshops on "The Hygiene of the Child's Life from Babyhood to Puberty." Other women including Dr. Nettie Bainbridge Powell (Grant County, Indiana) and Dr. Harriet E Turner (Marion County, Indiana) also gave free workshops. They also worked with the local boards of health, but recognized more instruction was needed. In one year alone, they reached over 2,100 people.

- Member, American Medical Association (July 1909-death)
- Assistant in physical diagnosis, Medical College of Indiana 1905-1907 (non-paid)
- Assistant in physical diagnosis, Bobb's Free Dispensary 1905-1911 (non-paid)
- Member, Indiana State Medical Society
- Member, Indianapolis Medical Society: On September 18-30, 1910 Dr. Knabe spoke to the Indiana State Medical Association members about rabies. She advocated muzzling dogs to prevent the spread of rabies, but believed it needed to be a state law to stop the imperfect enforcement of local laws and ordinances.
- Nu Sigma Phi (women's medical sorority (1909-death): based at Indiana University[115].
- Member, Washington Lodge 1352, Knights and Ladies of Honor until 1910- she believed fraternal orders were one means to uplifting the common people.
- Indianapolis Civic League (who depended on her plans for its public physical welfare section)

Paying Teaching Positions

- Young Women's Christian Association (YWCA): Hygiene and home nursing classes
- Flanner House: classes on sanitation and hygiene circa 1909-1911 [116]
- Associate professor of Physiology and Hygiene, The Normal College of the North American Gymnastic Union (April 1910-death)
- Elected faculty, Chair of Parasitology and Hematology, Indiana Veterinary College
- Member and Instructor, Young Women's Christian Association[118]
- Women's Club: Instructor of Hygiene [119]

From 1896-1906 Dr. Knabe lived at 1151 Bates Street (later renumbered 1205 Bates Street). Two years after Dr. Knabe graduated, she moved to the Ardmore Apartments where she stayed until 1910. For two of these years she roomed with Dr. Ada Schweitzer, who would replace her at the Indiana State Board of Health and become known in her own right for programs such as Healthy Babies. Dr. Knabe then moved to the Delaware Flats and lived there until her death.

Top: The Knights and Ladies of Honor Lodge that Dr. Knabe attended.

Book Illustrations and Journals

In addition to her work and membership in professional organizations, Dr. Knabe also contributed to journals and created medical illustrations. Art was an important part of Dr. Knabe's medical profession. Whether she was paid for the work is not known, but her artistic renderings are contained in several books. Each of her drawings contains her signature.

Four known books contain her drawings. They are:
- Physiological and Clinical Chemistry (1903) Dr. John F. Geis, Professor of Toxicology and Forensic Medicine and Director of Chemical Laboratory at the Medical College of Indiana/IU School of Medicine
- Disease of the Ears, Nose and Throat (1906) Dr. John J. Kyle, Lecturer of Laryngology, Rhinology and Ontology and Assistant to Chair of Surgical Pathology (Dr. Clark) at the Medical College of Indiana/IU School of Medicine
- Emergency Surgery (1909) Dr. John Sluss, Professor of Anatomy at the Medical

College of Indiana/IU School of Medicine
- Life with Health (1906) Dr. J.N. Hurty, Lecturer on Hygiene and State Medicine: a short run book that was written toward elementary school children.

Dr. Knabe's art was also featured in medical journals although none have been found to survive. She did, however, contribute to "*The Medical Student,*" the IU School of Medicine student journal. In 1907 she wrote, "Do Death Certificates Tell Tales," which was a humorous piece based on her experience at the State Board of Health[120]. She also wrote an article in the same issue entitled "A Parting Word to the Class of I.M.C, 1907" in which she talked of how students were about to embark on their careers and how they would lean on each other for support, but that they would also lean on their knowledge, books, microscopes and the Indiana State Board of Health for help. She talked of making "micro-pictures" from Klebs-Loeffer bacilli and how beautiful they were [121].

At the time of her death, Dr. Knabe had also entered a medical art piece in a contest about hygiene and cleanliness. The whimsy and clear message are apparent in her work.

Additionally, doctors were very courteous in giving her proper credit for her

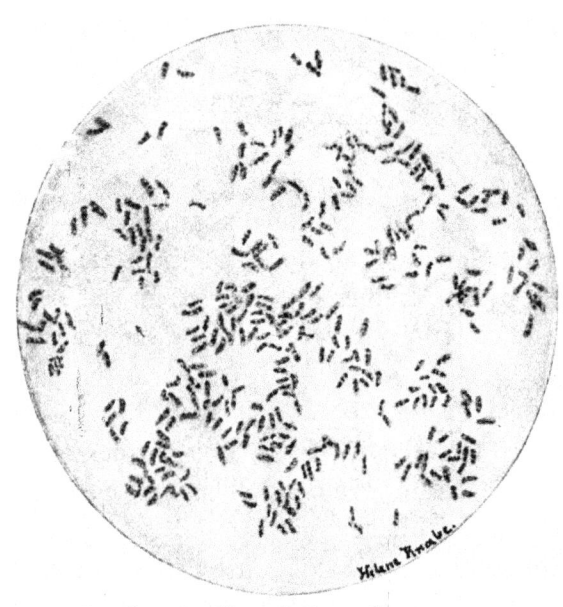

FIG. 46.—KLEBS-LÖFFLER BACILLUS.

Left: A drawing by Dr. Knabe of those "beautiful" Klebs-Loeffer bacilli.

She Sleeps Well   69

JOHN FRANK GEIS, M. D.

DR. JOHN W. SLUSS.

Three of the doctors to whom Dr. Knabe provided medical illustrations:

Top left: Dr. John Geis
Top right: Dr. John Kyle
Bottom: Dr. John Sluss

examination and data. In the Journal of the American Medical Association, "Neisser Bacterin in Chronic Gonorrheal Urethritis," Dr. George Lake thanked Dr. Knabe for allowing him to use the results of her microscopic examination[122]. In the *Indianapolis Medical Journal*, Dr. F.C. Heath's "Report of a Case of Tumor of the Optic Nerve," Dr. Knabe provided the pathological report for the research[123]. In 1909, Dr. George Henri Bogart recognized her as "brilliant" in helping him diagnose walking typhoid that was later reported in a research report in *The Medical Summary*[124]. In co-authoring research with Dr. Frank Wynn, Dr. Knabe published research on the suprarenal glands of cattle[125]. This paper was presented at the American Medical Association's annual session in 1904[126].

Top: The Traction Terminal in Indianapolis. Dr. Knabe contended that the prismatic glass caused her fall and subsequent fractured ankle. Although she was not successful in her suit, it was the first time anyone in Indiana had used X-Rays in a court case.

She Sleeps Well   71

Illustrations from John Sluss' Emergency Surgery. Dr. Knabe illustrated a variety of procedures.

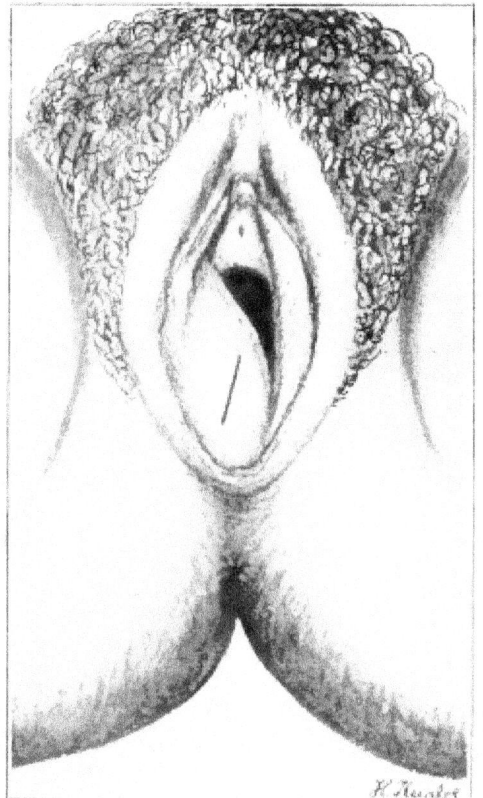

Fig. 316.—Vulvo-vaginal abscess. Direction of incision.

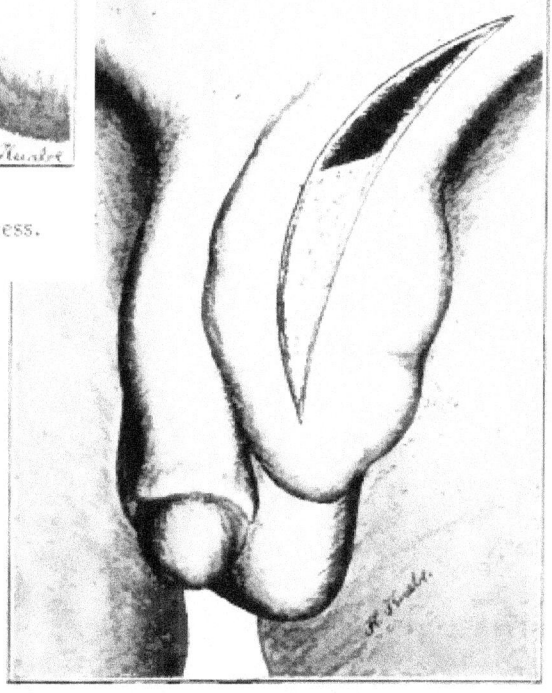

Fig. 458.—Strangulated inguinal hernia; primary incision.

72 *She Sleeps Well*

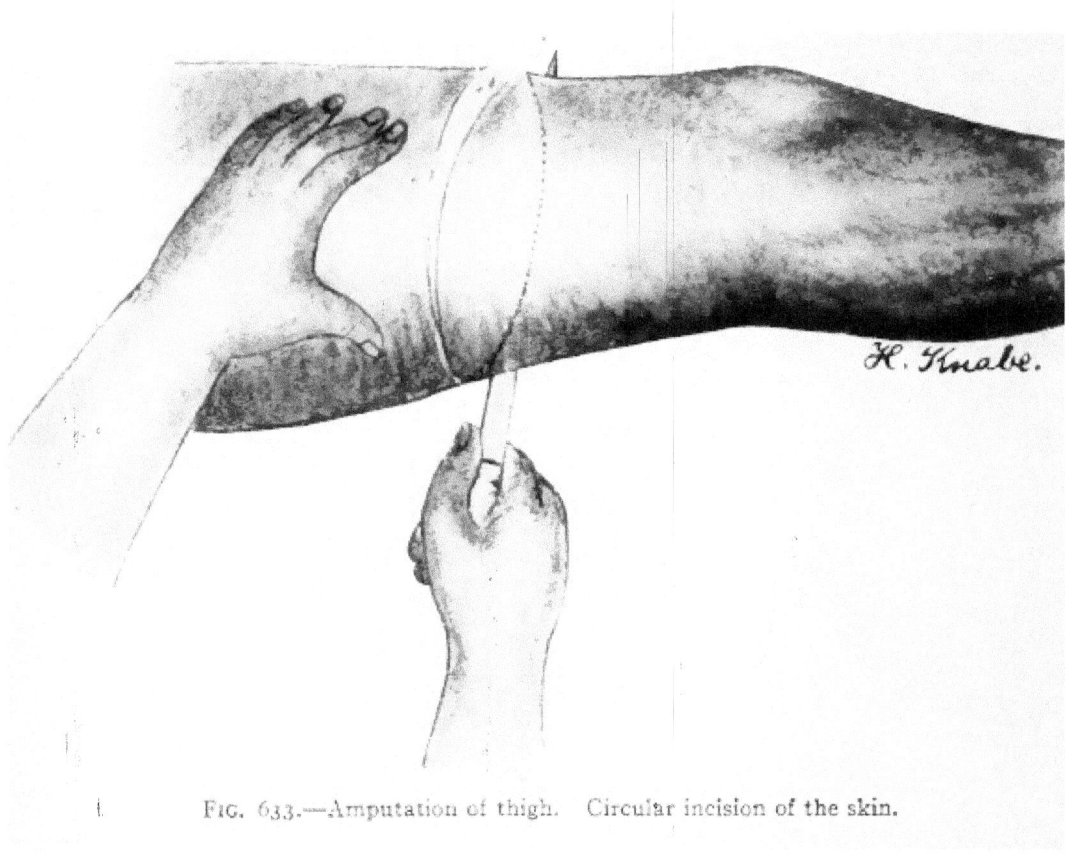

Fig. 633.—Amputation of thigh. Circular incision of the skin.

Illustration from John Sluss' Emergency Surgery.
Opposite: Illustrations from Dr. John Hurty's Life with Health. Dr. Knabe always signed her name "H. Knabe" or "H.K."

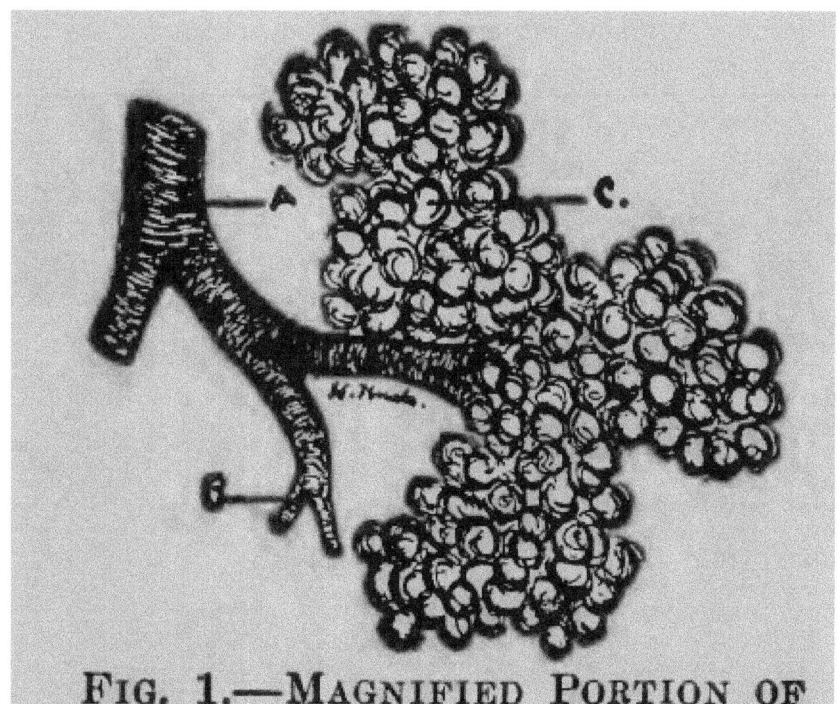

FIG. 1.—MAGNIFIED PORTION OF THE LUNG.

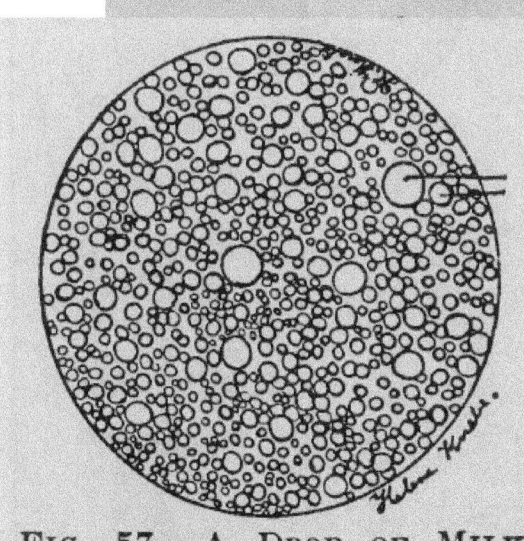

FIG. 57.—A DROP OF MILK, MAGNIFIED, SHOWING FAT GLOBULES.

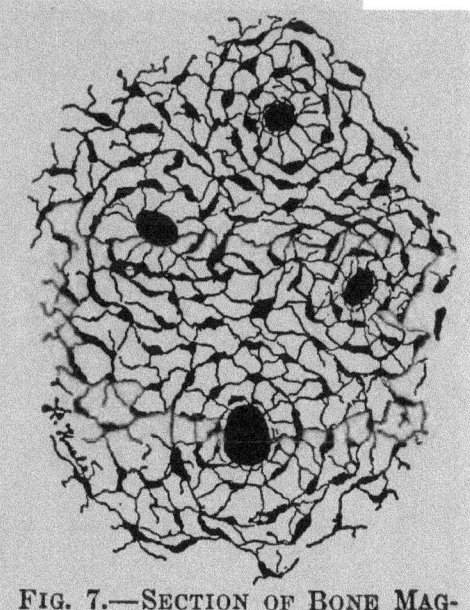

FIG. 7.—SECTION OF BONE MAGNIFIED.

Below and opposite: Dr. Knabe's entries into the medical art contest.

She Sleeps Well

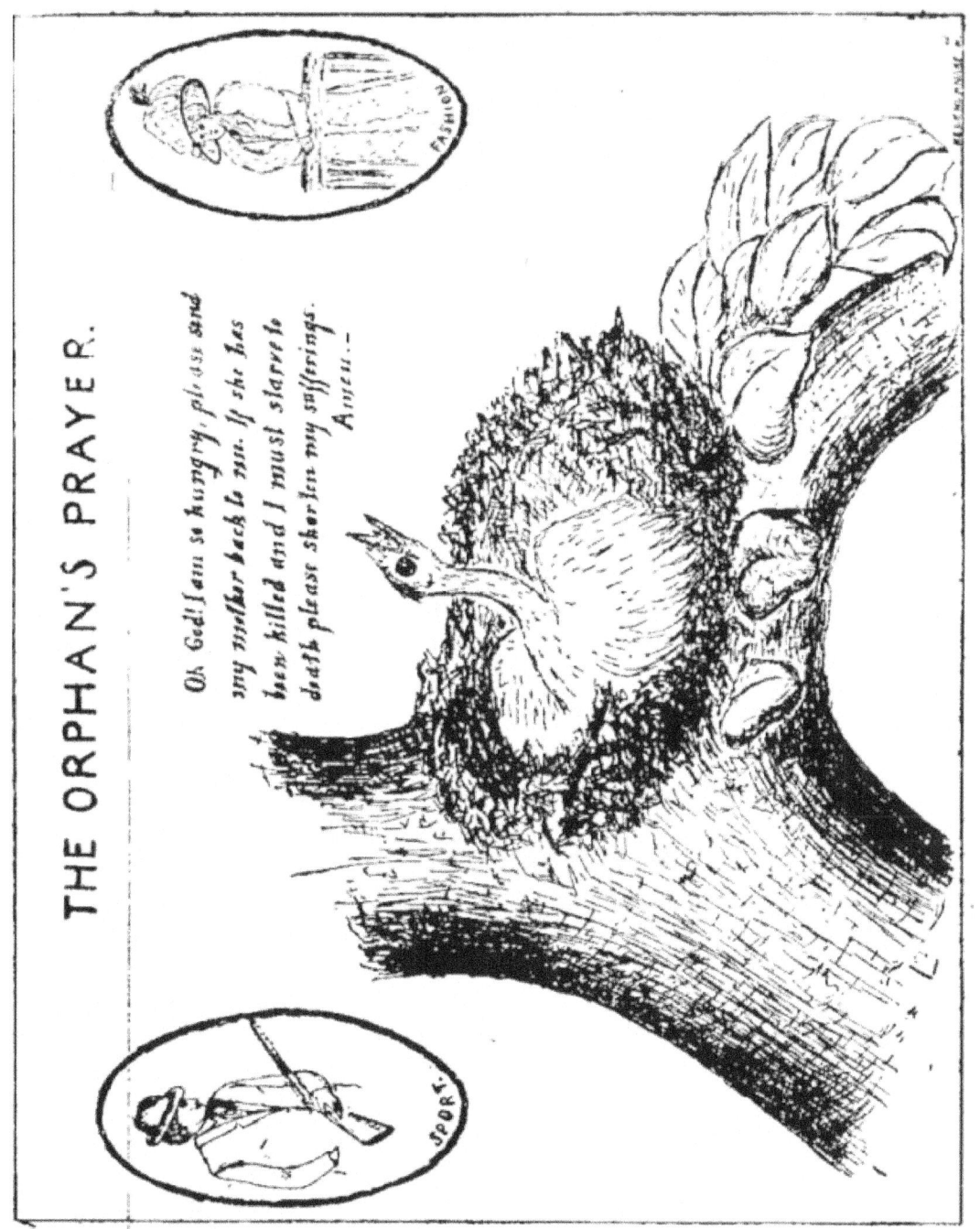

Using Modern Medicine in Court

On the evening of April 12, 1907 Dr. Knabe was turning the corner of Illinois to Market Street after a long day of work and she fell on the prismatic glass at the Traction Terminal Station. Bystanders carried her into a drugstore where she was then transported to St. Vincent Hospital[127] in the City Dispensary ambulance with Dr. J.E. Hughes. In January 1908 Dr. Knabe was the first person to exhibit an X-Ray[128] showing a "Pott's fracture" as evidence in a court proceeding. Dr. Knabe was detained in St. Vincent's Hospital for 35 days.[129] She held the glass accountable for the fractured ankle and filed suit against the Indianapolis Traction and Terminal Company for $5000 damages[130]. She had missed work and was still struggling with the travel and climbing stairs on her injured leg[131]. The picture proved the fracture of the ankle and saved much cross examination of witnesses. The jury tested the sidewalk by pouring water over it and then slid to see how it would work. This was a very poor test, however, as the weather in Indianapolis from April 8-12, 1907 had been snowy every day [132].

The Medical Student staff stated the students keenly missed her presence at the commencement at the Grand Hotel, but that she had been "sentenced to 30 days" at St. Vincent, her "crime being a Pott's fracture .[133]"

The Normal College of the North American Gymnastic Union (NAGU)

It should be no surprise that Dr. Knabe participated in, advocated for and taught for the North American Gymnasts Union[134], which was founded in part due to the *Turnvereine*. This organization and the *Turner* movement actually began in 1811 when Friedrich Ludwig Jahn created the first *Turnplatz* , which is a place for physical training, in Hasenheide, Germany (near Berlin.) Jahn had lived through many wars that had reduced the once strong Germany to deep humiliation. The original reason of the *Turnplatz* was to create sound minds and bodies as well as create a sense of patriotism in the young men who participated. With Napoleon's thumb on Germany, the idea was to free Germany from his tyranny by creating the fervor and trained bodies to do so.

In the same year, Jahn and other people founded the *Deutsche Bund*, an organization with the purpose of defying the foreign powers in charge of Germany. With this new organization came the *Deutsche Burschenhaft*, the student arm of the original organization.

Through this organization, Jahn helped restore Germany to rightful power. During this time, he also wrote books about gymnastics and was able to prove his system in the form of the Turners who fought for Germany. He lectured extensively on political topics which eventually led to his *Turnplatz* and others like it closing at the demand of the government.

Later members of the student organization became violent. As a result the *Deutsche Bund* and *Deutsche Burschenhaft* were accused of being anti-government. Jahn suffered the most. He was imprisoned and suspected of treasonous activities long after his release. However, people became more discontented with the government. In 1848 he was thrust in to the role of representative for the national German Parliament at Frankfurt on the Main. He was not capable of holding such a role, having been demoralized over the years. He stepped down, estranged from the Turners who put him in the role, and moved to Freiburg where he died in 1852.

During this time, in addition to Jahn, Carl Beck, Carl Follen and Francis Lieber were avid Turners who fled to the United States. Beck was a Lutheran minister and taught Latin in Switzerland where his stepfather had been banished after writing a letter to an assassin of August Friedrich Ferdinand von Kotzebue. Follen, like Jahn, was accused of treasonous activities and escaped to Basel, Switzerland, where he taught. Both Beck and Follen were wanted individuals and when the law came too close, they moved to New York and arrived on Christmas Day 1824. They started a boy's school in Northampton, Massachusetts and set up a *Turnplatz* there. Dr. Francis Lieber followed to the United States soon after.

Due to various circumstances, Beck, Follen and Lieber were forced at times to stop teaching gymnastics and take up other teaching or clergy work. Later Follen would introduce gymnastics to Yale University.

These men had an easier time than most. When the first gymnastic society was founded in the United States as the *Cincinnati Turngemeinde* on November 21, 1848, the German influx of refugees was met with less than open arms. *Turnvereine*, gymnastic clubs with members who had been part of the *Deutsche Bund* or *Deutsche Burschenhaft,* wanted to establish new clubs in the United States. However, the Know-Nothing party, which was in a position of influence, opposed anything foreign and made establishment of these organizations difficult[135].

In order to strengthen the Turner movement, the *Philadelphia Turngemeinde* organized a festival, the *Turnfest,* for all the organization to attend, which was a huge success. Many other cities signified intent to join the *Turnerbund* (later the *Sozialistischer Turnerbund*). Because of these cities' support, the Turnerbund gained a footing and these organizations spread across the US and into schools.

The organization once again entered politics by denouncing slavery. Slowly, debts from unpaid subscriptions to the *Turnzeitung*, the organization's newspaper, and the organization itself put the organization in the position of ignoring gymnastics and concentrating only on politics. As the aging Turners left the organization or died, there weren't large numbers of new men to take their place because the younger generation did not have the same interests or ideals as the old Turners.

In 1856 a gymnastic festival was held in Kentucky, across the border from Cincinnati. Fights broke out and the Turners sought refuge in the Newport, Kentucky gymnasium, where they defended their position all night. The next day 107 Turners were arrested, with a bond of $1,000 apiece. The entire sum of $107,000 was paid by two citizens of Newport. No one was sentenced to jail time.

During the Civil War, the Turners continued to be under fire. Their Baltimore facilities were burned to the ground. The Turners were some of the first to volunteer for the Union. Festivals were still held in the North during the Civil War. Following the Civil War, the Turners organizations declared that it, as an organization, should promote thinking that followed the laws and constitution of the US, including a zero exclusion law for people of any race, creed, color or nationality, and that they would continue to be politically active in the interests of the US. Finally they declared that the Turners would work to raise the intellectual standards of the people and would establish schools.

After the Civil War, the Turners prospered and in 1911 there were approximately 232 societies in 24 districts with an enrollment of 38,751.

The school in which Dr. Knabe taught for and enrolled in was The Normal School of the North American Gymnastic Union. It was founded in 1866 and started as a traveling institute and later turned into bricks and mortar institutions across the United States. Several types of teaching certifications were offered, including for teaching gymnastics for both men and women, and a special certification for students who had knowledge of the German language. Later another course was offered for students who wanted to teach in American high schools.

The Normal School of the North American Gymnastic Union (NAGU) was opened in *Das Deutsche Haus* on September 23, 1907. In 1910, around the time Dr. Knabe decided to take courses there to become a teacher, the Indiana State Board of Education accredited the institution as a Class A college, which meant applications for positions in public schools and high schools in Indiana were exempt from examination.

Students had to pass a physical education exam, a medical physical, examination in subjects that the student cannot provide proof of and examination in elementary and special subjects for students interested in those areas of study.

Dr. Knabe was an Associate Professor of Physiology and Hygiene. She also

Top: Second Girls' Class of the Sozialer Turnverein (social Turners' Club). This picture was taken in the Gynmasium of Das Deutsche Haus (now the Athenaeum Foundation building), which is still used for exercise today.

Top: The auditorium in Das Deutsche Haus (now the Athenaeum Building). Dr. Knabe attended dissections, speeches and medical society meetings in this room. Today the room is used for meetings and weddings.

Top: A selection of exercise equipment. This picture was taken in the Gymnasium, which is still used for exercise today.

MEDICAL EXAMINER'S ROOM.   PART OF PHYSIOLOGICAL LABORATORIES

Top: In the early 1900s, the NAGU used this room as the Medical Examiner's room. This is where Dr. Knabe worked, performing physicals and other examinations on students. Today, the room is used for meetings and special events.

served as a medical examiner for the students to conduct their physicals prior to acceptance into the school. Dr. Knabe also planned and gave a series of lectures on "The Hygiene of the Body"[136]. Her plan was to continue her practice but to teach gymnastics and hygiene classes in the gymnastics school, and also in public schools. This would not only afford her more money and a steady income, but would allow her to continue to practice medicine. On April 26, 1911 she was well on her way to this goal by reading how medical work and physical culture were related. By October 1911 she was enrolled and attending classes as a junior[137], presumably because of her previous school experience [138].

Dr. Knabe started teaching April 10, 1910 at the NAGU and made $16 per month from teaching one hour a week. At the NAGU, Dr. Knabe was paid the same amount as her male peers and sometimes more. One male fencing instructor, Alvin C. Herrmann, made $11 per month for the same hours taught. When Dr. Knabe died, Dr. Harriet E. Turner took over her classes. The flowers the NAGU sent to Dr. Knabe's funeral cost $5.

Marion Craig, William Blair Craig and Indiana Veterinary College

Dr. William Blair Craig always maintained he met Dr. Knabe through her treating his daughter for an ailment. What the ailment was or how Dr. Knabe came to treat Dr. Craig's daughter is not known. However, as the doctor circle was small, it was inevitable that she would have met him through the State Board of Health. Dr. Hurty was an advocate for pure foods and as part of that, he would visit the stockyards. There he worked with veterinarians and other doctors who oversaw the sanitary conditions and the feed and care of the cattle, swine and other animals at the stockyards.

Dr. Craig's backstory reads like something out of novel. His family was wealthy, owning about 960 acres of farmland named "Drumshang Farm House" in Ayshire, Scotland. In 1871 the house employed 24 men and women[139].

William came to America on a horse boat that his uncle had in 1882 when he was 14. He loved the idea of America and how free it was. He knew that being the youngest of five children, he would not inherit, so he went off to seek his fortune. This turned out to be a good thing, because his oldest brother, Robert, gambled the estate away[140].

Dr. Craig had been widowed in 1905 when his first wife, Elizabeth Comingore, the daughter of the stable owner where he was working, died of diphtheria as did his son. However, Dr. Craig did have an older daughter named Marion with Elizabeth before her untimely death.

Because he seemed to be of a somewhat cranky nature, he decided to become a veterinarian, because the animals didn't complain like people did[141]. He became a part of the Indiana Veterinary College (IVC) staff and faculty. Dr. Craig was the Dean of Students at the IVC and later also a lecturer in the Theory and Practice, Comparative Medicine. Dr. Knabe lectured for the school and was the Chair of Hematology and Parasitology at the IVC. Academics have argued that she was not a real head of any department, because no one at that time was called a department head, as the school was a small, non-university affiliated proprietary school (and stayed so until its closure). In 1921, three years before its demise, the same was true. However, she was considered the resident expert on hematology and parasitology and colloquially that is what she was known as.

Dr. Knabe continued to see Marion on a social basis and Marion was projected as being Dr. Knabe's friend, although not one word was written about Marion's grief over the loss of her friend.

Indiana Veterinary College (IVC)

The Indiana Veterinary College began in 1892 as a rudimentary school in comparison with today's veterinary curriculum[142]. It was founded by Drs. George H. Roberts and Louis Adolph Greiner, D.V.S. Greiner also owned L.A. Greiner & Son, which owned the Indianapolis Veterinary Infirmary at 14-16 S. Alabama Street. Many of the staff and teachers were medical doctors with no veterinary training other than

Top: The Indiana Veterinary College. This lecture was held in the back part of the building.

Top: The Indiana Veterinary College. The right side of the building was where many lectures were given and demonstrations with animals.

real world experience.

In the early 1900s, veterinary science was barely considered a science. The practice of calling someone an "old horse doctor" would seem to support this. Licensing for this type of work only took two years in 1893 despite an 1892 by-law adopted by the United States Veterinary Medical Association (USVMA) that required three years and six months instruction. By 1904 this amount of time was extended to three years, as the school could not be in good standing with the American Veterinary Medical Association (AVMA) without it. In 1904 the AVMA did a survey of all veterinary schools in the US and found at the IVC there were 10 professors and seven lecturers, five of whom were veterinarians.

The first two years provided 132 course hours of teaching and the last 144. (Compared with the Medical College of Indiana, this number was paltry!) Tuition was $75 a year. By 1906, Dr. A.W. Bitting who had been at the head of the Veterinary Science

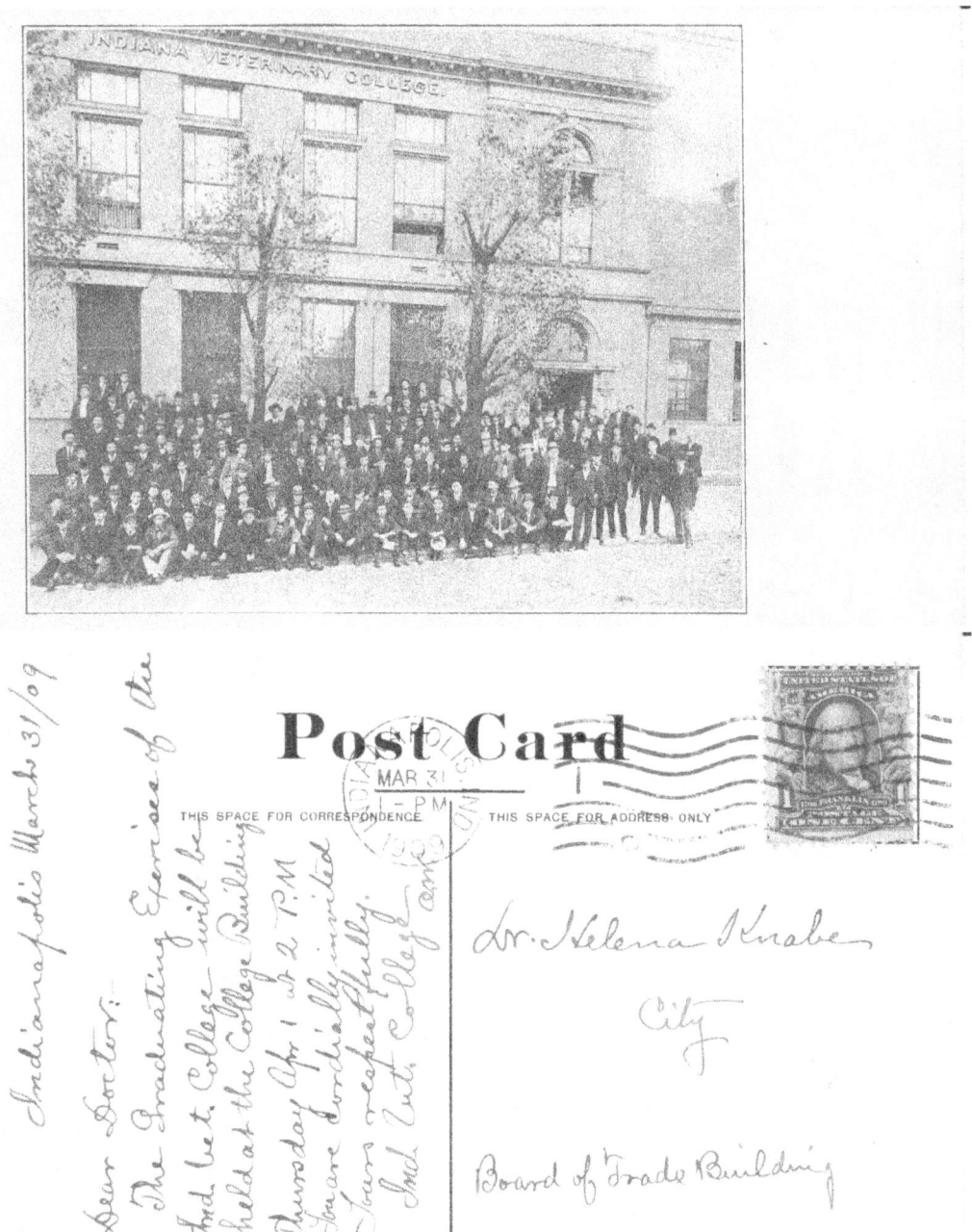

Top: One of the author's most prized possessions. A postcard sent to Dr. Knabe by Ferdinand Adolph Mueller from the Indiana Veterinary College.

Department at Purdue University and the State of Indiana Veterinarian, reported on the IVC. He was generally favorable about the school in that the paperwork submitted by Dr. F.A. Mueller, the secretary of the school was in order, and that the faculty members made a greater effort and did better work than many of the other veterinary colleges in the US. He did fault them for not having any laboratory work, such as chemistry, bacteriology, histology and pathology. However, he did state that there was a new building under construction that would allow for such clinics.

The building, which was completed somewhere between 1909-1910 and featured in a 1911-1912 catalog, occupied a quarter of a city block at East Market and North Davidson Streets in Indianapolis. It had special labs for chemistry, zoology and physiology, histology and pathology as well as a large clinic, operating rooms and lecture rooms. By 1911 the curriculum was still three years but the faculty rose to 21 members. Five of those professors were medical doctors and one being the first woman to teach at a veterinary school in Indiana- Professor Dr. Helene Elise Hermine Knabe. To gain admittance to the school, one had to have a diploma from a college, normal or high school. Without diploma, they had to pass an exam that consisted of five questions in U.S. History, U.S. Geography, arithmetic, 20 words in spelling, penmanship, copying from plain copy and a composition of no fewer than 125 words on a given subject. They also needed 70% to pass.

By 1912 a more complex curriculum was in place. New laws and requirements from the state of Indiana and professional organizations made a more robust curriculum necessary. Gone were the days of a medical doctor doubling as a veterinarian, although many medical doctors were grandfathered into the teaching field because of their years of experience. Others obtained a veterinary science degree (DVS) and others became doctors of veterinary medicine (DVM). The school compared law, dentistry and medicine to the benefits of its school. The school stated the average salary was $1,400 starting off ($18,785 in today's money). By 1922 the curriculum spread to four years.

School work consisted of field work, where students were able to work with real animals and organizations such as businesses that kept animals and relied on veterinarians for their wellbeing and production. Students also had case work in which animals were brought to the school and lectures and hands on practice were given. Also, students were required to attend lectures and participate in the theory and practice as well as surgery in a variety of areas including the theory and practice of comparative medicine, ophthalmology (anatomy, physiology and disease of the eye), surgery, obstetrics, hospital and clinical work, hygiene and sanitation, histology and parasitology, bacteriology, pathology and zoology, zootechnics[143], law, laboratory

Members of the IVC faculty and staff:

Left: Dr. Alfred Jaeger, Professor of Comparative Pathology, Histology, Embryology

Right: Dr. William B. Craig, Dean of Students & Faculty and Professor of Theory and Practice, Comparative Medicine.

Members of the IVC faculty and staff:

Left: Ferdinand Adolph Mueller, Ph. G, Professor of Materia Medica, Chemistry, and Pharmacy

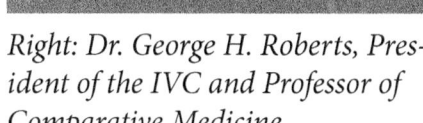

Right: Dr. George H. Roberts, President of the IVC and Professor of Comparative Medicine.

diagnosis, meat inspection, and chemistry, physics, toxicology and botany.

The school required four terms (i.e., freshman, sophomore, junior, senior years) within the school which were satisfactorily passed along with final exams. School ran from September 18th to May 18th. The curriculum was as follows:

Freshman	**Sophomore**	**Junior**	**Senior**
Anatomy Histology*/** Zoology* Embryology Physiology Breeds and Breeding Judging Inorganic Chemistry Physics Botany Bacteriology Clinics Medicine, Surgery, Restraint and Dentistry	Anatomy Physiology Organic Chemistry General Pathology Dentistry Materia Medica*** Clinics Bacteriology	Feeds and Feeding Toxicology Materia Medica*** Pharmacy Practice Com. Medicine Surgery Surgical Exercises Lameness Obstetrics Clinics Dairy Inspection Pathology	Anatomy Applied Laboratory Diagnosis Therapeutics Parasitology* Meat Inspection**** Autopsies Practice Comp. Medicine Surgery Surgical Exercises Soundness Lameness Shoeing Jurisprudence Hygiene Clinics

* These were the areas in which Dr. Knabe taught before her death. Zoology taught the fundamentals of life and the relation of animals to each other and how they develop.
** This involved learning about the tissues and learning about organs and functions.
*** This was a series of lectures around natural properties of chemicals, a review of specimens and drugs and their value and creation/compounding.
**** This was added when pure food laws came into effect. It taught students laws and ways to ensure meat sold for human consumption was pure.

Top: The Young Womens' Christian Association. Dr. Knabe taught at this location and throughout the community with her outreach programs.

The 1921 guide for the school seems to really push how much veterinarians are needed and how much money one could make as well as the prestige one could obtain, versus the care and commitment needed for such a career. The catalogue also speaks to how being a veterinarian can help elevate a man's status in the community and the respect they are given. "As their importance grows, their social position and their income becomes greater, and the calling is more attractive."[144]

Outreach

Chautauqua assemblies, traveling adult education opportunities, were conceived of as late as 1878 and became very popular in the 1920s and 1930s as part of social reform. However, outreach programs were a new concept in Indianapolis in the early 1900s and classes for women or medicine (geared toward women) were unheard of- until Dr. Knabe and other female doctors made them happen. They broke class and race barriers with their course offerings. Dr. Knabe worked with the Women's Club, an organization for African-American women, the Flanner Guild (later Flanner House), which was an African-American community center, and the Young Women's Christian Association (YWCA), which worked with African-American and Caucasian women.

Through these programs, Dr. Knabe proved herself a remarkable instructor. She always had the gift, whether it was teaching students at the medical college or in a clinical setting. At the Indiana State Board of Health, she demonstrated her ability to gain the trust of her colleagues around the state and of her patients.

The class and pay records for these organizations are spotty at best, but there is a public record of classes offered and their locations.

Young Women's Christian Association (YWCA)

The Young Women's Christian Association was established in Indianapolis in 1895. Originally, it was a place where working women could have lunch in a safe and clean environment[145]. During its early days, it was uncommon for women to go to restaurants alone. Within a few years, however, women were more likely to eat in restaurants and later, the YWCA added amenities. It provided low cost housing for single women. Two branches served the women of Indianapolis. The Phyllis Wheatley branch was for African-American women and the other branch served Caucasian women [146, 147].

Dr. Knabe gave a class on October 19, 1906 on "The Human Body and Its Functions in Health." She also started a nursing class on October 26, 1906 on personal hygiene, which was all about bathing and germs. In 1907 she continued these classes and she expanded to home nursing in which she gave practical application for home first aid. It was only available for members of the YWCA and not to the public[148]. She also showed her skills at evaluating her own classes by adding specific bathing and ice pack techniques to her class on personal hygiene[149]. In November she added Disinfection and Disinfectants" "When, Where and how to Disinfect Scarlet Fever, Diphtheria, Typhoid and Tuberculosis;" "The Necessity of Disinfection of Houses Without the Presence of Infectious Disease."[150] Also in November was a class on "Nursing Diseases of Childhood: Croup, Whooping Cough, Diphtheria, Chickenpox, Measles and Scarlet Fever."[151]

In 1908 she continued her current classes, revised her home nursing course and added a second set of them, and gave a lecture[152] on "Infections of the Upper Air Passages."[153]

In 1909 she added yet another class, "The Care of Typhoid Patients."[154] Her hygiene class at the YMCA in 1910-1911 stemmed from taking over from Dr. Hannah

Graham.[155,156] Her Hygiene and Sanitation course was on Friday night from 7:30 to 9 p.m. Single lectures were $0.50 and the whole ten week course was $3.50. In addition to lectures she also took participants to different places in the city, both sanitary and otherwise. The point was to show both sides of the sanitation coin and give tips for improvements. She used specimens, charts, drawings and photographs. Dr. Knabe touched on the causes of infectious diseases, their prevention and recognition and the consequences of infections. She also taught the laws of quarantine.

Sexual hygiene gave women avenues to protect themselves from unwanted pregnancy, sexually transmitted disease (for which some had no cure) and generally allowed them to understand their bodies more. She would also teach "First Aid to the Injured." Her students could write for a pamphlet on the subject. She also taught home nursing from 1906-1911. Dr. Knabe taught hygiene and nursing classes on a part time basis to women of all races and ethnicities. Dr. Knabe also went into different parts of Indianapolis wherever she could find space (normally at organizations for women or churches) and taught hygiene, safe food preservation and cleanliness techniques.

In 1911 Dr. Knabe was the head of home nursing and created a certificate program for nurses to become certified for work in private homes [157].

One of the final teaching lectures she gave was gymnasium work and physical fitness from a medical standpoint. As Miss Mabel Ford of the Cleveland, Ohio YWCA stated, women were not interested in sanatorium type day camps and working on needlepoint. They want to swim, be outside and have walks in the woods[158].

While teaching at the YWCA, Dr. Knabe demonstrated her ability to know her participants needs and build on that, evaluating and improving her courses for future teachings. She pulled from her personal knowledge and experience for the classes. Since she was a fine networker and connected at so many levels to her profession, she was able to keep her teaching current. She was also very practical in her approach and allowed her participants to be very hands on so they not only understood why something was important, but also understood how to perform the work. Dr. Knabe's maxim of mastering the work by knowing all the details certainly proved valuable.

This was one of the few teaching opportunities Dr. Knabe had that paid, although the rate was not listed in available records. Her outreach extended outside of Indianapolis with similar programs being given throughout Indiana. After she was murdered, no one taught hygiene or nursing at the YWCA.

Social Life

Dr. Knabe was described as someone who did not have patience with superstition and blind faith. She believed in law and consequences. Indeed, although most genteel ladies were to go to church and cling to their faith, she seldom went to church services, preferring to read and study alone. Dr. Knabe was so intent on study and so thirsty for knowledge that she was always looking at new lines of study in and out of the medical profession. Her professional obligations included meetings, donating time to instructing future doctors, working in her laboratory researching samples and disease, and attending functions, such as graduations and professional conferences.

With all of these attainments, Dr. Knabe was not without a fun side. She wrote that although she was "enthusiastic in her profession" and "indefatigable in her devotion"[159] to her work, she wasn't all work and no play. She enjoyed plays and programs at a variety of places including the Athenaeum Building (*Das Deutsche Haus*) and enjoyed shopping and having tea with her friends. She had a piano and was taking lessons from a patient.

Dr. Knabe is also known to have done many of the things ladies of the day did as well as keeping her time filled with professional obligations. She met for tea and shopping with many of her friends and her cousin, Augusta. She enjoyed listening to commentators and orators at *Das Deutsche Haus*.

Additionally in 1906 Daniel and Clara Ehmke visited Dr. Knabe. The ship, SS Kaiserin Auguste Victoria (later RMS Empress of Scotland) left from Hamburg and stopped in Cuxhaven (Germany), Southampton (England) and Cherbourg (France) before completing the trip to New York. They had a steerage compartment. Both stayed with her for a month. Daniel did not like Indianapolis and despite requests for him to stay, he returned to Germany with Clara.

The rich and fulfilled life *Frau Professor Doktor* Helene Elise Hermine Knabe worked so hard for was about to end.

Murder Investigation

On October 24, 1911 Augusta Knabe had a dream. In it she saw a big black snake winding its way between her and her cousin, Dr. Helene Elise Hermine Knabe. The snake, with its sharp, spiky fangs, leered at the two women, almost begging them to make a move. They were frozen with fright, clinging to each other. It was ready to strike, and it was only a matter of time before it had its way.

Augusta awoke with a start, drenched in sweat. Her eyes darted around the darkness and as her mind came out of the dream, Augusta heard familiar sounds- the ticking of her clock, a horse clopping down the street, the creaks of her stepfather's house on Bates Street. Augusta was sure she was just feeling guilty. She'd decided not to have tea with Helene yesterday after shopping. It was just that the streetcars got so crowded around that time…Slowly, Augusta returned to a fitful sleep.

When she awoke in the morning, Augusta made her way to school No. 33, Whittier School to teach German for the day. Shortly after she arrived at school, Katherine McPherson, Dr. Knabe's assistant, phoned her, "Something terrible happened to Dr. Knabe."

Augusta arrived at Dr. Knabe's apartment within half an hour. She noticed the blinds in Dr. Knabe's laboratory and bedroom were up and lights were burning. Katherine met Augusta in Dr. Knabe's office.

The consensus in the available witness testimony is that somewhere between four and six o'clock Monday evening, Jefferson Haynes saw Dr. Knabe with her cousin, Augusta Knabe, on Michigan Street. Augusta Knabe said she left Dr. Knabe about 5:50 p.m. Dr. Knabe worked with Katherine McPherson until about 6:00 p.m. when Dr. Knabe began preparing her office for the next day's work. Katherine left at that time, noticing nothing amiss. Dr. Knabe told Katherine she was going to study that evening and bid her farewell.

It is apparent Dr. Knabe left her apartment that evening. First, she posted a letter received by Dr. Nettie Bainbridge Powell and noted as postmarked the evening before

96 *She Sleeps Well*

Top: Dr. Nettie Bainbridge Powell and one of her children. Dr. Knabe wrote to her and mailed a letter the night of her death. Dr. Powell was scheduled to meet Dr. Knabe the following week at the Federation of Women's Clubs.

her death. Second, Dr. William B. Craig's housekeeper, Nancy Tenant[160] (sometimes listed as Tennant), stated in her testimony Dr. Knabe paid a visit to Dr. Craig during the dinner hour.

In fairness, the police were behind the eight ball. They didn't know what they didn't know. Forensics only had seen a jump in application and technique in the 1880s when Jack the Ripper killed several prostitutes in London. Each victim was examined for wound patterns[161]. Fingerprinting and blood grouping were developed in the late 1800s [162].

In the early 1900s, forensics and criminal justice were self-taught. No schools or degrees existed for this type of work. The only curricula that existed for this type of work was created in 1902 by Swiss Professor R. Archibald Reiss at the University of Lausanne, Switzerland culminating in 1909 in a school dedicated to forensics. It would be 30 years before forensics and criminal justice would be offered in the United States.[164]

Police and societal attitudes were a different matter. For hundreds of years, the police existed in one form or another. During the early 1900s, many policemen were hired because of family members being a part of the force but also they were appointed due to political influence. Social and political progressivism[163] lead to much police reformation well into the 1970s[165].

Coroner's Inquest 1911

In addition to an autopsy, Coroner Durham questioned many people. Jefferson Haynes and Katherine McPherson were the first two people to be questioned and the first to be cleared. Augusta Knabe was questioned next. Her story matched Katherine's except that Augusta stated she'd put a pillow on the body. The police did not think this difference to be of great significance. They attributed it to possibly Katherine confusing Augusta's movements of placing a sheet over the body and the pillow.

Augusta did shed some light on Dr. Knabe's finances and her life. The line of questioning went to Dr. Knabe's structured routine and habits. Augusta reinforced that Dr. Knabe had high morals and had worked hard her whole life for what she wanted. Dr. Knabe, Augusta said, worked among the poor of Indianapolis and provided many of her services for free, despite her financial needs. In fact, at the time of her death, Dr. Knabe was worried about her finances and owed Augusta five or six hundred dollars. The furniture in the apartment was Augusta's[166].

The Unfortunate Katherine McPherson and Others Who Followed

Miss Katherine McPherson worked with Dr. Knabe as her office assistant for more than two years. She started working for Dr. Knabe because Katherine was being treated for a "nervous disease," which was not fully described . However, due to some of her reactions in relation to the finding of the body, the strain of providing testimony and some of the minor inconsistencies in her stories, it seems she was a woman who did not deal with stress very well.

The morning of October 24, 1911, Katherine McPherson stopped at Stout's Shoe Store to pick up a pair of repaired gymnastic shoes for Dr. Knabe. Having completed her task, Katherine walked the block and a half to Dr. Knabe's office-apartment located in apartment number two in the Delaware Flats. She inserted the key into the lock and turned it. They key seemed to turn rather easily, as if the door was unlocked, but Katherine did not pay much attention to it at the time. Stepping inside the door shortly after 8:15 a.m., Katherine was surprised Dr. Knabe was not up and about, as she was normally a very early riser. Katherine noticed the windows were open with the blinds drawn to the lower window sill, as was Dr. Knabe's custom. (Later it would be found that one of the windows in her office at the corner of the building was closed, but the blind was still pulled down as usual.)

Katherine called out to the doctor, and not hearing a reply, she made her way from the door, into the doctor's examination room. Katherine noticed the electric lights were on and she was puzzled. Dr. Knabe did not normally have lights on when it was daytime. Not seeing the doctor and hearing nothing, she tentatively moved toward the curtain that led to Dr. Knabe's private quarters. Katherine swept the doors open and stepped into the room. She saw Dr. Knabe in bed and went to the foot of the bed, thinking the doctor must be ill.

Later Katherine McPherson would state that she thought she would "literally faint" from the sight of Dr. Knabe with a horrible gash in her throat. Katherine could not tear herself away from the gruesome sight, but the very shock of the situation kept her in the room.

Dr. Knabe lay with her head almost under the headboard of her narrow super-single hospital bed, her throat so deeply gashed that it was severed down into her spinal column. Her bedclothes seemed be neatly tucked under her body, but a pillow had been placed upon her torso. Under the pillow, Katherine could see Dr. Knabe's pink nightdress [167] was bunched under her armpits. Katherine could not tell if Dr. Knabe had done it or if someone else had.

Upon closer inspection, Katherine saw a little blood on Dr. Knabe's right hand, which seemed to come from a wound on her arm. She also noticed some drops of blood on the floor. What Katherine did not remember was the large pool of drying blood that stained the wood floors.

Katherine's first coherent thought was to call a doctor, which she attempted for over 15 minutes. She called Dr. Frank B. Wynn first, then Dr. Clark and Dr. Kyle. Most of the doctors were on their morning rounds.

Many of the doctors' wives appeared first in lieu of their husbands. Katherine recalled that two articles were disturbed in the room. First, Katherine always placed two pillows on the window seat in Dr. Knabe's medical office. They had been moved and put in an upright position and thrown there with great force.

Augusta arrived next. When Augusta Knabe arrived shortly after from School Number 33 Whittier School, she rushed to Dr. Knabe's side. She said, "She can't be dead." When testifying, Augusta told Coroner Durham that someone had murdered her "little girl."[168, 169]

When Katherine said she had been trying to reach doctors, Augusta said she should get the police or any doctor she could find.

Drs. Ernest C. Reyer, Frank B Wynn and Charles Ferguson arrived first. Seeing the state of Dr. Knabe, they called the police, who arrived around 9:00 a.m. During that time, a sheet was placed over Dr. Knabe's body. When Dr. Ferguson arrived, Augusta asked him to help her "little girl." He believed it might be a sick child, but found Dr. Reyer already phoning the police. He stated Dr. Ferguson couldn't help Dr. Knabe. Dr. Ferguson checked for a pulse and found that to be true. He believed Dr. Knabe killed herself and asked where the knife was. Augusta and Katherine denied finding a knife and said Dr. Knabe had been murdered.

Mrs. Frank B. Wynn, who had arrived before her husband, also questioned Augusta and Katherine stating, "You know the responsibility of concealing a knife if there was one?" Augusta insisted there was no knife. Her words were enough to convince Mrs. Wynn that Dr. Knabe had not committed suicide.

Augusta was shocked. The last time she saw Dr. Knabe alive was on the previous evening at 5:50 p.m.. They had just finished some shopping and Dr. Knabe invited her home for some tea. Augusta said she was too tired and the street cars would be too busy and she just wanted to go home.

That night, Augusta has a horrible dream and awoke about 11:30 p.m. She dreamed a big black snake hung between them from a tree. She and Dr. Knabe were speechless with fright and they held each other closely as if every moment would be their last. Augusta awoke in great fear and slept badly the rest of the night.

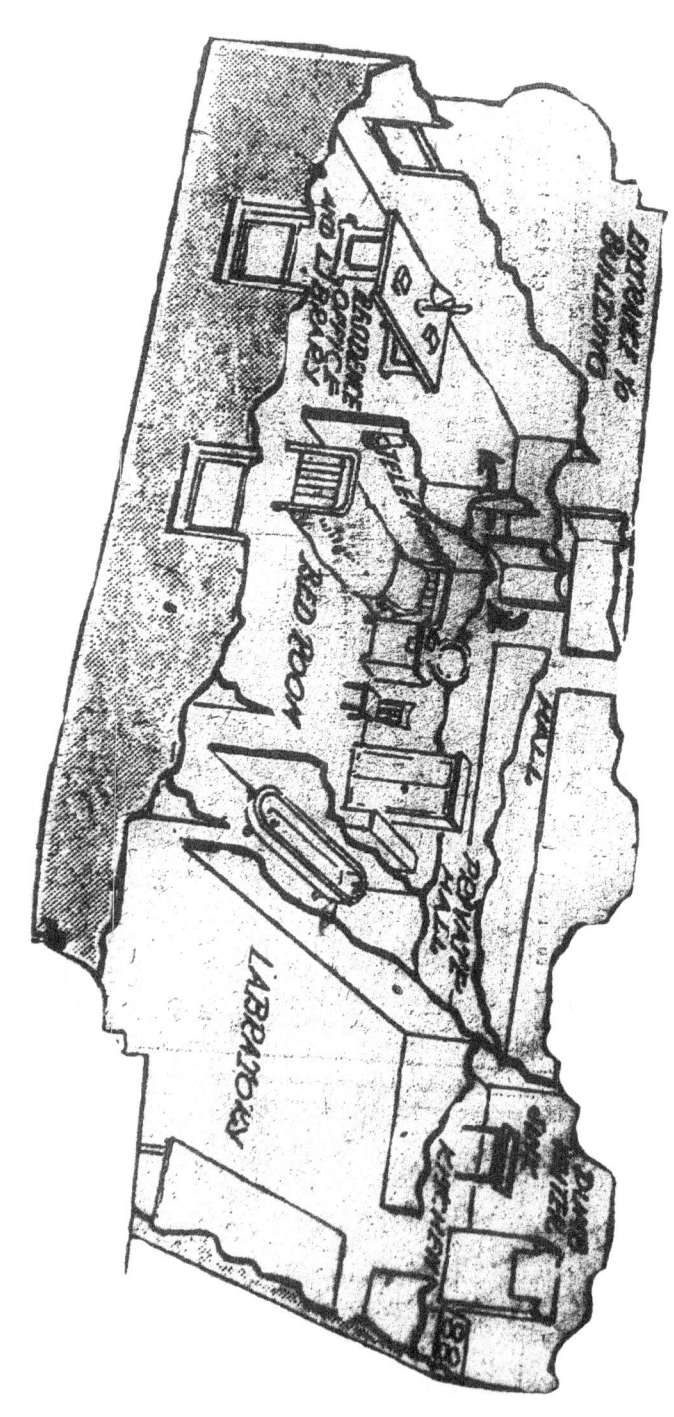

Top: Map of Dr. Knabe's apartment. Today, Dr. Knabe's apartment is home to housing and offices managed by the Salvation Army. Her bedroom is now a restroom.

Top: Katherine McPherson (left) and Augusta B. Knabe (right). These women were the first two people on the murder scene. Katherine was being treated by Dr. Knabe for a nervous disease and in turn, Katherine helped Dr. Knabe run her office. Augusta Knabe was Dr. Knabe's cousin and friend. Both women were distraught over finding the body, the incessant questioning and relentless scrutiny by men in the community.

During the investigation, Katherine McPherson told investigators the ventilation window in Dr. Knabe's apartment was always unlocked but when they viewed it, the window was found to have been nailed shut.

Katherine also remembered no blood stains on the wall, but given her state of mind at finding Dr. Knabe's body, it would have been easy to overlook them. Coroner Durham said he'd found blood spots and had taken a piece of the wallpaper as proof. Katherine did not know where the keys to the flat were. The police did not find them on an initial search. Later they appeared on a dresser. She did mention that Dr. Knabe was very orderly and in the habit of putting her slippers next to her bed. They were found in two locations in her room. A corner of the bedroom rug was also skewed.

Augusta's Testimony

Augusta had been called to the police station on October 28, 1911 but did not make it there because she was so distraught to the point she had taken to bed.

"Please spare me this." Augusta Knabe uttered when asked about what she saw in the room. Tears rolled down her cheeks as the coroner explained how important it was to understand and record all the details of her story. Reluctantly she began. Augusta said Dr. Knabe was on the bed with her head pressed against the metal bars. Her body was unclothed from the waist down. Augusta picked up a pillow and put it over her body. She indicated there was no knife, that Dr. Knabe did not kill herself and that she believed Dr. Knabe was murdered, although she had no idea who the murderer was.

Augusta said she didn't understand what McPherson said at first but once she did, she asked the principal of Whittier School Number 33[170] for permission to leave, grabbed her hat and coat and ran two blocks from Twelfth and Sterling to get the East 10th Street car. Mrs. Wynn arrived shortly after Augusta at 8:55 a.m.

The coroner asked if Dr. Knabe believed in Buddhism because some of her correspondence Dr. Knabe mentioned it. Augusta said she didn't believe Dr. Knabe practiced Buddhism.

She also said she told Katherine McPherson to "Call a physician, call the police or get a man." McPherson contradicted this by saying Augusta Knabe told her "Oh, no, don't call police. They are a rough and an ignorant class and I don't want them around." Regardless, the doctors and police were called.

Jefferson Haynes Testimony

Jefferson Haynes was the janitor of the Delaware Flats and lived in the basement below Dr. Knabe. He was the former pastor turned deacon of the Shiloh Colored Baptist

Church. He could not read or write and had been employed most of his life as a janitor in various apartment houses. He and his daughter Eva and his helper, Mrs. Fannie Winston[171], had all been detained early on in the investigation but released when no proof was found to implicate them in Dr. Knabe's death. Haynes testified that the screens on Dr. Knabe's windows weren't fastened and there was no way to fasten them. He also stated that her windows were unlocked at the time of the murder. Finally, he said that no one entered the dumbwaiter because he would have heard it.

During his testimony to the coroner, Haynes stated that he was making rounds and making fires in the common room fireplaces until around 8:00 p.m., when he was called to flat number 11 to take care of a noise, which turned out to be a mouse. Afterwards, he stayed in his flat until 11:00 p.m., when he went to bed. Later, and at another time, (some accounts say unknown time, others say shortly after 11:00 p.m.), he heard something like a body fall off a table or bed. As he listened, he also heard three screams and three moans that he thought came from Dr. Knabe. These moans caused him to shudder in the darkness of his room. He also heard footsteps go toward the area he heard the noises and a muffled conversation ensued. These noises were something

Top: The Delaware Flats, scene of the murder. Dr. Knabe's apartment is the corner one next to the men. The second window on the first floor is the window to her bedroom.

Haynes did not relate to the police in his first interview, for unknown reasons. Haynes stated he fell asleep believing that Dr. Knabe was treating a patient in pain.

He awoke at 5:30 a.m. when he heard footsteps in Dr. Knabe's rooms. He stated that when he signaled later that morning for the trash to be put on the dumbwaiter, someone placed it there and it was sent down. McPherson and Augusta Knabe deny putting anything in the dumbwaiter.

Later Katherine McPherson and Augusta Knabe declared they had not placed the can in the dumbwaiter. People in the room with Katherine and Augusta at the time of the signal said that no one put a garbage can in the dumbwaiter.

The latter statements are impossible if we believe that McPherson was in the apartment only after 8:15 a.m. and Augusta Knabe came later at her request. Additionally, the dumbwaiter was inside Dr. Knabe's apartment. If she had done it after 5:30 a.m., the time of her death would be significantly off. If it was after 8:15 a.m., it would not have been possible since Dr. Knabe was visually verified as dead.

Haynes also stated that there was nothing improper about her conduct, that Dr. Knabe often treated late night cases. In all cases, it was women accompanied by their husbands. This is something Katherine McPherson and Augusta Knabe denied, but perhaps Dr. Knabe told them this to ease their mind about a woman allowing people into her apartment late at night. They could have been in denial because they could not conceive a woman could or should allow someone in (especially a man) at night.

Ernest Haynes, Jefferson Haynes' son would be called before the grand jury as one of the last witnesses in 1912.

Franz Kropp's Testimony

Franz Kropp[172] who was 70 at the time of the murder, was Dr. Knabe's step-uncle. He was married to Augusta Knabe's mother, who had passed away some years ago. He was called by Knabe and McPherson and arrived before the police[173]. On November 3, 1911 he said he refused to express an opinion on whether she had been murdered or killed herself[174]. He believed if there had been any weapon, Augusta would have told him about it[175]. "And she tells me nothing. She only grieves." He said he thought the case was perplexing enough that one could not say if it were murder or suicide. He also denied that Dr. Knabe's parents were from German royalty. He said when he lived in Germany he knew them both personally and lived about 15 miles away from them[176].

Witnesses

During the inquest Captain of Detectives Holtz said that no new clues of importance had been discovered, despite many leads. One problem with moving forward was that many leads were repeated by different reports, doubling police efforts.

The investigation extended all over the United States, wherever Dr. Knabe had conducted business and had friends. Correspondence as to her life were sent to the police after inquiry but seemed to uncover no clues.

Mr. Joseph C. Carr

Joseph C. Carr, a plumber , told the police at 11:00 p.m. (although some reports say 12:45 a.m.) he heard two screams that seemed to come from Dr. Knabe's apartments the night of her murder and later he saw a man walk quickly away from the alley at the rear of her building and south onto Delaware Street . The man was about five foot eight or nine inches tall, weighed 170 pounds, and wore a dark suit and dark, soft hat. The police discounted this idea after taking measurements and deciding there was no way he could have heard screams from where he was and could not have seen the man leave her apartment in such a short time after the screams. The murderer, they reasoned, would have to have gone out of Dr. Knabe's apartments, out the west door, turn north then east, down a flight of stairs and through an alley in a short amount of time for Carr to have seen him after the screams. The police tested the theory and found it impossible.

Mr. Harry W. Haskett

Harry W. Haskett[177] said there was a prowler near the Delaware Flats on the night of Dr. Knabe's death. He also said around 11:20 p.m. he saw a man stepping from the air shaft north of the building. His description did not match Carr's. Haskett said the man had dark hair, a mustache and weighed about 180 pounds. He wore a dark hat and long dark cravenette[178] . This theory was "exploded" by the police as Leo Kahn, a tenant of the Vendome Flats, attached to and just north of the Delaware Flats. Kahn said he had gone to the theater with his wife and they returned about 11:20 p.m.. The lights were off and his wife was scared so he walked in the air shaft to the custodian's apartments in the basement to tell him to turn on the lights. As he emerged, Kahn met Haskett. Kahn wore a soft, dark hat and a long dark coat. He weighed 171 pounds. Haskett denied Kahn was the person he met by the alley.

Mrs. Frances Mount, Flat No. 14

At 8:00 p.m. on November 23, 1911 Mrs. Mount heard a noise at her screen and she became frightened as she was alone and left her home as soon as possible. *All of*

Top: The scene of Dr. Knbe's murder. Her body was freshly removed. The bloody sheets are still on the bed. Dark blood stains mar the floor. The pillow which would be found a bloody handprint is still on the bed.

DR. ERNEST C. REYER.

DR. CHAS. E. FERGUSON.

Top: This is a detail of her chiffonier top. Notice the pictures. Could one of these be her mother or even Daniel Ehmke and Clara?

Top left and right: Two doctors called to the scene. Dr. E.C. Reyer (left) belived Dr. Knabe was murdered. Dr. Charles Ferguson (right) sat the fence believing Dr. Knabe had no reason to kill herself, but could see no reason why someone would want to murder her.

the apartments near Dr. Knabe's were not rented because they were "dark." She told the police that a prowler tampered with the windows at the Delaware Flats the night Dr. Knabe died. At 8:00 p.m., she heard someone rattling the windows between the alley on the east side and Michigan Street.

She moved out the day after the murder.

John Grace Testimony

John Grace was the custodian of the Emmet Flats, directly to the south of Dr. Knabe's apartment. He said a prowler peeped in her windows several months ago and gave a description. The man had turned toward John Grace. The man was 5 feet 8 inches, about 140 pounds with a dark complexion, clean shaven. He wore dark clothes and a dark, stiff hat. The man had an expressionless face and to Grace looked like a "sodden degenerate, with baggy watery eyes and a weak mouth."[179] Grace tried to chase him but to no avail. The man had not been seen since August 1911.

Mrs. J. W. Smith Testimony

A neighbor to John Grace, Mrs. Smith saw the same man several times and reported it to her son, who worked at the *Indianapolis Star*. She also pointed him out to Grace who approached the man and said, 'Good evening." He was answered with a grunt. Mrs. Smith's description was similar but she said he weighed closer to 160 pounds. The night of Dr. Knabe's murder she saw him about 11:30 p.m. approaching Dr. Knabe's window. McPherson did say that Dr. Knabe had been frightened one night when a screen was raised and a hand came in the window. That evening Dr. Knabe stayed at home in case a burglary was planned but the event was not repeated.

Testimony from People Called to the Scene
Dr. Charles E Ferguson's Testimony

Dr. Charles E. Ferguson testified that he was called about 9:15 a.m. and that he was needed at Dr. Knabe's flat. He knocked at the door.

Augusta Knabe was distressed, according to Ferguson and she asked him to save her "little girl." At first Dr. Ferguson thought Dr. Knabe needed assistance with a child. He stepped into Dr. Knabe's bedroom and saw Dr. Reyer at the phone and then at her body telling her Dr. Knabe was dead and that it was a case for a coroner and the police. He then assisted Dr. Reyer finding the telephone numbers of the police and coroner. He asked Dr. Reyer if it was suicide and he said he didn't know. Then he asked where the instrument was and he said that they should probably leave things as they were until the coroner arrived. Ferguson said Augusta Knabe asked why the doctor didn't do something and she told Augusta that it was too late, that Dr. Knabe had been dead for a while.

Ferguson said he didn't believe Augusta Knabe really thought her cousin was dead until he told her. Dr. Ferguson went to the bed and looked under it. The blood had soaked through the mattress and pooled on the floor. He went to the west side of the bed which was more or less in the corner and looked behind it to see if anything had fallen behind it, which he didn't see.

Dr. Knabe's body was resting on top of the mattress with no pillow under the head. Her head was thrown back so far that he could see the opening in the trachea. Her thyroid gland was extending up into the wound. The left arm was over the edge of the bed and the hand had some blood on it. The head was up by the metal headrail. The right hand was extended and had spots of blood on it. The body was covered in a sheet from about midway up the waist to the shoulders. There were no bloodstains on the floor or anywhere else in the apartment. A blanket that was usually turned down at the foot of the bed, as it was just for show, was nowhere to be found[180].

When Dr. Ferguson heard the patrol wagon, he went into Dr. Knabe's office area where Mrs. Wynn was. When the police arrived, he motioned for them to come in and was asked who discovered the body. McPherson said she had. Many of the police at that time very emphatically said it was murder. Augusta echoed this idea. When the coroner came in, they lifted the sheet. Dr. Knabe's left leg was straight and the right was flexed and rotated outward. There was a pillow from the waistline down to the knees.

The police were concerned about a missing microtome blade. Dr. Ferguson was able to identify the microtome blade he lent Dr. Knabe. He stated that he did not have any reason to suspect that Dr. Knabe committed suicide but he also had no reason for why someone would want to murder her.

Dr. E.C. Reyer

Dr. E.C. Reyer was questioned and his testimony matched Dr. Ferguson's. He stated he believed there had been a struggle due to the condition of the bed clothes and Dr. Knabe's night gown. It looked as it if it had been pulled or twisted in a struggle.

Mrs. Frank B. Wynn's Testimony

Mrs. Wynn was the third person on the scene. She believed McPherson and Augusta Knabe thought Dr. Knabe was murdered and did not kill herself. McPherson called and asked for Dr. Wynn but she said he was out, so she went instead. When she

Top right: Dr. Loy McAffee Inghram's 1904 Medical College of Indiana portrait.
Top left: Dr. Loy McAffee's military portrait.

entered the apartment Augusta Knabe said that Dr. Knabe had been murdered. Mrs. Wynn did not go into the sleeping room but stayed in the front room trying to console Augusta while McPherson tried to reach doctors.

Mrs. Wynn stated that she had never seen Dr. Knabe be anything other than bright and cheerful. She did not see a knife and no one mentioned a knife. McPherson did say, when Mrs. Wynn commiserated with her about how horrible it must be to find someone in that condition, that at first she wanted to run but then she felt she needed to call a doctor.

Testimony of Dr. Knabe's Friends
Dr. Loy McAfee Inghram

Dr. Loy McAfee Inghram of New York graduated with Dr. Knabe from medical school in 1904 as the second of two women who graduated that year. Dr. Inghram worked with her husband as a stenographer in his New York City office and edited medical literature.

She assisted the police in their investigation, but would not talk with reporters. It was reported that she met several times in a three day period with police and she was trying to find a motive for the murder. None was found before she returned to New York.

Dr. McAfee Inghram said Dr. Knabe would not have taken her life even if she was discouraged because she'd known Dr. Knabe for a long time. She said, "If the mystery is dropped by the police as suicide, then one of the most atrocious murders ever perpetrated on the continent will go unavenged."[181] She went on to say that her faith and love for Dr. Knabe was as strong as ever, just as strong as when they sat on the stage of the English Opera House to receive their diplomas.

Mrs. E.D. Brocking Testimony

Mrs. E.D. Brocking of 309 E Wyoming Street, mother of Dr. Ernest R. Brocking, who was a classmate of Dr. Knabe's and a close friend. She said Dr. Knabe was not in love, nor had company with any men that she knew of and that Dr. Knabe made enough money to live well. Mrs. Brocking also said Dr. Knabe did not seem to worry much and seemed to be happy with her life. "She seemed to have no cares but to live and be satisfied with her portion."[182]

Other testimony

The afternoon before her death, Dr. Knabe borrowed some notes from Alvon

G. Hermann, physical director of the Social Turnverein at the German House. She wanted to borrow the notes he took the previous year when he was still a student. She promised to return them on Tuesday.

Men and their testimony

On November 18, 1911, four men were in attendance and gave testimony but their identities were kept secret by all involved. One of them said he could name Dr. Knabe's killer. Their identities remain a secret.

Alonzo Mayfield Ragsdale, Undertaker Testimony

Alonzo M. Ragsdale was a business acquaintance of Dr. Knabe's and became the executor of her estate at the request of Augusta Knabe.

Ragsdale started as a druggist in Trafalgar, Indiana. At the time of Dr. Knabe's death, he was an undertaker in Indianapolis. His undertaking establishment was at 231 Massachusetts Ave (now in newer building bordered by Delaware, New York, Ohio and Pennsylvania Streets). In testimony, he said he passed by Dr. Knabe's apartment every night. The night of her murder he passed by shortly before midnight. He didn't notice anything unusual but said a light was on in her apartment.

In fact, he told Durham at his office that shortly before her death, Dr. Knabe nodded at his building and told him, "You'll have me in there one of these days." [183] Ragsdale firmly believed she killed herself.

Coroner's Investigation
Post-mortem

Coroner Durham attended to the post-mortem of Dr. Knabe. In addition to being the coroner, he was also a professor of surgical anatomy at the Indiana Medical College. Dr. Ralph S. Chappell, a deputy coroner, attended the post-mortem of Dr. Knabe's body conducted by Coroner Durham. On October 27, 1911, Dr. Chappell explained to the police that he did not believe Dr. Knabe had, or could have, committed suicide. Dr. Chappell explained the carotid arteries had not been severed and only the left jugular vein was partially cut but the right was untouched.

The wound was made by drawing a very sharp, medical grade instrument across Dr. Knabe's throat from right to left. There were three slashes. The first cut severed the trachea, causing her death. The second was a false start on the left side. The third cut pressed deep into her throat (causing the nick on her spine) and was drawn up to the left side .

The fact that there were two viable slashes disproved the suicide theory. After the first cut, Dr. Knabe would most likely be unable to breathe and in her case, she was cut below the larynx, which made her unable to call out even with her last breath. Additionally, the trachea was cut and minor veins were bleeding into her throat, causing her to choke. Dr. Knabe could not have cut her trachea and been able to complete the second cut. Also, there was a defensive cut on her arm which would call into question the suicide theory of the police.

Although Dr. Knabe's estate would be over $500 short (see section on Dr. Knabe's estate), Coroner Durham said her accounting books showed that she was not overdrawn in her finances, rather, her medical practice was growing.[184] Even the *Indianapolis Star* took up the cause. It stated that the police believed she committed suicide over $500 or $600 dollars. "People can be found in every block who owe that much money, without paying it soon as she had, yet have no notion of ending their lives. In view of the struggle made by Dr. Knabe to master her profession and the difficulties she overcame, a debt of that size could not have been a very large mountain to her." The paper stated plainly a better reason for suicide would have to be made before the people who really knew her and cared for her would ever believe suicide.[185]

From the beginning, Dr. Charles O. Durham said he would bet his last dollar that Dr. Knabe had been murdered rather than had killed herself. On December 28, 1911, Coroner Charles O. Durham released his verdict.[186]

> *I, Dr. Charles O Durham, Coroner of said County having examined the body of Dr. Helene Knabe and heard the testimony of the witnesses, do hereby find that the said deceased came to her death October 23, 1911 at apartment #2 Delaware Flat Indianapolis, IN from hemorrhage & shock following a cutting wound of throat at hands of unknown person or persons- murder.*

This 50 page document detailed his findings and records of the testimony of 12 people. To date, this document has not been found. There were two known copies. One was placed with the cold case file, which was destroyed in 1977[187], and one that was filed with the county clerk, which is either missing or unable to be found in the microfilmed files of the coroner. Immediately, Superintendent Hyland pointed out inconsistencies in Durham's work and said he still believed suicide more than murder.

Durham said there were misunderstandings in Dr. Knabe's life that may have been the basis for murder, but he would not give details. Hyland stated he didn't believe

Left: Coroner Charles O. Durham believed after his inquest that Dr. Knabe was murdered. His verdict was met with scorn by the politically fueled police department. Nevertheless, he moved forward and the case went to two grand juries.

Top: Coroner Durham's murder verdict. The 50 page document that should accompany it has been lost.

Durham could make such statements and presume murder. He called the statement that Dr. Knabe couldn't have cut her own throat "ridiculous" and that the question of if she could have done it had been answered by other suicides. He said also that suicide was likely because of the lack of a struggle in the room[188].

The *Indianapolis Star* asked, 'How much progress can the police force make toward solving the Knabe mystery, with the suicide theory urged upon them by Superintendent Hyland? Not much, it would seem, if there is anything in the law of suggestion.'[189]

The coroner's verdict was met with scorn from Superintendent Hyland of the Indianapolis Police Department. Even after the verdict, Hyland clung to his belief that Dr. Knabe committed suicide. He called Durham's report ridiculous. Hyland argued that Dr. Knabe could have killed herself had been proven in an unnamed case that happened since Dr. Knabe's death. Hyland said there was no evidence that would sway his opinion. Hyland stated that there was no evidence of a struggle (despite dissenting voices from police and physicians) and in his over 25 years of police experience this supported the suicide theory. He also believed, with a somewhat sexist attitude, that the reactions of Katherine McPherson and Augusta Knabe were unnatural. After the women saw the body, Katherine went calmly to the door and met the postman, telling him nothing about what had happened. Augusta asked Katherine to call a man and when the postman showed up, they did not ask for his help. Superintendent Hyland stated, although it is nowhere else documented, that when Katherine suggested getting the police, Augusta said she didn't want the police around because they were a "rough and ignorant class."[190] Also according to Hyland, when Augusta was asked about why she didn't call the police, she said it didn't enter her head. When in Hyland's mind, it had. Hyland found it unusual that neither woman screamed for help. For Hyland, this was just not womanly behavior or the behavior of someone who believed a dear friend had been murdered (versus suicide).

From this attitude, the police on the case may have experienced some pressure to dispose of the case as quickly as the media would allow. Hyland was the head of the police and his voice trickled down through the ranks. However, for all purposes of the media, the investigation went on. Even the newspaper in its editorials did not believe Dr. Knabe had been a victim of her own hand. Additionally, Hyland failed to mention the defense wound found on Dr. Knabe's arm and the bruising on her left hand, which might have been from hitting her assailant.[191]

Women and men were split. The women physicians believed
- Dr. Knabe was generally cheerful and had no reason to kill herself.
- She would have used drugs instead of a knife.
- In the event of suicide her body would have been clothed.
- She often said suicide was the mark of a coward.
- They did not believe the wounds could be self-inflicted.
- There were prowlers and suspicious characters about that could have done it.
- There seemed to be a cover up by the police to make it look like a suicide.

Men physicians believed:
- Dr. Knabe was despondent over her financial situation.
- The knife used by her for dissection would indicate suicide.
- The idea to kill herself may have come on suddenly without care to the arrangement of her clothes
- The fact that she'd talked of suicide as cowardly proved she had thought of ending her life.
- The knife could have been hidden before the police arrived.
- The very nature of the wounds show they could be self-inflicted.
- No evidence of a break in made it look like suicide.

Suicide Theory

Several reasons for the suicide theory exist. First, some people believed Dr. Knabe made the cuts herself because she was despondent. There was no evidence of robbery that anyone could see and the apartment didn't look as if a struggle had taken place, despite the defensive wound on Dr. Knabe's arm. Additionally, the police believed there was a significant time lag from when the body was found to the time they were called that Augusta and/or Katherine may have removed the weapon. Third, at some point it was decided because there was no weapon, which was definitive proof Dr. Knabe killed herself. Fourth, the police felt the reaction of the women was abnormal. Also, a semi-famous detective-turned-writer analyzed the newspaper accounts and gave his opinion, stating it was murder, based on the "evidence" he read about. Finally, a few professionals in Indianapolis decided to call unfounded innuendo into the case by suggesting Dr. Knabe was unhappy because she was a lesbian. At the very least she was unhappy because she was a difficult woman and had no friends, therefore she was a failure and decided to end it all.

Editorials came almost weekly. One asked the simple question "About how long and loud would Dr. Knabe have had to scream before the neighbors and passers-by would have thought she might need assistance ?"[192] Another one a few weeks later said, "Listen to the voice of medical wisdom in the Dr. Knabe case and you will be even more in doubt than ever."

What actually happened was that instead of looking at the case objectively, the police were less than helpful from the onset. They waffled back and forth from suicide to possibly murder and back to suicide due to lack of evidence. They either did not know what they were looking for, or were so steeped in denial and provincial thinking that it clouded their judgment.

Suicide and Women

Not once in the newspapers, in the trial or from the doctors were any statistics about suicide given. It is hard to completely pinpoint exact statistics but from what the Centers for Disease Control reported in 1911, we can see the likelihood of Dr. Knabe using cutting as a method of suicide is highly unlikely. At the time, the only ethnic distinctions made were black and white.

In 1911 Dr. Knabe was 35 years old. According to the Centers for Disease Control, Indiana in 1911 experienced 199 deaths that were white male and female suicides in the 30 to 39 age group.[193] Indianapolis saw 42 suicides of males and females in all age groups, white and black. In the United States there were 2,076 total suicides in the 30 to 39 age group with 144 suicides from cutting or piercing in the 30 to 39 age group from whites and blacks. This method was the sixth most used method. The top five methods were poison, asphyxia, hanging/strangulation, drowning, and firearms. Although a specific analysis of male versus female methods or percentages is not available, one can see the percentage of total people using cutting or piercing as a suicide method is less than seven percent which makes white females and even smaller fraction of that number. If we were to use seven percent for the 42 total suicides (i.e. male and female, all races) seen in Indianapolis in 1911, that would mean less than 3 of them would be by cutting or piercing and the chances of a white woman doing it would be even less.

Even today, women are highly unlikely to use cutting as a method of killing themselves.[194] According to the Centers for Disease Control and Prevention, suicide ranks the fourth leading cause in people aged 35 to 54. Firearms, suffocation and poisoning are the top three methods. Cutting is the fifth most used method in the 35 to 44 age group (2%). Of those in the age group of Dr. Knabe, only 1.5% of females who committed suicide used cutting or piercing as their method of choice. In 2014 that was 25 women across the United States.[195] When we look at the Midwest specifically, that number drops to one percent of 308 deaths or about three white females .[196] When we look specifically at Dr. Knabe's age of 36, there were 22 suicides in the Midwest in 2014. Cutting was not even a method for this age.[197]

The Cuts

The suicide theory started after Coroner Durham looked at Dr. Knabe's body. The police said that the marks left on her clearly proved Dr. Knabe committed suicide. To do this, Dr. Knabe would have had to hold the blade in her left hand. People who had known her for years asserted that she was right handed, discounting this theory . Hyland's issue was that it was astounding that the killer was able to leave the building without leaving a blood trail throughout including shoes, fingerprints and smears. Later he added that there was no motive, as she had not been sexually assaulted or robbed.

There was some blood on the wall, as Coroner Durham took a sample of the wallpaper as proof. The coroner lifted the left arm and they saw an incised wound on the outer aspect of the left forearm, midway between the elbow and wrist. Her mouth was shut and her eyes were almost closed. Blood was lightly spattered by the light switch and on the west wall. Although Dr. Ferguson and McPherson had corroborating stories about the bedroom scene, Dr. Reyer also added he believed the bed clothes were twisted as if a struggle had taken place, and as if they had been dragged or pulled during the struggle. Her nightdress bunched under her shoulders as if she'd been on the bed, backing into the corner away from someone by using her feet to propel her. This nullifies the suicide theory again.

Second, there was a defensive wound on her arm as if she tried to ward off the blows of the knife. Some doctors would assert she had tested the killing instrument to ascertain how deep she would need to cut before she killed herself. Why would Dr. Knabe, who was intimate with medical knowledge, try this at all? She would already know how deep she needed to cut to be effective.

Third, the assailant had intimate knowledge of the human body. The way her throat was cut indicated the person was deliberately trying to kill her in a way to minimize the blood spurting. The first cut killed her and she drowned in her own blood, the majority of which went down her throat. The second cut finished the job with the same purpose, missing the same arteries as the first. With so little blood spurting, it is possible that there was minimal blood that could be concealed with a coat and the clothing disposed of later. It is also conceivable that the killer brought other clothes to change into or covered up his blood-stained clothing with an overcoat and changed later. This assailant was narcissistic enough to come in and gain her trust and kill her without having anyone come to help her. The killer could have washed up in her bathroom, taken his clothes with him and disposed of them later. The residue blood tests in 1911 were non-existent.

Additionally, the cut on Dr. Knabe's throat was from left to right and then right to left, suggesting the killer was right handed. She had only flecks of blood on her hands. If she had killed herself, she would have had a lot of blood on her hands and the weapon would have been bloody and dripped onto her fingers, which was not the case.

The second cut could not have been made as the first cut severed her windpipe and filled with blood, effectively choking her to death. The second cut was just as strong as the first, which, would have been impossible when she was choking.

The *Indianapolis Star* called attention to an article in a current periodical about suicide and throat cutting. What it said was that most cuts are done left to right because most people are right handed. They start with a bold stroke and end with a weaker one. With Dr. Knabe, the opposite was true. Hers started on the right side and ended abruptly and then a second cut was made on the left side, with equal pressure. Unless Dr. Knabe had been ambidextrous, this would have been impossible to do. Had she had wielded the knife, her hands would have been bloody, rather than just spotted.

The writer of the journal article said most often the victim of an assailant had defensive wounds on their hands, mainly cuts. Dr. Knabe didn't have cuts on her hands, though she had a defensive wound on her arm. There were reports that she had a bruised fist, however, in the coroner's report and testimony, no mention of this was made.

Professor Emeritus Dr. Richard Miyamoto from the Indiana University School of Medicine, Department of Otolaryngology–Head and Neck Surgery was interviewed about this case by the author. He believed that Dr. Knabe could have made the first cut, but not the second. The first could have been superficial enough to hit the jugular vein, which is a return vein and would not have caused spurting. He believes it is possible that if the bleeding could have been stopped at that point and the airway cleared, Dr. Knabe could have lived. However, the act itself would have opened up the larynx or trachea and cause her to choke on blood very quickly. The second cut was deep, all the way to the spinal cord. Dr. Miyamoto does not believe Dr. Knabe could have been able, after the first cut, to complete the second or miss the carotid arteries. In fact, he would be surprised if anyone could complete any cut to the back of the neck and miss the carotid artery, which would have caused massive spurting. Additionally, he also noted that her hands would have been very bloody, versus spotted. It is possible, he reasoned, that the killer could have waited until she was dead to open up the second cut, hit the jugular vein and have minimal spurting, however, that is not what was reported by Coroner Durham and his staff. Dr. Miyamoto agreed that the cut on Dr. Knabe's arm was most likely a defense wound.[198]

Time Lag

When the police were called, they consistently complained about the amount of time it took for them to be called. In comparison, the citizens of Indianapolis and the family of Dr. Knabe didn't see any progress. Yet if there had been any complaints from her family, those were never published.

The Weapon or Lack Thereof and the Mystery of the Keys

The police also believed that various investigations show that no one broke in through the windows. Whoever came in either had a key or was admitted by Dr. Knabe. Hyland also believed since a microtome blade[199] lent to her by Dr. Ferguson was missing, that she had done it herself and the blade hidden. Ten days after the murder, the missing blade was found without blood, covered in dust between a stack of dusty papers by Hyland's own detectives William Morgan and Elmer F. Hall, with Alonzo M. Ragsdale, who had assisted in many searches for evidence. As executor of Dr. Knabe's estate, he had full access to the apartment and her possessions.

When Dr. Knabe's possessions were auctioned, the police found a semi-stained knife in a dusty case and took it for testing. It was found in a case behind a suitcase in her laboratory. Coroner Durham attached no importance to this item as he believed the dusty case spoke to the knife's disuse.

At the time of her death, Dr. Knabe's personal set of keys was missing. It is not a stretch to imagine that someone who knows her may have come in, taken the keys and left, only to return to kill her. These missing keys were found the same day as the microtome blade. They were on her chiffonier, a place that had been searched multiple times, by multiple people. Captain Holtz preferred to say that it was found because the detectives had missed seeing it. The police were stunned by the discoveries. Augusta Knabe was questioned again regarding the key and denied having had any but her own keys.

The police also believed Dr. Knabe's sheets were undisturbed under her. At least one doctor stated he saw that the sheets did look disturbed. It was a double sheet folded over and the fold placed to the side of the bed. The police said if there had been a struggle that the fold would have been disturbed. The author conducted her own experiment using cotton sheets folded over on a bed. She used her feet to try to get away from someone. The sheet under her had some wrinkles but no large displacement. Naturally, the author was not trying to fight for her life, nor was she the height or weight of Dr. Knabe, nor was the mattress exactly the same.

Furthermore, Dr. Durham believed Dr. Knabe did not commit suicide. The murder weapon was not found in the apartment. It could have been concealed but the people who were in the room stated with the exception of putting the sheet over her body, they left everything as it was and did not move anything. Dr. Durham had no reason to disbelieve them as he was acquainted with many of the people involved, and they were questioned for a long time after the event. The way the cut was made would have made it impossible for her to have so deeply cut from ear to chin and still give Dr. Knabe time to hide the weapon. The wound was not jagged; it was clean. Dr. Durham believed it would have been impossible at the angle Dr. Knabe was found in, to have inflicted such a clean set of cuts. Additionally, Dr. Durham was able to conclude the cuts were made at a different angle than Dr. Knabe was found. The cuts were made from right to left, then a second cut from left to right. The cuts extended from ear to ear. They went from the extreme right of her neck, through the part of the left jugular vein, severing the windpipe and extended all the way back to the spinal column, where it was nicked. With the first cut, he concluded she would have drown in her own blood and been unable to make the second or position herself as she was found in death. Coroner Durham examined the wound on Dr. Knabe's arm, which was two to three inches deep. It was obvious that she had her arm up in self-defense.

There were a few drops of blood under the light switch at the foot of the bed, seven feet from where she lay. These may have come from her arm wound when she was trying to fend off the attack. If she had killed herself, she would have had to have made the cut before she slit her throat and then threw herself back so hard that her head was driven under the horizontal iron cross piece on her headboard. Hardly. Dr. Knabe slept with her head at the foot of the bed near the telephone so she could be near it should it ring at night.

Four separate people heard screams- Jefferson Haynes, custodian; Mrs. Andrew Powell, third floor tenant; Mrs. Ella Hitt, lived across the street on Michigan Street, tenant and wife of Dr. Thomas Hitt, and Joseph Carr, the plumber. If suicide was truly the case, then Dr. Knabe would have been framing an imaginary person for murder. Dr. Knabe by all accounts was direct and plain speaking and did not like to deal with deceit or strategy politics.

It is believed Dr. Knabe died in the dark. Carr saw no light burning when he came by. By 2:45 a.m. Walter Slayer, the linotype operator at the *Indianapolis Star* came home and said an electric light was burning in her bedroom. If Dr. Knabe killed herself she would have had to have died later than thought and turned on the light before she killed herself.

Despite the fact that the missing keys had been found on her chiffonier ten days after the murder, a place that had been searched by multiple detectives and multiple people, including multiple times by Alonzo M. Ragsdale, the suicide theory persisted with police. Captain Holtz did eventually say that either she was murdered or a person intent on hiding a suicide had replaced the keys.

Ten days after the murder, when the keys were found and when the missing blade without blood was found, would have been November 5, 1911. This was four days after Ragsdale, funeral director and executor of her estate, had done a final walk through and inventory of her apartment. He would later be indicted for her murder.

Augusta Knabe and Katherine's McPherson's Behavior

Detective Martin J. Hyland was the worst critic and the most vocal about the unnaturalness of Augusta and Katherine's behavior. He said from the start the crime looked to be a suicide based on testimony and behavior from McPherson and Augusta Knabe. He said they did not want the police there, yet, they did call doctors, who in turn called the police. There seemed to be a vibe that the women hid the weapon or threw it out. However, it was proved that there was no weapon thrown out in the apartment building by the testimony of the janitor. It also seems highly unlikely that police and onlookers would have overlooked a weapon had it been thrown out the window.

Additionally a mailman, George Deming, came to the door at 8:50 a.m. but was not told of the tragedy. McPherson asked Augusta Knabe if they should call the police and she said no that she didn't want them around. When the police said they could only see one reason for not calling them- a cover-up- Knabe said that she thought her cousin had been murdered.

Neither woman knew who had committed the murder, if it was murder.

Dr. Harry Dunn Tutewiler[200], the former coroner, stated he had not been involved in the case in any way but that in his experience the first idea is to call the police if someone suspects murder. He stated nine times out of ten if it is a suicide, the police will not be called and family members will try to hide the disgrace. Again, this logic is faulty. The women were not in the habit of identifying dead people and therefore didn't know that she was dead, they thought she might be helped, so they called the physicians first. When the physicians couldn't help, the doctors called the police without any incident from the ladies. Dr. Tutewiler stated that when he was coroner, Dr. Knabe, as student, had watched Dr. John M. Geis perform autopsies for Dr. Tutewiler many times and performed the work herself. During that time, she used a large, flat knife, which he believed was the same weapon she used to kill herself. He made these statements without knowing that in fact, there were two cuts and a sharper medical grade instrument was used. He also stated that in life, if she was disappointed that her plans didn't go well, she became despondent. There were no examples given of this despondency or of how despondent she became, so this could mean she simply was disappointed and that Dr. Tutewiler was gender biased.

Perhaps neither wanted the police there. Perhaps Augusta Knabe really did think the police were ignorant. However, there is nothing in existence that proves that Augusta Knabe or Katherine McPherson were anything but cooperative in any of their dealings with the police. They did call someone in authority- the physicians and the police. It doesn't seem unusual given that Augusta Knabe and McPherson were both around doctors due to their personal and professional relationships with Dr. Knabe. Furthermore, Detective Hyland stated that because of these conflicting statements, the fact that his detectives were working 24 hours a day on the case and no reasons for murder had been uncovered, suicide had to be an option. Hyland also admitted they had a few cases were motive was not found and the case was still considered a murder. He concluded his statement by saying a friend of Dr. Knabe's stated she had commented a few days before the murder, "It will not be long before I will be over there."[201] and that Dr. Knabe nodded her head in the direction of a funeral director's office. He also went on to say that many of her friends indicated Dr. Knabe had made indirect threats against her life. As the comment could have been taken out of context, this comment could have meant she aspired to being a funeral director, or that she was dreading going to the funeral home for work soon[202]. It was never proven who these friends were that said she was contemplating killing herself, as all of her friends staunchly refuted this notion. The people who did accuse Dr. Knabe of suicide were accused of playing at petty professional bickering by Reverend Blunt and the Indianapolis newspapers[203].

Grinding of Professional Axes

Dr. William T.S. Dodds, taught Dr. Knabe at the Medical College of Indiana as a professor of bacteriology.[204] He was also a former deputy coroner and former Associate Professor of Clinical Diagnosis at the IU School of Medicine (a paid position in comparison to Dr. Knabe's). He worked with Dr. Knabe, teaching upperclassmen at the dispensary. He also had a private practice in the Claypool Hotel in rooms 341-343. Dodds said he believed Dr. Knabe killed herself because he knew her personality. He said her characteristics were such that he believed she would end her life by cutting her throat. He also said she was failing in business, though that was proven untrue. Coroner Durham reviewed her records and saw she was making a profit. Dodds believed she cut her arm first to test the knife to determine what force was necessary to cut her throat. These ideas are extreme. How he knew she was going to kill herself because of her predisposed personality traits was never explained. Dr. Knabe was a doctor who had performed autopsies. She would already know what pressure needed to make an incision. If she was going to kill herself, would she worry about missing the arteries and jugular veins and blood spatter? Dr. Knabe had conversations about suicide and apart from it being distasteful to her, she was able to recite many medications that would produce the same results and much less pain[205]. With her access to medications and drugs, it seems far more likely she would have chosen pills.

Dodds seemed to have a personal axe to grind with Dr. Knabe and was perhaps a bit misogynistic (although he was married). He called her arrogant, headstrong, and merciless, stating that she was so ambitious that she "would not hesitate to sacrifice anyone to achieve it ."[206] He was never able to back up this statement with examples, and from Dr. Knabe's supposed impoverished level of life, this seems highly unlikely. Dodds further claimed to be well acquainted with "the woman" and was not surprised to hear of her death[207]. While she was a state health officer, Dodds also stated that she made herself so disliked Dr. Knabe was asked to resign from the State Board of Health. Dr. William Niles Wishard[208], a long time member of the State Board of Health until June 1911[209] and Dr. John N. Hurty, Secretary of the State Board of Health, denied the accusation stating she rendered excellent service. At the time she resigned, the newspaper reported the same from Dr. Hurty and Dr. Knabe gave her reasons as the long hours and lack of pay, as well as being discriminated against. Dodds stated she couldn't keep her own practice going and that she was a failure at her pathology work. He also called her mentally unbalanced and said many of her friends believed that as well, without providing substantiation.

Again, Dr. Durham stated he had examined her books and found she was making money, negating Dodd's assertion she was failing. Dr. Durham stated that any woman who was on her own financially may become somewhat despondent at any time. He went on to stay that Dodd's statement did not credit him or the medical profession in which Dr. Knabe was so highly honored. Interestingly, not one of her

Top: Dr. W.T. S. Dodds, one of Dr. Knabe's professional acquaintances. He was very harsh in his judgment Dr. Knabe after her death. Because she was ambitious and because he felt she had not achieved success, Dr. Dodds believed Dr. Knabe killed herself.

professional or personal friends stated she was mentally ill. Only Dodds. In fact, three doctors, Drs. Martha B. Keller, Marie Rimmelin and Hannah Graham all believed she would have never taken her own life. Rimmelin pointed out that she knew of many drugs that would have caused her death with no pain within minutes so why choose this way? Keller believed she would have never committed suicide having been so happy with her success.

On a final note, Dodds said Katherine McPherson should be locked up until after the investigation- for what reason, he did not articulate. Katherine McPherson and Augusta Knabe always made themselves available for questioning and explained themselves to the full satisfaction of the grand jury.

On November 3, 1911, the Hancock County Medical Society censured Dr. Dodds stating his remarks, "in no way reflects the common feeling or belief of the doctors who have come in contact with Dr. Knabe and that the society censures Dr.

Left: Dr. Hannah Graham later in life at an event to bring equality to all, regardless of ethnicity or gender.

Dodds for his hasty and unwarranted remarks."[210] On November 5, 1911 Reverend Harry Blunt, pastor of the First Congregational Church censured the police, Drs. W.T.S. Dodds and Tutweiler for their unfounded judgments in Dr. Knabe's case. He stated that the investigation should be open and above board and above all, decently for Dr. Knabe's sake. He stated McPherson and Augusta Knabe had been treated unfairly and that this would always be a blot for these women because of the horrific nature of the crime- and the way they'd been treated. He finished out his sermon with "Judge not lest ye be judged."

Coroner Durham examined Dr. Knabe's financial records. She was not suffering from a lack of funds, Durham explained and in fact, the books showed Dr. Knabe's business was growing. The conditions of Dr. Knabe's finances would give a reason for suicide. She had borrowed small sums from various people and was contemplating teaching physical culture in schools.

When private detective Harry C. Webster began piecing her life together in February 1912, he started with right before the tragedy. He said the only real suicide theory advanced was that she was short of money. He examined her books and found she took in more than $1,500 from January 1, 1911 to October 23, 1911. She took in more than $300 in cash in September alone. While it is true that the summer months had been someone leaner because of the floor work done inside her flat. She had brought in at least $150 a month during the last year. In 1911, that was just not suicide income. Webster said she probably had a just as good, if not better, practice than most of the women physicians of the state. Given her life in Germany and her beginnings in coming to the America, she was used to hardship. If things were a little straitened at times, it was no more than what she'd been able to work through at other times of her life.

Additionally, because Dr. Knabe was a fighter and scrapper, bad finances were hardly something to ruin her life. She had strong friends to help her when needed. In fact Mrs. Blanche Lindley made her an offer in a letter, and in her reply of October 1, 1911, Dr. Knabe stated she was glad to know she had such good friends but she was not ready to "squeal." Dr. Knabe had also told Dr. Frank B. Wynn that she had three Pasteur cases which paid her about $75 each. They were in cash payments so she had some money set by.

William J. Burns, America's Sherlock Holmes

By October 28, 1911, Captain Holtz stated that they believed they could not prove suicide because no weapon had been found. They were almost convinced it was murder and that it was probably the greatest criminology mystery in Indianapolis history. They promised to continue following up on leads.

Adding fuel to the suicide pyre, on November 7, 1911, William J. Burns [211], known as "America's Sherlock Holmes" and owner of the William J. Burns International Detective Agency, was in Indianapolis. He'd been in the Secret Service, then opened his own detective agency. Burns would go on to notoriety as his exploits were published as true crime pieces in various detective magazines. During the time in which he owned his own detective agency, he was also the director of the Federal Bureau of Investigations.

Although Burns' official stance was that he had not been retained by the police or anyone else (and he was on his way to St. Mary of the Woods College near Terre Haute to visit his daughter,[212]) Burns stated that after making a study of the facts and

Left: William Burns, Detective. He believed, based solely on what he read in the newspaper, that Dr. Knabe killed herself. Much of what he had to say was based on attitudes of the time.

In his mind, no normal woman would be so ambitious. If she dared to be so selfish, once she met with resistance and failure, she would kill herself.

Further, he believed that Katherine McPherson and Augusta Knabe were not normal for not immediately opening the windows and screaming for help.

the newspaper[213], he was puzzled as to why there was any mystery. He concluded Dr. Knabe killed herself. His theory was that if there was a murder, there would have been motive. According to the police, robbery and assault had been disproved. Dr. Knabe's stellar reputation also disproved a secret meeting between her and a lover. Because a light was burning the morning after Dr. Knabe's death (when witnesses stated there was no light when they passed by,) it couldn't be murder because murderers didn't commit their crimes with lights on and window shades up. At the very least, the flaws in Burns' theory are that Katherine McPherson had already stated *in the newspapers* that the blinds were *down*. If Burns read the newspapers, he would have known this. Additionally, although there was not the psychological profiling that we have today, we know now that crimes of rage and passion, premeditated or not, have been committed for a very long time. It is interesting that Burns does not account for the defense wound on Dr. Knabe's arm. It may not have been mentioned in the paper for a purpose, but if he examined the facts (which he would have had to have gotten from the police, the coroner, and the newspapers), he would have known this even if he couldn't say anything directly in the newspaper about the wound.

Dr. Knabe, Burns reasoned, was ambitious and had unrealized ambition, possibly because of her gender, and so she decided to end her life. Burns went on to say that because Katherine McPherson and Augusta Knabe were calm and collected about the discovery of Dr. Knabe, coupled with their closeness with her, it would be a catalyst for covering up a suicide. Burns could not believe that any woman could, or would, enter the bedroom, see the scene before her and not open the windows (they already were) and scream for help. Also, Burns asserted, because McPherson and Augusta Knabe weren't at the police station every day asking for updates, they seemed to know that she had committed suicide. Burns did not take into consideration that they were being questioned by the Coroner. They were probably overwhelmed and extremely trusting. They were both brought up in a time where authority was the ultimate word and it wasn't normally questioned. So why would they think anything other than everything was being done that could be done? Both of them had just lost a friend, a family member, and an employer. As they were in shock, they probably could only maintain and do what was asked of them.

Burns also believed because the investigation showed Dr. Knabe had financial difficulties, which was sufficient reason to believe it was suicide. He was adamant that if one physician said that she could commit the act herself, then this was enough to believe it was suicide.[214]

Innuendo

In addition to the police being directed by Hyland to treat it as a suicide more so than a murder, innuendo was cheap within the police department. They suggested that she was not strictly virtuous and that perhaps she was lesbian because of the page the book, *Psychopathia Sexualis* book was opened to[215]. Additionally, there was a rumor that persists still today that she was involved with Janet Flanner, the daughter of Frank W. Flanner of Flanner and Buchanan Mortuary. Further, it's been stated that Frank Flanner paid someone to kill Dr. Knabe because she had dallied with his daughter Janet.

Frank Flanner was prominent, being the first licensed embalmer in Indiana and owning the second crematorium in Indiana. During his height of success with his partner, Charles J. Buchanan, it was expected that anyone who was anyone would be buried with the Flanner and Buchanan mortuary. Their success was based on giving special rates to the different lodges and clubs so that there was not so much of a financial burden on the widows, and to the ambulance service used to expedite the railroad injured to medical help. Additionally two women, Ann Murphy and Nettie Thomas, pioneered "lady embalmers" to handle the female dead. Flanner had been born into the Quaker faith, married a Quaker from Muncie, Mary Ellen Hockett, and wandered through his life spiritually, finally dabbling in Protestant religions and Christian Science . On February 17, 1912, he went to three different druggists and then went to his funeral home at 320 N. Illinois Street and told his nephew, Paul Buchanan that he was going to have a rest. He proceeded to go into the mortuary chapel and drink carbolic acid, strychnine, and morphine. Flanner was said to have killed himself because of despondency over the ill health he'd recently experienced [216].

In the 1950s, the *Indianapolis Times* did some retro pieces in the publication. During one interview with retired Herron Art School professor, Ian Frasier, he mentioned there was some talk of Janet Flanner being sent to Europe to end the affair between her and Dr. Knabe, but this has no merit. Dr. Knabe was not a child predator. Janet Flanner was in Tudor Hall School for Girls (now Park Tudor School) in 1911. In 1912 she enrolled and attended the University of Chicago in 1912. There is no record of her on a passenger ship in 1910 or 1911. She returned briefly to Indianapolis in 1914 to become a film critic and then in 1918 she married William "Lane" Rehm, who Janet admits was a convenient excuse to get out of Indianapolis. That same year, she met Solito Solano with whom she had an on-again/off-again relationship with until her death. In 1926 Janet divorced Rehm, although they remained friends until his death.

During her life, Janet wrote as a war correspondent from Paris, introducing Americans to Paris. She was also a close personal friend of Ernest Hemingway. Janet wrote for the *New Yorker* on a variety of topics and covered the Suez crisis and the Soviet invasion of Hungary. On November 7, 1978, she died due to unknown causes.

The Flanner rumors persist largely because people love salaciousness. The truth of it is that the rumor doesn't wash. If her relationship with Dr. Knabe had been a huge deal (if indeed there had been any kind of relationship), why wasn't it mentioned in her biography? Surely if there was a lesbian affair with Dr. Knabe, it would have been one of Janet's first, and therefore memorable enough to write about. Janet was not shy about herself and it seems unlikely she would have shied away from the rumor about her family. After all, she was a writer and she knew what made a good story. Everyone loves murder and if it is for salacious reasons, so much the better.

It is true that Dr. Knabe worked with the Flanner Guild (later Flanner House.) The Flanner Guild was located in Lockerfield Gardens and served as a "Negro

Left: Janet Flanner as a young woman. Innuendo flew that Janet and Dr. Knabe were lovers, although there was no proof, nor was Janet ever questioned. There were four mystery men questioned and her father, Frank could have been one of those.

Dr. Knabe worked with the Flanner House but it unlikely this rumor is true. Dr. Knabe did not have access to Janet, nor did she socialize with the Flanners.

community center." Dr. Knabe provided hygiene and home nursing classes to the organization. However, as a philanthropic organization, it is highly unlikely that Frank or Janet Flanner would have been overly involved in its running. Boards of Directors, Presidents and other volunteers would have largely been in place for this purpose. The likelihood that Dr. Knabe had a lot of access to either Flanner family member is low. Based on what we know, she did not make a lot of trips anywhere and the only ones we know of are related to medical conventions and work.

Second, Frank Flanner had mental issues as far back as February 1911 and had returned after Dr. Knabe's death from an extended trip to Europe. His partial recovery waned and he began talking of killing himself to get out of his troubles. Flanner started taking trips to the South to try and recover. Flanner had mental issues, but it sounds like he was focused on killing himself, and not others or hiring a gun to do the job for him.

Third, by the time Janet had come out, Dr. Knabe was dead. It was at least by 1918 that she really fully came into her own as a semi-out of the closet lesbian. By that time, Dr. Knabe was dead.

Fourth, during Janet's life, she was a frequent guest at her mother's house, so her life style must not have been that important to her. Although we don't know if that could be said for her father during the time, it seems highly unlikely that anyone in her family would have wanted to off Dr. Knabe because of a lesbian relationship. If this is true, why not do the same to Solito? After all, in 1918 lesbianism was not looked upon as it is today.

Finally, Jefferson Haynes, the janitor in the building, also stated he did not know why she would want to kill herself or why anyone would want to kill her. He had never seen anything inside the building that would have made him doubt the propriety of her conduct.

Reality and Reaction

Dr. Knabe was a very strong woman emotionally. Overcoming what could have been crippling challenges, such as not having her parents in her life for very long, made her into the woman that arrived in America in 1896. She was encouraged by her uncle and cousin to become a doctor. Her Uncle Daniel visited her in 1906 with his daughter, Clara. Augusta and her stepfather, Franz (Dr. Knabe's step-uncle) fully supported her by having her live with them from the time she arrived to the time she was able to make her own living and build her practice. The treatment she received in her life after her arrival in her domestic work, her studies and in her social life further served to mold her.

After Dr. Knabe's death, the people who knew her for many years lauded her as a doctor dedicated to her profession. She was someone detail oriented, curious, and always searching to improve a process, diagnose a disease and make sure it didn't come back. Dr. Knabe proved this in the way she worked as a health officer, as the acting head of the Department of Bacteriology at the State of Indiana, and in all walks of her personal and professional life.

It was hard for a working woman in the early 1900s. Most women worked in the home taking care of their families or they sold vegetables, canned goods or did sewing to make ends meet. Some women worked in factories and mills, or as secretaries, and shop girls till they married. Whether married or not, professional women were even fewer and far between. These women had to compete doubly for what they had in a man's world. Doctors were no exception. If it was difficult for men to build and maintain a practice, it was twice as hard for women. They had to find people who would patron them, despite the fact they were women. They had to fight the values and conceptions they'd been fed as children that they were delicate, that women didn't do certain things and that treating men was wrong or in some way unwomanly or unwholesome. Even the time of day in which they treated patients was up for scrutiny. Men could treat anyone at any time. A woman, especially an unmarried one, who was on call at night was suspected of being up to no good.

The idea that Dr. Knabe would kill herself was an impossible one for Katherine McPherson. She stated that Dr. Knabe talked of people who committed suicide as being "cowards." In fact, Dr. Knabe said many times if anyone wanted to kill his or herself, which it could be done with a minimum of pain by ingesting drugs, which Dr. Knabe listed. The idea that Dr. Knabe would choose a painful method to end her life did not make sense.

Katherine McPherson, who had been one of the closest people to Dr. Knabe in terms of everyday interaction, felt Dr. Knabe had no known enemies. She admitted that some of Dr. Knabe's colleagues who had professional jealousies towards her but Katherine said Dr. Knabe had never discarded friendships with these people.

Dr. Etta Charles of Summitville, Madison County

Dr. Etta Charles wrote to the *Indianapolis Star* and related a couple of stories which she thought might benefit the police. As a woman doctor, she said many people assumed they would dress or put a wrapper on before letting a patient in at a late hour.

Another assumption was that women doctors would never treat a man at a late hour.

Augusta Knabe didn't seem aware of any male patients who called at night. If Katherine McPherson knew, she wasn't saying. As Dr. Charles put it, if a doctor was hustling to get a valuable patient (read, hurrying to get a paying client), then dressing or excluding men was probably not going to happen.

She let a man in who claimed to have an ailment, only to be told he had some surgical knives he wanted to sell. He wouldn't leave so she stood in the light of her office as he peered out to see if anyone was watching. Dr. Charles wanted to get her revolver but she knew if she walked past him to get it, he would grab her. Finally, she bluffed him out of her office 15 minutes later.

Another time, a man came in with a problem and she told him there were male doctors that could better help him, but he wouldn't leave. Dr. Charles was standing

ETTA CHARLES, M. D.

Left: Dr. Etta Charles in later life. She was an established doctor by the time Dr. Knabe was killed and understood how and why women worked the way they did.

close to her office door and speaking loudly. The man put his hand on her shoulder and just as Dr. Charles tried to get away, the husband of a neighbor came in and chased the man away.

Her point in relating the stories was that Dr. Knabe may have not dressed or let a man in. She may have put herself in harm's way in search of taking care of a patient, as many doctors might.

A few weeks later, Dr. Charles wrote to the newspaper again and related a story from another woman physician. This physician heard a knock on the door and asked who was there. She heard in answer the name of a male doctor, who was a husband, father and twice grandfathered. She let him in because her relationship had been a father/daughter type while she was in school. She put on her kimono and let him in. What happened was that they fought all over the room and turned over all the furniture until she was able to get him leave. Dr. Charles stated that we don't know what took place in Dr. Knabe's office. She was adamant that no women physician would scream unless she was in mortal danger at risk of being the object of ridicule, and by then it might have been too late for help. Dr. Charles also believed Dr. Knabe was not murdered by a transient or low-life. She believed it was a man with family and friends because "he would have everything to lose and Dr. Knabe would have proved a relentless foe if she survived an assault."

Dr. Hannah Graham, Friend of Dr. Knabe

Dr. Hannah Graham[218] was an Indianapolis doctor who was quite active in the Women's Suffrage Movement.[219] Dr. Graham stated three weeks after Dr. Knabe's death that she did not believe McPherson and Augusta Knabe told everything they knew. She was not accusing them of committing the murder but Dr. Graham believed they should have been detained and their stories checked out in detail till they matched immediately. It is interesting that Dr. Graham should say this, because the police later found out the two women were together after the murder for two days. They took lunch at a small restaurant on Massachusetts Avenue.

Dr. Graham also believed Dr. Knabe was murdered. But if she were wrong in that thought, she also believed Dr. Knabe would have been insane at the time she committed suicide because she would have never chosen that way to kill herself.

Graham said that Dr. Knabe would be missed deeply. She was "Very much above the average. She was an energetic woman, always just in her profession and perfect in her ethics."[220] Graham also said she was a big supporter of the suffrage movement even though her profession caused her not to be an active part in it[221].

Other Colleagues

Dr. W.T. Gott , Secretary of the Board of Medical Certifications, went through his records to help find Dr. Knabe teaching positions. He was especially complementary of her, stating that she was a remarkable woman who was a strong individual and devoted to her extraordinary work.

Dr. John N. Hurty, Secretary of the State Board of Health, stated that Dr. Knabe was a woman who never hesitated to let people know where they stood with her. She "shot from the shoulder" and offended people with her blunt speaking. However, this man could have been biased because of the way Dr. Knabe parted with the State over her working conditions and pay. He did go on to say that she was skillful with a microscope, a good lecturer. Dr. Hurty became cryptic when he said her skills, enthusiasm, and appreciation for the work were "unusual." It is unknown if he meant this in a sense for a woman in comparison to a man or for people in general.

Dr. Mary E. Ash, a friend of Dr. Knabe's, said she did not think that Dr. Knabe killed herself. She said that she believed the police would do better to find the fiend in a man, one whose soul secrets were bared to his wife through her microscope and work as a pathologist. No evidence to this effect was reported, however, police stated they tracked down the lead nonetheless.

A man named Otto von Tesmar was listed as a doctor in the newspaper and said he grew up 20 miles away from Dr. Knabe in Germany. They had always been friendly there and good colleagues. Two days before her death, she passed him in the

Left: Dr. W.T. Gott was part of the Board of Medical Certifications and had helped Dr. Knabe find work. He had a very high opinion of her work and ethics.

hall in *Das Deutsche Haus* and he said she wouldn't look at or talk to him. He was employed to articulate skeletons, as she had been, as well as a taxidermist at a shop 720 S. Delaware, where he also made his home.

Miss Olga M. Tetley, a friend, didn't believe she killed herself. She said Dr. Knabe wanted to make a name for herself and enjoyed life. Her pastimes were studying and attending good plays, especially *Dante's Inferno*.

Dr. Jane M. Ketcham[222] believed Dr. Knabe to be of high ideals and knew her when she was a student. They usually saw each other at least once a week. She did not believe she committed suicide, rather than a man had broken in because he saw the woman physician sign as an invitation to kill.

In her testimony, Augusta Knabe stated she did not know of anyone from the Indiana State Board of Health or abroad in Germany who would wish to see Dr. Knabe dead.

It is also unlikely that as a woman of refinement, Dr. Knabe would have put herself in the position she was found in death. She wouldn't have wanted anyone to find her with her breasts bared and she probably didn't want anyone to find her in night clothes. Nor would she have been able to stage the voices heard after her death. Rigor mortis sets in between two to six hours from death. She had to have died by 1:00 a.m. to have been in the condition she was in when found. So, knowing this, were the 5:30 a.m. footsteps heard by Jefferson Haynes also part of an imaginary frame up?

Dr. Knabe also slept with her windows open and blinds closed. If she staged her death and the screens and footsteps, wouldn't she have kept them open so the world could hear? McPherson found everything closed when she got to the office.

Dr. Knabe's hair falls and rats were found on the chiffonier. During a time when a woman's hair was considered feminine and her crowning glory, would Dr. Knabe really have left these items designed to enhance her appearance lying out for anyone to find after her death? She had also laid out clean clothes to wear the next day. If you commit suicide, you don't worry about your next day's clothing.[223]

Dr. Knabe had signed up for a teaching course at the North American Gymnastics Union. Why would she do this if she planned to kill herself? It was clear she loved her work, her courses, and life.

Dr. Knabe had an appointment with Miss Maud Neill, stenographer at the 501 Lemcke Annex building, at her flat the night of her death. She called Miss Neill and said she had something important to tell her and wanted Miss Neill to come by when she could stay for a time as it was a long story. She promised to come Monday night but was called away from the city on Saturday and did not get to keep the engagement. She got the news on Tuesday of Dr. Knabe's death.

Also, Dr. Knabe had an appointment with Miss Mary Brigham, a school teacher at 5:00 p.m. on the Tuesday she was found dead. She had also left a pair of shoes to be repaired at Stout's Shoes and asked for them to be repaired *immediately*. Mr. Meyer said he couldn't do it then but would do it early so she could have them in time for her classes. These are the shoes McPherson picked up.

Dr. Knabe had also bought a piece of cloth goods from the W.H. Block Company for $25 and had it taken to a woman's tailor on Massachusetts Avenue to have a dress made for $70. It was to have been fitted the day of her death. Mr. Dixon telephoned from the tailor and asked if she would be coming in. Augusta Knabe said she couldn't come in that day. This proves two things. First, she was not contemplating suicide. No one gets a new dress made if they are never going to wear it. Also, her finances must not have been too bad if she, an accomplished seamstress, was having a dress made- something she could have easily done herself. A $70 dress was worth almost $2,000 in today's money. Surely this was not just an everyday dress. Silk ran about $1-$2 a yard in 1911.[224] Depending on what the material was that Dr. Knabe was having made into a dress, it could have been 10-12 yards or more of fabric. An average dress for a woman her size would have been around 4-5 yards. This was an extra special dress. Perhaps even a wedding dress[225]. This theory might even be supported by a picture of Dr. Knabe inoculating a guinea pig. She seems to have an engagement ring on her finger (see p. 55).

Dr. Knabe had arranged to meet Dr. Nettie Powell of Marion, Indiana the following Wednesday at the Claypool to attend the annual meeting of the Federation of Women's Clubs. She had also agreed to meet Mr. VanBuskirk and his wife of Eaton, Indiana on Tuesday. Dr. Knabe was to take them to the office of Dr. John Kolmer[226] to have Mrs. VanBuskirk examined for an operation. She agreed to spend a week with the couple in the fall[227].

Dr. Knabe also asked friends to come to visit in an October 15, 1911 letter to Blanche Lindley. Dr. Knabe said something had happened and she wanted Mrs. Lindley to come to Indianapolis to tell her about it. Lindley said it must have been very important, as Dr. Knabe usually exhibited the utmost freedom in her writing. Webster hardly thought Dr. Knabe wanted to tell Mrs. Lindley she was going to kill herself.

Does a woman who is going to kill herself make all these plans?

Still, the police would not let the suicide theory rest. The police detectives were split on the murder/suicide theory. Captain of Detectives Holtz continued to state that he would not say for sure that she had committed suicide. He believed that until an investigation was complete, it would not be fair or just. However, Holtz negated this statement by saying the police still had more reasons for suicide than murder. As amazing as it seems, there was little written about their efforts except that they tracked down false leads, incredulously inaccurate leads and the like.

Reactions of Augusta and Katherine

Augusta and Katherine were devastated. Augusta went on with her life and worked at school while dealing with the inquest. At one point she did take to her bed so deep was her grief. She was lucky to have her coworkers and Franz Kropp to help support her emotionally during this time as well as her family of teachers and the teachers through the Robert Nix Memorial Association.

Katherine was equally crushed. After the inquest, Katherine was present for the trial. She became a stenographer and disappeared from all records as of 1951. [228, 229]

Friends of Augusta Knabe

The teachers at Whittier School were getting a fund together for a private detective. They hoped to get $1,000 but they couldn't solicit directly at the school because it was against the rules.

Franz Kropp's Reaction

Franz Kropp resented the intrusion into his life and that of Augusta Knabe. They lived on Bates Street where working class people lived. A railroad track ran behind the home. He was a bricklayer. The home was small and unassuming. The neighbors talked well of the tight knit family. He said that Augusta loaned small amounts to Dr. Knabe. Augusta said she never loaned Dr. Knabe $500 and called it a lie. He didn't like that his daughter (notice that he did not say step-daughter) was being questioned as he knew she had nothing to do with the murder and was not hiding anything.

Reaction from Germany

Dr. Harry Meyer sent a letter to the mayor of Rügenwaldermünde asking for information about Dr. Knabe. This would have been a normal thing to do as the mayor would have facilitated finding the information from the *Standesamt*, or City Hall regarding Dr. Knabe's birth and life in Germany. In Prussia after 1874 , people in Germany had to register in the town they live in, a practice that continues to today. A letter was received by Meyer from Dr. Schrader, mayor of the German city. In it, her biological father was an engineer in government employ. The mayor confirmed her father and mother were dead, although records show her father was awarded a fourth class Prussian Red Eagle on November 25, 1911. It does not seem to be posthumously given. The information about Dr. Knabe's mother's side of her family sent by Meyer could not be confirmed. It was found, however, that her mother's father was a rough-tanner and her maiden name was Krolow.

From a young age, she was raised by Daniel Ehmke. Ehmke took Dr. Knabe's death very hard and wanted to know how to get her personal effects and how to find out if life insurance existed (it didn't.) Augusta Knabe testified about five years prior she and Dr. Knabe has sent money to relatives to have Ehmke and others come over. They begged him to stay but he didn't like it so he left.

Other Reactions

Laurel Thayer, a local journalist said, "…a beautiful life has been lived among us, a life purse, strong, unselfish, helpful- and who shall say it failed? If we did not appreciate this life, ours the blame; if a criminal ended it, there shall be justice sometime, somewhere."[230] She was quite vocal in calling for more people to step up to find out the facts and to donate money to the reward fund.

The YWCA where Dr. Knabe taught released a statement which said Dr. Knabe had been an honored and valued faculty member and that they denounced the murderer(s). They wanted to publicly acknowledge appreciation of Dr. Knabe as a woman and a physician.

Dr. Nettie Bainbridge Powell of Marion, Indiana received a letter from Dr. Knabe on the day she was found postmarked 9:30 p.m. on Monday. The letter stated that Dr. Knabe was expecting a visit from Dr. Powell. It also gave a vague reference to Dr. Knabe's finances as Dr. Knabe ordered a book and asked that it be delivered to the Claypool Hotel upon Dr. Powell's arrival. Dr. Knabe stated that Dr. Powell could pay for it as she probably had more money than Dr. Knabe. It is not clear if this book was a shared resource or if it was solely Dr. Powell's book, or if it was Dr. Knabe's book.

Two days after Dr. Knabe was found, Governor Marshall and the women's clubs of Indianapolis became interested when no arrests were expected. The City Council asked the Finance Committee for an appropriation of $1,000 as a reward for evidence leading to the capture of the murderer. Councilman Johnson thought they should hold off on the measure. He believed the police would either be insulted or negligent if money were offered. Captains Holtz and Crane believed the money should be appropriated immediately, deeming part for information and part for conviction of the murderer. Governor Marshall spoke with Mayor Shank and said he would raise funds for a reward. Three days later, the City Council was unable to obtain a quorum to approve a $500 reward from the city and $500 from the State of Indiana. Councilmen Blumberg, Copeland, Denby, Johnson and Rubens attended the meeting. Councilmen McCarthy, Troy, Stills and Owen did not. By October 28, 1911 the Governor was asking Police Superintendent Hyland if he considered it murder and until it was decided, the reward that was pending by the state (which was fluctuating between $500 and $1000) would not be offered to the public. On October 29, 1911 the City Council agreed to vote and pass a measure to offer $1,000 for information leading to the arrest of all murderers (there were three cases that were included in the reward money). It would be available through January 1, 1913. Frank M. Cantwell of the Madison Flats agreed to donate $25 towards finding her murderer. Finally on October 31, 1911 The City Council approved the $1000 reward.

Dr. Amelia Keller of the Indianapolis Local Council of Women and the Women's Franchise League met with Captain Holtz to discuss raising money for a reward.

The Woman's Franchise League of Indiana expressed its regret at Dr. Knabe's death and called upon the city to offer a reward. It asserted people were not safe because of Dr. Knabe's death and other murders. It was signed by Dr. Amelia Keller and Mary Strong, secretary.

Left: Dr. John Kolmer, one of her supporters.

Bottom: Dr. Amelia Keller, a Dr. Knabe's friend and part of the Local Council of Women. She hoped to raise reward money.

The Indianapolis Civic League felt her absence acutely. Dr. Jane M. Ketcham, chairman of the physical welfare section, said that they relied on her greatly for her work with the league and their work would be slower without her. They believed she was murdered.

The Local Council of Women asked for a committee to raise funds for the apprehension of Dr. Knabe's murderer. Headed by Miss Margaret Hamilton[231], supervising principal of Benjamin Harrison School, the board said it had no money to pay anyone on a committee. Hamilton said "womanhood" of Indianapolis demanded action. She suggested women be included as part of the police force to patrol movie theaters, parks and other recreational places women might frequent as an added layer of protection.

Dr. John L. Freeland[232], Superintendent of the City Hospital, suggested during an Indianapolis Medical Association meeting that everyone donate $5 toward a fund that would help solve the murder case. The donations failed to appear.

Drs. Frank Wynn and John Kolmer praised her life as they knew her professionally and socially. They commended her for her bravery in coming to America and completing medical school. They stated she had special gifts for the work and was outspoken and that even her most unfavorable traits showed a strong character. Dr. Wynn said her eccentricities should be forgiven by those who were affected by them. Dr. Kolmer spoke of the oppressions of the struggles in her life that caused her to have a suspicious nature and somewhat pessimistic view at times. But he praised her work, stating she had a constant fear of not being as perfect in her work as she should be. Her life, he said, was an unfailing example of fortitude, vigor and faithfulness. Others who knew her said they city has lost one of its most conscientious workers, a great student of learning and a wonderful person.

Even the *Indianapolis Star* had a kind and fair word for Dr. Knabe. In an article on the day the microtome blade and keys were discovered, an editorial piece questioned whether Dr. Knabe was getting a fair shake from everyone involved. After all, "proof of suicide is as completely absent as proof of murder. Theories are not facts." They showed her as a resolute and aggressive character, who was not cowardly leaning toward suicide and quitting, but rather, she was a fighter whose mental attitude was toward life. The writer went on to say that although her death may always remain a mystery, that people should be more kind in how they speak of her. She may have been "drawn to self-destruction by the whips and scorns of time, the pangs of disprized love, or the spurns that patient merit from the unworthy takes" but that she should be remembered at the very least in sorrow instead of "unclean suggestion, unmanly detraction or professional spite". The writer bid her well in the closing, "After life's fitful fever, she sleeps well."[233]

Funeral

More than 750 people visited Alonzo Ragsdale's funeral parlor to view the body of Dr. Knabe on October 25-26. Many of the people who attended were her friends and companions, associates of her medical profession, her students, her former instructors, nurses whom Dr. Knabe had interacted with, family and others who had known her in life. Accounts of the time note that many people cried unabashedly as they passed her funeral bier.

The funeral was held at the same establishment on October 27, 1911 at 2:00 p.m. The service was conducted by the Reverend A.B. Philputt, pastor of the Central Christian Church and Reverend J Christopher Peters, of German Evangelical Zion Church. Reverend Philputt praised Dr. Knabe's spirit for the work she did, especially the work for which she did not accept fees. He condemned the city of Indianapolis for not acknowledging her work while she was alive.[234] Reverend Peters spoke in German for the funeral goers who could not understand the English sermon.

Many people were turned away, though they stayed outside on the pavement, listening from their positions outside the building. People who attended included professional acquaintances, personal friends, former classmates and patients, many of whom were from poor areas of Indianapolis. With them, they brought small bouquets of flowers.

The pallbearers were Dr. Frank B. Wynn, her former preceptor, Dr. John J. Kyle, for whom she provided book illustrations, Dr. Charles E. Ferguson and Dr. Ernest C. Reyer, Dr. John Kolmer and Dr. Edmund D. Clark (sometimes referred to as M.E. Clark), former instructors, colleagues and peers. During the service, Augusta Knabe would clasp Dr. Knabe's hands and press her lips to Dr. Knabe's brow. Katherine McPherson trembled as if cold, and so she was, having lost a good friend.[235]

Burial was at Crown Hill Cemetery in Indianapolis, Indiana (Section 43, Lot 6950). The Butler College male quartet sang hymns including "The Dark and Cloudy Day" as her casket was lowered into the grave. Many of the people from the funeral home came to the graveside service. Reverend Peters gave a short prayer in German and Philputt gave a eulogy. His closing words were, "Life grows mysterious and we wonder upon human motives and human deeds. We believe that finally some power will make things just and right; will trim down the superfluities and even up the deficiencies so

145   *She Sleeps Well*

Top: Dr. Knabe's grave marker in Crown Hill Cemetery. The author and her husband raised funds and gave numerous ghost tours in order to pay for the marker.

that a life of struggle and sacrifice shall be impossible . "[236]

After the service, after all the people had gone, Augusta Knabe was left, a solitary mourner. It was Augusta Knabe who threw the first clod of dirt onto the grave after which she turned from the lonely grave.

It seemed, even the people there were grateful for Dr. Knabe's kindnesses in the tributes they gave her, but for the majority, they had never penetrated her life. She lived apart and bore the burden of being self-reliant and always there for her patients.

No one provided a headstone for her until 2006 when Nicole and Michael Kobrowski gave ghost tours for and raised the money for her stone. They bought her a rose colored granite stone and made it look as if it had been there from day one, which it should have been. On December 22, 2006 on Dr. Knabe's 131st birthday, the stone was set in place and *Frau Professor Doktor* Knabe was toasted with champagne.

Suspect Leads

Prosecutor Frank P. Baker and his chief deputy, Fred McCallister, said the evidence collected supported four theories: attempted criminal assault, attempted robbery, possibly suicide and possibly murder without either an attempted assault or robbery. As would be proven by Coroner Durham, the only assault was the murder itself with the defense wound on Dr. Knabe's arm. No suicide weapon was found. Nothing was taken. To quote Sir Arthur Conan Doyle,"when you eliminate the impossible, whatever remains, no matter how improbable, must be the truth." In this case, murder. Coroner Durham went so far as to say he would bet his last dollar Dr. Knabe had been murdered.

Other notable people in Indianapolis were asked about the theories by the newspaper. Dr. Charles E. Ferguson and Dr. E.C. Reyer, who were some of the first to arrive, believed it was murder. Two days later, Dr. Ferguson changed his mind and said it was suicide based on the position of Dr. Knabe's body. He believed this until Augusta Knabe and Katherine McPherson both testified in front of a grand jury that they had seen no knife around the body. Michael A. Ryan, an attorney, believed it was murder. Interestingly, Thomas F. Colbert, a former police superintendent, refused to choose a theory because unless you were on the inside you couldn't have enough facts to support your stance. Dr. J.A. Hauser disagreed with the other doctors. He believed it was murder, but that unless a narcotic was given to Dr. Knabe, she would have struggled and he felt that evidence of a struggle was completely lacking in this case. He did not take the defense wound into consideration, nor the fact that her night dress was not just pulled up and her covers turned down on the bed, but rucked up as if she

Heads of the Murder Investigation

MARTIN J. HYLAND, SUPERINTENDENT OF POLICE

Top left: Martin J. Hyland, head of the police investigation into Dr. Knabe's murder. He supported the suicide theory to the point of hindering the investigation.

Top right: William A. Holtz, Captain of Detectives at the time of Dr. Knabe's death. He went to far as to say she was murdered or someone intent on suicide hid and later replaced the missing keys.

THE DETECTIVES AND INVESTIGATORS

George M. Stewart
John W. Morgan

John Mullin
Otto Simon

William Morgan
Elmer F. Hall

Adolph Asch
Jerry Kinney

were backing away from someone on the bed. Dr. Knabe's acquaintances were split on whether she'd killed herself. Many other physicians thought she'd killed herself because she was worried about finances although they could not say this for sure. Her friends stated that she would not have killed herself as she was always in the habit of worrying about money and always found ways to fix her problems.

On October 28, 1911 Lieutenant of Detectives Jerry Kinney was assigned to the case full-time. He was a tenured policeman, but even he was reluctant to say that he'd be able to solve the case. Days later there was squabbling amongst the police as some believed Kinney was in charge of the detectives in addition to his role on the Knabe case- something denied by Kinney and Captain Holtz.

Initially, janitor Jefferson Haynes was questioned because of his proximity and access to Dr. Knabe's apartment. His questioning may have also been racially charged. Mayor Shank, Captain of Detectives William A. Holtz, and Coroner Durham questioned him.

Oscar Franklin, who sought treatment at City Hospital for a deep cut on his left wrist, was also questioned. Franklin had been asleep at the Mrs. Mattie Ennis' boarding house when someone entered his room and tried to cut him. Ennis was arrested on suspicion and Franklin was taken to the hospital ward of the prison and charged with assault and battery. Later Ennis posted bond but was rearrested for public intoxication and disorderly conduct. The police could not question her at the time to corroborate Franklin's story but stated if they could not do so, they would investigate further. Also, there was a trail of blood from Franklin's bed to the door, which bore out part of the story that he'd called for another roomer in the house after he was cut. Franklin was not mentioned again as a suspect. By October 28, 1911, Franklin had been cleared. When the truth came out, it was found that Franklin had many cuts on his body and a bloody butcher's knife was found in his room. Ennis welded the knife used against Franklin. She was taken into custody-again.

Over the first few days, many people from in- and out-of-state sent letters, some by special post, to the police. Some letter writers claimed to have interviewed clairvoyants or claimed to have supernatural powers themselves. Captain Holtz said these letters may prove useful and every clue in the letters would be tracked until it was proven or disproved.

On November 11, 1911 Mrs. Ella Hitt, wife of Dr. Thomas Hitt, reported she heard screams and brisk walking on the night of the murder. She and her husband were in Oklahoma for a time after the murder and she had not been able to communicate with the police before then. She and her husband lived in the Belmont, which was on the south east corner of Delaware and Michigan Streets. Their apartment was in the north west corner of the second floor. Their bedroom faced the Delaware Flats. She said about 1:15 a.m., she heard screams and then a man walking briskly east on Michigan Street. This was believed to be Joseph Carr. But Mrs. Hitt was convinced that she heard Dr. Knabe's death cry as it sounded as if she were terrified for her life.

Mrs. J.W. Smith lived in the Emmett Flats, which is to the south of the Belmont. She was accustomed to sitting on the porch till late because her son was a pressman at the *Indianapolis Star* and would come home at midnight for his lunch. In June, she saw a prowler near Dr. Knabe's window. Mrs. Smith said Dr. Knabe did not pull her blinds down as far as "she might have done" and with a little effort, anyone could creep up on tiptop and look inside her apartment windows. She saw the same prowler several times, always with the lights burning in Dr. Knabe's apartment. One night she pointed out the man to Mr. John Grace, the janitor at the Emmett. Grace approached the prowler with a "Good Evening" which elicited a grunt from the prowler. She described the man as about five feet seven or eight inches tall, and 160 pounds. He always wore dark clothes and a soft felt hat.

The police thought this might be the same work of the man Mrs. Mount described that night. Even Dr. Knabe said about a year before her death that once she was about to leave her apartment and went into her office when suddenly the screen moved and a hand thrust into her apartment window. Dr. Knabe told Katherine McPherson she'd been scared and stayed in her apartment because she feared robbery. Since that time, there had been no other disturbances.

More proof that there was a prowler was given when Miss Catherine and Miss Grace Blackwell, daughters of former Coroner John J Blackwell, stated a man and woman were seen loitering around Dr. Knabe's apartment.

Mayor Shank Gumshoeing

Mayor Samuel Lewis Shank went to Cincinnati to talk with a woman who said she might have some information that would help the detectives. When the mayor returned, he said he had uncovered information that detectives would be interested in reviewing. Mayor Shank would not provide the name of the woman to the press but said he'd relayed information to the police. We have no record of what that information was. He also said in early November 1911 that he favored the suicide theory because there were motives for suicide and none for murder had been uncovered.

In the same breath he praised the police for the work they'd done and said he thought Dr. Knabe wouldn't have committed suicide without leaving a note, of which none were found. He said he thought Dr. Knabe would have left a note for McPherson and told her not to tell anyone about it and left further instructions for how to cover up the deed.

Nothing ever came of this information if it existed.

More False leads

Many people sent letters to the police with not so helpful advice and clues. Some of them came from dreams- "wild eyed dreams" as the newspaper called them. Others were just unreasonable or of very little help:[237]

> "Dr. Knabe was murdered by a man. Find the knife and you will find the man and also prove she did not commit suicide."

> "Dr. Knabe is not dead. She was kidnapped by a German nobleman and some other body was placed in her bed. He kidnapped her very likely because she was about to inherit a large fortune."

> "Search the garbage cans for the knife."

> "I wish to state that the person who returned the key to the doctor's apartments is the murderer. Had the office girl or this relative had the key, they would have been smart enough to have destroyed it. The key was returned by the murderer to throw suspicion on the two women. In this case possibly the one that is talking the loudest is the criminal."

> "An ape broke into her apartment and killed her."[238]

Some people believed she had escaped a man who had supposedly courted her in Germany and due to his family not wanting him to marry a poor girl, she rejected him. The theory was that he came over to woo her and when she rejected him again, he killed her [239]. There is no evidence any such person existed.

The police spent valuable time looking for a black woman that was known to be Dr. Knabe's charwoman. McPherson stated that Dr. Knabe had three such women in her employ but that at the time, there was no regular person who came to do housework. On November 12, 1911, Mrs. Mary Scott of 914 N. Scioto Street told the police she may

Top: Mayor Shank. The mayor did some investigation but nothing came of it.

have been the person they were looking for. She had been engaged to do cleaning the Tuesday Dr. Knabe's body was found but Dr. Knabe told her on Monday that she didn't need to come. She told the police she was used to coming regularly with the exception of when hardwood floors were installed in the apartment. Recently Dr. Knabe wanted her to resume her work but Mrs. Scott said she had a lot of other work and hadn't really been back. The police continued to search for the woman they believed may have been permanently engaged by Dr. Knabe but nothing ever came of this lead.

In 1912 W.L. Benton of Brownstown said the slayer of Dr. Knabe was dead and that he knew all, but wanted to get the $3,000 before he gave up his secrets. Needless to say, this lead went nowhere fast [240].

An African-American from Lockland, Ohio, William Ellison, was investigated. He was up on robbery and assault charges. Witnesses swore he was in Indianapolis during the time of her murder and after, when he returned to Ohio, was flush with money [241].

The Prince

Prince Constantinos Paleologos (also Palailogos and known as Constantine Aristides Mammonas), moved from Greece to Chicago in 1907 and lived in Chicago and worked as a bank teller[242], lawyer, and later as the Director of the Greek-Italian

Left: Seth Nichols- the man who said he killed Dr. Knabe and later recanted his statement.

division of the great Chicago Central Trust company of Illinois.

The night of Dr. Knabe's murder, he was in Indianapolis. Paleologos had been scouting Indiana and wanted to see if it was a suitable place to do business. He told police that about 10:30 p.m., he walked by Dr. Knabe's apartment and noticed her talking to a man sitting on the window seat that was on Delaware Street[243]. (Katherine McPherson said the pillows on the window seat were positioned as if someone had been sitting on them.) Captain Holtz thought the prince must have been mistaken about this, however, because five people who lived on North Delaware told him they passed by at that time and that they saw no lights on. Still, the police swore they would continue to find the prince and investigate the story. They lost his track in Chicago where he told friends he was going.

Seth Nichols

In April 1912 Seth Nichols, who was 21 years old [244, 245], said he was the murderer of Dr. Knabe and received $1,500 for it from a man named Knight[246]. Nichols was in need of money and bill collectors were nipping at his heels. Nichols stated he and Knight hid in the building and waited. "Then we went in the bedroom. She was lying in bed. The covers did not reach up to her breast. Her nightdress was open at the neck, and showed her round throat that was all white in the reflection from the light from outside. Just as we reached her bedside, she moaned and moved a little. Then she opened her eyes. I will never forget those eyes. I think I would have reneged if she hadn't wakened. But—well, she turned toward me, and I lunged with the knife Knight had given me. It was sharp as a razor. And…that's all."[247]

Nichols also alternated between saying he left Indianapolis the next day and saying he didn't leave Indianapolis for three days and nights because Knight kept him drugged. He said he stayed in a room in Wonderland Park, North Washington Street and first met the man at the Washington Street Skating Rink in Indianapolis. In any case, he was held at the Rockingham County Jail, New Hampshire for an unrelated crime of carrying a concealed firearm. Later on the day he was taken to jail, the Boston police said he was wanted on a $180 larceny of property charge lodged by a Mrs. Della Lyons. She and her husband George Lyons, brother in law to Nichols, said he robbed them while living with them after the death of his wife. Nichols stated, "It is all off me now. I don't care what becomes of me, now my wife's dead."[248]

His aunt Mrs. William Knight didn't believe his story and his aunt Mrs. Glenn Gilbert [249] from Lafayette, Indiana, said he fell several times when he was four and injured his skull and he'd never been right since. He was allegedly a Navy deserter.

The officials at the Brooklyn Navy Yard said they had no record of desertion but many of the men knew him as a bad character. Sometimes they did not pursue deserters because having them gone was better than having them there. Others came forward and said he'd been to the Naval Branch of the YMCA.

Nichols' sister, Mrs. Robert L. Blakeman, said, and records showed he was also on the USS Dixie on October 23, 1911[250] when the crime happened. Lieutenant Kinney went to Portsmouth, New Hampshire where Nichols was to see how his revised story bore out. Nichols swore he talked with the record keeper of the Dixie to "fix up" the records as if he had been on board when he hadn't been[251].

Later that month, Nichols said[252] he made it up because he'd been drinking. He also said he was distraught over the death of his own wife and after reading the newspaper accounts of Dr. Knabe's death, he "conceived in some strange manner" that he'd done the deed. He said the story was ultimately, "only a child of my brain."[253]

A former roommate and firefighter told the newspapers that he believed Nichols was faking insanity to keep from going to prison for deserting.[254] It didn't seem to work. On April 23, 1912 he was sentenced for deserting and larceny of clothing to serve time in the Concord Reformatory.

J.E. Guthrie

In May 1912 J.E. Guthrie confessed he shot Dr. Knabe. Superintendent of Police Hyland said it was nothing but a fake lead. "Undoubtedly 'confessions' on the Dr. Knabe case will come from 'dope' fiends and diseased minds for years to come."[255]

Unusual Facts of the Case

On the Friday previous to her death, Dr. Knabe met Dr. Amelia R. Keller on the street and said she had something to tell her and wanted to meet. Dr. Keller said Dr. Knabe was very worried and asked her to call on her at her office but Dr. Knabe said that wasn't possible as there were too many interruptions and the story would be a long one. Dr. Keller was not able to make an engagement with her and so she never heard Dr. Knabe's story.

Distracted students

A chalkboard containing test questions written by Dr. Knabe was taken down, photographed and put into storage in an unused room at the Indiana Veterinary College around November 4, 1911. The request was made by faculty. The students would become distracted by the object and become unable to concentrate. Dr.

Knabe's successor had yet to be named.

Ouija Boards and the case

On November 18, 1911, the *Indianapolis Star* reported that a Ouija board session was conducted at the house of Deputy County Prosecutor John F. Engelke. He and friends were playing with a Ouija board at his house. He demanded the name and address of Dr. Knabe's murderer. The location was not mentioned in documentation. Following this, Engelke's office received numerous calls from people wishing him to divine other information for loved ones and pets. Engelke vowed to get even with the fellow who gave it to him as a Christmas present.

Curious Sightings

John Hildebrand of 1023 N. Rural Street said he saw Dr. Knabe the night of her death at the German House (the Athenaeum) at a lecture. Although many of Dr. Knabe's friends were there, none reported seeing her. Later it was found that another woman came forward and was found to be the person Hildebrand saw.

Even today, visitors report seeing Dr. Knabe in the Max Kade room as well as the gymnasium of the YMCA on the east side of the building- the former North American Gymnast Union. During one television interview with the author of this book, the doctor was seen floating into the Max Kade room. Rushing into the room, the participants sought to see Dr. Knabe. Although she was not caught on film, a breeze did pass by the interviewer, camera operator, and author. Many times since then visitors have communicated with her through dowsing rods and digital voice recorders in the same room.

In another instance, paranormal investigators, including the author were in the YMCA gym, which had been converted into an exercise machine room. The author was struggling with how she was going to go forward with her weight loss. She asked if Dr. Knabe was present and the dowsing rods indicated yes. The author asked Dr. Knabe, "You know what I've been struggling with. What would you suggest?" Dr. Knabe answered by turning on one of the exercise machines with a media panel. It was set to German and it had the word "*Los*" on it, meaning "go."

Feelings of Apprehension

Charles S. Tariton of 230 E. North Street was attacked by unaccountable feelings of horror and uneasiness while passing the Knabe flat on the night of the murder. Could this have been a premonition similar to Augusta Knabe's dream?

Dr. Richard A Proctor who contributed an article to the *Electric Medical Magazine* on "Some Strangely Fulfilled Dreams" says that even in ancient days, supernatural origin of dreams was accepted. On the night before President Lincoln was assassinated, Secretary of War Stanton had a prophetic dream. He said it is not incredible that some psychic mode of communication exists by which one brain may receive the same impressions which affect another"[256] The fact that Tariton was a stranger allowed him to receive only vague impressions.

The Fake Crime
Alma Hagan was 14 years old when she slashed herself with a penknife a week after Dr. Knabe's death. She hid the knife and some jewels and lowered the shades in her bedroom. Alma then lay down on the floor until she was discovered by her sister.

Alma's sister, Miss Genevieve Hagen, a nurse, revived her from a drug induced stupor and Alma told of having a man enter the apartment and attacked by a man and threatened her life. He tied a handkerchief over her eyes until she drank from the bottle he offered. Alma drank and said she passed out. When Genevieve heard this, she searched the house, fearing a robbery and found jewels missing.

The police investigated the fishy story and Sergeants Barmfurher and Ray were able to get her to confess to the fake attack. Alma said she'd heard about Dr. Knabe's death and wanted some excitement and notoriety. She admitted it was all an act.

Her sister was attending a patient when Alma made her stage act. She stated Alma, who was noted as being exceptionally large for her age, was in seventh grade and was inclined to be romantic. Genevieve said she would consult a doctor to examine her sister. [257]

The Fantastic Bloody Story
A woman claiming to be Dr. Carrie Gregory from Indianapolis told Coroner Durham in Elwood that they should track down a nurse named Mills who could tell them more about Dr. Knabe allowing two other doctors to drain two quarts of blood from her body, which was supposed to be taken to an Indianapolis hospital in a thermos bottle and put into a woman who was suffering from a blood ailment that destroyed the red corpuscles. The Coroner could not verify the patient was in the hospital. Although Dr. Gregory gave her address as Indianapolis, she was described as not being known to local physicians. Her name was not in any of the city directories for Indianapolis or Elwood. Additionally, there are no licenses on file at the State Archives in their records for Dr. Carrie Gregory in Indiana, which means after 1904 she could not have truly

practiced recognized medicine without it .[258]

Suicide attributed to Knabe Mystery

Miss Lulu Clemens, 28 years of age, of 1018 St. Paul Street locked herself in the bathroom on October 29, 1911 and slit her throat with her brother's razor. She wrote a 28 page letter talking about life, love, immortality, the Bible and blamed the Board of Health. She said that they keep you from taking poison but not from things that prompt people to talk about their lives.[259] Dr. Mary A Spink, neurologist said she didn't want to diagnose the patient but it could be because she felt the tragedy deeply. Or it could be that she was simply a morose and pessimistic person. Miss Clemens had been in ill health for a long time prior to her suicide.

Beyond the Police Investigation

The *Indianapolis Sun* asked on October 25, 1911 why the police were not doing just service to the case or the people of Indianapolis. Regardless of the fact they lost about an hour at the apartment because of the time they were called, the police chief put inexperienced detectives on the case. The apartment was not thoroughly investigated and now there was a mess. To say that because someone had been in there for an hour before the police blew the entire case was a bit unprofessional. At one point it was suggested the killer brought his own change of clothes and blade, but because of the slowness of the police, this doesn't seem to have been investigated. It denounced the police for haranguing Augusta and McPherson when they had done nothing wrong.

A month after Dr. Knabe's murder, the *Indianapolis Star* declared that the women of the city who put up money to help find her murderer shouldn't have had to take on the responsibility- the Medical Association should have. But since they had, everyone should pitch in and help. That includes understanding that unless the murderer was caught, it would continue to blight the name of the city. The editorials on this continued for weeks because it seems the money was slow to trickle in. At one point the paper declared, "If Drs. Jameson (Dean of the Medical College of Indiana), or Burckhardt, or Cole or Pantzer [260], or Pfaff or any other well-known male physician, had been found with his throat cut, consider the energy with which his professional brethren would have sought for the perpetrator of the deed. Why is it that the doctors show such indifference to the murder of Dr. Helene Knabe ?"[261]

In contrast a widow, Mrs. Amelia Mendel, who had six kids to provide for when her husband burned to death, received after one week almost $2,000, most from contributions and $400 from insurance in the span of a week. Dr. Knabe's fund after eight weeks was zero.

In another article the *Indianapolis Star* stated that the more the investigation went on, the finer Dr. Knabe's character seemed to be. All the vulgar innuendo and discussion, when sifted through, proved out to be rumors only started by ugly men.

Six weeks after her murder, the paper asked what the six police officers and the superintendent had been doing for six weeks and why not more progress had been made.

Apartment after her death.

Dr. Knabe's apartment was rented on November 14, 1911 by Mr. and Mrs. J.E. Wailther (sometimes Walther). He was a senior at the I.U. School of Medicine. They both said they were not superstitious and spent a good first night in the flat. Bars had been installed on the windows to prevent peeping Toms and other issues.

Policewomen come to Indianapolis

A committee of women, consisting of Dr. Amelia Keller, Mrs. Harry E Barnard (wife of Dr. Barnard), Mrs. W. Barnes (wife of the doctor), Mrs. Graco Julian Clarke, Miss Margaret Hamilton, Mrs. Felix McWhirter, Mrs. Robert H Strong, Mrs. John F Barnhill, (wife of Dr. Barnhill), attended a city council meeting to discuss adding police women to the force. Mayor Shank had had so many requests, he approved two positions.

Robert Nix Memorial Association

The Robert Nix Memorial Association was founded by German teachers in Indianapolis who taught in the public schools. It was founded to commemorate Robert Nix, the former director of German in the city schools[262], who died on October 16, 1910. They provided entertainment at *Das Deutsche Haus*, the Murat Shrine Temple and other venues throughout the year as well as a large annual show. The additional earnings up were put into a teacher's pension fund and 25% of the additional earnings were turned over to the general fund of the city. (If they disbanded, all the additional money would be put in the teacher's pension fund.) It is not mentioned after 1915 in the local newspapers.

In 1911 Augusta Knabe was the first vice president of the association. Dr. Knabe was part of it as well and they adopted a resolution for annual entertainment at the German House in March. Mrs. Carl H. Lieber was the chairman. Mrs. Minna Broich and Mrs. Robert Elliot were in charge of the press committee. [263]

Local Council of women

There were still no solid leads by the beginning of 1912. Coroner Durham was still pursuing the murder theory. The local women decided to take matters into their own hands.

The Local Council of Women hired Harry C. Webster, manager of the Webster Detective Agency located in the 525-526 Indiana Pythian building. He said he was confident the mystery would be solved. He said there were a lot of people in the public that knew more than what they were saying and they need to step up and get rid of the fear of getting mixed up in the case. He gave the example of the people Miss Blackwell saw at the corner who were there at 8:00 p.m. and still there at 10:00 p.m. If the people would just come forward (because he doubted they had anything to do with the death) they could clear that part up. A man and woman called on Dr. Knabe the night of her death and talked with her till 11:00 p.m., but Webster said they knew nothing about them and needed the public's help to solve the crime.

Grand Jury One, June 1912

In April 1912, the paper remarked, 'With the unsolved Knabe case turning up to bother it every now and then and now with the Health Board row on its hands, it must be said that the administration has its troubles."[264]

A grand jury was called after the murder verdict by Coroner Durham. A silken kimono which Dr. Knabe wore while working at night was a subject of focus. The kimono had been missing several months but was found with Ragsdale and turned over to the grand jury several months later when he was asked to do so. When asked about the kimono, Ragsdale said he thought it was a discarded garment and was wrapped around some other old clothing and put in with Dr. Knabe's other effects. When he was originally asked for the item, he didn't recall it until its colors were described to him. Only then did he find the garment- and kept it until the grand jury asked for it and he turned it over to a detective working the case, instead of to Harry Webster, who had requested it in February 1912.

Fred McCallister, the deputy prosecutor who conducted the prosecutor's part of the grand jury investigation, believed the kimono was never lost and said he knew about it for six months.

How could this be? If Ragsdale had turned it over to any grand jury several months later, this is a lie. There was a coroner's inquest in November 1911. The first

Left: Detective Harry C. Webster was hired by local women to help find Dr. Knabe's murderer. He worked for pay at first and stayed on because he believed there was a job to do that went beyond a pay scale.

grand jury was in 1912.

Much of the focus outside of the testimony was having the grand jury try to determine if the spots on the garment were blood and if they were human blood spots. No one who saw the body said the kimono was on her body, which would indicate it had been removed later.

Dr. R.P. Noble, an analytical chemist, made an appearance and examined the garment. Several pillows were also sent to the grand jury, one with a bloody handprint.

The grand jurors asked for all Dr. Knabe's correspondence to review it. Captain Holtz appeared and stated he believed she committed suicide. Coroner Durham appeared as well and said he believed it to be murder.

Others we know to have appeared to give testimony include Katherine Agnes Fleming[265] of Hendricks County, Ferdinand Adolph Mueller, a druggist and secretary of the Indiana Veterinary College and Otto Wagner, former superintendent of the college. Dr. John D. McLeay (office at 157 N Illinois Street), who is connected with the veterinary college, and Nathan Kahn who resided in the Vendome Flats at the time Dr. Knabe was killed. Detectives John Mullin (Mullen)[266] and Adolph Asch appeared. Dr. John W. Sluss, superintendent of the City Hospital, Judge Ross of Probate Court, and Miss McPherson were also called. Alonzo Ragsdale was in the grand jury room for a whole day. Dr. Eva B. Templeton and Thomas H. Neilan of the Indianapolis Sanitary Company were also called to testify.

Grand Jury Two July – December 1912

The second grand jury was formed to decide what action to take based on the evidence from the previous grand jury. Dr. Eva B. Templeton, Dr. John Kolmer, who Dr. Knabe did pathological work for, Dr. Lillian Crockett-Lowder, a close friend and someone fighting for the search for her murderer, and Dr. Amelia R Keller of the local Council of women appeared. Drs. J.H. Vaught, who had an office in the Claypool Hotel, W.T.S. Dodds and Charles Abraham Pfafflin, an alternate officer of the Marion County Medical Society, were called. Miss Alice T. Shea of the Indianapolis Sanitary Company, Miss Maude Neil (Neal) a stenographer, Miss L.B. Riley, connected with the art department of a local store testified. John M. Maxwell, a newspaper man, Miss Louisa Bush, employed at Woods ' Livery and Dr. R.P. Noble, who examined some of Dr. Knabe's clothing for blood, testified.

The Grand Jury was comprised of John C. McCloskey, a foreman in real estate, Louis J. Blaker, real estate, J.F. Reister, real estate, James E. Broden manager of the Industrial Supply Company, Jonas Joseph retired, and Thomas P. Kane, retired .

Oddly enough, the grand jurors complained of the sanitation and ventilation of the quarters in which they had to deliberate. [267]Dr. Knabe would have had something to stay about that!

Interestingly, John Maxwell, a newspaper man, had questions of his own. He had been in the apartment several times as part of his job. He stated in a newspaper letter that he couldn't understand where this kimono had come from. The police and coroner had searched, so had Drs. Ferguson and Reyer. Maxwell was sure the kimono hadn't been in the apartment and was curious as to how it had gotten into the mix of evidence months later.[268] In another letter, he chastised the police for continuing on with the suicide theory. When the bloody handprint on the pillow was shown to the grand jury, it was obvious that she had not done it as not much blood was on her hand. Additionally Dr. Ferguson could find no evidence of blood having been cleaned up. Maxwell asked why this piece of evidence wasn't processed by the authorities (fingerprinting was in existence) and why was the pillow slip burned? Why was Dr. Knabe's bloody gown burned? Who authorized them to be burned and why?[269]

Harry Webster received personal attacks during this time. He stated there were people that believed he would continue "to dig up dirt" as long as he got paid. Well, the joke was on them. He had not been paid a cent since Spring of 1912. He had continued on at his own expense because he believed the perpetrator would be brought to justice and should be[270]. This fact was verified by Dr. Amelia Keller and she went on to state that Webster had no additional promise of payment from the women.

One year anniversary

On the one year anniversary of Dr. Knabe's murder, Superintendent Hyland still clung to suicide and Coroner Durham to murder. Hyland said they never completely dropped the case but he still believed it was suicide and he didn't know if they mystery would ever be solved. Dr. Lillian Crockett-Lowder received threatening letters telling her to back off from investigating the murder. She ignored them.

INDICTMENTS AND TRIAL

Among the many letters and communications found in Dr. Knabe's flat and which were examined by the grand jury was a sheet of paper giving her "philosophy of life."

Dr. Knabe had written as follows.

"If only I had done differently! "

How often we hear those words voiced by sad-faced individuals, in most instances followed by: "If only I could live that time over again"

Now, my dear, be sincere with yourself a moment. If you were put into the same circumstances again, possessing the same amount of knowledge, experience and strength (moral and physical) that were yours at the time when that which you bewail happened—would you not do the same again?

Regret, if not accompanied or followed by good results, is but a waste of time. Therefore, if you realize that you could have done better, begin at once to put the lesson to a practical application.

Make the best of what is left! There remains always an abundance of good. Use that to its fullest, capacity and there will be no deficit when the final balance is taken.

Many of the trials which seem so hard to bear are necessary to bring out the best in us.

Then why worry over that which is past? Why look back when our path leads forward? If we are to make the best of every opportunity life affords, it will keep us busy.[271]

Fifty-one Witnesses

Court records show a list of 51 witnesses who were subpoenaed in the case. They were:

Catherine (Katherine) McPherson, Dr. Knabe's assistant
Auguste (Augusta) Knabe, Dr. Knabe's cousin
Mrs. Frank B. Wynn, Dr. Knabe's friend and first on scene
Dr. Alfred S. Yaeger (Jaeger), IVC
Dr. Otto Wagner, IVC
Ila McPherson, Katherine McPherson's sister
Mrs. Samuel T. Marshall, witnessed prowler
Ferdinand Adolph Mueller, IVC
Alice Duden
John M. Maxwell, newspaper
Margrette Mueller
Jeff Haines (Haynes), lived below Dr. Knabe
Joseph Carr, witnessed prowler
Harry Haskett, witnessed man the night of the murder near the apartments
Dr. Charles Ferguson, Dr. Knabe's colleague and first on scene
Dr. Ernest C. Reyer, Dr. Knabe's colleague and first on scene
Dr. Charles O. Durham, performed autopsy
James Paul White, newspaperman who had interviewed Dr. Craig
Edward M. Tutt
Dr. George J. Cook, IVC
Dr. J.D. McLeay, IVC
Dr. Lillian Crockett-Lowder, Dr. Knabe's friend and colleague
Dr. John Kolmer, Dr. Knabe's colleague
Dr. R.P. Noble, did blood testing on kimono
Dr. Jewel Vaught

Miss Lauzenia B. Riley, L.S. Ayres & Co. Art Department

Maud Neil (Niell), stenographer

Dr. Eva B. Templeton, Dr. Knabe's friend and colleague

Henry Meyers, worked at Stout's Shoes

Mrs. J.W. Smith, witness prowler

Dr. Ralph Chappell, conducted autopsy

Dr. M.C. Leeth, conducted autopsy

L. A. Kiefer

Taylor Power- Power's Grocery Store (Delaware and Michigan Streets)

B. Frank Dixon, tailor

Alonzo Burton, Indianapolis Sun

Ray Baughmgartner (Baumgartner), Indianapolis Star

Froeda Sondermann, Miliner

Dr. George H. Roberts, President of the Indiana Veterinary College

Anna Louisa Bush, employed at Woods Livery

Miss Elois Tousey, worked in Dr. Wynn's office

Walter E. Plater, saw light in Dr. Knabe's apartment the night of the murder

Florence Hulen, worked at the Indiana Veterinary College

Blaine Patten, Indianapolis Star News Bureau Editor

James W. Pierson, Indianapolis Star Financial Editor

Miss Marry K. Brigham, taught at Public School Number 50

Dr. Ernest E. Lawler (left the city in the employ of the government)- worked for Indiana Veterinary College

Mrs. M.E. Powell (neighbors said she left to avoid the trial, but she did testify)

Ella B. Hitt (moved to Florida), Dr. Knabe's friend

Maud McGreger (moved to California)

Ray C. Dodge (left city in July)- worked at Block's Restaurant (possibly where Augusta and Katherine saw Dr. Craig drop his pie).

168 *She Sleeps Well*

THE ACCUSED

Left: Dr. William B. Craig, Dean of Students and Faculty at the Indiana Veterinary College.

Dr. Knabe worked with him and treated his daughter for an ailment.

Opposite: The indictment paper for Dr. Craig and Alonzo Ragsdale.

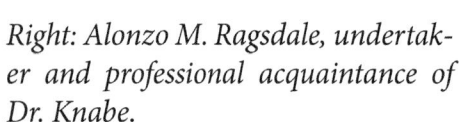

Right: Alonzo M. Ragsdale, undertaker and professional acquaintance of Dr. Knabe.

No. ~~Shelby Circuit Court,~~ day of Term, 190

~~Comes now the Grand Jury for the Term aforesaid and present in open Court the following indictment, to-wit:~~

The ~~"State of Indiana, Shelby County, ss:~~ Criminal Court of Marion Co.
Brown
~~Shelby Circuit Court.~~

THE STATE OF INDIANA,
vs.
Indictment for Murder in First degree

~~The Grand Jurors of Shelby County, in the State of Indiana, good and lawful men, duly and legally impanneled, charged and sworn to inquire into felonies and certain misdemeanors in and for the body of said County of Shelby, in the name and by the authority of the State of Indiana, on their oath present that one~~
~~late of said County, on or about the day of A. D. 190 , at said County and State aforesaid, did then and there~~

The Grand Jurors for the County of Marion and State of Indiana upon their oaths present that William B. Craig & Alonzo M. Ragsdale on the 23rd day of October 1901, at and in the County & State aforesaid did then & there unlawfully, feloniously, purposely and with premeditated malice kill and murder one Helene Knabe by then & there unlawfully, feloniously, purposely & with premeditated malice striking, cutting, stabbing & mortally wounding the said Helene Knabe with some sharp instrument to the Grand Jurors unknown with said instrument the said William B. Craig & Alonzo M. Ragsdale then & there held in their hands of which mortal wound so inflicted as aforesaid the said Helene Knabe then & there died

contrary to the form of the Statute in such cases made and provided, and against the peace and dignity of the State of Indiana."

Frank P. Baker
, Prosecuting Attorney.

Indorsed. A true bill,
, Foreman.
Witnesses: Dr. C O'Durham, Henry Webster, Augusta Knabe, Katherine McPherson, Louis Bush, Alice Thea, Dr. A Muehler, Ernest M. Fath

Indictment on December 31, 1912

Dr. William B Craig, veterinary surgeon, and Alonzo M. Ragsdale, funeral director and executor of Dr. Knabe's estate, were indicted by the grand jury, placed under arrest, and charged with the murder of Dr. Knabe.

Some of the witnesses to the grand jury included Charles O. Durham, coroner; Harry C. Webster, private detective; Augusta Knabe, cousin to Dr. Knabe; Katherine McPherson, Dr. Knabe's assistant; Miss Louise Bush, Wood's Livery Stable, Miss Alice Shea, Indianapolis Sanitary Company at 630 Kentucky Avenue, Ferdinand A. Mueller, Indiana Veterinary College; Mr. E.M. Tutt, Mr. Joseph Carr, witnessed men outside Dr. Knabe's apartment; Harry W. Haskett, witnessed men outside Dr. Knabe's apartment; Mrs. Samuel T. Marshall[272], Mrs. Frank B. Wynn, first on the scene; Mr. Ella B. Hitt, wife of Dr. Thomas Hitt and one of the first people at the crime scene; Mr. Jefferson Haines, janitor of the Delaware Flats; Dr. E.C. Reyer, Mr. Ray C. Dodge, an employee of a local department store; Dr. Lillian Crockett-Lowder, 204 Penway Building; Dr. R.P. Noble, 10 W Ohio St; Miss Maud Neal, 401 Lemecke building; Miss L.B. Riley, L.S. Ayres store; Dr. J.H. Vaught, 217 ½ N. Illinois St; Dr. Eva Templeton, 816 Harrison Street; Dr. William T.S. Dodds, 720 Hume Mansur Building; Dr. Charles Pfafflin, 422 Newton Claypool Building.

Also present were Detectives Captain Adolph Asch, Otto Simon, and Captain John Mullin.

Dr. Craig knew he was under investigation. He was sitting quietly in his office at the Horace Wood Transfer Barn when he was informed. He said, "What do you know about that?" in a startled tone. "Come here, Wood,"[273] he said to his friend Horace. "They say I am indicted. What do you know about that." Dr. Craig said he would not talk about the case. "I have nothing to say. I did not seem to be trying to run away, did I? I am going right ahead about my business. They can find me here any time they want me."

Fred McCallister, deputy prosecutor, told Judge Markey at the bond hearing that he had been involved with the grand jury during the investigation and recommended that Dr. Craig be admitted to bail, as was Ragsdale. With cases of murder, normally the State opposed bond issuance if it has a strong case. In this case, the evidence against both was circumstantial, but the State had good witnesses in Craig's housekeeper, Mrs. Tennant and two witnesses who saw Dr. Craig leaving the building.

Dr. Craig's bond was $15,000 and Ragsdale's was $10,000. Both men appeared with bondsmen with several million dollars, and were allowed to go home under the bonds. Many people accompanied Craig to the bondsman. It was signed by 11 of Dr. Craig's friends and attorneys: Frank H. Wheeler, owner of Wheeler-Schlebler Carburator Company and a founder of the Indianapolis Motor Speedway; Horace F. Wood, of Wood's Livery; A.W. Thompson, who was in financial services; Edward M. Crawford, druggist[274] and a close neighbor of Dr. Craig; Lucius M. Wainwright, president of Diamond Chain and Manufacturing Co.; Frank F. Churchman (of Jeffery, Churchman and Drake), Live Stock Commission Salesmen; Dr. Charles A. Pfafflin; John Ruckelshaus, of the law firm Ryan & Ruckelhaus; Joseph R. Morgan of the law firm Morgan & Morgan; Elliot R. Hooten and Oren A. Hack, both attorneys.

It was unsurprising Dr. Craig declined to make a statement in court. His attorneys Hooten and Hack also said nothing, and said they would say nothing until the trial. To that, Dr. Craig stated "I have said nothing in regard to the case except what is true."

This was in reference to the grand jury investigation in June when he was asked for a statement after being informed of the trend of the detective's theory. At that time he told the *Indianapolis Star*,

> *"I had known Dr. Knabe for years and had a very high regard for her. She taught in the school and I regarded her the same as I would anyone with abilities. She has been to my home and was a close friend of my daughter's. I have been in her office, but had not been there for about six months before her death. I had not seen her for some time before she died.*
>
> *I obtained some business for Dr. Knabe, I believe. I called her in some cases of rabies. Frequently when we lectured at the school at night, she would go to her home in my machine, but our relations at all times were simply those as will exist between two men in the same business, who had a high regard for each other's ability."*

Dr. Craig then spoke about her visit to his home the Sunday night before her death, saying she had returned a borrowed book. He also said he had loaned her small amounts of money and that Dr. Knabe had treated his daughter for a minor ailment. "I knew that Dr. Knabe was contemplating closing her office and going into physical instruction work."

He also said that he was at the sanitary plant office and talking about a new contract when he received a call from his office to call Dr. Knabe's apartment as something awful happened. He thought his daughter was ill and had been taken to

Dr. Knabe. A woman answered the phone. He told her who he was and asked what happened, and she told him Dr. Knabe had been found dead. After he left the sanitary plant, he went to the veterinary college and it was there he learned her throat had been cut.[275]

This information triggers many red flags. If his daughter was such a close friend, why was she never once mentioned in any of the articles in the newspaper, especially the one about her funeral? Additionally, why would he say he loaned her money? It could have been lunch money. Why didn't he treat his own daughter?

Ragsdale had an equally jolting indictment notification. Ragsdale learned of his indictment while he was in Columbus, Indiana where he was conducting a funeral. He said he had no statement to make, "I have no comment." He picked up the coffin and took it into the house in which he was conducting the funeral. Afterwards, Ragsdale went directly to the bondsmen, then to the sheriff to post bail. Ragsdale made a statement, "I am absolutely innocent. Further than that I have nothing at all to say about the matter." His demeanor was described as vexed and irritated but he laughed and chatted with the posse of men accompanying him. He repeated often when asked about the case that he didn't care to discuss it and that he was innocent.

Ragsdale's bonders were Myrtillus J. Voris (sometimes seen as Voids) of Franklin $20,000. He was in the mercantile business. Walter R Beard of Indianapolis gave $10,000. He was in the furniture and stove business. John W. Ragsdale of Franklin and brother of Alonzo Ragsdale; and Horace G. Winnings and Theodore M Carriger of Winings & Carriger, proprietors of the Meridian Stables (142 N. Alabama Street) also signed the bond. The men only commented to ridicule the charge against Ragsdale, declaring it an outrage.

Ragsdale was arrested as an accomplice because it was believed he laundered the kimono, altering any evidence, while it was in his possession. Augusta Knabe reported that she gave it to Dr. Knabe for Christmas 1910. It was blue with a red flower design and it was brightly colored. What was retrieved from Ragsdale was not. It was faded and in poor condition. Augusta Knabe asked McPherson if she'd ever washed the kimono and McPherson said once and that it came out beautifully. Dr. R.P. Noble did an analysis on the remaining stains and they were found to contain human blood. The fact that he could do this once it had been washed was an amazing piece of science at the time. However, determining whose blood it was not possible.

Ragsdale and Dr. Knabe's Estate

For her own personal reasons unknown at this time, Augusta Knabe put Alonzo Ragsdale in charge of Dr. Knabe's estate. By November 11, 1911 he filed a list of items with the Probate Court. These items would be sold to pay for outstanding debts, according to probate judge John P Leyendecker, judge pro tem.

On November 16, 1911 Dr. Knabe's possessions were sold at auction in Ragsdale's undertaking business on the second floor in a cell-like room. Hundreds of people attended the sale of her furniture and her medical instruments. Her microscope, which was expected to sell for $35 sold for $60 and her books sold for as high as $25 apiece. Popular novels sold for 25-75 cents apiece. A Battenberg lace piano cover went for $2. Dr. John Kolmer bought her near new medicine case for $5.

In December 1911 Mrs. Myrtle K. Matthews sued Ragsdale to recover possession of a $60 diamond ring which went into Mr. Ragsdale's possession as administrator of the estate. She wanted the return of the ring and $10 in damages. She had given the ring to Dr. Knabe as security for a debt, part of which had been paid, but the rest she was ready to pay. ($9). Eventually Mrs. Matthews did receive her ring.

The bed on which Dr. Knabe was found murdered sold for $10. (name not given)

Augusta Knabe bought much of the property including jewelry, clothing, furniture and bed clothes. Many items had very little value except as keepsakes.

Medical books and surgical instruments were bought by physicians. The Bethany Assembly bought an ice chest valued at $4. The piano was sold to W.E. Probst for $225. Forty-three items as well as miscellaneous articles did not sell. Another public sale was conducted including books and medical instruments.

In November 1912 Ragsdale stated he couldn't file a report because he needed to collect accounts first. He was to file the report within a month, which didn't happen. Alonzo M, Ragsdale [280] filed a report in 1913 stating the final total was $614.23 and that he did not directly or indirectly buy any of the items. Only some of the names of the people who bought items were included. Ragsdale said he couldn't keep track of all the names of all the purchasers. The newspapers, however, reported her estate was minus $500, which as we can see, was not true.

As soon as Ragsdale was arrested, Judge Frank B. Ross said that his final report for the probate court on Dr. Knabe's estate had to be filed immediately to close the estate. It had been over a year since the liquidation of her possessions, yet, he still hadn't filed a report. By the middle of January 1913, he had filed the report stating he had about 50 articles left and nearly everything sold for above appraised value, for a total of $614.23. The largest amount was for the piano. It sold for $122.50. Judge Ross approved the report and ordered the rest of the property to be offered at private sale within three days. Ragsdale was to make another report in 10 days .[276]

Also, Katherine had asked in 1911 about a quilt that was always on Dr. Knabe's bed. It was presumed missing until after the last report was filed. Alonzo Ragsdale had it the whole time.

The probate court shows several charges to Dr. Knabe's estate between 1911 and 1913:

Person/Organization	Date	Owed	Distributed
Augusta Knabe	March 8, 1912	$480	$256.28
A.M. Ragsdale	October 24, 1912	$139.98[277]	$139.98
Freda Sondermann (Milliner)[278]	March 31, 1913	$41	$31.73
William H. Armstrong Co.	May 3, 1913	$24.93	$19.31
W.V. Hargrove Co.	December 12, 1913	$11.96	$9.25
Abbot Alkoloid Co.	April 3, 1913	$20.92	$16.19
G.V. Mosley Musical Book and Publishing Co.	April 3, 1913	$8.00	$6.19
Lewis Publishing Co.	July 22, 1913	$63.90	$49.45
Joseph & E. S. Stern**	December 6, 1911	$22.50	$22.50
	Total	$813.19	$550.88[279]

** This entry is hard to read and who these people are is unknown

This final report was not filed until March 11, 1913, nearly two months late. According to Ragsdale, the estate was insolvent and the claims on her estate were paid at 77 35/100% of the claim. Many things didn't add up in this scenario. The claims totaled $813.19.[281] Paid out at the 77 35/100% the total paid would have been $629. The total listed amounted to $550.88. The mysterious Joseph & E.S. Stern received full payment of $22.50 presumably, although it isn't listed in the distributions, there is a note saying it was paid in full. Additionally, Augusta Knabe was short changed. Her claim was for $480 and she should have received $332.61, but she only received $256.28. Alonzo Ragsdale received his full $139.98.

Regardless of these individual figures, none of what was printed by the newspapers or said by Alonzo Ragsdale adds up. The estate was not insolvent by $500, nor was the final total $614.23 because otherwise the court fees and the amount distributed to creditors could not have been done.

Augusta Knabe and Detective Webster's Reactions

Augusta Knabe was very appreciative of the indictments, thanking Dr. Amelia R. Keller, the Local Council of Women, and all the other good women who assisted. She stated that if people had known Helene that they would know she did not do this to herself. She stated that the men who were so interested in the beginning had lost interest because it didn't affect their families or lives. She made the offer to help Mr. Webster in any way.

Augusta told reporters that she and Dr. Knabe had lived together many years, and even when she moved out they would spend time together every day- or almost. When they hadn't had time, Dr. Knabe would always greet her cousin with a cheerful, "Well hello stranger, where have you been?"

Private Detective Harry C. Webster, hired by women to find her killer and who had not been paid in almost a year, was surprised the men were let out on bail. He said, "The Craig-Ragsdale release has made a very bad impression. We are either in earnest in this matter or we are not. For my part I mean business."[282]

Following the indictments, the press started the year with a prophetic message.

> *"Secrets are in some, human knowledge that could make all the mysteries plain before this morning's sun has set, whether it was murder or suicide; and if confession is never made, those secretes may never be known by any but the murdered breast where they are hid."*[283]

The Rationale

Detective Webster believed that the friendship between Dr. Craig and Dr. Knabe became objectionable to the man and he wanted to break it off. Many things happened to show Dr. Craig was bitter towards her. According to the detective, they were expected to marry but trouble about the work at the Indiana Veterinary College (where Dr. Craig was Dean of Students and Dr. Knabe was a lecturer and Chair of the Hematology and Parasitology Department) was part of the reason he wanted to end the relationship. The detective also believed that Dr. Craig knew of her death before anyone else in her apartment did. Detective Webster believed Dr. Craig had already told people at the sanitary house something had happened by the time he received Katherine McPherson's call. Webster also believed Craig told the people at the veterinary school that Dr. Knabe had been murdered before he went to her apartment, though he had not been told of her death.

According to Augusta Knabe, Dr. Knabe became acquainted with Dr. Craig when she worked as the Acting Superintendent of the State Laboratory of Hygiene. There she did some pathological work for Dr. Craig, quite possibly rabies cases. When Dr. Knabe left the Indiana State Board of Health, he offered her the position of assistant laboratorian at the Indiana Veterinary College. Dr. Knabe accepted her position as the assistant to Dr. John McLeay, and she lectured on hematology and parasitology. She lectured from 1909-1911. Her work was praised by Ferdinand Mueller, secretary of the college, who said her presence had "distinctly strengthened the college".

Dr. Craig paid much attention to Dr. Knabe during her time at the college from 1909-1910. He often took her to and from the school in his automobile. One member of the faculty stated that Dr. Knabe would sometimes hurry through her morning lecture in order to be done at the same time that Dr. Craig finished so they could ride home together. Today it is a six minute car ride from where the school was to her apartment. In 1910, it was a 20 minute walk, or an even longer trolley ride.

Sometimes, Augusta said that Dr. Craig did not take Dr. Knabe all the way home, but dropped her off a block away. Dr. Knabe liked it this way because she didn't want him to go out of his way to drop her off. Later they abandoned the plan and he began driving her all the way home. He also once insisted that she go to the theater with him whether she was dressed up or not. She wrote Mrs. Blanche Lindley that she stood before a looking glass and "William commented on the fact that I looked beautiful." This comment implies much more than a passing friendship or working comradery. Or even, as Dr. Craig said, an admiration for a colleague such as he would have for another man.

By Spring of 1911, the amicability was gone. Dr. Craig decided he no longer wanted to be so friendly with Dr. Knabe. In fact, he was supposed to take her to the senior class banquet in May 1911. Instead he went alone and early, sitting by himself at the head of the table. Dr. Knabe came somewhat later and took the seat assigned to her. He also did not take her to the graduation exercises. However, whatever this difficulty was, he was friendly with her during the summer months and Dr. Knabe treated his daughter for a small ailment in June.

At the same time Dr. Knabe worked for the IVC, she used the Pasteur diagnosis of rabies to help earn her living. She went to New York to learn it and bring it back to Indiana. She made an average at first of $75 per case, but later, the state began giving free Pasteur treatments and three other doctors entered the field so part of her income disappeared.

She went to former Superintendent of Schools Kendall and asked him if she could teach hygiene and physical culture. He said she needed to get a certificate of graduation from the North American Gymnastics Union, then she could find positions all over the U.S. for her teaching.

She asked Dr. Frank Wynn, who had been her psychology instructor and preceptor at the medical college, for $600 to get her through the two-year course and asked him if he thought other doctors might help her raise that amount through their contributions.

At the time, it didn't seem the plan had gone further, but later, Dr. Knabe did arrange to take the certification curriculum. She called again on Dr. Wynn and asked for $60 to pay her first semester's tuition. He gave it to her, with the blessing of his wife, who knew Dr. Knabe well. The records show she paid $62.50 to the school on October 6, 1911.

This course was about four hours a day, Monday through Friday; therefore a large part of her medical practice time was unavailable for money making. She started on September 15 and seemed to enjoy her classes as she wrote in her letters to Mrs. Blanche Lindley in Marion, Indiana.

Normally Dr. Knabe would have lectured at the veterinary college in the mornings, but since she had class for herself in the morning she couldn't. She called the school several times about changing her lecture time and asked McPherson to take care of it, but McPherson and Dr. Knabe were unable to get a satisfactory answer. The first week of classes at the veterinary colleges started without any lectures from Dr. Knabe.

Drs. Craig and Ferdinand Mueller were two of the earliest employees of the

Indiana Veterinary College. Mueller's brother in law Otto Wagner was president of the Indianapolis German Fire Insurance Company. Mueller lived with his three children at Wagner's house. Wagner had retired from Vonnegut Hardware Company after 30 years' service and took the superintendency of the school for finance.

Wagner said when he came in Dr. Craig and he did not get along. Lecturers were paid at $1.50 per hour and many times Dr. Craig would challenge the payments. Wagner was also responsible for lecturer schedules. He called a meeting on September 29 with Dr. George Roberts, president of the college, and Dr. Craig to get a schedule made. Dr. George Roberts said he would be glad to switch classes with Dr. Knabe and give her his 1:30-2:30 p.m. slot. Wagner asked Dr. Craig about switching classes and he said, "oh, ----- tell her to go to ----!"[284]

Wagner said he'd do no such thing and Craig turned and walked away. Wagner, not knowing what to really do, and rightfully concerned about having the proper coverage for lectures, called McPherson and told her that Dr. Knabe could take Dr. Roberts' hour. Then he told her that Dr. Knabe should take Dr. Craig's class from 2:30-3:30 p.m.

That afternoon, Dr. Knabe taught. Dr. Craig drove into the barn, and looked for his class which should have been in the ground floor demonstration room. When he found out Dr. Knabe had his class, he became thoroughly enraged and left the school.

Dr. Knabe detailed this in a letter from October 1, 1911 to Mrs. Blanche Lindley. Dr. Knabe said after she finished her class, she went to Wagner and asked how she was given the class. Wagner said Craig had left the school incensed at her. Dr. Knabe said it wasn't her fault and wrote to Mrs. Lindley. She went to Dr. Craig's house and talked with him. Dr. Craig said he believed Wagner did it on purpose and he was tired of teaching and wanted to resign and make Mr. Mueller pay him more money. Dr. Knabe remonstrated with Dr. Craig, asking him to reconsider. However, Dr. Craig refused to budge and resigned in a letter to Dr. Roberts.

Craig did not appear at school the next week so Wagner went to his office at Woods' Transfer Barn on Monument Place (now the Hilbert Circle Theater) to smooth things over. Dr. Craig called him a "----snake in the grass" and refused to discuss the matter.

Because of the resignation, the school was in jeopardy. On October 5, 1911 there was a board of trustee meeting where Wagner's resignation was called for, which he gave under protest (later he was rehired). Dr. Knabe lectured the next day (Friday). On October 9, 1911 Dr. Craig came back in as dean. Dr. Knabe, who was set to lecture on October 13 and 21, never lectured again according to the records of the school.

Dr. Knabe, according to McPherson, tried several times to have her lecture hour straightened out. The Sunday before her death, she went to Dr. Craig's house at 809 N. Delaware Street about the "quarrel "[285] but he was not home. She went back to her apartment where Augusta Knabe and her stepfather Franz Kropp stayed until 6:00 p.m.

Dr. Eva B. Templeton told detectives that Mrs. Nancy Tennant, housekeeper of Dr. Craig, told her that Dr. Knabe came to Craig's house 7:00 p.m. the day before her death to return books she'd borrowed. A fight started between them. The word "marriage" was used and Dr. Knabe told Dr. Craig, "You can continue to practice and I will continue to practice." When they sat down at the table, Dr. Knabe was in tears and Dr. Craig said, "I will have none of this!" He took her by the arm, leading her out of the house. Dr. Craig did not return until midnight.

Harry Haskett testified that it was Dr. Craig who came out between the Vendome Apartments and Delaware Flats at 11:15 p.m. the night of the death. He said he would have shot the man if approached because his actions were suspect. Haskett picked out Craig's picture from a handful of photographs and identified him personally by saying, "If that is not the man I saw, then he has a double in the community."

Further, Mrs. Tennant told Dr. Templeton that Dr. Craig came home late the night of the murder. He changed his clothes completely upon returning, left the house early the next morning with a bundle of clothing, and left instructions that if anyone should call, Marion, his daughter, should answer it.

Superintendent Hyland continued to believe Dr. Knabe's death was suicide.[286]

Pre-trial Days

The newspapers enjoyed taking Superintendent Hyland to task for his perceived shoddy overseeing of the investigation. They were quick to point out that Webster had done in less than a year what they couldn't do with more men in over two. The newspapers delighted in asking why Hyland still clung to the suicide theory when a plausible motive had been found. They theorized, perhaps the public would finally know why the men especially in the medical profession had shown so little care and definite indifference in helping solve or contribute to the solving of the case.

The newspapers raked the Indianapolis police over the coals for the lack of action to this point for the innuendo and the smear campaign on Dr. Knabe's character. They cheered her family on for their day in court, declaring that the family should be happy that the day had come to publicly defend Dr. Knabe, admitting this was something that should not have to be, rather the focus should have been, from day one, on catching her killer.

The media also said that friends of Dr. Knabe were first insulted at having to provide details about Dr. Knabe and themselves, knowing that they would be investigated and all would be brought to light. These facts were brought in the Webster report as a way to prove the murder, although her detractors were gloating over them at the time. If the people who suffered from suspicion in the case could not put themselves to right, hopefully the case in the courts would do that for them.

Finally, the *Indianapolis Star* ran an item about a sailor in London who had been cut up, sewed in a sack and thrown in the river. The London police seemed to think the circumstances pointed to something other than murder. The newspaper asserted that if the Indianapolis police had been on the ground in London and assisted with that case, perhaps they wouldn't continue to think Dr. Knabe had committed suicide.[287]

Rumors

Webster continued to try and clear up rumors about McPherson and Augusta Knabe. They only had five minutes together, which was not enough time to conspire. Some rumors included cutting up bloody garments and flushing them into the sewer. He traced the source of the rumors and "the source was just as I expected. There was no truth in the stories. Miss McPherson told the truth and should be thought of as a very courageous woman. She tried to get first aid to Dr. Knabe as she'd been taught by the doctor. Nothing more, " Webster stated.[288]

The bloody knife in the trash can was also a rumor. Haynes whistled for the trash bin at 9:30 a.m. Someone put on in the dumbwaiter, according to Haynes. However, Dr. Reyer was there at 9:10 a.m. and Dr. Ferguson at 9:20 a.m. Wouldn't one of them remembered if the can was sent down as Haynes said it was? Haynes said there was no knife in the can.

However, not all the garbage had been removed, if indeed any really had. Augusta said the garbage had stayed in the apartment till November 2. The can stank with the food scrapings that had never been removed and were covered with mold.

There was also a rumor right before the trial that Dr. Knabe had confided her love for, and the quarrel with Dr. Craig to psychic mediums, which the prosecution denied.

Dr. Knabe's Art at the Center of the Controversy

The book "Emergency Surgery" by Dr. John W. Sluss, superintendent of the City Hospital, had an engraving that Dr. Knabe drew depicting a cut throat similar to how hers was cut. The police believed she killed herself because she knew how to do it

She Sleeps Well   181

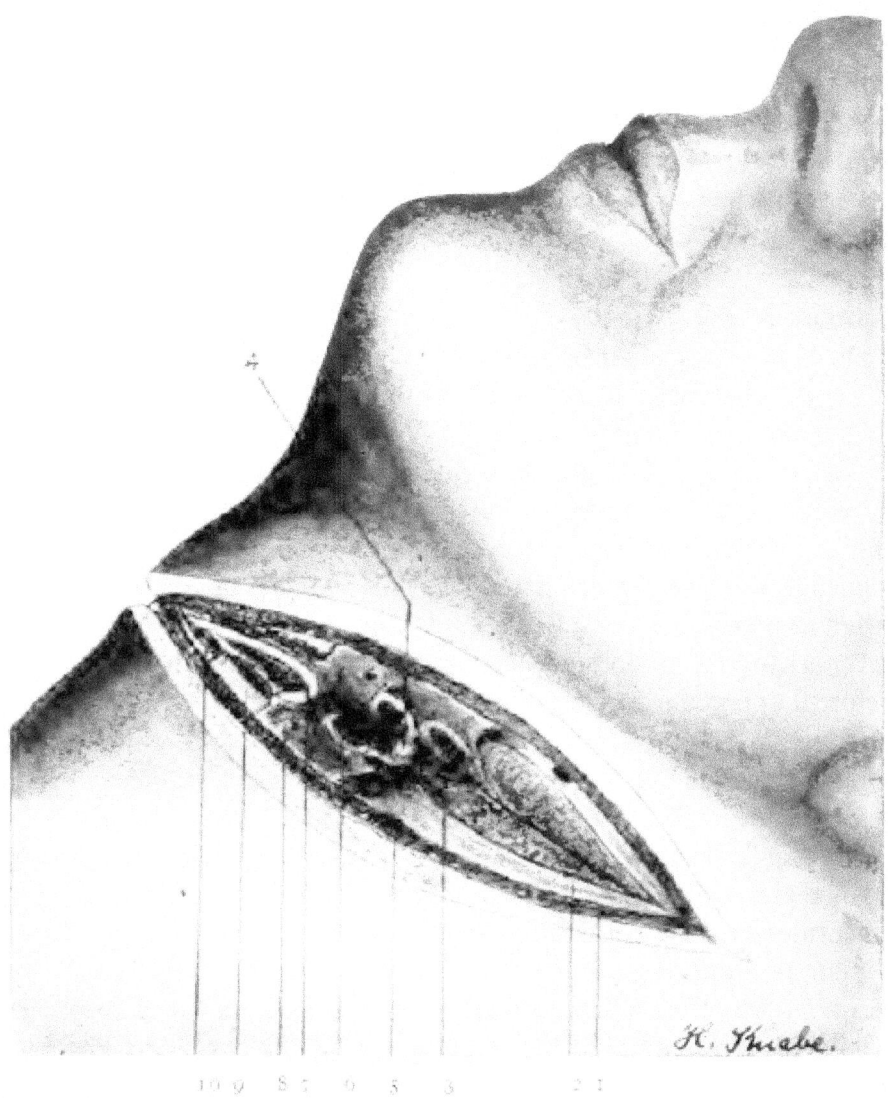

FIG. 64.—Incised wound of neck involving the larynx. 1, platysma; 2, sterno-mastoid; 3, int. jug. vein; 4, vagus nerve; 5, ext. jugular vein; 6, com. carotid art.; 7, upper part of wound in thyroid cartilage opening into larynx; 8, sup. thyr. art.; 9, st. hyoid muscle; 10, sterno-thyroid musc.

Top: The picture of a throat wound from Dr. Sluss' book as drawn by Dr. Knabe. The police and defense thought because Dr. Knabe drew the picture that she killed herself.

based on the drawing in the book. It is not the same cut nor is it from the same angles.

The plan backfired when a copy of this book was obtained from Dr. Craig by Detective Asch, and was presented to the grand jury in July 1912 by Captain Holtz. One of the grand jurors thought it was odd that the inscription page was glued to the title page. He successfully pried the pages apart and it stated, "To Dr. William B. Craig, complements of Helene Knabe."[289] The fact Dr. Knabe did not use her title of doctor when inscribing the book seems to indicate more than just a professional comradery to their relationship.

Craig's Innocence

Dr. G.M. Waggaman believed Dr. Craig was innocent. He was Dr. Craig's associate and first assistant from April 1911 to April 1912. He was almost always with Craig in the days following the murder.

Waggaman said the night of the murder, the college had its regular association night. Craig was president and present. Dr, Waggaman was out of town early the next morning and he didn't see Craig until noon on Tuesday. When Waggaman got back, he was filled in and he explained how Craig called Knabe's apartment at 3:00 p.m. and asked what happened.[290]

Detective Webster found it interesting that Waggaman had never volunteered to go before the grand juries. He felt sure Craig must have explained to Waggaman why he hadn't gone to the flat when asked by the pitiful voice of Katherine McPherson over the phone. Webster offered to pay for Dr. Waggaman's trip to Indianapolis if he would give testimony before the current grand jury.

Dr. Craig's daughter Marion was being treated by Dr. Knabe and was to have stopped by that morning while on her way to school. This point is interesting. This was never mentioned before the indictment. If Marion was to stop by Dr. Knabe's office before going to Shortridge High School, which was just a couple blocks away from the apartment, why would Dr. Craig tell his housekeeper to have Marion answer any calls that day? By this reasoning, Marion, it seems, should have been the first person to find Dr. Knabe, had Marion actually stopped by before school. Finally, even if Marion wasn't the first one, even if she were going to stop by at 8:00 a.m. and go to school late, it makes no sense to tell the housekeeper to have Marion answer calls. And why didn't Marion show up at Dr. Knabe's as she was supposed to? Was she being naughty or was she every really supposed to go to Dr. Knabe's offices?

Dr. Craig went to the Indianapolis Sanitary Plant and was talking with the superintendent when the telephone rang. Dr. E.E. Lawler, second assistant at Craig's office, was on the phone. He told Craig something had happened to Dr. Knabe but he knew none of the details. Craig telephoned at once thinking something happened to his daughter. When Dr. Craig learned that Dr. Knabe was dead, he told Waggaman he was dumbfounded.

Dr. Waggaman was at Dr. Craig's house for supper that evening and of course, Knabe was the topic of conversation. He reviewed his long acquaintance with Dr. Knabe and talked of her good work and ability. Waggaman said Craig seemed completely normal. "If he is guilty he proved a superb actor," Waggaman said. Craig said he regretted the affair but he didn't seem upset. Dr. Waggaman said that the relationship between the two were friendly and most of the professional men they knew also knew Dr. Knabe was in not terrific financial shape. Dr. Craig had often loaned her money and assisted her in many ways, but only assistance that a gentleman might offer. But nothing more specific was suggested or offered by the defense.

Dr. Waggaman went on to say the Dr. Craig was family man and doted on his daughter. As he was the first assistant, he knew where Dr. Craig was most of the time. He could not think of Craig as guilty and believed Dr. Knabe committed suicide.

The Dream and the Umbrella Link

Detective Webster stated that he'd heard a lot of stories relating to communication beyond the grave but the only one to give him pause for real thought was the one about the missing umbrella.

Mrs. Blanche Lindley of Marion, Indiana, a friend of Dr. Knabe's, and by all accounts a very rational and cultured person, had a dream in which Dr. Knabe visited her. Dr. Knabe and Mrs. Lindley became acquainted when her daughter was bitten by a pet. The Lindleys went to Indianapolis for treatment by a physician. Mrs. Lindley heard Dr. Knabe's name and she decided to take the Pasteur treatment.[291] From that grew a mutually respectful friendship lasting until Dr. Knabe's death. In fact, when Mrs. Lindley heard of Dr. Knabe's death, she was prostrate with grief for about two months. It was during this time the dream occurred.

Mrs. Lindley was not a believer in the occult or mystics. However, one day as she lay in her bed, Dr. Knabe appeared before her and said, "Hello, dear." She looked and acted much as she had in life.

Mrs. Lindley stared and said, "Hello, doctor! How are you?"

"If you will find out to whom the umbrella belongs that hung over the banister in the hall, you will learn something." Dr. Knabe replied. "Also inquire about (Homer or Himer) and he can tell you all about it if he will." That was all. Dr. Knabe disappeared as quickly as she'd come.

Mrs. Lindley was astonished and unable to speak at first. Despite her physical condition, she got on a train and went to Indianapolis. First she went to Katherine McPherson's home on Spruce Street and asked if she'd ever heard of an umbrella hanging over the banister in the hall of the Delaware apartments. Katherine said she had no recollection of any such article.

Not to be deterred, Mrs. Lindley went to Augusta Knabe on Bates Street and told her of the dream. Miss Knabe clasped her hands together and said she remembered the umbrella from the day the body was discovered. It was hanging behind the newel post at the bottom of the stairs but she had attached no importance to it given the circumstances of the day. The umbrella, according to Knabe, hung there until November 2. She'd taken the umbrella to Detectives Hall and Morgan said perhaps it should be included as evidence. Detective William Morgan took it and looked it over, concluding perhaps someone from the apartment building had mislaid it.

Augusta Knabe told Morgan to take good care of it as everything in the case was important. The last she saw of it, Detective Morgan still had it in his possession. When Detective Webster asked Detective Morgan about the umbrella, he said there must have been a mistake, because he knew of no such umbrella. Webster had heard of someone with a name such as Homer or Himer, and was still searching for the person. Although one could loosely interpret this as Elmer (perhaps Elmer Hall, a police officer involved on the case), nothing came of this lead.

THE PLAYERS

Judges
Judge Joseph T. Markey, Marion County Courts
Judge Alonzo Blair, Shelbyville Circuit Court

Lawyers
State
Prosecutor Frank P. Baker: wanted to have an early Spring trial
Thomas H. Campbell of Wray & Campbell
John C. Cheney, prosecutor at Shelbyville, direct charged of prosecution
Former Prosecutor John W. Holzman, State
William A. Ketcham, was paid for by many of the Indianapolis women physicians out of their own pockets.[292]
Ephraim Inman, prosecution, hired by the local council of women, one of the best known criminal lawyers in Indiana
Fred McCallister, chief deputy to Prosecutor Baker
Albert F. Wray of Shelbyville, counsel for the state of Wray & Campbell

Dr. Craig Defense
Elliot R. Hooten of Hooton & Hack
Oren Hack of Hooton & Hack
Charles Hack Meiks & Hack
George H. Meiks of Meiks & Hack
Henry N. Spaan

Ragsdale Defense
James A. Pritchard, former criminal court judge, of Pritchard & Pritchard

Dr. Craig Jury *(Name, occupation, age)*
Alfred Arnold, farmer, 61
Kimball E. Barnes, farmer, 61
Martin Good, farmer, 58
Ollie Harrell, farmer, 37
Perry Hurste, farmer, 55
William Lemasters, farmer, 51
Ralph Swinford, farmer, 25
Louis Weinantz, farmer, 49
Elbert Wicker, farmer, 44
Elbert D. Willard, farmer, 41
Walter V. Wright, railroad employee, 34
Marcus Young, farmer, 51

JUDGE AND STATE PROSECUTION

ALONZO BLAIR
PRESIDING JUDGE

FRANK P. BAKER
MARION CO. PROSECUTOR

JOHN W. HOLTZMAN
FOR STATE

JOHN C. CHENEY
SHELBY CO. PROSECUTOR

WILLIAM A. KETCHAM
FOR STATE

A. E. WRAY
FOR STATE

THOMAS H. CAMPBELL
FOR STATE

EPHRAIM INMAN
FOR STATE

FRANK MCALLISTER
MARION CO.
DEPUTY PROSECUTOR

Dr. Craig's Defense Team

GEO. H. MEIKS
FOR DEFENSE

CHAS. HACK
FOR DEFENSE

ELLIOT R. HOOTON
FOR DEFENSE

OREN S. HACK
FOR DEFENSE

HENRY N. SPAAN
FOR DEFENSE

Funding

In January 1913, Dr. Lillian Crockett-Lowder asked for help from the Marion County Medical Society to get support for the defense fund movement. This had been agreed on by Dr. Laura J Cloud, Dr. Rose J. Buttz, Dr. Emma J. Fitch, Dr. Rebecca Rogers George, Dr. Hannah M. Graham, Dr. Alice L. Hobbs, Dr. Martha E. Keller, Dr. Jane M. Ketcham, Dr. Martha J. Smith, Dr. Mary A. Spink, Dr. Urbana Spink, Dr. Elizabeth Conger, Dr. Mabel Tague, Dr. Mary Ella Ash, Dr. Amelia R. Keller.[293]

They felt responsible as women but believed this should be something for the whole medical community. To this point the Marion County Medical Society had been chastised for its indifference. Dr. Lowder presented five points:

1. Dr. Knabe had died and had been until her death a member of the society and was entitled to the ethical protection while living. Now that she was dead, she was entitled to the moral and civic protection of the organization.
2. The legal verdicts indicated murder and the grand jury chose to indict.
3. Dr. Knabe was murdered.
4. Since the organization was composed of people who were supposed to conserve life and alleviate suffering, to do their religious and civic duty, they should join the women who had already started the movement and donate to the legal fund.
5. She asked them to affiliate with the women to bring the killer to justice.[294]

The message fell on deaf ears. When the Indianapolis Medical Society was contacted, they tabled the idea stating they did not want to be known as a collective body that endorsed the indictments. Dr. John Oliver made the motion to table the issue.

The *Indianapolis Star* wrote that until the city pulled together and brought her killer to justice, life was a cheap commodity to the police. It went so far to say that although Hyland had said the police had good luck catching perpetrators in the last year, he didn't comment much on Dr. Knabe's case. And in its opinion, the uncommonly stupid way the case was handled was not offset by luck on the other cases.

Dr. Lilian Crockett-Louder, with the Nu Sigma Phi sorority, believed that if the 100 woman physicians in the state would donate $10 that would go a long way. She suggested that many private women might want to contribute too. She was meeting with Keller so that they could work together to get money. The money was collected by several people and also directly sent to the Union Trust Company. No final tally for the fund was provided.

Dr. Amelia Keller, president of the Local Council of Women, said that Dr. Knabe didn't have a lot of friends, but that she always looked at her job from a humanitarian viewpoint and that she was not one to advance wealth. That she was so cruelly taken from Earth left a stain on Indianapolis and Indiana unless her killer was brought to justice. Dr. Keller also said that she thought first-degree murder was a non-bailable offence, but she was pleased as things progressed that the state believed it had a much stronger case than when they recommended bail.

Dr. George D. Marshall of Young America, Indiana

When Dr. Knabe was sent to Young America to look at malarial patients in Howard and Clinton Counties for the State Board of Health, she stayed with Dr. Marshall and his wife. In her report, she was honest about the Howard County physicians. She stated that they were unprofessional, started rumors and tried to get a confidential statement of her opinion regarding the situation. She said she told the physicians she should not be offering her opinion, that the State Board of Health would offer help after her report was filed.

Despite what some people may have considered harsh opinions, Dr. Marshall stated she was the hardest working woman he ever knew. She would spend the entire day looking at cases and the night making analyses. She was exceedingly independent and worked on her own without asking for help.

Based on his knowledge of Dr. Knabe, he could not find it even possible that she would kill herself. She had graduated the same year – she from MCI and he from the Central College of Physicians and Surgeons. In his opinion, she'd overcome adversity in her homeland and made her own way including being a scrub woman and working in the kitchens of restaurants.

But, Dr. Marshall said Dr. Knabe was ambitious and wanted to be a doctor. She skimped and saved and went to night school and finally was accepted to medical school. She was successful in her profession and it was growing. If she had been wanted to kill herself, her earlier struggles would have made a more fitting time.

Dr. Marshall commented that she was a rather masculine woman and not one that most men would be attracted to. She always struck him as someone who was not attracted to or attracted by men.[295]

Delays

From the beginning, Prosecutor Baker was against the trials. Once the grand jury indicted the pair, he wanted to try Craig and Ragsdale together. This was partly for judicial economy.[297] If the evidence was the same against them, why would you want to have to repeat the same testimony and process twice? That did not happen and the plan was then to try them separately. Also, there would have been strength in numbers.

With the two accused people together, it would have presented a better intertwining story to the jury and been much stronger for the prosecution to be able to present the story in this way.

The trial was originally set for February 1913. By the middle of January, the prosecution stated that they did not know when it would take place, as the defense wasn't ready. If they tried to force the defense, it would just ask for a continuance and probably get it. One of the reasons for the delay was that John W. Holtzmann, who was involved with the case from day one, was in Europe and now engaged in a political campaign. They delayed the trial until the end of his campaign.[298]

In May 1913 Prosecutor Baker said he was ready to try the case but it seemed that all of Craig's attorneys were quite busy and of course, there were vacations. In June 1913 a witness was supposedly ill and the State said more leads were being tracked down. Later it was set for October 23, 1913, the two year anniversary of Dr. Knabe's death.[299] Everyone believed it was merely a coincidence, however later it was said it was chosen after the prosecution met.[300]

Everything had been mismanaged thus far, and why should preparation for the trial be any different? The state prosecutors, Judge Markey and Dr. Craig's attorneys searched for the autopsy report. It was found many weeks later wrapped in the kimono under the bloody pillow in a storage room off Judge Markey's chambers.[301]

Additionally, on October 3, 1913, Craig's attorney, Elliot Hooten, asked for a change of venue due to alleged prejudice against Dr. Craig in Marion County. The motion was granted. Ragsdale's case was to remain in Marion County and was continued. His attorney James A. Pritchard was not sure if they would ask for a change of venue. Eph Inman, one of the State's attorneys, was surprised by the request of a change of venue.

When a change of venue is made, it is treated as an entirely new case on the course dockets. Additionally, the prosecutor of the county it is placed in acts as the prosecutor and the prosecutor from the original county only assists. Once filed in the county, the clerk has 10 days to prepare the paperwork for transfer.

Because Craig asked for the change of venue, in a criminal case, that means although Ragsdale was indicted at the same time, the request for the change of venue allows now for two separate cases to be tried.

Judge Alonzo Blair did not know when the case would be tried as it was swiftly transferred to Shelbyville, the seat of Shelby County. Judge Markey in Marion County had to choose the county as the attorneys could not come to an agreement.[302]

Top: The Shelbyville Courthouse. The venue was changed by the defense because they didn't believe Dr. Craig could get a fair trial in Indianapolis. Judge Markey in Marion County had to chose the county because the lawyers on both sides could not come to an agreement. New lights and communication wires were installed for the trial.

Top: John H. Butler was the bailiff for the Shelby County Circuit Court. At one point, he was ordered to find the people cheering in the courtroom and have them arrested. No one was found or arrested, however.

Top: *The jury poses in the sheriff's office. Unfortunately, this picture was unlabeled so it is unknown who each man was.*

194 *She Sleeps Well*

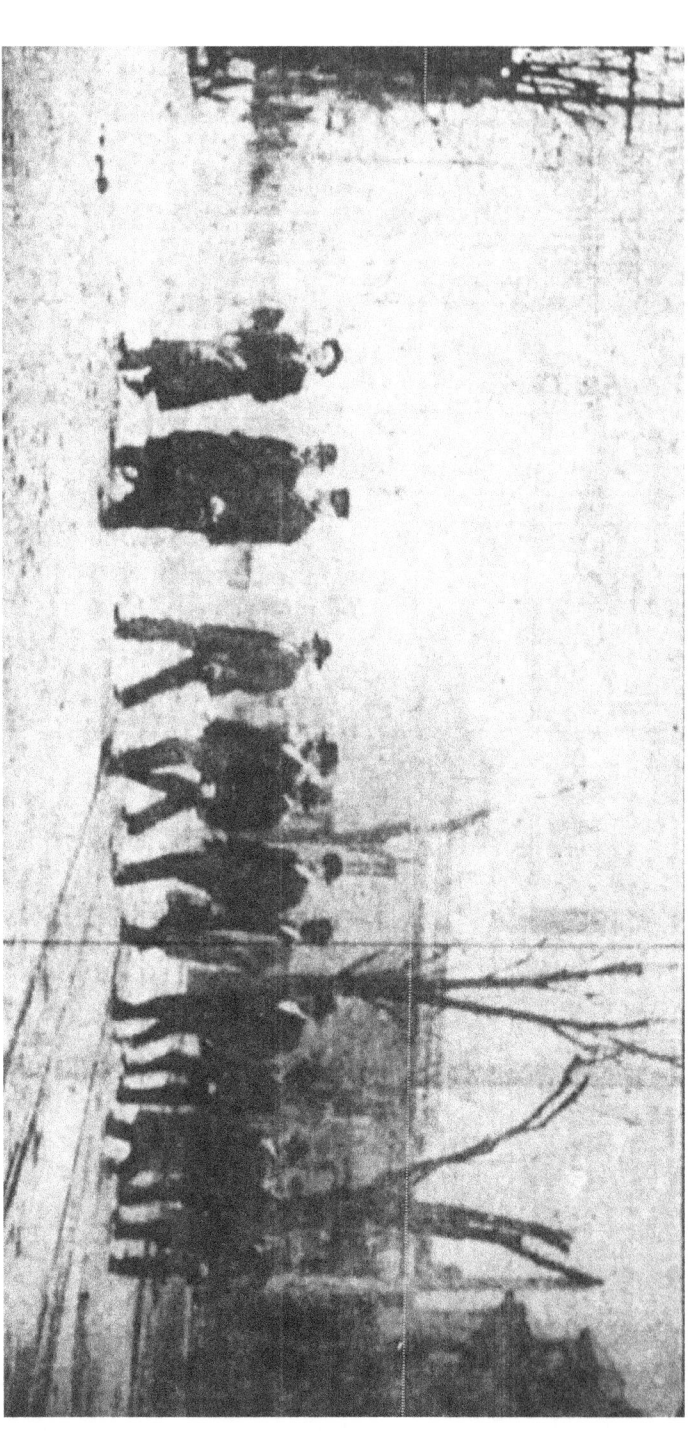

Top: The jury on its way to court. Unfortunately, this picture was unlabeled so it is unknown who each man was.

Small Town, Big News, Bigger Change

Shelbyville was a quiet town…but for a time, that was to change. Not much had been discussed about the case in the last two years. In fact the day of Dr. Knabe's murder, less than half a column (above the fold line) was devoted to her story in the *Shelbyville Republican* and *Shelbyville Democrat*. From that point, the case didn't affect the county seat because no one there knew her, Craig, Ragsdale or any of the other players in the saga, and so not much attention was given to the case.

Until the change of venue to Shelby County.

The excitement brought to the city was in the preparations that were made for the trial including the hiring of Shelbyville attorneys for the case. By this time, the case had been covered in small part all over the country. Indianapolis newspapers were going to report the trial step by step every day.

New electric lights were installed in the courtroom so they could stay and attend the trial as long as they liked. Conveniences for the newspaper men and the jury were added as well. Two telegraph wires were installed. The chairs were elevated and foot rests were added. A solid wood banister was added to the jury box to keep them away from the court officials and attorneys. A venire of 50 men was chosen and the attorneys got down to the last 15 before finding a full jury.

Newspapers from Indianapolis, Shelbyville and reporters from the *Chicago Examiner, Cincinnati Enquirer,* United Press, Associated Press and dozens of photographers invaded the farming community, creating quite a bit of intrigue and excitement.

The prevailing thought was that the State's case was weak and the majority didn't think the State would be able to pin the murder on the what people considered a handsome man.

Set in a park, the courthouse in Shelbyville was described as old-fashioned having been built in 1862 and remodeled in 1878. One would reach the courtroom via a narrow tunnel in which city luminaries were recognized. Once in the courtroom one would notice how small the space was. A few chairs on the south were reserved for onlookers. The majority of the people sat in an upstairs gallery. The attorneys sat on the east side of the room, with the judge in the middle and the jury in a box on the west side.

October 29, 1913

By October 29, 1913, eleven of the twelve jurors were seated. More women than men were in the courtroom and it was a daily race to see who would be able to get seats. Lawyers and newspapermen outnumbered the public. Dr. Craig sat unperturbed by his daughter, Marion. Craig arrived at 8:30 a.m. with his daughter, followed by Elliot R. Hooton. Craig chatted freely with attorneys and court attachés. When Craig left, he didn't want his picture taken but his attorney told him to stop and let the boys in the press have a few.

Jefferson Haynes attended court on October 29, 1913. Augusta Knabe arrived accompanied by Mrs. Ernest Fuehring, her friend, and Franz Kropp. Katherine McPherson didn't come to court until October 30, 1913.

During the day's activities, Mr. Spaan questioned witnesses about their faith in clairvoyants. All said they had no beliefs in such things .

November 28-30, 1913

After another month, court was in session again. On November 28, 1913, Craig was summoned to court by 9:00 a.m. A mysterious man was being sought and a warrant for his arrest at hand but the prosecutor and the sheriff's offices deny any warrant has been sworn out or offered for service. *The Shelbyville Democrat* noted Craig wore a dark grey suit.

The next day, a Saturday, Craig appeared again and his daughter Marion Craig became agitated. Craig calmed her saying he was not guilty and there was nothing to fear. She says that he loves all domestic animals, always has a smile on his face and could not have killed Dr. Knabe as she was his friend.

On Sunday, November 30, 1913, court started at 9:00 a.m. and 75 witnesses were to be examined.

December 1, 1913

On Monday, the trial truly started. The State continued to deny rumors of use of clairvoyants. Many mediums circulated rumors about the case and information obtained in that way. Inman said the state will present nothing obtained by clairvoyants or mediums. The first witnesses would appear once the jury selected. One of the first witnesses was Dr. E.D. Clark, who was called when Dr. Knabe was found. Dr. Wynn also appeared for the defense.

In his opening statement on December 1, 1913, Eph Inman painted Craig as a monster of immorality. He intoned that the State would prove he killed Dr. Knabe during a quarrel following his announced intention of breaking a promise to marry Dr. Knabe. "Craig indulged in a system of making engagements to women and then breaking them. He seduced a high school girl and when she asked him to marry her, Craig replied, "I pay cash ."[303] He did the same thing with another girl and offered to compromise. This girl, just before the trial opened, mysteriously turned up in Florida.' Inman also shouted "Dr. Craig has other methods. He watched Dr. Knabe when she was unaware he was in sight. We will prove that he peeped into her windows at night."

Inman admitted it was unfortunate that the State could produce no witnesses who say Craig cut Dr. Knabe's throat, but said they had overwhelming evidence to prove it did happen. He said likewise they had no direct evidence that a marriage engagement existed between Dr. Craig and Dr. Knabe but they had overwhelming evidence tending to show the fact. "Dr. Knabe bought presents for her wedding which was to be in New York City and she told friends she was engaged to marry a man with an ungovernable temper. She fully expected him to complete the marriage contract." They stated a housekeeper of Dr. Craig's, Mrs. Nancy Tennant ,[304] said he came home the night of the murder carrying a bundle. Although Nancy Tennant still lived in Indianapolis, she did not attend the trial. Her testimony had been given before State witnesses and was admissible. However, this testimony, presented as an affidavit, had far less impact than if Tennat had been in the room testifying. [305] Inman also said that Dr. Craig had taken one of the three keys to Dr. Knabe's apartment. McPherson had one, Dr. Knabe had one and Augusta's went missing shortly before the murder and showed back up in Dr. Knabe's things that were in Alonzo Ragsdale's possession.

Inman added, "….it is conceded by the state at the onset that the defendant should be asked to clear up no mystery or to prove his own innocence in relation to the death of Helene Knabe." The State accepted the responsibility of proving Craig's guilt.

December 2, 1913

The next day was short. The jury was sworn in at 11:30 a.m. They were housed in the Lockwood House and would not be permitted to separate during the trial.

Spaan was quite dramatic when he took the floor. He stated that the State of Indiana had at no time been fair to his client and would continue to be unfair. He questioned the veracity of McPherson, stating she'd been alone with the body (five minutes was the actual number.) He fairly yelled, "Heaven help the State of Indiana if it tries to hide the facts in this case by keeping men off the witness stand ."[306] He went on to try and smear Dr. Knabe by saying she lectured as a "horse doctor" and she was the only woman among the men. He called her extremely masculine, ambitious and full of German blood which means that "Dutch death ."[307, 308] He tried to say that she was only a lecturer at a "horse college " and not at a college for human anatomy, which was untrue as she had been employed by the Medical College of Indiana, Purdue's short-lived medical school, and the Indiana University School of Medicine since she graduated. [309]

Inman addressed the jury concerning Dr. Craig's private life and Spaan objected. This was sustained by Judge Blair. The court said that it was however, proper for the State's attorney to tell the jury that Craig apparently had broken an engagement to marry Dr. Knabe.

Spaan said Inman was unprofessional after Inman said that Craig had been engaged to marry Dr. Knabe and that he made a practice of this sort of thing. Inman said he was just presenting facts. Spaan said, "That is just what we do not want you to do present the facts to the jury. The jury ought to be out of the room when matters of this kind are discussed." The jury was asked to leave.

During the professional posturing, the witnesses were kept from the courtroom and Spaan made a complaint to the court when he saw John M. Maxwell, a former Indianapolis newspaperman in an anteroom. The court directed the bailiff to keep witnesses from within earshot of the court room. The only exception was made for Craig's 15 year old daughter, Marion. Spaan told jurors that Craig was being persecuted. Not only could he establish the doctor's reputation for clean living through the testimony of 100 witnesses, but who also could produce other witnesses to swear he was elsewhere until a late hour on the night that he is alleged to have killed Dr. Knabe. Women were in the courtroom during the trial, which was unusual for the time, but not unusual for the trial, given who had died. Many people in the gallery had a hard time hearing Inman as he spoke low, slow and measured about the life of Dr. Knabe. Occasionally during this speech, Dr. Craig would turn pale and his hands would clutch at the arms of his chair but otherwise, he showed no emotion. His daughter, Marion, was equally detached despite being described as a friend of Dr. Knabe.

In order to refute the idea of suicide, Inman told of Dr. Knabe's actions the night before- being cheerful, taking her shoes to be repaired, all the way through to Dr. Craig finding out about Dr. Knabe the next day. Inman said the State would prove that two hours before he was informed by Miss McPherson over the telephone that something had happened at Dr. Knabe's flat, Craig had informed persons at the veterinary college that Dr. Knabe had been found dead in her rooms. Inman also said that Dr. Craig told Miss McPherson that he was "in the country' when in fact he was at the college. The State said it would not show how the key reappeared.

Inman told of how screams were heard and how Dr. Knabe was found. He said her rug was crumpled and one of her slippers was askew as if someone had moved them or had left in a hurry. He mentioned the second woman who Dr. Craig broke an engagement with had disappeared and the prosecution couldn't find her. Back in the early 1900s breaking engagements was a sometimes criminal offense and damages were due to the woman upon a man who was in breach of contract. Additionally, damages were awarded on whether or not the couple had had premarital sex and the degree of emotional distress for the woman. A woman who had sex before marriage was usually awarded more money as her chance of marriage and establishing a household was greatly diminished. Dr. Knabe could have sued Craig and made his life difficult had he broken an engagement.

Inman said whoever cut Dr. Knabe's throat had an intimate knowledge of the human body because the arteries were avoided and death followed immediately and there was no violent spurting of blood.

The State said that they would get the truth from Craig's former housekeeper about him and his clothes bundle. When Inman tried to make a comment about 100 Indianapolis businessmen vouching for Dr. Craig, the defense made an objection based on the counsel had no right to forecast what the defense would be and it was sustained by Judge Blair.

Spaan said they would prove Dr. Craig was kind to Dr. Knabe and even attended her funeral. He said the first time Dr. Craig entered her apartment was at her invitation. She gave him medicine because of the condition of his heart.

December 3, 1913
The defense immediately began its campaign to prove Dr. Knabe killed herself. It focused on five points:

1. Dr. Knabe, who and what she was
2. The wound on her arm
3. The weapon
4. Could she kill herself
5. Dr. Craig's relationship with Dr. Knabe

Spaan made an opening statement. He said the defense experts proved the wound could have been self-inflicted, and that Augusta Knabe had remarked she feared Dr. Knabe would commit suicide. He also stated that Dr. Knabe was masculine, aggressive,

200 *She Sleeps Well*

Top: Augusta Knabe walks with her friend, Mrs. Ernest Feuhring.

ambitious, and wholly able to take care of herself. Spaan said he would show that detectives and attorneys had been employed to obtain circumstantial evidence against Dr. Craig, and that Ferdinand Adolph Mueller worked against the defendant and assisted in obtaining the indictment against him. The entire morning was taken up with the opening statement. Testimony began in that afternoon.

None of the witnesses threw new light on the details of Dr. Knabe's death. All the witnesses talked about wound on her arm. Spaan asked if the cut couldn't have been made through convulsive moments and they all answered yes. They were asked if they had seen anything in the bathroom to indicate a weapon had been washed or cleaned. All said no.

Dr. Ernest C. Reyer, one of the first doctors on the crime scene, said he knew her for about five years and that he was called to her apartment at 9:00 a.m. and arrived 20 -25 minutes later. When he arrived Mrs. Wynn was there. He said he didn't remember the exact words but that Augusta said something terrible had happened to her dear girl. The room was orderly, but after examining Dr. Knabe, he called the coroner and the police. He also saw a paring knife. Spaan asked if Augusta Knabe had said she didn't want the police there, and asked if there was anything in appearance to suggest suicide. The State objected and it was sustained so the question went unanswered.

Dr. George J. Cook, a second doctor who came to Dr. Knabe's apartment the day her body was found, did say there was blood on her hands. The right hand was sprinkled and the left hand had a smear of blood. There were no bruises on the hands to indicate she had struggled with an assailant.

Dr. Charles E. Ferguson, another doctor who arrived at the crime scene, said he found all her surgical instruments in the cases where she kept them. There was no disorder except on one that might have had a blood stain. He also noticed a paring knife in the apartment. He said Dr. Knabe was of the masculine type. He said she was only aggressive when pushed and was a fighter for what she wanted and believed. He said the only disturbance in the room was that the rug was mussed. Dr. Ferguson corrected Spaan, as Dr. Knabe's head was not under the rail, but her head had been cut so deep that the muscles released and threw her head back so that it looked like it had been shoved there.

Dr. Frank B. Wynn said he examined the hands and found no blood on them.

Spaan detailed the first meeting for Dr. Craig and Dr. Knabe and recalled the lecture hour dispute which the state alleged caused an estrangement between them. Spaan said two Sundays before her death Dr. Knabe went to Dr. Craig's house while they were eating dinner and he insisted she join them. He was anxious for her to have some fresh cider he had received from the county. She sat at the table but didn't eat, as she'd already eaten. She spoke with him about the trouble at the college and he said, "Why no, that's all right, it is all over now."

Spaan also said that Dr. Knabe had told several doctors including Drs. Frank A. Morrison of Indianapolis, Dr. E.D. Clark and Dr. Wynn, that shortly before Dr. Knabe's death Augusta Knabe said Dr. Knabe wasn't making much money and that she was afraid she would commit suicide. The defense said when Dr. Knabe's estate was settled that it was insolvent, furthering the suicide theory. First, Dr. Durham went over Dr. Knabe's books and showed that she was making money. The issue with Dr. Knabe's finances was that she was her own sole support and the sole support of an aged man, her Uncle Daniel Ehmke, in Rügenwaldermünde. Second, her estate was insolvent but only insomuch as there were over $880 worth of accounts from her practice that Ragsdale declined to pursue for payment.

He also described how the arrangement of the bedroom was to preclude easy access of an intruder in the room. The cords connecting the telephones were placed in such a manner that made it difficult to reach the head of the woman's bed. Spaan also brought up the Sluss book and her drawing, implying it provide she knew how to kill herself in the way she'd died. He blamed McPherson and Knabe for having strange conduct with regard to getting help. He hinted that they covered up the suicide for fear of scandal. He said when Webster talked to McPherson she changed her story. He denied that Dr. Craig had left his home earlier than usual the day they found the body. Spaan also said Craig did not tell anyone of the death at the school before he was called. He denied Dr. Craig said he was in the country and that he said he was at the sanitary company.

W.A. Ketcham objected to Spaan telling the jury what the defense expects to prove in cross-examination.

In an effort to taint the efforts of Harry Webster, the defense also produced a contract between Webster and an Indianapolis clairvoyant named Mrs. Rose (Rosa A.) Cooper for $300 if she could produce the name of the person responsible for the death of Dr. Knabe. The same attorney denied this contract existed a week earlier. No mention of it was made in Spaan's opening statement or by the witnesses. Although Rosa was a palmist and lived at 415 N. Alabama Street, the State declared the contract a fake, as did many people interested in the case. It stated:

Left: Harry Haskett, saw a man fitting Dr. Craig's description leaving the alley by the Delaware Flats.

February 3, 1912
To Mrs. Cooper, City

Dear Madam,
I will agree with you thus if you shall render information or assistance which shall lead to the capture of the guilty person or persons in the Knabe murder case to pay you $300 of the reward money when the same has been collected by me.

HC Webster, Supt the HC Webster Detective Agency[310]

Durham testified that the cuts on Dr. Knabe's throat were right to left, then left to right. The State used this to try to disprove suicide. He also talked about the scene of the crime. Dr. Knabe was found on top of the bed covering. The cut was an inch and three-fourths inch deep on her arm and there were three cuts on her neck. Two on the left and one on the right. One on the left was a false start. He said that the first cut was from right to left and the left to right cuts came after. A right handed person, like Dr. Knabe, would have started left to right. There was blood under the bed, by the light switch, a thumb print on the pillow, on the hands as if blood spurted on them. The paring knife was entered as evidence and Dr. Durham said it didn't cause the wounds. He was asked on cross examination if there were other knives that could have caused he wounds. He said her surgical instruments could have. Judge Blair sustained an objection from the State when Spaan asked the coroner if, on the morning he was called to the flat, he had not asked Miss Augusta Knabe for the knife which caused Dr. Knabe's death. Durham also said that death was within three to four minutes of first cut if not instantaneous.

Dr. Ralph S. Chappell, deputy coroner, testified about the wound in her throat. Dr. Moses C. Leath, deputy coroner, testified that his report was wrong and that the cut was right to left as in his testimony and not left to right as the report stated. Said death was from the right cut and within a minute. Dr. Leath insisted that the wound was jagged due to turning the weapon when it hit the thyroid cartilage (Adam's apple). He said the wound would have caused almost instant death. The wound on her arm, he testified, was 1.25 inches long and 1.5 inches deep.

December 4, 1913

Henry Spaan said he and his client believed that "no sweeter, purer woman ever lived "[311] and that the defense would not try to assail the character of Dr. Knabe. However, through innuendo, minimizing and diminishing her work and its value, and trying to paint a picture of who she really wasn't, they already had assailed Dr. Knabe's character and rained an assault down upon her lifeless form.

Henry (Harry) W. Haskett, who previously picked out Dr. Craig's picture from a group, was unable to identify him 100% when placed on the witness stand. Haskett said "he looks like the same man." Spaan asked him if he would swear positively that it was Craig he saw and Haskett said he would not, although he did say the man weighed about 180 pounds and wore a crushed hat and overcoat. He was questioned about having gone to the Wood's Livery stable with Webster to identify Craig and again, Haskett said, "He looks like the same man." Haskett lived at 112 E. North Street but formerly lived at 114 E. Walnut Street. He was also a former deputy sheriff in Hamilton County, Indiana, a former Noblesville, Indiana police officer and served as an officer at the Indiana Reformatory and State Prison. He saw the man as he was coming home from the Pythian Temple. He managed the billiard hall in the Castle Hall building for the Knights of Pythias. Haskett was about 41 with a wife and two children.

Otto Wagner testified about the lecture hours debacle and when he brought it up with Dr. Craig he said, "Oh tell her to go to H—l."[312] The defense objected to the presentation of that testimony and the jury was excused while the attorneys discussed it. Inman told the court he wanted to show Craig had expressed "his disgust and tiresomeness of Dr. Knabe" and that the testimony of Wagner desired to show the attitude toward her at the time of her death. Judge Blair ruled the testimony was proper for the jury.

When the jury returned, Wagner further testified that he had seen Dr. Knabe and Craig leave the college together several times and that she completed her lectures and hurried out to meet him. Other people from the Veterinary College (Dr. P.H. Riedel and Dr. W.H. McCann) testified but were unable to recall anything that established a relationship with Knabe and Craig.

Paul White, now an assistant in the state fire marshal's office and formerly and newspaper reporter in Indianapolis, was called to testify regarding interviews he had with Dr. Craig before and since his indictment. The State attempted to use White's testimony to show that McPherson had called Dr. Craig on the telephone on the morning following Dr. Knabe's death an hour earlier than the defense alleges. White said he heard Miss McPherson speak the words "Dr. Craig" over the telephone but Judge Blair sustained and objection of the defense that such testimony would be hearsay and did not permit it. White testified that soon after Dr. Knabe's death he called at the Woods Livery stable and talked to Dr. Craig. He asked Dr. Craig if he knew Dr. Knabe and he said yes. They discussed the incidences surrounding her death and Dr. Craig said he feared it was his daughter they were referring to over the phone when they said something terrible had happened. Craig told White he wouldn't be surprised if it developed that Dr. Knabe had committed suicide. After the investigation by the grand jury White went to Dr. Craig again and asked if he was the man being investigated and Dr. Craig said yes.

Ray Baumgardner, a member of the *Indianapolis Star's* staff, was called after White. Baumgardner said he called at Craig's house in June 1912 and talked to the vet about the Knabe case. Baumgardner said he was told by Craig that he didn't know anything else about Dr. Knabe's death other than what was in the paper. This statement was made after he was informed by Baumgardner and other reporters that the grand jury had begun an investigation. "We told Dr. Craig that it looked as if someone was trying to make him the 'goat' and he replied it was news to him." Craig asked the men if he would be called and they said they didn't know. Dr. Craig then asked what could be done to meet charges of that kind. Baumgardner didn't remember the answer given and Dr. Craig said he had a high regard for Dr. Knabe and he said his admiration of her was similar to that of which he would hold for a man whom he regarded highly. He told of having loaned Dr. Knabe small sums of money which were all repaid, except one small loan that he didn't expect to get back because she had treated his daughter.

In an effort to offset the contention of the defense that Dr. Knabe was masculine, John Nicolson, an Indianapolis photographer, identified a photo of Dr. Knabe taken three or four years before her death. Spaan objected to the photograph being introduced, but the objection was overruled and it was shown to the jury. The picture appeared to be that of an extremely feminine person.

Miss Katherine Agnes Fleming of Avon, Hendricks County, Indiana testified. Miss Fleming was the cousin of State Senator Stephen B. Fleming of Ft. Wayne, Indiana. Inman showed her a letter written by her cousin and asked her if she knew about it . She said no. Miss Fleming said she had known Dr. Craig for 17 years. He called on her near Avon every Sunday for over three years and his daughter had been there several times.

The State alleged she was engaged to be married to Dr. Craig and that Dr. Craig wanted to break off his engagement with Dr. Knabe so he was free to marry another. Most newspapers declared Fleming denied an engagement, with a slight smile, but when questioned by Inman said they had talked of marriage. However, the *Shelbyville Republican* reported that she and Dr. Craig were engaged and the wedding clothes bought and everything arranged and that the wedding had been postponed because of the trial. Either this is a bold lie designed to sell newspapers or the trial or something else was too much of a burden on their relationship, or the relationship was a lie, because the pair never married.

Inman asked if she had seen Dr. Craig since the opening of the trial. She admitted to having met him in the Traction Station. She was on her way to Ft. Wayne to see her sister but she had telephoned him to meet her there. Inman asked if she had made wedding preparations and she said no. Spaan asked if she had taken some clothes to Indianapolis for repairs and if this might not be the wedding preparations Inman referred to and she said, "Yes, I suppose it is." Inman tried to intimate Fleming was a hostile witness by entering into evidence the subpoena that was marked "not found" for her but Spaan said she couldn't be held accountable for the sheriff of another county's actions.

Fleming had been staying at Hotel Ray for two days before the trial although her name had not been entered on the registry. She was the owner and manager of a farm near Avon. She was 42 with grey-streaked-hair, although she appeared younger.

Top: The "other woman" in the trial, Miss Kathrine A. Fleming. She and Dr. Craig were friends and he visited her often, but they were not engaged.

Craig and Fleming first met 17 years prior at the American Hominy Company at Madison and Fountain Streets. She used to work as a stenographer but when she left in 1909, she had been stenographer, bookkeeper, and cashier. Craig was reported to have exhibited unusual interest in her testimony, keeping his eyes on her the whole time she was on the witness stand.

December 5, 1913

Three witnesses testified to noise in flat the night of the murder. Judge Alonso Blair sustained a motion to deny admission of the kimono into evidence at this time. The connection between Craig and the kimono had to be shown before it could be admitted.

Miss Mary Elizabeth Vail (sometimes identified in newspapers as Bales) Powell of 3303 E. 10th Street (lived on the third floor of the Delaware flats), Jefferson Haynes (sometimes seen in newspapers as Haines), and Joseph Carr testified. Mrs. M. E. Powell said her husband came home at 11:00 p.m. and two or two-and-a-half hours later she head the shrill short scream and another immediately after. Mrs. Powell's apartment was right above Dr. Knabe. She thought however, that the scream came from outside the building, perhaps a block or so away. Spaan concentrated on the fact she thought the screams came from outside the building.

Haynes said he heard a noise like someone falling out of bed and two screams, one after the other and groans after that and a low voice speaking. He heard light footsteps. About 4:00 a.m. he heard someone walking around the apartment. Inman asked if Haynes had seen a knife and he said no. He said if there had been any type of instrument or weapon in the can he would have seen it. He denied to Spaan that a woman's voice said "all right" when he called for the can. Spaan also asked if Detective H.C. Webster or John M. Maxwell had talked to him about the case. He said they had. Maxwell talked to him until they had a falling out and then he quit speaking with Haynes.

Dr. George Roberts, president of the Indiana Veterinary College, testified that Craig was at the school on October 24, 1911 between 10:00 a.m. and noon. There is a discrepancy in the time the state believed him informed of the death and the time the defense asserts he was first informed. Miss Florence Hulen, who was employed at the college, also testified and she agreed with Roberts.

Joseph Carr also said he heard screams in the Delaware Flats. He saw a man come from the direction of the flat soon after he heard them. He described him as about five feet nine inches tall and 180 pounds. He wore a derby hat and white cuffs.

Top: Hotel Ray where Katherine Fleming stayed secretly while newspapermen milled about.

Below: Lockwood Hotel, where many people attending the trial stayed.

Dr. R.P. Noble (sometimes listed as Robert C. Knoble), an Indianapolis chemist, analyzed the kimono and was not permitted to answer the question as to whether he found blood on it. The jury left the room while Spaan and Inman argued the question before Spaan cited some decisions on the subject. He said that State would not be able to show any conspiracy or relationship between Craig and Ragsdale. Inman argued that Craig and Ragsdale were not indicted for conspiracy but charge jointly with murder and the State will show the connection.

Lon V. Burton (some papers reported him as Whorton), an *Indianapolis Sun* newspaper photographer, was called to identify some pictures he had taken recently of the Delaware Flats. The pictures were introduced in evidence and shown to the jury.

In order to show Dr. Knabe's regard for Dr. Craig and vice versa, witnesses were questioned about the pair's relationship. Otto Wagner, former superintendent of the Indiana Veterinary College, was recalled and asked on redirect examination about the banquet given at the Denison Hotel by the senior class of the college in October 1911 before the death of Dr. Knabe. He said Dr. Knabe and Dr. Craig were at the banquet. On cross examination Spaan did not talk about that part of the testimony. The witness testified that there was a dispute about the hours Dr. Knabe was to lecture. Wagner said Dr. Craig spoke harshly of Dr. Knabe. He also said that Dr. Knabe took two cigars from a box which was passed at the banquet and that they were meant for Craig. They were not found in her room after her death.

Dr. Alfred S. Jaeger of the Indiana Veterinary College, testified about the banquet. He saw Dr. Knabe take the cigars but did not know what she did with them. He said they were found in her room after her death.

Walter E. Plater (sometimes Playther) of 523 N. Alabama Street, testified as to having seen a light in Dr. Knabe's apartment about 2:40 a.m. or 2:45 a.m. on October 24, 1911. He was passing by and noticed light under the shade.

J.W. Smith of 215 E. Michigan Street (across from Delaware Flats) sat on her porch and said she saw a man outside the Delaware Flats. He placed his hands on Dr. Knabe's windows as if trying to get in. The prowler always came about 11:30 p.m. to 12 a.m. each night for several weeks. When he tried to get in, she called the police. The officers watched the place for a week but he did not reappear. She said he was a large man and wore a soft hat pulled over his face. When asked if he was slender, wore gloves or other things, she said she couldn't say. Spaan asked her if he was tall and again, she said she couldn't say. Spaan said, "You saw him as many as 30 times and you can't say whether he was slender?" Smith said no.

Dr. Joseph E. Wailther (sometimes Walther) of Glenwood, Rush County,

Top: Photo of Dr. William B. Craig, his daughter Marion, who attended the trial, and his defense team.

Indiana occupied Dr. Knabe's apartment after her death. He identified a diagram of the apartment and said John M. Maxwell assisted him in making the diagram.

Fred McCallister, chief deputy prosecuting attorney for Marion County, made some measurements of the flat and testified about the measurements.

Miss Maude McGregor, stenographer at 125 W. Market Street, was called but was not present. The State tried to introduce the subpoena that was returned by the sheriff but the defense objected and it was sustained.

December 6, 1913

Augusta Knabe was on the stand. She cried for several minutes when the kimono was handed to her to identify. The State claimed there were blood stains on it. She said Dr. Knabe was a women who was well proportioned and was a regular woman with normal womanly instincts. [313] "Her form was very pretty, her hair light and silky and her hands delicately shaped." She testified Dr. Craig often took her on auto rides and visited her. No bloody knife was found in the apartments. Augusta also testified to her cousin's perseverance on coming to America and her career. The State planned to close its case, but McPherson was recalled for cross examination. McPherson was cross examined. A physician sat with her because of her delicate nature they thought she would collapse. She did draw away in horror when the bloodstained pillow was thrust into her hands; she turned pale and almost fainted. Katherine testified that she talked with Dr. Craig at 11:00 a.m. and he told her he was "in the country." She also said that after Knabe's death, she and Augusta Knabe met Dr. Craig in Summer 1912 in a restaurant and he appeared "nervous" and pale when he saw them. He also dropped pie in his beverage glass. She was asked how Miss Knabe was dressed on the occasion.

Katherine stated Augusta wore a white embroidered dress and a white hat. Inman asked if she looked like her dead cousin at the time of the meeting in those clothes but Judge Blair would not allow the question. Katherine said she had known Dr. Knabe for two to three years and Dr. Craig for about that long as they were introduced by Dr. Knabe at her office one evening. She said he came to Dr. Knabe's office three times in 1911 and she was in his car quite often. Katherine was shown a photograph of Marion and Dr. Craig and asked how Dr. Knabe got it. Marion had given it to her. The night before Dr. Knabe died she asked her to pick up shoes from Stout's Shoes. Which she did. She also stated that when she got to the flat, the key didn't want to work as normal. The defense failed to shake her original story.

Dr. Craig expected to leave the court a free man this day. Dr. Craig's daughter said "Daddy will go home with me tonight a free man, won't you daddy" as she stroked her father's hair. He smiled and nodded at the direction of the court. Spaan said he would move to take the case from the jury after the State rested. The State, he said, has proved Dr. Knabe was a victim of murder and not suicide, but it did not connect Craig with the tragedy. None of the witnesses would swear positively that it was him they'd seen. The chief reliance of the State would be that Dr. Craig told someone at the school Dr. Knabe was dead at 10:05 a.m. when he wasn't called till 11:00 a.m.

The defense said if the judge did not take the case from the jury they would produce newspaper extras showing the word on the street of Dr. Knabe's death was at 10:00 a.m. and that he told McPherson he was at the sanitary plant and not in the country when he spoke with her.

Ferdinand Mueller said Dr. Craig was at the school shortly after 10:00 a.m. and told him that Dr. Knabe was found dead. He was normal but pale.

Samuel T. Marshal of 713 N. Delaware testified as to have heard someone running rapidly north on Delaware between 2:00-3:00 a.m. on the night of Dr. Knabe's death.

Joseph Carr said he saw a man coming from Delaware flats about 12:30 a.m. He did not meet him on the sidewalk. Carr was on the south side of Michigan and the man was on the north. He walked eastward and the man crossed the street diagonally and they didn't meet. Carr was on his way home from work and had escorted a woman friend back to her home on Illinois Street. He said the man wore a derby hat but others witnesses said he wore a soft hat. Spaan tried to prove that Carr was drunk but was unable to do so.

Dr. Charles O. Durham was asked about finding the keys. He got keys from Capt. Holtz and later Augusta Knabe. Holtz got his key from Miss McPherson.

Dr. John Kolmer went to her apartment the Saturday after her death to appraise her property. He found a bunch of keys on a chiffonier. They were given to Mr. Milnor who was also appraising property with him and then from there they went to A.M. Ragsdale.

Miss Ila McPherson of 1148 (later 1152) Spruce Street Indianapolis, sister to Katherine McPherson, and a teacher in the Indianapolis schools, testified she saw Dr. Craig in Dr. Knabe's apartment on October 24, 1911 about 3:10 p.m. He was sitting in a chair talking to Augusta Knabe. He had a mustache at that time (there had been some dispute to this fact.)

Arnold Moore, 21 and a cabinet maker of Shelbyville, Indiana, testified he saw a man loitering near the flats before Dr. Knabe's death. He had lived in the Emmet Flats across from the Delaware Flats. He approached the man and asked him what he was doing there. Moore was told to keep his mouth shut. Moore then went back into the flats. When asked if he saw the man in the room, Moore pointed to Dr. Craig. Craig and his daughter stared steadily at the witness. He had also gone to the livery to see if he recognized Craig and he said he looked like the same man. When asked if it was, Moore said, "Well, there are so many men who look alike." The lawyers wrangled over how the question was worded but Moore did not identify Craig positively. Spaan cross examined and he said he met Detective Webster on June 1, 1913. Moore went to Webster's office and was shown pictures of some men and was told pick out the one that seemed to be the one at the flat. He had not been told about a reward. Inman redirected and asked him how many other men he has seen who looked like the man at Delaware Flats and he said one, a Mr. Merlatt. When asked if it was Mr. Merlatt at the flats, Moore said no.

Mrs. Frank B. Wynn testified she was admitted to Dr. Knabe's flat by Augusta Knabe and that Katherine McPherson was there. They were busy calling friends and trying to reach physicians. The State wanted to show that the pair did not delay in getting help.

Fred McAllister, deputy prosecuting attorney of Marion County was asked if any testimony had been offered to the grand jury concerning the kind of instrument that caused Dr. Knabe's death and he said none except it was a short instrument.

The Craig case adjourned at noon until Monday morning .

December 7, 1913

The people in the courtroom were disappointed by the lack of thrills in the trial. Some believed that her death had been caused by an ape man who came into her apartment in the night. [314]Others came to gather what they could from the life of Dr. Knabe and Craig. Many women had been turned away for lack of seats. Those women, who had been able to find seats, brought their lunches to stay in the court and keep their seats. The gallery was full to capacity and the supports, which were very frail and seemed ready to collapse.

Augusta Knabe identified the kimono saying she gave it to Dr. Knabe on Christmas Day 1910. It had been a navy blue with pretty red poppies, not the dull color it was now. At Ragsdale's funeral establishment, it had been all crumpled up when given to the grand jury in June 1912. She had last seen it the Sunday before Dr. Knabe's death and it was in good shape then. She told of coming to America and Dr. Knabe immigrating. Dr. Knabe worked as a "second girl " in private families till she learned English. She talked of Dr. Knabe and her work at the Indiana State Board of Health and working in the Board of Trade building and then working at the Indiana Veterinary College. Augusta said that Dr. Knabe was 158 pounds, had a pretty form, beautiful hands and dark brown hair, which was very fine and silky but very short. How short her hair was or why (e.g. medical, preference) is not known. She mentioned Dr. Knabe thought everything had a place and everything should be in that place. For example, her spectacles were always put in a case and her hair pieces put in a net.

The first time Augusta met Craig was in 1908 before Dr. Knabe retired from the Indiana State Board of Health. Dr. Knabe was walking with her when Dr. Craig approached. Dr. Knabe made the introductions. Later, Augusta saw Craig standing by his car at Monument place and told him that her cousin wanted to leave the city. Craig said "Oh, she won't go away " and waived his hand dismissively.[315] Augusta said that Dr. Knabe was pleased to go riding with Craig in his auto. She believed that Craig and Knabe were good friends because they frequently joked about trivial things.

Spaan cross examined Katherine McPherson. He wanted to show that Dr. Craig's photograph was not the only picture Knabe had of male friends. She was asked if Knabe had photographs of professors or lecturers at the Indiana Veterinary College and Katherine said no. She was asked if she had not told the police that the door was locked when she arrived. She said she could not remember having said that. The State wanted to show the door was unlocked. If that could be proved, the murder theory had additional merit. She said she did not do anything with the garbage can the day Dr. Knabe was found. Inman stated that Miss McPherson recalled Dr. Knabe brought home a steak for supper before her death which was found in the garbage at least seven hours after the body was found.

As Augusta Knabe left the courtroom, Dr. Craig moved out of her way and tipped his hat. He was met with the cold, hateful stare of a broken-hearted woman.

December 8, 1913

The defense believed yesterday the trial would end. The defense believed again today that the trial would end.

The defense still argued that the kimono should not be introduced until it was proven it belonged to the doctor and it was proven that no one put the blood stains on it. Because it didn't seem the State would be able to do this, when the State rested, the defense asked for an acquittal.

What we know at this point was that the State proved Dr. Knabe and Dr. Craig were good friends and they spent a lot of time together. The State did not prove he was the man prowling around the flats.

Augusta resumed her testimony. She recounted the day she found out her cousin was dead. She went to school, to the apartment, and then, she saw her cousin. Augusta stated that Dr. Knabe's head was nearly off her body and she could see the gold tooth Dr. Knabe had shimmering slightly. Augusta was understandably distraught and asked for water. She also stated she was in a draft and the windows were closed. Augusta was asked to identify the pillow she'd placed so tenderly on her cousin's torso. She did, saying it was from home (Germany), and kissed it. "I covered my poor cousin with a sheet."[316]

She said Katherine had called Dr. Craig at his home and office. She knew McPherson called Dr. Craig around 11:00 a.m. because a clock had stopped working and Mr. Allen came in to fix it. He used his watch to reset the time which was a little after 11:00 a.m. Augusta said Katherine called Dr. Craig at no other time. When Dr. Craig came it was between 2:00 p.m. to 3:00 p.m. and he sat in a rocking chair. Augusta said she talked but he didn't. Dr. Craig put his hands to his face and looked through his fingers. He had never acted that way before and he stayed that way a long time. When she said, "Isn't it awful?" Dr. Craig said "Yaas." Augusta "drawled" his yes the same way he said it.[317]

She also testified when she and Katherine McPherson saw Dr. Craig last summer in the restaurant, he was nervous. Later, Katherine was walking with her at the Circle and Dr. Craig was in front of his office. He made a motion to go into his office and then stood and stared at the pair. Then Dr. Craig stepped on one foot and the other and put his hands in and out of his pocket. He did not speak to Augusta at that time or any time since the day in Dr. Knabe's apartment.

The council for both sides argued about taking the case away from the jury. Many spectators watching said the State didn't have a strong case. When Ketcham called Dr. Craig a murderer, Spaan and Ketcham clashed so violently that Judge Blair had to admonish them. Prosecutor Baker was most notably silent.

In his closing remarks, Spaan admitted the State made a good case for murder instead of suicide, but did not prove Craig did it, nor had anyone identified him. The death was as much a mystery now as ever. The State failed to show motive with Dr. Craig. Ketcham accused the defense of coming to Shelby County to get away from Marion county where Dr. Knabe was well known. The defense said they did it because they couldn't get a fair trial there. Spaan said his client had been branded a murder. "This man has been harassed more than can be imagined. He ought to be allowed to walk out of this court room a free man with a crown of honor upon his brow. This is the first time he has been able to confront his accusers. It is the first time the white light of investigation has been brought forth ." [318]

Wray argued for the prosecution that there was motive. Dr. Craig wanted to get Dr. Knabe out of that way and there was no other person under God's heaven who had such a desire. He said the State had shown the estrangement through their quarrel at the school. Augusta Knabe said Dr. Knabe went to Dr. Craig's to return a book Sunday afternoon and returned in 15 minutes when she did not find him at home. When Dr. Craig found out that she had been there (after he came home from Miss Fleming's home), he became angry. Dr. Craig planned her death and executed it. He incriminated himself when he went to the school at 10:00 a.m. and talked of Dr. Knabe being dead before he got a call about it, which he admitted was the first he'd heard of it. Wray said if the case was taken from the jury, it would be contrary to the constitution of the state which provides that a jury shall review such cases. He said it didn't matter how the murderer got in or out but just that he was there.

The attorneys argued on and Spaan said if the court requires the defense to offer testimony, they will put Haskett, who said he saw Craig, on the stand and prove that it was Leo H. Kahn (now living at 2444 North Meridian but at the time he lived in the Vendome Flats next to the Delaware Flats). He was looking for the janitor to get help with the lights in his apartment. Prosecutors would also offer testimony to offset the witnesses who said they saw a man and woman in front of the flats.

Sadly for Dr. Craig, his freedom was not secured this day.

December 9, 1913

Sadly for the Knabes, Dr. Craig's freedom was secured this day.

Judge Blair came in 30 minutes later than usual and began reading his decision without the jury present. When the jury was allowed to come in, Judge Blair did the incredibly rare, especially in cases where there is no technical error, and ordered a directed verdict. What this means is that in cases where someone cannot be convicted beyond a reasonable doubt, the judge can act as a thirteen juror and ask the jury to return a "not guilty" verdict. He wrote 15 pages for his justification of his decision. Dr. Craig was presumed innocent until proven guilty, the evidence was circumstantial and the State failed to connect Dr. Craig with the death of Dr. Knabe. "Reasonable doubts are to be resolved in favor of the defendant, whether they arise as a result of the evidence from conflicts in the evidence or from the absence of evidence." He conceded that the State proved Dr. Knabe had been murdered. Judge Blair also believed Dr. Knabe and Dr. Craig were friends, but no more. "To my way of thinking, these attentions showed kindness and respect rather than love and infatuation. There is no evidence whatever that the defendant was ever engaged to Miss Knabe, or that they ever contemplated marriage, or in fact that he knew what Miss Knabe had any other feeling toward him than that of friendship. The evidence discloses that their relations were pure and honorable."[319]

In his review of Dr. Craig telling Dr. Knabe to go to hell, the reports of prowlers, the witnesses who could not identify the men seen around the apartment building, he was equally as underwhelmed. In the matter of the incident where Dr. Craig stared oddly at Augusta Knabe, Judge Blair stated that it proved nothing. [320]

Finally, Judge Blair stated, "Defendants counsel for the purpose of the argument to motion now before the court, conceded that Helene Knabe was murdered. If Helene Knabe was murdered it's as a brutal, atrocious murder and the person who committed this awful crime ought to be given the extreme penalty. "[321]

Spaan echoed the judge's words stating that Dr. Craig had been harassed more than was able to be borne by any one person. The State argued it had presented evidence to show that Dr. Craig wanted to get Dr. Knabe out of the way and that there was an estrangement via their quarrel at the Indiana Veterinary College that proved Dr. Craig wanted to get rid of Dr. Knabe. Mr. Wray argued for the State that to take the verdict away from the jury would go against Indiana's constitution.

All the words in the world made no difference. The jury looked perceptibly relieved by the judge's words and came back a short time later with the acquittal signed by Louis Weinantz, the foreman. Craig was released immediately.

Dr. Craig received the news as calmly as he had sat there the entire time. Miss Marion was visibly affected when the jurors filed out to do what the court asked. Dr. Craig greeted the jurors as they filed past him. Miss Marion snuggled on the shoulder of Elliot R. Hooten and sobbed.

The people in the court room cheered, but Judge Blair stopped it. He directed the bailiff to arrest anyone who cheered, but no one was arrested.

Dr. Craig and his attorneys made no statement after the case. Dr. Craig shook hands with Judge Blair and they chatted for several minutes. He also shook each juror's hand. His daughter talked with some women and thanked the judge profusely.

Eph Inman said "The State fully realized it was a difficult case to make. The State has no criticism to offer in any way and the attorneys for the Prosecution feel Judge Blair's ruling in directing a verdict of acquittal came from his conscience and that he was absolutely sincere in his view of the evidence. The Prosecution sought to develop and represent the evidence to the jury fully and honorably and the Prosecution takes no exception to any action of the courts."[322]

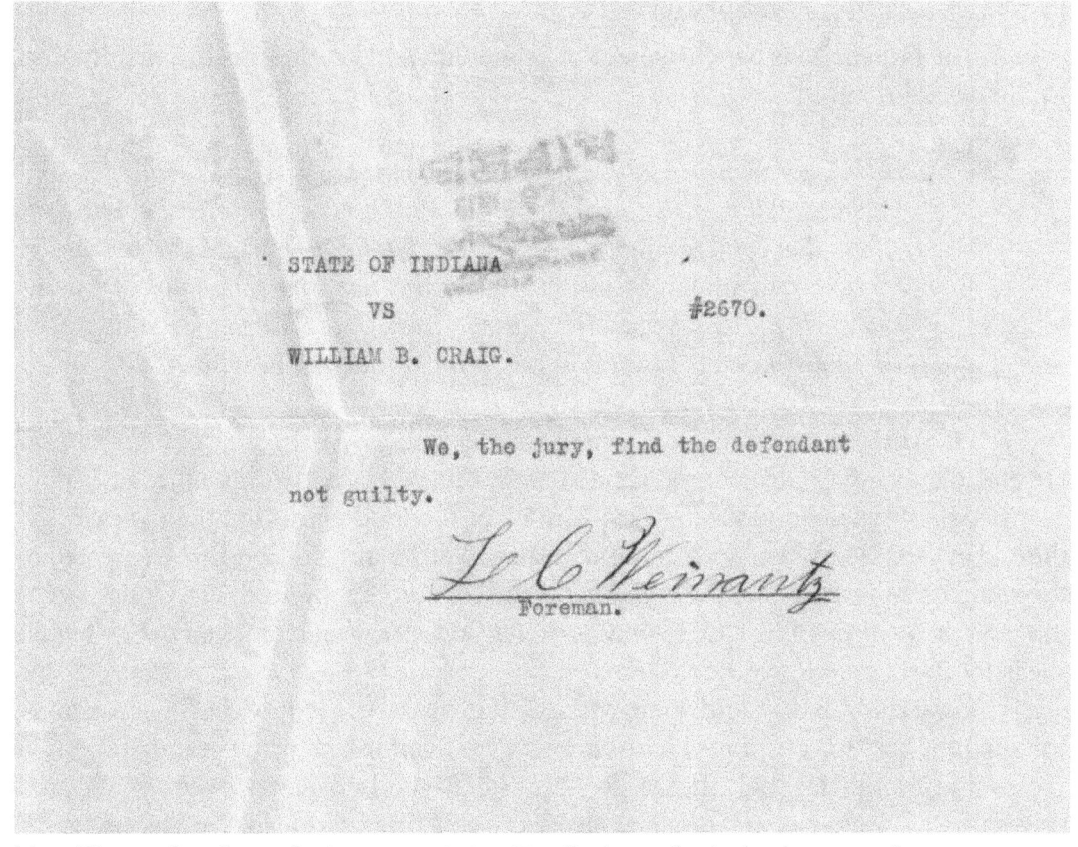

Top: *The verdict from the jury acquitting Dr. Craig as the judge instructed.*

The defense never had to fully present its case.

Life Goes On

The *Shelbyville Republican* roasted Augusta Knabe and Katherine McPherson after the verdict was declared, "The way was plain. It was the right thing to do. Quite a good many people are of the opinion that Miss McPherson and Miss Augusta Knabe acted strangely in not notifying the police more quickly upon discovering the dead body, and also that possibly they could have told more of the case. Be that as it may, the case is now over. Dr. Craig is freed and the death of Helene Knabe is a mystery and probably always will remain so, for the person or persons who do know about it, if any such there be, will never tell ."[323]

The Indianapolis papers were more eloquent, and kept to the idea that the case would never be solved.

> *"The only change of solution apparently is the eventual unbosoming of some guilty breast now securely locked. It is not an improbable thing that confession may clear up the details of Dr. Knabe's cruel and distressful taking off and certainly from the standpoint of justice to the living, both the accused persons and the dead woman's intimate friends, it is a consummation devoutly to be wished ."*[324]

Dr. Craig returned to Indianapolis on December 9, 1913 shortly before noon. He and his daughter went home immediately. Later he went to his office at Woods Transfer Barn where friends and acquaintances met and expressed their pleasure at the end of the case. When he went to the Indiana Veterinary College, he was greeted by the students and was presented with a pipe and tobacco by the students. Craig said he did not care to discuss the case saying he preferred to let what happened in Shelbyville speak for itself.

Prosecutor Baker and Fred McCallister, his chief deputy, had been against bringing the case to court but their opinions were overlooked by the grand jury.

Even after the trial, the debate- and lies[325] and cover up- went on. Alonzo Ragsdale was cleared as well because the case with Craig crumbled. On December 18, 1913 the Marion County Prosecutor Frank P. Baker made a motion to nol-pros (i.e. dismiss) the charges against Ragsdale. He said that the State had said something about the kimono Ragsdale was accused of laundering.

Baker stated that when the kimono was brought in front of the first grand jury, it had no stains on it. [326] He intimated that he did not know what happened between the first and second grand jury when Detective Webster had the kimono in his possession. When it was presented for the second grand jury, there were stains on it.

Deputy prosecutor Fred McCallister said he would have testified to the same thing if he'd been asked. He said that he saw the kimono in June and that no stains were found. He couldn't imagine that as thoroughly as it was examined by him and the grand jury that the stains could have been overlooked.[327]

Judge Markey asked Baker if he meant the stains got on the garment after the first grand jury investigation. Baker said that is exactly what he meant. Judge Markey sustained the motion.

When Private Detective Harry Webster heard about the comments by Baker, Webster did not hesitate to call Baker a liar. He stated that in March 1912 he sent Augusta Knabe and Katherine McPherson to retrieve the garment from Ragsdale. They were told by unknown persons that Ragsdale didn't know anything about the kimono. In June 1912 during the first grand jury, Ragsdale was put in front of the grand jury and was able to produce the garment.

In fact, Webster stated, Baker was the one to tell him that there were stains on the kimono. After the first grand jury reviewed it, Webster took the garment to Dr. Lillian Crockett-Lowder who helped take it to another physician (Dr. R.P. Noble) for testing. That physician stated that the stains were blood and the grand jury itself said that the garment had been washed.

The garment was turned over to the second grand jury and then given to John W. Holtzman, one of the attorneys assisting in the state prosecution of the case. When the kimono was given back to Webster, the stains were still quite evident.

Baker responded to these comments by saying he could say things about Webster that may impeach Webster as a witness. He said Webster was mistaken. Baker stated that he put the kimono on at the first grand jury and the grand jury examined it on him and then he took it off and everyone had an opportunity to examine it separately. Baker did concede that the kimono was crumpled and did appear as if it had been washed but that there were no stains on it.

He explained away the information given to Augusta Knabe and Katherine McPherson. Ragsdale had said he didn't have the kimono but later, as he was the executor of the estate, he found it crumpled up among some other items. Baker said Ragsdale had sent a man up to Dr. Knabe's flat to gather some things and the man had found it hanging on the door of a closet, placed it on the floor and wrapped the items in the kimono.[328] When the second grand jury took place, there were new stains on the kimono.

Baker further stated that when he was at Shelbyville for the trial of Dr. Craig, he told the attorneys for the state if he were asked to testify he would have to say that if there were any stains on the kimono when it was presented to the first grand jury, Baker didn't see them.

Webster had good reason to call Baker out on his statement. This entire statement by Baker is a lie. Dr. Knabe was killed on October 23-24, 1911. The newspaper reported the police and Ragsdale did a final walk through of the apartment on November 1, 1911 to ensure everything was inventoried and to officially turn over the flat's contents to Ragsdale as executor. By November 11, 1911 Ragsdale had filed his first report with the

Top: *The Delaware Flats as the Barton Hotel.* Bottom: *The lobby of the hotel.*

probate court. It would be assumed that by that time he had ascertained the full value of the estate, and enumerated anything included in the estate. Dr. Knabe's apartment was rented on November 14, 1911. Webster was employed by the Local Council of Women in February 1912. Further, Ragsdale paid claims from the estate starting on December 20, 1911. One would believe if Ragsdale had done his job properly, that he would be in full possession of what the value was and what was contained in the estate via a list. By the time Webster asked for the kimono, there was nothing left at her apartment to send a man for, as Baker indicated because it was already rented as of November 14, 1911.[329]

This means Ragsdale had the items in question well before the first grand jury in June 1912. Additionally, the grand jury examined the stains on the kimono during the June 1912 session. At that session, Baker told the grand jury that the kimono was never lost and he knew about it for six months, meaning he would have known about it from January 1912 at least. So who is to say what happened to it when Baker and Ragsdale were known to have known about and possessed it for six months before the grand jury?[330]

Baker never wanted to prosecute the case against either man. Once Craig was acquitted, Baker wanted the case against Ragsdale to go away and he wanted to save professional face. Baker simply lied to make it so. One has to wonder if the case against Ragsdale had gone forward, with the evidence that was available, if it would have made any difference. Would Ragsdale have at last turned on Dr. Craig and shed new light on the case?[331] Unfortunately, even if Ragsdale had provided new details, the case against Dr. Craig could never be retried.

Top: Augusta Knabe's grave marker in Concordia Cemetery, Indianapolis, Indiana.

WHERE ARE THEY NOW?

The building in which Dr. Knabe was murdered still stands. In 1914 the apartments became the Barton Hotel. Later it was the Barton House nursing home. Finally the Salvation Army bought it and turned it into the Barton Center of Hope. The Salvation Army restored the lovely bay windows and brought it back to life. Occasionally, the author stops by the building. The tenants say Dr. Knabe still roams the halls. They say she hates messes and no one stays for long in what was her office and bedroom.

Dr. Helene Elise Hermine Knabe was buried in Crown Hill Cemetery, Indianapolis, Indiana Section 43, Lot 6950 in an unmarked grave. In 2006 the author and her husband, Michael raised money to buy and set a tombstone for her. It was set on her 131th birthday, December 22, 2006. Dr. Knabe was toasted with champagne and her favorite flower, gardenias were placed on her grave.

People Close to the Family

Augusta B. Knabe was born in March 9, 1867 in Stolp, Pomerania, Prussia, Germany. After her move to America on June 28, 1894, she lived at 1205 Bates Street until she died. Augusta was born in Germany and came to Indianapolis for good at the age of 28. She attended Butler University and taught German at Whittier School No. 33 at Sterling and 12th Streets for 25 years. After World War I she taught in School 72 (Emma Donnan at 1202 E. Troy Avenue) and School 7 (Thomas Jefferson on the north side of Bates Street between S. Concordia and S. Davidson Streets) for another 15 years. Augusta was naturalized on March 28, 1921. She retired from teaching in 1933. Augusta was a member of the Second Evangelical and Reformed Church. She died at 87 on August 14, 1954 due to acute gastric dilation caused by para-esophageal hiatal hernia. Her funeral was on August 17, 1954 at Meyer-Abdon Funeral Home and she was buried in Concordia Cemetery. She was survived by her nephew Lorenz Kropp and several cousins.

Katherine M. McPherson was born in January 1888. She stayed in Indiana for many years after Dr. Knabe's death. She lived with her mother and several sisters for many years. By 1935 she was a religious education worker living at 1148 Spruce Street, where she'd lived since she'd known Dr. Knabe. Katherine McPherson disappeared from the city directory in 1951. Her death date and final resting place are unknown.

Franz F.W. Kropp was born in December 24, 1841 in Bielefield. He was a seaman in the Germany military and barber before he immigrated in 1879 to Indianapolis.

Franz came with his wife Karoline (Caroline) Kropp and his son, Karl (Carl) Frederick (Fred) Wilhelm Kropp. He worked at Indianapolis Chair Manufacturing Company at the corner of New York and Canal Streets and later as a bricklayer. In 1903 Franz was naturalized. Franz F.W. Kropp lived at the 1205 Bates Street address until his death on August 29, 1921 at 79 years old. Franz died of larynx cancer from which he'd been suffering for five months. His wife died July 27, 1896 from hepatitis and his son died on October 23, 1921. Franz and Karoline are buried in Crown Hill Cemetery, Indianapolis, Indiana Section 54, Lot 2734 and Section A, Lot 3311, respectively. Karl is buried in Washington Park East Cemetery, Indianapolis, Indiana.

Jefferson Haynes: By 1914 the apartments were turned into the Barton House. Jefferson Haynes, died in April 28, 1915 in the building where Dr. Knabe was found dead. He was found in the bathroom of the hotel. He called for a doctor when he felt ill but died before help arrived. Haynes had a history of heart trouble. He is buried in Crown Hill Cemetery, Indianapolis, Indiana in Section F, Lot 5289.

Harry C. Webster was born in September 12, 1858 (although some records state September 13, 1855) in Philadelphia, Pennsylvania. He had two early marriages. The first with Mary E. Atherholt Webster resulted in the birth of their son John M. Webster who died six years later from scarlet fever.

With his next wife, Susan, he had a son, Harry J. Webster. Webster married a third time. Three other sons, Willard (b. 1885) (a cleaner in a cleaning plant), Earle (b. 1887) (a milkman at a creamery), and Buren (b.1891) (a chemist at an auto plant) were born. By 1899 Webster was widowed, although it is not known where or when it happened.

On October 1, 1899 he married his fourth wife, Fay (Fairy) E. Crull (b. November 1872) who was born and raised in Indiana as were her parents. The 1900 census shows he had no children after two years of marriage. He was widowed at some point and on January 18, 1910 he married his fifth wife, Pearl Weston Baldwin (b. 1873) who survived him. In 1930, Harry working in Detroit, Michigan as a packer in an auto plant. He also worked as a banker until 1933.

Harry died on August 29, 1939 of coronary thrombosis and interestingly enough, senility was listed as a cause. His son Buren bought the plot at White Chapel Cemetery in Troy, Michigan. His son Willard bought the headstone in 1940.

Otto Windschild: There is no indication Dr. Knabe had any contact with her father after he left during her early childhood. No mention is made of him and he is not interviewed in newspapers, nor did Otto travel to America to comfort other family members or collect any of his daughter's belongings. It was believed by Augusta Knabe and the mayor of Rügenwaldermünde that Otto was dead at the time of Dr. Knabe's murder, however, he received the fourth order of the Red Eagle and these were usually given while the person was alive. Given the distance between Otto and his daughter, it is possible that no one really knew if he was still alive or not.

The Accused and Suspects

Dr. William Blair Craig's life went back to the status quo after he was acquitted. During WWI, the Indiana Veterinary College was the only school called upon by the U.S. military to provide qualified veterinarians for the war effort through the Student Army Training Corps . He continued to play badly in the sandbox with his colleagues and was ousted from the Indiana Veterinary Association only to be reinstated a year later with another member and Dr. R.C. Julian, the state veterinarian. They had been kicked out because of conduct unbecoming a member of the profession. Dr. Craig had been associated with Dr. Julian and often acted as an assistant to him.

The Indian Veterinary College closed in 1924 after years of pressure by competition and stiffer regulation and academic scrutiny of private institutions. With horseless carriages becoming the norm and more mechanization, the immediate need for many veterinarians became obsolete. Stockmen and farmers either didn't see the need or could get services from public institutions and doctors who didn't come with high price tags. Automated agriculture after World War I also contributed to the lessening need for veterinarians .The school was eventually torn down for the inner loop of highways in Indianapolis, Indiana.

Dr. Craig died on February 16, 1938 at St. Vincent on Fall Creek (now where Ivy Tech has offices) after an illness of two months. He was 69 years old. He was born in Ayrshire, Scotland November 5, 1868 and came to the United States when he was 14 years old, as he was down the line in succession of the family inheritance. He worked at his brother, Robert Craig's farm near Southport, Indiana. Robert was an importer of steins and mirrors. William went to school near Southport until he was 18, when he was employed by Dr. Elliot, a veterinary surgeon. He graduated from the Indiana Medical College in 1893 and the Ontario Veterinary College in 1889. At the time of his death he was teaching short courses at Purdue and was the Secretary-Treasurer of the Indiana Veterinary Medical Association. He also did veterinary consulting around Indiana and surrounding states and conducted surgical clinics as well. He had become a leading trap shooter and an avid hunter.

Prior to meeting Dr. Knabe, Dr. Craig had been married to Elizabeth Comingore who died in childbirth to their son who also died in 1905. Elizabeth's father lived in

Indianapolis on a sheep farm and Dr. Craig's brother Robert lived nearby also owning a sheep farm. On October 25, 1914 he married Madge Roquet who survived him. In addition to Marion, who married Dr. T. Victor Keene, he also had three children by his second marriage, Mary Craig (who was a pre-med student at the time of his death at Indiana University), John Craig, a student at Purdue University, and Janet Craig. His funeral was held at Finn Brothers. Reverend George Arthur Frantz, pastor of the First Presbyterian Church officiated.

Dr. Craig was buried in Crown Hill Cemetery, Indianapolis, Indiana, as was his wife when she died. He had been ill since November 1937 and seemed to be improving until he developed deep vein thrombosis and his right leg was amputated. Following the operation he declined until his death. He is buried in Section 48, Lot 513 with Madge and Janet.

Marion Elizabeth Craig married Dr. Thomas Boone Victor Keene (b. February 19, 1881 Evansville, Indiana; d. December 12, 1961 Indianapolis, Indiana) in 1922 when she was 24 and he was 41. They had a son, also named Thomas Boone Victor Keene (b. July 15, 1923 Indianapolis, Indiana; d. July 23, 2010 Pacific Palisades, California). Marion Craig died in March 6, 1982 in Los Angeles, California. She is buried in Crown Hill Cemetery, Indianapolis, Indiana Section 48, Lot 23 with her husband .

Alonzo Mayfield Ragsdale was born in 1854 and died on April 22, 1920 at his home at 323 N Delaware after he'd been ill many months with a heart condition. His business largely went on after his indictment. His daughter Edna married Jacob Price in 1904 and they formed Ragsdale & Price undertaking. Ragsdale's funeral was on April 26, 1920 at his own establishment at 1319 N. Alabama. He is buried in Mount Pleasant Cemetery in Franklin, Johnson County, Indiana. On April 28, 1922 his wife Fidelia followed him.

Seth Thomas Nichols, the man who confessed to killing Dr. Knabe, which was later proven a lie, was born February 25, 1890 in Rensselaer, Indiana to Wallace and Caroline (Lax) Nichols. According to his own family, he was never a reliable person. While enlisted in the U.S. Navy as a seaman in 1909, he was admitted to the U.S. Naval Hospital in Pensacola, Florida, for measles. He spent six weeks in the hospital and was discharged May 18, 1909. After Dr. Knabe's death on November 6, 1911, Nichols married a 17 year old mill girl, Mary A. McHale, in Pawtucket Rhode Island. She tried to kill herself by ingesting mercury or cyanide of potassium (depending on the source) three months later, but she recovered. On March 11, 1912, she died of pneumonia. On April 23, 1912 he was sentenced for deserting and larceny of clothing to serve time in the Concord Reformatory. By 1917, he completed his WWI draft registration card stating he had a wife (presumably Ada J. Werling, who he married in February 26, 1914) and a child, Laura, and he was asking for exemption from draft based on this. In 1920 he was a machinist in Indianapolis. On December 24, 1920 he died of meningitis in Letcher County, Kentucky. He had been working as a track man in a coal mine and suffered for 36 hours with meningitis before he died. His burial location is unknown.

Witnesses

Dr. Charles Eugene Ferguson was born May 29, 1856 in Indianapolis. In 1882 he married Isobel Lamb and moved to Florida. In 1890, he moved back to Indiana and enrolled in the Medical College of Indiana where he graduated in 1892. He served at the City Hospital and as the Secretary for the State Board of Health where he and Dr. Knabe proved pollution in White River and got the government to install filters to rid it of typhoid bacteria. Ferguson worked with Dr. Knabe at the Medical College of Indiana and the IU School of Medicine. During his life, he fought in the Russo-Japanese War in 1905. In 1913 he watched the First Balkan War. He was a volunteer during WWI in the Medical Corps. He came home and worked in the classroom until the flu epidemic took hold of Indianapolis. Ferguson lost his eyesight in 1922, but he kept up with new ideas through phonograph records and books and radio courses through the University of Illinois. He was considered Professor Emeritus at Indiana University at the time of his death. Ferguson died on May 18, 1945. He had quite a penchant for science and kept up a correspondence with Charles Darwin, known for his theory of evolution by natural selection. He is buried in Crown Hill Cemetery in Indianapolis, Indiana Section 15, Lot 22.

Katherine Agnes Fleming, the other woman of the trial, was born on October 17, 1870 in Fort Wayne, Indiana. Fleming stayed in Indiana after the trial until a few years after the death of her mother. In 1930 she was living in Los Angeles, California to be closer to her sister. According to a family member, no one ever talked about the trial and the first anyone knew of it was during a genealogy search. Family members remember she was a very independent woman and did as she pleased. Fleming was to have moved to Alaska and become one of the state's first postmasters, however, this information has not been verified. Fleming died on September 14, 1959 in North Hollywood, California. Her body was sent back to Fort Wayne, Indiana and she was buried in Catholic Cemetery Section A, Lot 49.

Dr. Ernest C. Reyer was born in Indianapolis on January 16, 1864. He attended Shortridge High School and graduated from the Medical College of Indiana in 1885. He continued his study at Bellevue Hospital in New York in 1889 and later in Europe.

Like Dr. Knabe, he taught for the Indiana University School of Medicine. He was an expert in brain and nervous diseases. In his early practice, he worked with Dr. William B. Fletcher, the famed superintendent of Central State Hospital who abolished restraints for a time. After working at Central State for three years, he spent time in Europe, earning a diploma from Heidelberg University in 1890 and the University of Munich in 1891. He married Laura May Carothers Reyer on June 14, 1899. Later in life, he constructed an apartment house named, Reyer Apartments near his home.

Dr. Reyer died at the age of 54 on March 24, 1918 at his home at 1801 N. Capitol Avenue in Indianapolis. He was about to go on a medical call. He'd just cranked the engine of the car and was walking around to the side of the car, lost his footing and fell. Reyer died just 10 minutes after he was carried into his home. The autopsy showed the cause of death was due to a fractured skull. He was survived by his wife, and his children, Charlotte, Virginia, Ernest C. Jr. and an adopted son, Reverend Nelson J. Springer. He is buried in Crown Hill Cemetery, Indianapolis, Indiana Section 40, Plot 261.

Harry Haskett, who said he saw Dr. Craig come out of the alley next to the Delaware Flats but who would not swear to it under oath, was born 1863 and died in 1933. He worked as the head of the shirt department at the Reformatory in Jeffersonville, Indiana. He was then a deputy sheriff in Hamilton County, Indiana. He married Dorothy (Clara) Kreag in a secret ceremony in Jeffersonville in 1894. They were to celebrate a public wedding the following year but Dorothy's parents objected. Haskett became vexed and produced the original marriage certificate silencing his inlaws. After Dr. Knabe's death, he and Clara lived in Indianapolis until his death. He and Clara (died 1974) are buried in Crownland Cemetery, Noblesville, Indiana Section 13, Lot 41.

Dr. Thomas Smith Hitt/Ella Baxter Hitt: Thomas was born Jun. 26, 1846 in Urbana, Champaign County, Ohio. He died Jun. 29, 1937, Pinellas County, Florida. Ella Baxter Hitt was born March 8, 1857 in Champaign County, Ohio. She died July 26, 1934 at the Normadie Hotel, in Columbus, Ohio. They are buried in Oak Dale Cemetery in Urbana, Ohio.

Blanche Fleetwood Riddell Lindley was born May 20, 1880 in Warren County, Indiana. She died at the age of 43 on July 12, 1923 in Asheville, North Carolina where she'd been for several weeks. She'd been very ill but her condition had been improving. Her body was brought back to her 701 Nelson Street home. Her husband, LeRoy, known as L.R. (b. January 26, 1876/ d. April 1, 1937), owned Lindley Box and Paper Company (later a part of Morris Paper Mills). The primary business as of 1914

was providing boxes for department stores, clothiers, tailors, dry cleaners, laundries, bakeries, florists, milliners, printers and other industries . L.R. was well worth a million dollars at the time of his death in 1937.
She was survived by her husband, LeRoy, her daughter, Monaie, a foster daughter, Ruth, and her son, Floyd. Lindley is buried in Estates of Serenity in Marion, Indiana next to her husband.

John Milo Maxwell, the newspaperman who gathered evidence used by the Grand Jury and who claimed someone tried to kill him, was born in 1865 and died in a Martinsville Sanitarium on February 26, 1929 following a stroke. At the time of his death, he was shopping a manuscript entitled, *The Man Behind the Mask,* in which he tried to prove that Sir Robert Cecil was the real author of the Shakespearian sonnets and plays. He was also known for having given Theodore Dreiser, Indiana native and American novelist, his first Chicago newspaper job many years before . Dreiser tried to help him get his book published. It was printed in 1916 by Harrington & Folger in Indianapolis, Indiana. Maxwell's most famous work *The Killer* played for three years on Broadway. He is buried in Crown Hill Cemetery, Indianapolis, Indiana in Section 3, Lot 25.

Nancy C. (Harrow) Tennant (Tenant) was born in 1845 and died in 1927 of chronic myocarditis. She worked as Dr. Craig's housekeeper in 1911. According to the city directories in 1910-1914, she lived at 2226 E. Washington Street. It did not show her as a boarding house owner until 1912. By 1920 she was able to move, continue to operate as a boarding house owner and housekeeper and she was able to have a couple of servants as well. She married Samuel F. Tenant, who was a Civil War veteran. He made history of his own.

While in Company F of the Fourth Indiana Legion, a State militia, he was involved in a battle with Confederate soldiers at Panther Creek, Kentucky in September 1862. In 1894 he fought for a pension due to a musket ball in the right hip that stayed lodged there and invalided him. At the time, because he'd been in state militia and not the Federal government army, he was ineligible for pension. In 1895 he successfully secured his pension. He died in 1898.

Nancy may have been able to afford her boarding house due to this pension. The couple had one daughter, Bettie (Tenant) Girathey . Nancy was buried September 2, 1927 at Crown Hill Cemetery Indianapolis, Indiana Section 70, Lot 238.

Dr. Frank Barbour Wynn/Mrs. Carrie Louise (Arnold) Wynn: Frank was born in Springfield, Indiana on May 28, 1860 and became a medical doctor, graduating in 1885 from the Miami Medical College of Ohio. He worked in the Ohio Asylum for the Insane at Dayton from 1886-1888. He worked in Indiana in 1891 as part of the medical staff of the Northern Indiana Hospital for the Insane at Logansport (Longcliff). From 1892-1893 he studied medicine in New York, Berlin and Vienna . He started his career in Indianapolis as the first city sanitarian. From 1895 till his death, he was part of the Department of Pathology at Medical College of Indiana and later the IU School of Medicine, becoming the Chair of Medical Diagnosis. Dr. Wynn was a conservationist and belonged to the American Alpine Club and a local Nature Study Club. He also supported the Indiana Historical Society. An avid mountain climber, he died on July 27, 1922 while climbing Mount Siyeh, in Glacier National Park, Montana. It was later renamed to Wynn Mountain in his honor. It was reported by the *Indianapolis Star* that J.W. Oliver, the director of the state historic commission, wanted to go with him but couldn't and said he would like to go next year. Frank replied, "I may not be here next year ." He is buried in Crown Hill Cemetery Section 58, Lot 3 .

Carrie Louise (Arnold) Wynn was born in Columbus, Ohio in 1893 and was a Daughter of the American Revolution. Carrie was one of the members of the mountain climbing expedition who was with her husband when he died. She died December 31, 1926 at Long Hospital and is buried with Frank in Crown Hill Cemetery Section 58, Lot 3.

Dr. Knabe's Friends

Dr. Charles Omer Durham, who had dealt with the case as coroner with balanced cool calm, died of apoplexy (most likely precipitated by a cerebral hemorrhage or stroke) on December 18, 1924 while on his way to see a patient. Durham attended the Kentucky School of Medicine for several years and graduated from the Central College of Physicians and Surgeons in Indianapolis, Indiana. He was the Dean of the Department of Anatomy and Surgery at the college. Later he started his own practice and also became a thirty-second degree mason, a member of the Scottish Rite, a Shriner and the Knights Templar. Durham was also a Democrat. His tenure as coroner ended in 1915. Dr. Durham had maintained a practice till his death. He was taken to St. Vincent Hospital where he died at 7:30 p.m. Dr. Durham is buried in Crown Hill Cemetery, Indianapolis, Indiana Section 59, Lot 186.

Dr. Henrietta "Etta" Charles was born in May 17, 1860 in Jonesboro, Grant County, Indiana and lived in Summitville, Indiana. She came from a Quaker family. She published in many journals. She also was the head of the Madison County, Indiana Board of Charities for a time. She attended school in Fairmount, Indiana and for a few years she stayed with her family and kept house and taught locally. Later she finished the St. Louis Women's Medical College three-year course. She also was mentored by her twin sister Dr. Olive Wilson, who practiced medicine in Paragould, Arkansas. At one time, the pair opened an office at 301 Lincoln Avenue in Alexandria, Indiana.

Dr. Charles lectured extensively in Madison County and did an outstanding job publishing in journals. She also belonged to and was active in several medical societies. During WWI she assumed physician duties at several large companies that would have regularly employed male physicians who had been called to war. She, with Ella B. Kehrer, helped establish the Ella B. Kehrer Tuberculosis Hospital in Anderson (east end of 10th street). At the pinnacle of her career she was the head of anesthesiology at St . John's Hospital in Anderson, Indiana and was member of the hospital teaching staff. She worked out of her home at 203 W. 6th Street in Anderson Indiana. As early as 1900 the census showed her as a widow . In 1940, she was still using "Charles" as her last name but listed as a widow. We do not know who her husband was, if he did exist. He is not mentioned in any biographies of Dr. Charles. She died July 17, 1949 in Grant County, Indiana.

Dr. Lillian Crockett-Lowder, who headed the reward committee for the Nu Sigma Phi despite threats against her life, died in a nursing home on September 19, 1955. She was 78 years old and had been an invalid for the last 6 years of her life . Despite the devastation at losing her friend and colleague, Dr. Knabe, Dr. Crockett-Lowder patented several items including hygienic garter belts and a mermaid toy . She also went on to be a patron of the arts, challenging the Hays Code, which prohibited certain types of production, including anything too sexual or immoral. She specifically challenged Hays on the film, *Blonde Captive*. She also wrote at least one dramatic composition called *The White Flame*, under the pen name, Ann Pitt . She is buried in Newark Cemetery in Newark, Greene County, Indiana.

Dr. John Frank Geis was born August 26, 1868 and he died March 7, 1904 of pneumonia. Dr. Geis had been ill since February 28, when he went home early in a carriage from his office. During his early years he went directly from high school to college and did post-graduate work in New York and Chicago before coming to Indianapolis and setting up his practices. Dr. Geis was a professor of chemistry at the Indiana Medical College and a deputy coroner. He was ahead of his time as having testified at court cases throughout the state. He was also one of the few Indianapolis men who joined the Chinese Masons, which endeared him to the Chinese people. After Dr. Geis' death the Chinese Masons sent flowers to his family. He was only 35 years old. Dr. Geis lived at 622 S. Alabama with his wife, Pauline Mueller Geis, his mother, Magdalene, and two sisters, Louise and Mayme. His sister, Anna Geis Hergenrooter and his two brothers Frank and Henry, lived in Indianapolis and Chicago respectively. His funeral was led from his house to St. Mary's Church on March 10, 1904. He was buried in St. Joseph Cemetery, Indianapolis, Indiana.

Dr. Hannah M. Graham was born in 1874 and died at the age of 56 on May 24, 1929. She was a dedicated doctor and a suffragette. Graham graduated from the Central College of Physicians and Surgeons in 1897 and from the Indiana University School of Law in 1914. She studied medicine in Chicago, Berlin (Germany), Vienna (Austria) and Manchester (England). She belonged to and championed many causes including the Restricted Equal Suffrage Association, which wanted to educate women in politics, business dealings and all other areas of life which were typically left to men. Its target audience were working women and the men that worked with them or who married them. Unfortunately, the organization did not last long. But still, Dr. Graham didn't give up. She continued to educate women and support the suffrage cause for the rest of her life. She was buried in Charleston, Illinois at Mound Cemetery.

Dr. Loy McAfee (Inghram), Dr. Knabe's friend and classmate, was born April 20, 1868 near Atlanta, Georgia. Although she started her medical career with Dr. Knabe in school and later worked with her husband in his medical office, Dr. McAfee (as she was known after her divorce) became her own person. During WWI she was a contract surgeon until 1921. Women at this time were barred from serving in the military but she still wore the uniform and conducted herself in accordance with military policy. Postwar, she was given a civilian post as editor-in-chief and worked on a multi-volume history or wartime medicine, *The Medical Department of the United States Army in the World War,* with her colleagues until its publication in 1930. It is still an invaluable tool for researchers who want to know about statistics regarding illnesses of and surgeries performed on soldiers during wartime. She became a member of the Association of Military Surgeons.

Like Dr. Knabe, she was a lifelong learner. Dr. McAfee graduated in 1926 with a law degree from the National Law School in Washington. She died on February 17, 1941 of heart failure following a stomach operation. She is buried in Arlington National Cemetery in Arlington, Virginia Plot: Section SOU, Site: 4555.

Dr. Amelia Keller was born January 12, 1871 in Cleveland, Ohio. As a young woman she attended the Womens' Medical College (Chicago, Illinois) and graduated with a medical degree from the Central College of Physicians and Surgeons in Indianapolis in 1893. One of the first licensed woman doctors in Indianapolis, she, like Dr. Knabe, taught classes in and out of a university setting and was a proponent of public health. She was an Associate Professor of Childhood Disease at Indiana University

School of Medicine. She was also a suffragette and edited the suffrage column for *The Citizen* for many years. She stayed active in civic affairs long after the 19th amendment passed. In fact, when she married her husband Eugene Buehler in 1899, she did not take his name.

She died on January 28, 1943 in Indianapolis, Indiana. She is buried at Crown Hill Cemetery, Indianapolis, Indiana Section 58, Lot 34.

Dr. Jane Merrill Ketcham was born Feb. 18, 1880 in Indianapolis, Indiana and died at 90 years of age in September 1970 of arteriosclerosis. She was one of the first female faculty member in the Indiana University School of Medicine beginning her career in 1912. She taught at the school for many years and eventually was promoted to Clinical Professor of Medicine in 1934.

Dr. Ketcham was known for her charitable works and much as Dr. Knabe did, worked with the poor. In 1913 when much of Indiana was under water due to flooding, she headed medical relief efforts and set up a triage center at Manual Training High School. She retired from practice and teaching in 1953. She is buried at Crown Hill Cemetery, Indianapolis, Indiana.

Dr. John Kolmer, a colleague of Dr. Knabe, an appraiser of her estate and the buyer of her medical bag, was born December 15, 1865. He was born in Prussia, Germany and when he was 15, he immigrated with his mother to Indianapolis. He attended the Normal College at Danville and graduated in 1894 from the Jefferson Medical College in Philadelphia, Pennsylvania. From there he studied at several institutions in the United States and Europe. In 1901 he married his wife Mary (May) Aufderheide.

Kolmer was one of the first doctors in Indianapolis to recognize that not everyone who was put into a mental hospital should be there. In his mind, there were people who were insane and required the hospital and others who had nervous disorders and could benefit from other types of therapies and hospital environment. Kolmer was very instrumental in getting the New Union Hospital at 1315 N. Capitol Avenue equipped and opened in 1898. He was credited as the first doctor in Indiana to use trephining surgery to relieve bone pressure in cases where children exhibited criminal behavior.

Kolmer had a quite diverse portfolio. Not only did he have his medical practice and his apartment building, he owned farm land and stock east of Carmel, Indiana in Hamilton County. After his death, it was auctioned off. He was also a man with a sense of humor. He built "The Colmar" which was an apartment building bearing the alternate spelling of his name. The spelling came from the French around Alsace, which flip-flopped between France and Germany for many years. It still stands at 1622 Central Avenue, Indianapolis, Indiana.

About two years before his death, he had to give up his practice and underwent treatment for a serious ailment and seemed to be improved. However, an edema of the lungs (pulmonary edema) began. He died October 21, 1917 at 51 years of age. He is buried at Crown Hill Cemetery, Indianapolis, Indiana Section 39, Lot 70. His wife, Mary (b. May 4, 1876/d. February 26, 1957) survived him and is buried next to him. His daughter, Elizabeth also survived him and is buried with her husband Russell Veit in Crown Hill Cemetery, Indianapolis, Indiana.

Dr. John J. Kyle was born May 27, 1898. He graduated Miami Medical College in 1899. He taught at the Medical College of Indiana and practiced in Anderson, Indiana; Marion, Indiana; Indianapolis, Indiana; and Los Angeles, California. During the Spanish-American War, he was a surgeon in the 159th Indiana Volunteers and with the 160th Colonel Gunder's regiment, which served in Mantanzas, Cuba. He also worked with the 161st Regiment . His philosophy is that he gave at least one hour a day to medical writing. It is interesting to note on an excursion with some doctors the group was deliberately mislead by a local. When he figured it out, he was ready to go "whip this man to a finish." Others dissuaded him. They had a good laugh and said it just went to show that he was willing to fight if necessary. He was the President of the American Academy of Ophthalmology and Oto-Laryngology in 1911. He died in Los Angeles on August 29, 1920. He is buried in Inglewood Park Cemetery in Inglewood, California.

Dr. Nettie Bainbridge Powell was born January 5, 1868 in Columbia City, Whitley County, Indiana. She attended school first in Columbia City and later Alma College at St. Thomas, Ontario, Northwestern University and University of Michigan, where she graduated in 1892 as a doctor. She set up her practice in Marion, Indiana. She married Dr. Albert E. Powell on September 4, 1893, but didn't take his name. He met her while attending the University of Michigan. He served as assistant coroner and a health officer of Grant County, Indiana. They had two children, Emily and Edmund. Albert died on September 20, 1905. Nettie died on September 25, 1951 and is buried in Estates of Serenity Marion, Indiana.

Dr. Marie Theresa Rimmelin was born in Baden, Germany in February 1867 and immigrated to Indiana in 1898. Not much is known about this doctor. What we do know is that she was progressive, strong and like many Germans of the time, experienced discrimination .

In 1919 she showed how progressive the women of Indianapolis could be when she gave away her niece, Miss Pauline Schaefer to Alvin Berger in marriage. Alvin's father officiated the event in Dr. Rimmelin's home.

The same year, she applied for naturalization and was denied based on "information" that the inquisitor, Mr. M.P. McNichols, naturalization examiner, had that would make her an unfit candidate. During this time after WWI, many Germans experienced this type of dishonesty based on their registration with the German consul during WWI. She disappeared from the census after 1920. Her death date and burial location are not known.

Dr. John William Sluss was born in 1867 and died in 1961 at 94 years old in a nursing home. After Dr. Knabe's death, he went on to be a superintendent of the old City Hospital from 1912-1915. He continued to practice medicine until he was 92. Dr. Sluss had been a physician and surgeon since the 1890s and lived at 3657 Washington Boulevard until he was admitted into the nursing home. He was a native of Oakland and a veteran of the Spanish American and WWI. Dr. Sluss was buried in Cloverdale Cemetery, Putnam County, Indiana with his wife Cora Hart.

Dr. Knabe's Professional Circle

Dr. William T.S. Dodds was born December 23, 1873 and died at 11:30 p.m. May 22, 1916 at the age of 42 due to a brief illness brought on by acute heart disease. Ironically, he was a specialist in heart and lung diseases, most notably tuberculosis. He graduated from the Indiana Medical College in 1899 and served as deputy coroner under Dr. A.W. Brayton, Coroner. He was born in Ohio, near Bellefontaine. Dr. Dodds was married and had two daughters, Margaret and Gene. He treated malaria in the military camps during the Spanish American War and developed new research on malaria and amebic dysentery. Dr. Dodds helped found and fund the first anti-tuberculosis hospital in Indianapolis. He also used X-Rays often in his work and used them for lung disease diagnosis. His funeral was May 25, 1916 at 10:00 a.m. He was buried in Crown Hill Cemetery, Indianapolis, Indiana Section 51, Lot: 393.

Francis William "Frank" Flanner, who was rumored to have either killed or hired someone to kill Dr. Knabe, took his own life on February 17, 1912 by downing five poisons obtained from five separate pharmacies. His business partner Paul Buchanan found him dying in the Flanner and Buchanan Chapel at 320 N. Illinois Street. Flanner was survived by his wife, Mary Hockett Flanner, and his daughters, Mary, Emma, Janet, and Hildegarde. He was buried in Crown Hill Cemetery, Indianapolis, Indiana Section 48, Lot 17.

Janet Flanner (see also Innuendo). She died November 7, 1978 in New York

City, New York. She was cremated and her ashes were scattered with Natalia Danesi Murray's over Cherry Grove in Fire Island , near Long Island, New York. Flanner lived with Murray and her son during WWII and cared for Murray in 1975 until her death.

Dr. John Lyman Freeland (only male to suggest financial help from doctors) was born June 23, 1860 in Dearborn County, Indiana and died at 83 years of age in April 4, 1943 in Denver, Colorado. He obtained his medical education in Cincinnati, Ohio. During his life he first worked in a private practice and at the State Board of Health . Then he worked as the superintendent of the City Hospital from 1906-1912. In 1912, when politics threatened his position, Dr. Frank B. Wynn came to his defense stating that under Freeland, the hospital had flourished and donations, including a large bequeath, were on the uptick. Still, he left the position and practiced medicine for four more years before moving to Denver. In 1920, he returned to Indianapolis and worked for the City Board of Health. He is buried in Crown Hill Cemetery, Indianapolis, Indiana Sec: 56, Lot 376.

Dr. John Newell Hurty was born February 31, 1852 in Lebanon, Ohio. He married Ethel Johnston Hurty. Hurty came to Indianapolis in 1875 after graduating from the Philadelphia College of Pharmacy and the Jefferson Medical College. He started a pharmacy and chemist business and began to actively campaign for better water and eradication of disease, especially typhoid. In 1882 he was a lecturer on analytical chemistry and sanitary science in the Medical College of Indiana and continued to teach for the rest of his life. He also assisted founding the Purdue University School of Pharmacy and served as a dean. In 1886 he received a degree of Doctor of Medicine from the Medical College of Indiana and was a licensed physician. Later he became the secretary of the Indiana State Board of Health. He died March 27, 1925 of influenza at his home in Indianapolis and is buried in Crown Hill Cemetery, Indianapolis, Indiana Section 60, Lot 1193.

Dr. Harry Dunn Tutewiler married Julia Belle Goodhart on October 21, 1896 and had three daughters. He was also part of the Indianapolis Playground commission, children's aid association, part of the Scottish Rite, a Shriner, Indianapolis Board of Trade and Commercial Club, Columbian Club, Was the partial owner of Tutewiler and Son. He was also a member of the Board of Embalmers from 1900 to 1901 and he was the Marion County coroner in 1902 and 1904. He is related to Jacob P. Dunn, an Indiana author through Dunn's daughter being his mother.

In November 1931 he had an accident in which his moving car hit a parked car. He was arrested for driving under the influence and failure to stop at the scene of an accident. The driving under the influence charge was dismissed and a $10 suspended fine was imposed on him by the judge. He died on June 3, 1945 and is buried at Crown Hill Cemetery, Indianapolis, Indiana in Section 42, Lot 135.

Otto von Tesmar was born Germany in 1856 and died Chicago, Illinois on August 3, 1931. As a child, Otto studied bugs and insects and later reptiles and birds. Through this work, he was able to learn about the anatomy of humans. Before coming to the United States, he worked as a naturalist and taxidermist for the Prussian government, which required he become a pharmacist and chemist due to the types of chemicals and compounds he worked with. During his forced enlistment with the Prussian Army, he was given the Iron Cross for bravery at the front during the Franco-Prussian War.

On coming to America, von Tesmar worked for the State of New York in Albany, Yale University, University of Michigan, and the Scientific Museum at Denver, Colorado. He spent several years at the Smithsonian and National Museum, mounting birds and large animals. He enjoyed spending just enough time to learn another man's methods and then moved on to learn more.

Von Tesmar was a registered pharmacist and chemist, becoming a druggist in Paragon, Indiana, near Martinsville. He ended up paying fines and costs in two cases and agreed not to sell as a druggist anymore, provided all other charges were dropped. The papers reported him as an impoverished German count who was well educated and a taxidermist. He supposedly did not drink after taking the temperance pledge. His wife died of typhoid pneumonia in 1904.

Von Tesmar worked as a janitor and taxidermist for the Medical College of Indiana (later I.U. School of Medicine). It was said that the sawdust on the floor, coupled with smoking students working on dissections, was the cause of the 1894 fire that flatted the first Medical College of Indiana building on Pennsylvania Street. His techniques included using different colored wires to represent arteries and nerves to create specimens to be used at the college. In his workshop in the school were the books he learned from as a boy. His work was known as "frighteningly real" and his papier-mâché models uncanny.

The man had a sense of humor. He once bet Tim Griffin, custodian of the State House, if William McKinley won the presidential election, Griffin would have to turn cannibal and bite into one of the medical college's subjects. Griffin bet von Tesmar that if William Jennings Bryan, presidential candidate, was elected, von Tesmar would have eat grass off the State House lawn. We don't know if Griffin had to bite a corpse, but McKinley won!

In late 1906 he and Dr. John Morris were mentioned in a $25,000 suit by Richard

E. Houren, an attorney who was investigated for selling dead bodies. His defense was that he was representing the wife, who was poor and needed to raise money. The court dismissed the charge because they said he couldn't sell the body because it wasn't in his possession. Morris and Otto were named in the suit by Houren because he said they were instrumental in having him imprisoned and his reputation had been severely damaged. Judge Carter made the judgment himself that Houren had not presented a case of false imprisonment and the case was dismissed .

On October 18, 1907 von Tesmar wrote a letter to the *Indianapolis Star* asking how Napoleon's skull could be exhibited twice in one place at the same time. His nephew saw a museum exhibit which claimed to have the skull of a 12 year old Napoleon and another from after his death. "I would like to inquire if the people of Corsica shed their skulls every year like snakes shed their skin. This is something beyond my power of understanding."

While in Indianapolis, he cured and mounted a black bear's head from a Riverside Park bear named Dick. The bear died of blood poisoning. The mounted head hung in the park office.

He is buried at Holy Sepulchre in Chicago, Illinois.

Indianapolis Police Department, Officials, and Attorneys

Captain Adolph Asch was born in Strassburg, Alsace on May 30, 1860 when it was under French control and died December 31, 1914 of pneumonia at City Hospital, Indianapolis, Indiana. In 1895 he immigrated to Indianapolis. He was a woodworker for a time and then, with the help of Albert Sahm, a county commissioner, he was appointed a guard at the Marion County workhouse. Three years later, with the help of Albert Mathey, who was a Frenchman by birth, he was placed on the police force. He was most famous for arresting Rufus Cantrell and the other grave robbing ghouls. He was interred in the Indianapolis Hebrew Congregation Cemetery South, Indianapolis, Indiana.

Frank Pierce Baker, the State's prosecutor in Dr. Knabe's case, went on to become a judge in the Indianapolis criminal courts from 1931-38. During his career, he was a criminal court prosecutor from 1906-10, a prosecuting attorney from 1911-1938. He was known as a "stern but just" arbiter. Baker seemed to be against liquor, specifically Paul V. McNutt, who served as Indiana's thirty-fourth governor. McNutt established the liquor licensing system Indiana has in place today. He was also against all forms of gambling and his investigators frequently raided establishments suspected of gambling activities. Baker was a Democrat, belonged to the Methodist church, the

Modern Woodsmen of America, the Indiana Bar Association, and was a mason. He had been a semi-invalid from 1945 beginning with a series of strokes, and Baker had been confined to his bed for the last year and half of his life . The *Indianapolis Star* stated, "Judge Baker has the respect of the public as a good citizen." He was born in Ohio on April 3, 1875 and died July 18, 1948 at his home at 1635 Woodlawn Avenue in Indianapolis, Indiana of a cerebral hemorrhage. He is buried at Crown Hill Cemetery Indianapolis, Indiana next to his wife, Rebecca J. and his son, Frank H. Section 59, Lot 646 .

Judge Alonzo Blair, the Shelbyville presiding judge on Dr. Craig's trial, was born in 1870 and died on August 10, 1943 at his daughter's house in Hammond, Indiana. He'd been ill for two years. From 1896 to 1900 he was a prosecuting attorney in Shelby and Johnson Counties. In 1910 he became a judge of the Shelby and Rush County circuit courts. He stayed in this capacity until 1913 when Rush County got its own judge. In 1916 he was reelected and served as a Judge until 1922. He was buried at Forest Hill Cemetery in Shelbyville, Indiana .

William J. Burns continued to run his detective agency until he retired. His son, Raymond was instrumental in catching John McNamara and Ortie McManigal, the suspected *Los Angeles Times* newspaper bombers who were arrested on August 14, 1911, shortly after Dr. Knabe's death.

In 1921-22, Burns had a part in the Teapot Dome scandal. Harry F. Sinclair was on trial for conspiracy to defraud. Sinclair Oil executive Harry Mason Day requested Burns investigate the jurors, which he did by hiring 14 agents. Day arranged for their compensation and in return, received their daily reports. Half way through the trial this deception was discovered and the judge declared a mistrial.

He moved to Sarasota, Florida and published crime and detective stories until his death in 1932.

John F Engelke, the deputy county prosecutor who received a message about Dr. Knabe while playing with a Ouija board, died on May 8, 1945 at his home at 2818 Talbot Street. His work included his deputy prosecuting work for Marion County as well as working with the State Department of Conservation. He was a mason and a Republican.

He was survived by his wife Frances W. Engelke, his daughter, Jean, and his son, John F. Jr. He is buried in Crown Hill Cemetery, Indianapolis, Indiana Section 66, Lot 825.

Elmer Frederick Hall, always called Elmer, was a night desk clerk in the detective office when he retired in 1923. He started his law enforcement career in the merchant police and then became a bicycle patrolman in Indianapolis. His former comrades remembered him tricking rookie cops into going out on calls by throwing his voice as a ventriloquist and making it sound like a real order from an officer. His highest rank was Detective Sergeant. He moved to Michigan to start a vineyard. Four years before his death, he'd become very ill. His wife, Eva Powell Hall was the only known next of kin. Hall was born in 1875 in Ohio and died in Berrien Springs, Michigan on January 18, 1946. He is interred with his wife in Oak Ridge Cemetery, Buchanan, Michigan.

Captain of Detectives William A. "Cap " Holtz was born in Indianapolis on August 22, 1867 and died at his home at 2910 E. 11th Street on November 19, 1943 after an illness of six weeks. He rose from bicycle patrolman to captain during his time at the Indianapolis Police. He was a deacon at Centenary Christian Church. Holtz was survived by his wife, Estelle and is interred at Memorial Park Cemetery, Indianapolis, Indiana.

Martin J. Hyland was born March 4, 1860 on a Clay County, Indiana farm and died June 27, 1940 in his home at 2101 Park Ave. After Dr. Knabe's death, Hyland went on to be the city commissioner. He retired from the police and went into the insurance and fire business. He was interred at Holy Cross Cemetery, Indianapolis, Indiana Section 6F, Lot-695 Sp-4.

Ephraim "Eph" Inman , was born in Martin County, Indiana on October 25, 1865. During his life he was a teacher and served in the Indiana legislature. During Dr. Craig's trial, he was part of the prosecution team for the State, was hired by the local council of women and became one of the best known criminal lawyers in Indiana. In addition to working on Dr. Knabe's case, Inman defended David Curtis Stephenson, the Grand Dragon of the Ku Klux Klan who kidnapped Madge Oberholtzer, raped, bit, pummeled and chewed her body until she took mercury bichloride tablets. When Stephenson realized what she'd done, he took her home. She died almost a month later. Inman wasn't completely successful because Stephenson was sentenced in 1925 to life in prison but paroled in 1950.

Inman died in Indianapolis on February 8, 1935 at his home at 33 E. 16th Street after a six week illness. He is buried at Crown Hill Cemetery, Indianapolis, Indiana . Sec: 49, Lot 390 .

William A. Ketcham was hired for the State prosecution for Dr. Craig's trial. He was paid for by many of the Indianapolis women physicians out of their own pockets. He was born in Indianapolis on January 3, 1846 and died of "acute indigestion" (i.e. possible heart attack in modern terms) on December 27, 1921 . In addition to being an attorney, he served as an Indiana Attorney General. Ketcham was a Captain in the Grand Army of the Republic and served during the Civil War. He was also a board member for the Soldiers and Sailors Monument and fought hard to keep all advertising off of the monument, which he felt was highly inappropriate. He also spoke in front of the Daughters of the Southern Confederacy and discouraged them from creating a monument for "the monster of Andersonville," Captain Wirz . His daughter, Dr. Jane M. Ketcham, was a friend and colleague of Dr. Knabe's. He is buried at Crown Hill Cemetery, Indianapolis, Indiana.

Lieutenant Jerimiah "Jerry" Kinney, the detective in charge of the Dr. Knabe murder investigation, served on the force for 44 years and was chief two different times. When he died, his reputation as a detective had become nationwide. He was born in 1865 and died June 9, 1931. Kinney had the most seniority on the force.

When he died, a black wreath was hung on the door of his office. Police of all ranks talked in low voices in reverence around the area. While Jerry lay in state at his brother's home at 3664 Kenwood Avenue, people from all walks of life praised him after his death. His loss was described by the Associated Employers of Indianapolis, as a "grievous loss of a progressive, superior, sincere, and scrupulously honest police executive whose rare gifts and intelligent service in police work stand unsurpassed in the nation's record of modern criminology and law enforcement.. Jerry Kinney's integrity and earnestness in his work was never questioned during his forty-four years of valiant service ." Many people remembered him fondly.

Kinney, it was pointed out, was honest as the day is long as he refused, as a Democrat, to become a superintendent in Mayor Jewett's term because the mayor was Republican. Despite that, the former mayor stated Jerry's friendship, "was a rare treat" for him.

Several people involved with the Dr. Knabe investigation had good things to say about Kinney. Former prosecutor Frank Baker, now Judge Frank P. Baker of the Criminal Courts stated, "I have known him as an efficient officer for over 30 years ." Former Chief Martin J. Hyland stated, "He was a great police officer ." John Mullin, Captain of Police, stated, "I have worked under him and over him and knew him for the real man he was and for his exceptional ability as a police officer ."

Kinney's body was treated to a full escort of police cars and motorcycles during the trip to St. Bridget's Catholic Church. Policemen from as far away as Marion, Indiana came to be part of the honor guard . He was interred at Holy Cross Cemetery, Indianapolis, Indiana.

Detective William A. Larsh was born in 1859 and died in 1940. He resigned from the police department after a special meeting of the Board of Safety in 1923. The board demoted him and another cop named Duncan from detectives to patrolmen. After his resignation, he became a night watchman in the 1920s, and a packer in the 1930s. By 1940, he was living in Montgomery County, Indiana with Charles and Ollie Cravens as a boarder and had become a farmer . He is buried in Darlington Odd Fellows Cemetery in Darlington, Montgomery County, Indiana with his wife, Louida W. Larsh.

Fred McCallister, chief deputy to Prosecutor Frank Baker during Dr. Knabe's murder investigation, became a Municipal court judge. McCallister was born on May 8, 1875 on a farm near Shannondale, Indiana and graduated from Wabash College. He walked home each weekend he was at college to be with his family. He graduated from law school and worked with S.E. Perkins, later becoming deputy prosecutor under Elliott Hooten. In 1912 he went into partnership with Ira M. Holmes in Holmes and McCallister. In 1925 McCallister practiced with Oren Hack and Earl Cox. In 1926 he became a judge. He also taught law at Indiana Law School and Benjamin Harrison Law School.

On December 28, 1927 he shot and killed himself at his home 3834 Byram Avenue. His son and wife, Hattie, tried to stop him. He was despondent over money and the thought he would not be reappointed by Governor Ed Jackson as a judge. (Although several people stated he would have been reappointed and the Governor stated if anyone had told McCallister that he would not be reappointed, it was without his knowledge, consent or decision.) Hattie was cooking breakfast when someone called to speak with him. McCallister spoke on the phone and told his wife he would be down soon after he changed. She followed him to wake up their son, Vance, who was home from Wabash College. Hattie saw the gun in her husband's hand. She screamed and she and her son went in to stop him. But the deed was done.

McCallister was survived by his wife and two sons, Vance and Ralph, and his daughters, Lois and Mrs. Leon Cope of Battle Creek Michigan. He was buried in Shannondale Cemetery in Montgomery County. He was 52.

Judge Joseph Thomas Markey was born on June 11, 1881 and died on October 30, 1952. He served as a law clerk before graduating from law school in 1902. He believed if a man and a woman had children it was their duty to stay together for that child. From 1911 to 1914 he was the judge of the Indianapolis criminal courts. In 1919 he took the position of attorney for the New York, St. Louis and Chicago railroad as well as keeping a general practice. In 1935 he was appointed to Superior Court 1 and in 1947 he served as judge for Municipal Court 1. He is buried at Holy Cross Cemetery,

Indianapolis, Indiana.

John W. Morgan was born 1851 in Indiana and died December 23, 1919 at 4178 Guilford Avenue after a two month illness He was 68 years old . Before becoming a police officer, he worked in the liquor trade. Throughout his career, he was promoted and demoted and even did a stint as a circus detective. His specialties were pickpockets and con men. Described by the newspapers as compared to England's Inspector Buckett, Morgan was "wonderfully patient, affable, alert, imperturbable, and sagacious." He was survived by his wife Margaret, and several daughters. He is interred in Crown Hill Cemetery, Indianapolis, Indiana Section 16, Lot 91.

Detective William M. Morgan was born in England in 1867. He immigrated in 1872 and was naturalized in 1875 . By 1926, he no longer listed himself as a police officer and on the 1930 census he no longer listed any occupation. He was divorced for many years before his death. His death date and resting place are unknown.

Captain John W."Bulldog" Mullin was lauded before and after his death in the public eye. During one interview, he remembered a shootout on Warman Avenue as the biggest day as a policemen while he was still a bicycle patrolman. Two men were sent to prison that day and it brought him a promotion to Detective Sargent. In 41 years, he estimated he sent 500 people to jail. Even 47 years after the fact, he still recollected Dr. Knabe's case involved suicide. Mullin was always President Roosevelt's bodyguard when he visited Indianapolis. He retired in 1944 and his wife, Mae, died in 1954 . Mullin was born in 1877 and died October 12, 1958 was interred at Holy Cross Cemetery, Indianapolis, Indiana Sec-H-2G, Lot-18 Sp-4.

Mayor Samuel Lewis "Lew" Shank : was born January 23, 1872 and died September 24, 1827. He was mayor from 1909-1913 and again from 1922-26. He died at his home in Golden Hill. He was 55. He died of heart disease brought on by acute indigestion. Shank supposedly gave away most of his salary during his time as mayor and when he decided to go into vaudeville after his first term, the money for the tickets to get to his gig was advanced to him. He was known as the "potato mayor of Indianapolis" because he'd buy food throughout the Midwest and auction it to housewives. Instead of paying $.45 for eggs, they would pay $.30. Shank had good success in vaudeville, but decided to go back in politics . Generally, he was seen as a good mayor because of his charitable acts and that he cleaned up prostitution and gambling in Indianapolis. He is interred in Crown Hill Cemetery, Indianapolis, Indiana Section 60.

Otto Henry Simon was born in 1872 and died October 25, 1938 at his home at 2118 S. Emerson Avenue. Before becoming a police officer, he was a driver. Simon was a detective for a time but at the time of his resignation, he was a patrolman. He died of acute heart dilation. He is buried in Memorial Park Cemetery, Indianapolis, Indiana in Section 4 .

Henry N Spaan, defense attorney for Dr. Craig, was born in 1851 in Gelderland, Holland December 13, 1851 and died May 18, 1935 at his home at 2829 N. Meridian Street after a three week illness. He was born Hendrik Spaan and was naturalized on September 3, 1860. His family immigrated to the U.S. on 1852 or 1859, depending on the source. His father helped make bricks and he helped too, saving his money to go to law school . He retired six years prior to his death. He belonged to several law organizations. He enjoyed flowers, gardening and reading. When his wife died, he understood why a man might be able to endure agony, but he didn't understand why his wife, whom he loved, should go through such a trial. Through her death, he saw that women were much stronger than men . Although in his obituaries, many cases are mentioned, Dr. Knabe's was not one of them. William Remy, a former Marion County prosecutor stated, "His quick analysis of courtroom situations, his ready wit and his almost uncanny ability at cross-examination made him a dangerous antagonist." He is buried at Crown Hill Cemetery, Indianapolis, Indiana Sec: 35, Lot: 289 He is buried next to his second wife, Helen May who he married on December 23, 1902.

George M. Stewart (bicycle squad): Sometimes his middle name is listed as V. but it is M. He was born in 1878 and died on March 4, 1928. Before becoming a policeman he was a salesman. He had been despondent over his ill health and separated from his wife and lived at the Puritan Hotel at Market and New Jersey Streets. He waved his gun at the front desk clerk, demanding the locked door between his room and the next be opened . Stewart, who had been drinking, swore his wife was in the next room. The clerk got him calmed down and returned to the lobby. That is when he heard a shot. Bert Atkins, the proprietor of the hotel, ran to the second floor room. Stewart had a smoking gun in his hand and a hole in his chest. He smiled, "I am almost dead." He had been commended in the 1909 battle in which John Mullin, also a cop, was promoted. The Saturday prior to his death, Stewart had been given a letter of commendation by the police chief when he said he was considering moving to Minneapolis, Minnesota and joining the force there. He was buried at Washington Park East Cemetery, Indianapolis, Indiana.

About the Author

Nicole R. Kobrowski began writing at 13 year old. She's written in many areas including newspapers, magazines and books. Her genres include academic, paranormal, history and romance. She and her husband, Michael, own Unseenpress.com, Inc. and give ghost tours throughout Central Indiana. Nicole's two children, Christopher and Brittany are grown up and out on their own. In her daylife, Nicole is a healthcare trainer. During her free time, she enjoys attending concerts, reading, gardening, and ghost hunting. Currently, Nicole lives with Michael in their über haunted home in Westfield, Indiana.

Top: Current picture of the author.

Bottom: Nicole (left) with Jerzy (far right), his wife (second), daughter (third) and a friend (fourth) in Darloko/Darlowo, Poland in 2007.

Author's Notes

My purpose in writing this book was to bring Dr. Helene Elise Hermine Knabe's life, work and accomplishments to light. For too long she's been a footnote to the medical and feminist community.

No longer.

In this purpose, I also wanted to correct misinformation. Too many people have only scratched the surface of her life and the events and nothing is really what it seems. For example, the book "Historic Indianapolis Crimes: Murder and Mystery in the Circle City" has a picture of where she was supposedly killed. It isn't the right location. The author also states that Harry Webster presented his findings to a grand jury in 1921 when it was actually 1912. Other people have either painted her as a loose woman or an uptight bitch. Although I do not know her personally, she is neither. Dr. Knabe was assertive when necessary, somewhat socially awkward and progressive.

As with any historical work, many questions remain unanswered, several of which I included in the book as analysis. It has been and will continue to be a gloriously torturous adventure as well as a painful reminder of the death of someone who gave so much of herself to those around her.

I chose to repeat some information for context. Some of the way it was presented changed at the trial. Some people may chose to read some parts of the book but not others. Apologies if anyone is upset by that.

As I edited the trial, I didn't want to. I didn't want to relive what I'd written. What I know the truth to be, which is that Dr. William B. Craig did kill Dr. Knabe. But I told myself I should. I must. It was the right thing to do, cathartic or not. Indiana and the Indianapolis police failed Dr. Knabe. I would not.

It was not simply Dr. Craig killing Dr. Knabe. It was William killing Helene in a rage. I believe he had wanted out of their relationship for long time. She referred to him as William in her letters to friends. Helene signed William's medical book with her name versus her title. I believe he had proposed marriage or at least gave her reason to believe he wanted to get married and strung her along enough to keep her interest. Perhaps he even allowed her to believe what she wanted and didn't correct her beliefs because he was a player. He didn't want anyone to know about their relationship and gluing those pages in the book together was his way of trying to ensure no one ever found out. When Dr. Knabe attempted to reason with him time and again, William decided to get rid of her. The cataylst was the night she died. She had already intimated to friends she wanted to talk to them about something heavy and it was a long story.

When Helene brought up the subject of their marriage that fated Monday evening, William wanted out in the worst way. After all, he was used to buying off women he ruined and his ego certainly couldn't have a woman in his life that was as successful or moreso than he was. William escorted her out of his house and back to her home and tried to break it off for good.

Whether Helene was having none of his guff or whether he finally just snapped, I believe he left the apartment, found liquid courage in whiskey and came back under the pretense of making up. But he was really there to kill her.

William Craig worked with sheep and other animals and had intimate knowledge of the human body. He was a strapping man. The newspapers called him handsome, but he was a big man. At least six foot tall and broad. Judging from the photos of him in the courtroom, he had to be over 200 pounds. Helene was five feet six inches tall and 160 pounds. She was not small, but she was smaller than him.

When William returned, he found her in her night gown. Whether they had a sexual relationship or not, they were comfortable with one another and she let him in. They talked and he sat on her window seat in the office. Then he made his move. He grabbed one of Helene's microtome blades.

Helene had enough time to dive for the phone. William got to her first. She twisted away from him and backed into the corner of her bed. She held her arms up and he cut one of them. Then he held her down and cut her throat, the first being enough to choke her to death. But he was mad, mad enough that he wanted to make sure she was out of his life. So he cut again, but it wasn't in the right place to miss the carotoid artery. So he started again and cut her deep, all the way to her spine. In that moment, I believe he truly hated her. He wasn't as careful and knicked her jugular vein anyway. Since she was close to dead, there wasn't as much spurting. When he withdrew his blade, he did it with such force that it spattered the wall.

I don't believe they were having a sexual relationship. I do believe he took the opportunity to look at what Helene denied him and that is why she was found with her nightdress pulled up to her shoulders. He took perverse delight in touching in death what he couldn't have in life. William Craig left her exposed to further humiliate and degrade Helene. Just as he sat with Augusta in Helene's apartment the day Helene was found, I believe he sat there for a long time, trying to figure out what to do. Lucky for him, not much had been disturbed. Dr. Craig took the blade with him and her keys. He could clean it and return it before anyone found her body.

When he left, he bumped into Harry Haskett. Dr. Craig hurried away. When he returned home, he cleaned the blade and himself. He put his clothes in a sheet that he'd dispose of later. He noticed he had cut himself and wondered if he'd left a trail.

Dr. Craig left his home and returned before daylight to dump his clothes, return the blade and ensure he hadn't left a trail. He saw her kimono had blood flecks on it. Blood typing was new in humans but relatively established in animals. Dr. Craig couldn't have them find anything on her clothes that might be considered suspect. But he kept her keys just in case. He hung her kimono on the back of the door. Then he left. When he realized that they were not just going to call it a suicide and let it go, he had to find a way to get the kimono. His friend, Alonzo Ragsdale was around the corner and would be good for a cover up, assuming the price was right. He enlisted his help to get the kimono. When the family asked for it, Ragsdale tried to clean it with chemicals. After all, he had been a pharmacist and worked with the dead.

When the scheme blew up because the grand jury saw the blood stains, he began building his defense long before he was indicted. He paid off Ragsdale, he paid Katherine Fleming, or at least sweet talked her into her testimony when they met at the Traction Terminal, and he certainly paid off the women he had previously wronged so they wouldn't testify. I also believe he paid Mrs. Tennant to stay away or at least lay low. Other key witnesses were also most certainly paid off or frightened away.

Societal attitudes of the day didn't hurt Dr. Craig's case either. Dr. Knabe was a determined woman working in a man's field. She was not popular for that and because she was a serious and assertive person. Men couldn't believe a man of upright, good standing in the community would do something so heinous, yet he did.

After the murder and trial, Dr. Craig kept up his facade. I spoke online to a family member and the person stated that Dr. Craig maintained Dr. Knabe killed herself, despite what his own attorneys admitted and what Judge Blair believed the State proved. Must be nice to have selective recall. He kept up this pretense because he was in denial and tried to keep the coverup going. Dr. Craig didn't want his family and peers later in life to know it was considered a murder after he was tried. After all, it would tarnish his standing in the community and cast doubt on him with his family. If Dr. Craig had ever had any true affection or feeling for Dr. Knabe, friend or otherwise, he would have been more sympathetic or sad about her death. He was cold, cruel and calculating as always.

Aside from being pissed off and angry about Dr. Knabe's murder, I am angry for everything she had left to do and couldn't. She was three years away from WWI. In WWI women were given valued positions as doctors in areas that traditionally they wouldn't have even been considered for. But because of the desperate need for physicians, women were put in positions of heads of departments, hospitals and even positions in the military. Once they proved their capability, it became more mainstream and by the 1920s, women physicians had so many doors open to them, although their struggle has never really ended. I am angry because Dr. Knabe never got a true chance to use her skills and live up to the potential she knew she had.

Of course, I cannot prove any of this. The case evidence was mishandled from the beginning and destroyed in 1977. However, much as Dr. Craig maintained Dr. Knabe killed herself, I can maintain that she did not. While Dr. Craig based his views on guilt and fear, mine is based on evidence to the contrary.

For years, I believe now I have searched for something that doesn't exist- the transcripts of the trial. Even today, trials are not transcribed unless they go to an appellate court. Recordings of trials are kept for a period of time and unless you pay to have them transcribed, they never are. In Dr. Craig's case, it didn't go to the appellate court and so it would have most likely never been transcribed. The only evidence of the trial would have been legal filings, possibly shorthand notes from the court recorder and the judge's 15-page decision. None exist in Shelby or Marion County. One newspaper article contains the entire transcript of Judge Blair's notes. I suspect this is the same case for the grand jury notes. So very sad.

At one time, Dr. Knabe was supposed to be my doctoral dissertation. My committee believed there was not enough primary documentation to build her life. I don't think one can say that when you're talking about history. This book is proof.

Regardless, I had the good fortune to walk through Dr. Knabe's apartment a few times before and after it was remodelled. I've included some pictures in the book. Enjoy!

She Sleeps Well 253

Top: This was her bedroom. Where the electrical outlets are on the right was the doorway to her office. This picture was taken in the early 2000s when the building was inhabited by transient people. The building had been used as a nursing home.

Top: The infamous dumb waiter door. This picture was taken in the early 2000s when the building was inhabited by transient people.

Top: This common area of the building nearby Dr. Knabe's apartment. This orb was not the only piece of possible paranormal activity the author has experienced in the building. The day this orb was captured, she also captured an EVP (electronic voice phenomenon) in Dr. Knabe's office that stated, "It's terrible."

Top: A glimpse of Dr. Knabe's office. This is where her desk sat. The window on the far side is where the window seat was.

Top: Dr. Knabe's office after remodel. Now it is used for transitional housing and offices. While under construction, the workers would hear her and they would find their tools scattered around the rooms.

Top: Dr. Knabe's bedroom and bathroom are now just a bathroom. One plumber met her face to kimono when she walked in wearing it. He crawled out of the bathroom and didn't return for a while.

Top: The hallway looking west. Dr. Knabe's apartment is on the left.

Top: *The first time the author stood on the beaches Dr. Knabe roamed.*

Chapter Notes

The author placed the footnotes as chapter notes for readability. The chapter notes are cited in the order they would appear as footnotes. Some chapters also include additional notes about specific points of the book.

Early Life and Family

1. Verlag von Frederich Nagel. (1892). Pommersches Güter-Adressbuch. Verzeichniss sämmtlicher Güter mit Angabe der Guts-Eigenschaft, der Gesämmtfläche und Flächeninhalts, des Grundsteuer-Reintrages, der Besitzer bezw. Stettin: Verlag von Frederich Nagel. Retrieved from http://bibliotekacyfrowa.eu/dlibra/docmetadata?id=oai:bibliotekacyfrowa.eu:582&from=http://fbc.pionier.net.pl
2. Genealoger.com (2012). Pomeranian Genealogy: Kreis Schlawe. Retrieved from http://www.genealoger.com/german/pommern/kreis/schlawe.htm
3. This has been one of the hardest areas to track down. Records were lost during WWII when the Russians came in and time has lost many others.
4. Familienforschung in Westpreußen. (n.d.). Verzeichnis westpreußischer Standesamtsregister, Zivilstandsregister, Dissidentenregister und Kirchenbuchzweitschriften. Retrieved from http://www.westpreussen.de/cms/ct/standesamtsregister.php
5. Baker, T. (9 December 1911). Who Killed Dr. Helene Knabe?. Colliers Magazine. 63(12). P.15-16, 27.
   Deutsche Bauzeitung. (28 July 1870). Hülfskomité für die Feld stehenden Architekten und Bau-Ingenieure. Deutsche Bauzeitung. p. 245.
   Deutsche Bauzeitung. (29 November 1873). Das preussiche Staats-Bauwesen. Deutsche Bauzeitung. p. 371-379.
   Deutsche Bauzeitung. (2 July 1890). Besuchstafel der Technischen Hochschule Berlin, bezw. Ihrer Vorläufer. Deutsche Bauzeitung. p. 317-368.
   Deutsche Bauzeitung. (9 July 1890). Personal-nachrichten. Deutsche Bauzeitung. p. 332.
6. NOTE: Men were required to serve in the military and perform community service. From the 1960s to 2011, unless they were exempt (such in the children of Holocaust survivors) every man was expected to serve in the military or perform community service between 6 to 18 months, depending on the year. If the person chose civil service, the time was longer than serving in the military.
   Dunn, J.P. (1910). Greater Indianapolis: The History, the Industries, the Institutions, and the People of a City of Homes (Vols 1-2). Chicago: The Lewis Publishing Company.
7. Dunn, J.P. (1910). Greater Indianapolis: The History, the Industries, the Institutions, and the People of a City of Homes (Vols 1-2). Chicago: The Lewis Publishing Company.
8. Augusta Knabe said she thought Dr. Knabe's father was dead at the time of her death, however this was not the case.
9. Deutsche Bauzeitung. (28 July 1870). Hülfskomité für die Feld stehenden Architekten und Bau-Ingenieure. Deutsche Bauzeitung. p. 245.
   Deutsche Bauzeitung. (29 November 1873). Das preussiche Staats-Bauwesen. Deutsche Bauzeitung. p. 371-379.
   Deutsche Bauzeitung. (2 July 1890). Besuchstafel der Technischen Hochschule Berlin, bezw. Ihrer

Vorläufer. Deutsche Bauzeitung. p. 317-368.

Deutsche Bauzeitung. (9 July 1890). Personal-nachrichten. Deutsche Bauzeitung. p. 332.

10. This award went back to 1792 in Prussia when King Frederick William II used the order of the black eagle , making the red eagle the second highest honor. However, in 1810 King Fredrick William III revised it and the red eagle became a fourth class honor.

11. and 12.

Burke, Bernard (1858). The book of orders of knighthood and decorations of honour of all nations. London: Hurst and Blackett.

Dunn, J.P. (1910). Greater Indianapolis: The History, the Industries, the Institutions, and the People of a City of Homes (Vols 1-2). Chicago: The Lewis Publishing Company.

Baker, T. (9 December 1911). Who Killed Dr. Helene Knabe?. Colliers Magazine. 63(12). P.15-16, 27.

13. Alexander Turnbull Library, (n.d.) Reverend Johann Heine. Alexander Turnbull Library.
14. Searches for this information have yielded nothing.
15. Indianapolis Star. (31 December 1911).Gives Light on Dr. Knabe's Life. Indianapolis Star. p. 1.
16. Ellis Island. (1894). Customer List of Passengers (Augusta Knabe). Ellis Island.
17. The National Archives at Washington, D.C.; Washington, D.C.; Records of the US Customs Service, RG36; NAI Number: 2655153; Record Group Title: Records of the Immigration and Naturalization Service, 1787-2004; Record Group Number: 85 (Franz Kropp)
18. FamilySearch. (1920). United States Census 1920.Retrieved from https://familysearch.org/ark:/61903/3:1:33SQ-GR66-DSY?mode=g&i=7&wc=QZJP-8Y1%3A1036470701%2C1036668101%2C1038501501%2C1589332834%3Fcc%3D1488411&cc=1488411
19. Crown Hill Cemetery. (1896). Burial Record Karoline Kropp. Crown Hill Cemetery
20. and 21.

Dunn, J.P. (1910). Greater Indianapolis: The History, the Industries, the Institutions, and the People of a City of Homes (Vols 1-2). Chicago: The Lewis Publishing Company.

22. The ships passenger list states she was a seamstress. In the date of death column, however, it is believed this is just a note from the recorder.
23. Bonner, T. N. (1995). Becoming a Physician: Medical Education in Britain, France, Germany, and the United States, 1750-1945. Baltimore, MD: Johns Hopkins.

Abram, R. J (Ed.). (1985). Send Us a Lady Physician: Women Doctors in America 1835-1920. New York: W.W. Norton & Company.

24. Dunn, J.P. (1910). Greater Indianapolis: The History, the Industries, the Institutions, and the People of a City of Homes (Vols 1-2). Chicago: The Lewis Publishing Company.
25. and 26.

The Medical Student. (1907). A Parting Word to the Class of I.M.C 1907. The Medical Student. Vol5 8(19. 21-25).

27. These people were supposed to be from her village but this cannot be verified.
28. Her grades were "average"
29. Which would have been OK. They only required semesters of time in school and a working knowledge of the subjects.
30. In Summer 2004 IU Pathology Newsletter it says prior to 1905, they could only get the first 2 years at Bloomington (1903-04) and they had to get the rest of their education at other institutions---

one of which could have been the Athenaeum.
31. Wilhelm Röntgen. Retrieved from https://en.wikipedia.org/wiki/Wilhelm_R%C3%B6ntgen
32. Indianapolis Star. (19 February 1932). Former Mayor of Kokomo Dies. Indianapolis Star. p4
33. Now known as the Athenaeum Foundation
34. Was controlled by the Flower Mission and maintained by public donations.
35. Aka Dr. Louis Burckhardt's Lying –in Hospital. It was established in 1894 for women who wanted to birth and be "confined" away from home.
36. The Medical Student. (1907). A Parting Word to the Class of I.M.C 1907. The Medical Student. Vol5 8(19. 21-25).
37. Wynn, F. B. & Knabe, H. (1904). Medical College of Indiana, University of Indianapolis. American Medical Association Transactions of the Section of Pathology and Physiology. p426-27
38. The Medical Student. (1903). Junior Class.. The Medical Student.Vol 1 4(20).
39. Indianapolis Star. (13 July 1903). King of Ghouls Writing a Book. Indianapolis Star. p.1.
40. He was later sent to the Jefferson Reformatory in southern Indiana. By 1912 he was out of jail and working in Anderson writing books of poems.
41. Indiana Medical Journal. (1904). Thirty-fourth Annual Commencement of the Medical College of Indiana. Indiana Medical Journal. p. 463.
42. Indiana Medical Journal. (1904). Thirty-fourth Annual Commencement of the Medical College of Indiana. Indiana Medical Journal. p. 463.
43. FindaGrave.com. (n.d). Clifford Burroughs Grave Memorial. Retrieved from http://www.findagrave.com/cgi-bin/g.i?page=gr&GSln=Burroughs&GSfn=Clifford+&GSbyrel=all&GSdy=1904&GSdyrel=in&GScntry=4&GSob=n&GRid=99246146&df=all&
44. He died on the eve of completing his classes. He was known for his cheerful disposition and kindness of heart. The class agreed they had a sense of personal loss now that he'd gone into the "Great Beyond". He would have gone into practice with an uncle in Shannondale, Indiana

Emersing Herself in Her Profession

45. ,Jacob Piatt Dunn's, "Greater Indianapolis : The History, The Industries, The Institutions, and The People of a City of Homes, Volume 1 and 2" chronicle some of the most influential people and business in Indianapolis at the time. It may have been a pay to be listed publication or a vanity publication or it could have been Dunn publishing his own work and the cost was to defray some of the cost of publication and the time of the person writing it. Many of the people profiled wrote much of their own biographies. Dr. Knabe was no exception.
When Dunn's book was published in 1910, Dr. Knabe had been in the United States for 14 years. Her English was excellent, as she was able to attend medical school only four years after her arrival, but as a 14 year English speaker, she was able to capture nuances of English to say more by way she phrased her biography. What she didn't write gives tremendous insight into not only her life, but the parts of her life from which she was possibly trying to minimize and from which she wished to redirect attention.
46. Indianapolis News. (4 January 1905). Dr. Ferguson Renders Bill. Indianapolis News. p.3.
47. Indianapolis Star. (29 September 1911). Gives Beauty Hint in Back Yard Art.Indianapolis Star. p. 3.
48 Another institution that got bigger than the people it was to serve. It exists yet today. As the author

trying to get any history or infomraiton from the institution around this event, was Ludacris. I was transferred to the wrong people 3 times, one person said she'd get back with me and didn't. And even veterans today call this hospital, "Hell" in the VA system. Ward, J. (2016, February 28). Electronic chat interview.

49. They were not available in the histories. Trustees present were AM Scott, Eli F Ritter, both of Indianapolis; William S Haggart, Lafayette, Louis B. Fulweller, Peru; Eli W Menaugh, Salem.
50. Indianapolis News. (4 January 1912). The State's Typhoid Fever. Indianapolis News. p.12.
51. Indianapolis News. (7 October 1905). Bad Water Causes Typhoid. Indianapolis News. p.5.
52. Indiana State Board of Health. (1905) Report of Indiana State Board of Health: Twenty-Fourth Annual Report. State of Indiana. Indiana State Archives Indiana Commission on Public Records. 5(1)
53. Indianapolis News. (11 October 1905). Farmer's Pride in Wells Handicap Typhoid Inquiry. Indianapolis News. p.18.
54. The test is ued to make a presumptive diagnosis of enteric fever (thyphod fever). It looks for bacterium Salmonella enterica serotype Typhi (S. typhi), usually transmitted through food and drinks contaminated with fecal matter. It is marked by symptoms that include high fevers, fatigue , abdominal pain, diahreah, constipation, weight loss and a rash. If not diagnosed early, intestinal bleeding or perforation can occur. The test is performed by detecting antibodies present in the infected person's blood sample and specific antigens of S. typhi, which produces clumping (agglutination) that is visible to the naked eye.When Widal tests were developed in 1896 it was at least a better tool than doctors had before.Widal tests are no longer used in the US but still used in developing countries. The problem with this test is that it can't distinguish from a current infection and a previous infection or vaccination against it. Additionally, there is cross sensitivity to other strains of Salmonella.
55. Indianapolis News. (11 October 1905). Farmer's Pride in Wells Handicap Typhoid Inquiry. Indianapolis News. p.18.
56. Indianapolis News. (14 December 1905). Flies Worst Insect as Disease Carrier. Indianapolis News. p.3.
57. Indianapolis News. (16 November 1905). Two Deaths from Typhoid Fever. Indianapolis News. p.14.
58. Indianapolis News. (29 December 1905). Learned His Disease at State Laboratory. Indianapolis News. p.8.
59. Indianapolis Star. (4 January 1906). State Laboratory Work. Indianapolis Star. p. 7.
60. Indianapolis News. (16 May 1906). Microbe That Causes Everlasting Sleep. Indianapolis News. p.1.
61. Treatment today are various medications for 1 to 3 days to kill the parasite and take additional iron to combat anemia, should it develop from the parasite feeding on your blood. Additionally, you may have to take nutritional supplements to combat any lost nutrients and if you have ascites, where you have a severe lack of protein and a buildup of fluid in your stomach, you would add additional protein to your diet. (Healthline. Hookworm Infections. Retrieved from http://www.healthline.com/health/hookworm#Prevention8)
62. Indianapolis News. (13 August 1906). Dogs Infected with Rabies. Indianapolis News. p.11.
63. Indianapolis Star. (09 February 1908). Dog Had Rabies. Indianapolis Star. p. 17.

Indianapolis Star. (12 February 1908). Finds Spaniel Had Rabies. Indianapolis Star. p. 3.
64. The Encyclopedia of Arkansas History & Culture. (n.d.). Rabies. Retrieved from: http://www.encyclopediaofarkansas.net/encyclopedia/entry-detail.aspx?entryID=6451
World Health Organization (2016). Rabies. Retrieved from http://www.who.int/mediacentre/factsheets/fs099/en/
65. Indianapolis News. (17 June 1908). Dog Died of Rabies. Indianapolis News. p.10.
Indianapolis News. (23 June 1908). Dog Had Rabies. Indianapolis News. p.3.
Indianapolis News. (20 July 1908). Dogs With Rabies Are at Large in Indianapolis. Indianapolis News. p.1.
Indianapolis News. (29 July 1908). Cases of Hydrophobia Among Dogs Increase. Indianapolis News. p.3.
66. Indianapolis Star. (26 July 1908). The Fight Against Hydrophobia in Indiana. Indianapolis Star. p. 39.
67. Indianapolis News. (12 March 1908). Spencer May Soon Be Made a Dogless Town. Indianapolis News. p.9.
68. Indianapolis News. (12 May 1908). Wish Calf's Head Examined. Indianapolis News. p.8.
69. Indianapolis News. (23 July 1908). Several Victims in Danger of Rabies. Indianapolis News. p.4.
Indianapolis Star. (26 July 1908). The Fight Against Hydrophobia in Indiana. Indianapolis Star. p. 39.
70. Indianapolis News. (27 July 1908). On the Trail of the Mad Dog. Indianapolis News. p.13.
71. Indianapolis News. (27 July 1908). On the Trail of the Mad Dog. Indianapolis News. p.13.
72. Indianapolis Star. (6 March 1908). Friend of Homeless Curs Bitten by Mad Dog. Indianapolis Star. p. 1.
73. Indianapolis News. (14 December 1907). Physicians Careless with Deadly Microbe. Indianapolis News. p.16.
74. Indianapolis News. (14 December 1907). Physicians Careless with Deadly Microbe. Indianapolis News. p.16.
75. We didn't have one until 1910
76. Indianapolis News. (27 December 1907). Fight for the Head of the Dog That Had the Rabies. Indianapolis News. p.2.
77. Indianapolis News. (13 January 1908). Will Begin a Crusade Against Tuberculosis. Indianapolis News. p.10.
78. Indianapolis News. (25 April 1908). Puro Water Analyzed. Indianapolis News. p.3.
79. Indianapolis Star. (15 October 1908). City Physician Named. Indianapolis Star. p. 14.
80. Indiana State Board of Health. (1908) Report of Indiana State Board of Health: Twenty-Fourth Annual Report. State of Indiana. Indiana State Archives Indiana Commission on Public Records. 10 (1-12)
81. Indianapolis News. (14 November 1907). Tuberculosis Killed 325 Last September. Indianapolis News. p.11.
82. Indianapolis News. (6 June 1907). Baseball Game. Indianapolis News. p.7.
83. Indiana State Board of Health. (1908) Report of Indiana State Board of Health: Twenty-Fourth Annual Report. State of Indiana. Indiana State Archives Indiana Commission on Public Records. 10 (1-12)

84. and 85.
    Indiana State Board of Health. (1908) Report of Indiana State Board of Health: Twenty-Fourth Annual Report. State of Indiana. Indiana State Archives Indiana Commission on Public Records. 10 (1-12)
86. Indianapolis News. (7 November 1908). Resigns from the State Laboratory of Hygiene. Indianapolis News. p.20.
87. Indianapolis Star. (2 December 1906). Dr. Rucker Begins Work. Indianapolis Star. p. 41.
88. Indiana State Board of Health. (1908) Dr. J.N. Hurty Correspondence. State of Indiana. Indiana State Archives Indiana Commission on Public Records. Pp. 6, 20, 48, 57, 62, 66,87, 88, 95-96, 334, 374, 449
    Indiana State Board of Health. (1908) Report of Indiana State Board of Health: Twenty-Fourth Annual Report. State of Indiana. Indiana State Archives Indiana Commission on Public Records. 10 (1-12)
    Indiana State Board of Health. (1907) Report of Indiana State Board of Health: Twenty-Fourth Annual Report. State of Indiana. Indiana State Archives Indiana Commission on Public Records. 9 (1-12)
89. Indianapolis News. (7 November 1908). Resigns from the State Laboratory of Hygiene. Indianapolis News. p.20.
90. Indiana State Board of Health. (1908) Dr. J.N. Hurty Correspondence. State of Indiana. Indiana State Archives Indiana Commission on Public Records. Pp. 6, 20, 48, 57, 62, 66,87, 88, 95-96, 334, 374, 449,
91. Interestingly her replacement Dr. JP Simonds left after 4 years and went to a university. Hurty wanted his assistant, Dr William Shimer to take over the position.
92. Indiana State Board of Health. (1908) Dr. J.N. Hurty Correspondence. State of Indiana. Indiana State Archives Indiana Commission on Public Records. Pp. 6, 20, 48, 57, 62, 66,87, 88, 95-96, 334, 374, 449
    Indiana State Board of Health. (1908) Report of Indiana State Board of Health: Twenty-Fourth Annual Report. State of Indiana. Indiana State Archives Indiana Commission on Public Records. 10 (1-12)
    Indianapolis News. (7 November 1908). Resigns from the State Laboratory of Hygiene. Indianapolis News. p.20.
93. Indiana State Board of Health. (1908) Dr. J.N. Hurty Correspondence. State of Indiana. Indiana State Archives Indiana Commission on Public Records. Pp. 6, 20, 48, 57, 62, 66,87, 88, 95-96, 334, 374, 449
94. and 95, 96
    Barnard, H.E. (20 March 1906). Unpublished correspondence. W.H. Smith Memorial Library, Indiana Historical Society.
    Barnard, H.E. (8 October 1905). Unpublished correspondence. W.H. Smith Memorial Library, Indiana Historical Society.
    Barnard, H.E. (30 March 1906). Unpublished correspondence. W.H. Smith Memorial Library, Indiana Historical Society.
97. University of Pennsylvania. (n.d.) University History: School of Medicine: A Brief History. Retrieved from http://www.archives.upenn.edu/histy/features/schools/med.html

Until 1910 and the Flexner report, this was not obligatory- with his report it became critical to have this—would have been a revenue stream. And she was luky to have the position- daught by preeminent physicians.

98. Bobbs Free Dispensary was formed after the Civil War but by 1870, it was known as Bobbs Free Dispensary for Dr. John Bobbs, who endowed it with $2000, and run by the Medical College of Indiana (and later the Indiana University School of Medicine). It sat first at 45 S. Pennsylvania Street and later at the corner north west corner of Market Street and Senate Avenue inside the School of Medicine. In this capacity, she not only dispensed medication, but it was really a precursor to emergency medical checks from today. She would have seen broken bones, colds, and even cases of STDs. It was also used to help medical students.

99. Other sources cite her as a lecuturer at the school. The truth is that all the lecturers were sometimes called professors and vice versa. At this small school, most faculty had more than one role, much as the doctors at the Indiana University School of medicine did. They would be the treasurer or a professor or associate and then have a private practices as well.

100. Indianapolis Medical Journal. (1910). The Indianapolis Medical Society. Indianapolis Medical Journal. 13 (188)

101. Indianapolis News. (7 October 1911). News of Colored Folk. Indianapolis News. p.27.

102. Journal of the American Medical Association. (1905 July-December). Society Proceedings. Journal of the American Medical Association. 45(485)

103. Bonner, T. N. (1995). Becoming a Physician: Medical Education in Britain, France, Germany, and the United States, 1750-1945. Baltimore, MD: Johns Hopkins.
From about 1870 the clinic versus the laborarory became a major fight. German, British and American doctors, who were considered the very best, argued incessantly over curriculum and the place of clinics and laboratories in the classroom.
German and Brittish curriciulum argued for clinics. Aneruca followed suit believing a lack of instructors in the field would be a detriment to making it a part of the curriculum.
Laboratory science was offered widely in medical schools by 1880, however it was only by 1900 that it was required by medical schools. Enrollment in these courses were modest in comparison to clinical courses.
Many doctors believed it was important to know the how and why but labs did little to help the patient at the bedside.
By 1900 with social welfare programs and rises in standards of living for many and class beginning to melt away, it wasn't a matter of the place of science and laboratories in medicine but rather, how could these be properly made accessable to students.
Still, by 1910 Abraham Flexner would advocate and continue to do so for years through his Flexner Report, to change the way doctors were educated. He believed in hands on approach and making it valuable to students. Students, he believed, needed hands on practice "The student no longer merely watches, listens, memorizes; he does." 293.

104. Indianapolis News. (9 June 1908). Medics' Meeting Pleased. Indianapolis News. p.16.

105. Indianapolis News. (2 September 1908). Nurses of Indiana to Hold Annual Meeting. Indianapolis News. p.5.

106. Indianapolis News. (2 September 1908). Nurses of Indiana to Hold Annual Meeting. Indianapolis News. p.5.

Indianapolis News. (9 September 1908). Dr. Knabe Gives Demonstrations. Indianapolis News. p.4
107. Indianapolis News. (9 September 1908). Dr. Knabe Gives Demonstrations. Indianapolis News. p.4.
108. The Board of Trade building has been razed and is now Chase Tower.
109. In 1911 Dr. Knabe was featured with other prominent women in the newspaper. Dr. Knabe's topic was making Indianapolis beautiful, in which she was able to work in the sanitation woes of the city.
110. Journal of the American Medical Association. (1910 January-June). News, Notes and Comments. Journal of the American Medical Association. 3(44)
111. State of Indiana. (1911). Officers of State, State of Indiana. State of Indiana. Indinaapolis, IN: Wm. Buford.
112. Indianapolis Star. (31 December 1911).Gives Light on Dr. Knabe's Life. Indianapolis Star. p. 1.
113. In sorting out her estate, the ring was returned to its owner. Indianapolis Star. (7 December 1911). Seeks Ring Given Dr. Knabe. Indianapolis Star. p. 5.
114. Indianapolis Star. (29 July 1909). Takes State Position in Health Movement. Indianapolis Star. p. 7. Indianapolis News. (6 October 1909). Women's Local Council Hears of Many Things. Indianapolis News. p.8.
115. The Journal of the Indiana State Medical Association, Volume 2 May 15, 1909 pp222. Has how it formed and by who. Lists Dr. K as Helen Knabe.
116. Indianapolis News. (1 July 1911). Notes of Colored People. Indianapolis News. p.14.
117. Indianapolis Star. (23 September 1911). Booths Depict Y.W.C.A. Work. Indianapolis Star. p. 7.
118. Indianapolis Star. (30 July 1911). News of Colored Folk. Indianapolis Star. p. 48.
119. Razed.
120. Indianapolis News. (15 January 1907). Students Write for Paper. Indianapolis News. p.16.
121. The Medical Student. (1907). A Parting Word to the Class of I.M.C 1907. The Medical Student. Vol5 8(19. 21-25)
122. Friedman, G.A. (1910). Supperative Perigastritis: A Case with Tumor formation following poefroated gastric ulcer of the grteater curature. JAMA. 1910;LIV(8):611-613 Retrieved from http://jama.jamanetwork.com/article.aspx?articleid=431320
123. Indianapolis Medical Journal. (1910). The Indianapolis Medical Society. Indianapolis Medical Journal. 13 (188)
124. Bogart, G.H. (1909 March). Report of a peculiar case of walking Typhoid. The Medical Summary. 31(139)
125. Wynn, F. B. & Knabe, H. (1904). Medical College of Indiana, University of Indianapolis. American Medical Association Transactions of the Section of Pathology and Physiology. p426-27
126. Wynn, F. B. & Knabe, H. (1904). Medical College of Indiana, University of Indianapolis. American Medical Association Transactions of the Section of Pathology and Physiology. pp. 426-27
127. Indianapolis News. (13 April 1907). Dr. Knabe Injured. Indianapolis News. p.3.
128. Indianapolis Star. (28 January 1908). Presents Picture of Ankle. Indianapolis Star. p. 12.
129. Indianapolis News. (17 May 1907). Ready to Leave Hospital. Indianapolis News. p.2.
130. The Medical Student. (1907). A Parting Word to the Class of I.M.C 1907. The Medical Student. Vol5 8(19. 21-25)
131. Indianapolis News. (27 January 1908). Wishes $5,000 for Sprained Ankle. Indianapolis News. p.3.
132. Indianapolis Star. (13 April 1907). Weather Makes Sad. Indianapolis Star. p. 1.

133. The Medical Student. (1907). A Parting Word to the Class of I.M.C 1907. The Medical Student. Vol5 8(19. 21-25)
134. Indianapolis News. (26 July 1911). No Action Taken on Kendall's Resignation. Indianapolis News. p.8.
135. Others included New York Turngemeinde (1848) and the Philadelphia Turngemeinde (1849)
136. Indianapolis News. (20 October 1911). Indianapolis School Notes. Indianapolis News. p.22.
    Indianapolis News. (7 October 1911). Indianapolis School Notes. Indianapolis News. p.19.
137. Indianapolis Star. (26 April 1911). Holds Leadership Day's Crying Need. Indianapolis Star. p. 6.
138. Mind and Body (1911 March- 1912 February) Notes from Normal Schools. Mind and Body. 18(297)
139. Tucker, S. (2008). William Blair Craig. Ancestry.com. Retrieved from http://mv.ancestry.com/viewer/bc8b2856-86bd-4832-9f16-f9a1d2600169/1587756/-1915861085
    Drumshang Farmhouse. (n.d.) rightmove. Retrived from http://www.rightmove.co.uk/property-for-sale/property-10946964.html
140. and 141.
    Tucker, S. (2008). William Blair Craig. Ancestry.com. Retrieved fromhttp://mv.ancestry.com/viewer/bc8b2856-86bd-4832-9f16-f9a1d2600169/1587756/-1915861085
142. Stockton, J.J. (Ed.). (1984). A Century of Service: Veterinary medicine in Indiana. Indianapolis, IN: The Board of DIrectors, Indiana Veterinary Medical Association.
143. Encompasses breeding, breeds, dairy inspection, stock judging, and feeds and feeding
144. Indiana Veterinary College (1921). Catalogue. W.H. Smith Memorial Library, Indiana Historical Society.
145. YMCA. (2008). About Us: Local History. YMCA. Retrieved from http://www.ywca.org/site/pp.asp?c=qkI3KgMTIrF&b=3841307
146. If they went to a fine dining establishment, they would often be turned away unless they had a male escort. The reason for this was that it was believed women would be accosted if they were out alone.
147. They merged in 1959.
148. Indianapolis Star. (2 December 1906). Y.W.C.A. Notes. Indianapolis Star. p. 26.
149. Indianapolis News. (5 November 1907). Y.W.C.A. Classes. Indianapolis News. p.8.
150. Indianapolis News. (9 November 1907). Y.W.C.A.Notes. Indianapolis News. p.23.
151. Indianapolis News. (23 November 1907). Y.W.C.A.Notes. Indianapolis News. p.14.
152. Indianapolis News. (13 January 1908). YWCA to Build Girls' Boarding School. Indianapolis News. p.3.
    Indianapolis News. (18 January 1908). YWCA Class Schedule. Indianapolis News. p.24.

Murder Investigation

153. Indianapolis News. (11 January 1908). YWCA Notes. Indianapolis News. p.21.
154. Indianapolis News. (28 October 1909). YWCA Notes. Indianapolis News. p.8.
155. Indianapolis News. (26 October 1906). Home Nursing Class. Indianapolis News. p.7.
    Indianapolis Star. (6 October1906). Class to meeting this evening. Indianapolis Star. p. 3.
156. Indianapolis News. (19 October 1906). Class in Home Nursing. Indianapolis News. p.25.
157. Indianapolis News. (30 September 1911). YWCA Notes. Indianapolis News. p.28.

158. Indianapolis News. (25 April 1911). YWCA Holds Session. Indianapolis News. p.5.
159. Dunn, J.P. (1910). Greater Indianapolis: The History, the Industries, the Institutions, and the People of a City of Homes (Vols 1-2). Chicago: The Lewis Publishing Company.
160. R.L. Polk & Company. (1910). Indianapolis City Directory. R.L. Polk & Company.
161. New York State. (n.d.) Forensic Science History. New York State. Retrieved from https://www.troopers.ny.gov/Crime_Laboratory_System/History/Forensic_Science_History/
162. Forensic Science Ireland (Eolaíocht Fhóiréinseach Éireann) n.d.) The History of Forensic Science. Forensic Science Ireland (Eolaíocht Fhóiréinseach Éireann) . Retrieved from ://www.forensicscience.ie/Services/History-of-Forensic-Science/
163. Unknown. (n.d.) Police; History- Policing Twentieth-century America. Retrieved from http://law.jrank.org/pages/1643/Police-History-Policing-twentieth-century-America-reform-era.html Cliff Notes. (n.d.) Progressive Police Reform. Cliff Notes. Retrieved from http://www.cliffsnotes.com/study-guides/criminal-justice/development-of-the-american-police/progressive-police-reform
164. New York State. (n.d.) Forensic Science History. New York State. Retrieved from https://www.troopers.ny.gov/Crime_Laboratory_System/History/Forensic_Science_History/
165. Archbold, C.A. (2012). Policing. Thousand Oaks, CA: Sage Publications. Retrieved from http://www.sagepub.com/sites/default/files/upm-binaries/50819_ch_1.pdf
Rennison, M.C. & Dodge, M. (2015). Introduction to Criminal Justice: Systems, Diversity and Changes. Thousand Oaks, CA: Sage Publications. Retrieved from http://www.sagepub.com/sites/default/files/upm-binaries/66074_Renninson_Chapter_4.pdf
166. Later on Kropp and Augusta say this isn't true, but she still took money from the estate.
167. The Day Book. (8 December 1913). The Craig-Knabe Case. The Day Book. p4.
168. In German, "kleines Maedchen" which means "little girl" is used quite often even between females who are not mother and daughter.
169. Indianapolis News. (1 November 1911). To Take Last Look at the Knabe Flat. Indianapolis News. pp.1, 17.
170. Named for John Greenleaf Whittier, now Whittier Apartments
171. Indianapolis News. (24 October 1911). Delaware Flats Where Dr. Knabe Lived. Indianapolis News. p.1.
172. State of Indiana. (n.d.). Marion County Naturalizations (Karl Kropp). State of Indiana. Retrieved from https://secure.in.gov/apps/iara/search/Home/Detail?rId=908317
173. Indianapolis News. (25 October 1911). Police Start Anew in Knabe Mystery. Indianapolis News. pp.1, 15.
174. Indianapolis News. (3 November 1911). Police Will Call Miss Knabe Again. Indianapolis News. p.1, 4.
175. Indianapolis News. (9 November 1911).Still Running Down Knabe Murder "Tips". Indianapolis News. p.2.
176. Indianapolis News. (3 November 1911). Police Will Call Miss Knabe Again. Indianapolis News. pp.1, 4.
177. Sometimes listed as Haskell but it is Haskett
178. Cravenette was a brand name of water repellant. In this case it was on a coat The Telegraph. (6 April 1946). Cravenette (Ad). The Telegraph.

179. Indianapolis Star. (12 November 1911). Phone Alarm Newest Clew in Knabe Case. Indianapolis Star. p. 1. 4
180. Later it would found with her estate things.
181. Indianapolis Sun. (2 November 1911). Suicide Impossible, Thinks College Chum of Dr. Knabe. Indianapolis Sun. p.3.
182. Indianapolis Sun. (24 October 1911). Dr. Helene Knabe Killed in Night, Janitor is Held. *Indianapolis Sun*. pp. 1-2.
183. Indianapolis Sun. (1 November 1911). Doctor's Property will be Searched for Minute Clews. *Indianapolis Sun*. pp.1, 3.
184. Indianapolis Star. (7 November 1911). Tells of Voices in Doctor's Fat. Indianapolis Star. p. 1
185. Indianapolis Star. (7 November 1911). Tells of Voices in Doctor's Fat. Indianapolis Star. p. 1
186. Indianapolis Star. (27 October 1911). Murder Clew Given by Carr is Abandoned. Indianapolis Star. pp. 1,13.
187. Rouse, W. (2016) Email regarding cold case files.
188. Indianapolis Star. (30 December 1911). The Knabe Murder Verdict. Indianapolis Star. p. 8 Indianapolis Star. (30 December 1911). Knabe Murder Verdict Ridiculed by Hyland. Indianapolis Star. pp. 1.
189. Indianapolis Star. (31 December 1911). Editorial. Indianapolis Star. p. 12.
190. Indianapolis Star. (2 November 1911). Hyland Holds Suicide More Likely Theory. Indianapolis Star. p.p 1,8
191. Indianapolis Star. (2 November 1911). Hyland Holds Suicide More Likely Theory. Indianapolis Star. pp. 1,8
192. Indianapolis Star. (12 November 1911). Editorial. Indianapolis Star. p. 1,7.
193. Department of Commerce Bureau of the Census. (1911). Mortality Statistics. Department of Commerce Bureau of the Census . Retrieved from http://www.cdc.gov/nchs/data/vsushistorical/mortstatbl_1911.pdf
194. Denning D.G, Conwell, Y. king, D. and Cox, C. (2000 Fall). Method choice, intent and Gender in compelted suicide. Suidice Life Threat Beahvior. 30(3):282-8. Retrieved from http://www.ncbi.nlm.nih.gov/pubmed/11079640
195. and 196, 197.
Centers for Disease Control. WISQARS. Data compiled by searching http://www.cdc.gov/injury/wisqars/leadingcauses.html
198. Miyamoto, R. (2016, March 28). Personal Interview.
199. A blade for making thin slices of tissue samples, usually for viewing under a microscope.
200. Findagrave.com. (n.d.) Harry Dunn Tutewiler Memorial. Findagrave.com. Retrieved from http://www.findagrave.com/cgi-bin/g.i?page=gr&GSln=Tutewiler&GSfn=Harry+&GSmn=d&GSbyrel=all&GSdyrel=all&GSst=17&GScntry=4&GSob=n&GRid=46036952&df=all&
Dunn, J.P. (1910). Greater Indianapolis: The History, the Industries, the Institutions, and the People of a City of Homes (Vols 1-2). Chicago: The Lewis Publishing Company.
201. and 202.
Indianapolis Star. (2 November 1911). Hyland Holds Suicide More Likely Theory. Indianapolis Star. pp. 1,8
203. Indianapolis Star. (6 November 1911). Decries Course in Murder Case. Indianapolis Star. p. 1

Indianapolis News. (6 November 1911). Dodds Statement Condemned. Indianapolis News. p.3.
204. Indianapolis News. (3 November 1911). Police Will Call Miss Knabe Again. Indianapolis News. pp.1, 4.
205. The Hancock County Medical Society denounced Dodds as well. Dr. JL Allen and Dr. Carl McGaughey in the society were classmates of hers. "unethical and ungentlemanly"
206. Indianapolis News. (1 November 1911). To Take Last Look at the Knabe Flat. Indianapolis News. pp.1, 17.
207. Indianapolis News. (1 November 1911). To Take Last Look at the Knabe Flat. Indianapolis News. pp.1, 17.
208. For which Wishard Hospital was named
209. Rice, T.B. (1946). Hoosier Health Officer: : A Biography of Dr. J. N. Hurty and The History of The Indiana State Board of Health to 1925. Indianapolis, IN: Indiana State Board of Health.
210. Indianapolis Sun. (3 November 1911). Is Helene Kanbe's Murder Playing Tag with Sleuths? Indianapolis Sun. p.1,22.
211. The paper reported he was journeying to SMWC where his daughter was studying.
212. Indianapolis Star. (3 November 1911). Burns Favors Suicide Stand in Knabe Case. Indianapolis Star. pp. 1,3.
213. Indianapolis Star. (3 November 1911). Burns Favors Suicide Stand in Knabe Case. Indianapolis Star. pp. 1,3.
214. He based this on the newspapers when he should have investigated further as Coroner Durham had. If Burns had, he would have found her finances in order.
215. Page 268 in an unknown edition
216. Indianapolis News. (17 February 1912). F.W. Flanner Drinks Poison; Dies in Chapel Indianapolis News. p.1.
217. Indianapolis Star. (15 November 1911). Bares Lite to Cast Light on Knabe Death. Indianapolis Star. pp. 1,7.
218. R.L. Polk & Company. (1910). Indianapolis City Directory. R.L. Polk & Company.
219. United Mine Workers of America. (1912). Proceedings of the United Mine Workers of America. United Mine Workers of America. Indianapolis, IN: The Cheltenham-Aetna Press.
220. Indianapolis Sun. (25 October 1911). Women Physicians of City Laud Life Work of Victim. Indianapolis Sun. p.2.
221. In 1912, the movement really geared up in Indianapolis. It is a shame Dr. Knabe could not have been a part of it.
222. She and Mary Spink had a downtown practice together for a time.
223. Baker, T. (9 December 1911). Who Killed Dr. Helene Knabe?. Colliers Magazine. 63(12). pp.15-16, 27.
224. Indianapolis Star. (3 January 1911). Loom Ends Ad. Indianapolis Star. p. 4.
225. Indianapolis Sun. (31 October 1911). None Will Don Suit Dr. Knabe Ordered. Indianapolis Sun. p.1.
226. Benesch, A.B. (1901). Men of Indiana in Nineteen Hundred and One. Indianapolis, IN: The Benesch Publishing Company.
227. Baker, T. (9 December 1911). Who Killed Dr. Helene Knabe?. Colliers Magazine. 63(12). pp.15-16, 27.

228. Another dead-end story was about a "German revolutionist" who got into hot political arguments with Knabe, perhaps at Das Deutsche Haus, the German cultural center now called the Athanaeum and the Rathskeller. This lead, too, led nowhere.

229. The IPD's apparent willingness to blow off this murder case angered Indianapolis women. With no progress made toward finding a culprit, the Local Council of Women, meeting at the Propylaeum on the Old Northside in December, started a private fundraising campaign to keep the investigation going. After this Jack the Ripper-style murder, women were scared. The Indianapolis News on December 8, 1911 cited the touching story of a mother who was putting her son to bed. This was told by Margaret Hamilton, principal of Benjamin Harrison School:

"There is a feeling of fear among women and children," she said, "A mother told me her little boy kissed her good night and said to her: 'I hope no one will kill you in the night, mother.'" ... Do you wish to live in such a community?" she asked. "Dr. Knabe was a woman who was self-respecting, and who lived not for herself, and should we say "how shocking" and do nothing? She left no kinsmen and no money, and we should apprehend the guilty one."

One other woman — 19-year-old Ruth Campbell — offered her own fascinating story about the night of the Knabe murder. Ruth Campbell had previously lived in the Delaware Flats, then moved down to the Marina Flats at the corner of Alabama and North Streets, a few blocks away. (Today this is the Murat Theater's parking lot.) That night, perhaps at the exact moment that Knabe was being killed, Ruth had a terrifying dream "where she saw a similar tragedy enacted."

In dream science and spiritualism, these are known as clairvoyant or precognitive dreams. There are thousands of well-documented example over the centuries. In Campbell's precognitive dream, she saw a female, aged between 30 and 35, hanging from a rope. The dead woman also appeared to have had her throat cut, since blood flowed out around the noose. If Campbell didn't just make the story up, the coincidence is amazing at the very least, since even though "Mrs. Campbell does not remember ever having seen Dr. Knabe," when she saw a photograph of Knabe the following day, Ruth recognized her as the hanged woman in her disturbing dream.

Dreams, of course, can give amazing insight into the waking world. Robert Louis Stevenson, after all, got the idea for his classic of medical crime fiction — Dr. Jekyll and Mr. Hyde — from a powerful dream of his own.

230. Thayer, L. (28 October 1911). Clasps Dead Woman's Hand and Presses Lips to Brow. Indianapolis Sun. p.1-2.
231. Indianapolis Star. (3 January 1913). Leaders of Bar May be Called to knabe Case.Indianapolis Star. p.1,3
232. Indiana State Board of Charties. (1907 September). The Indiana Bulletin of Charites and Correction. Indiana State Board of Charities.7 0-74(36)
233. Indianapolis Star. (3 November 1911). Respect for the Dead Indianapolis Star. p. 8.
234. Indianapolis Star. (29 October 1911). Card of Thanks from Augusta Knabe and Family. *Indianapolis Star*. p. 43.
235. Indianapolis Star. (28 October 1911). Dr. Knabe's Charity Praised at Funeral. *Indianapolis Star*. pp.1,6.
236. Indianapolis Sun. (28 October 1911). Miss Knabe is Now on Verge of Collapsing. *Indianapolis Sun*. pp.1-2.

237. Indianapolis Star. (10 November 1911). Wild Theories Given in Knabe Case Tips. *Indianapolis Star*. p. 6.
238. Indianapolis Star. (7 December 1913). Thrills Scarce in Craig Trial . Indianapolis Star. pp. 1, 9
239. Chanute Daily Tribune (3 November 1911). Hers was a Life of Mystery. Chanute Daily Tribune. p. 3.
240. Indianapolis News. (11 July 1912). Knows Knabe Murderer. *Indianapolis News*. p.4.
    Indianapolis Star. (12 July 1912). Would Name Knabe Murderer .*Indianapolis Star*. p. 10.
241. Indianapolis News. (16 July 1912). Echo of Knabe Murder. *Indianapolis News*. p.14.
243. Saloniki-Greek Press. (13 April 1918). Celebration of the Ninety-Seventh Anniversary of Greek Independence Mr. Constantine Mammonas Appeals for Third Liberty Loan. Retrieved from http://flps.newberry.org/article/5422062_5_0789
244. Indianapolis Star. (6 November 1911). Decries Course in Murder Case. Indianapolis Star. p. 1
245. Ancestry.com. Massachusetts, Marriage Records, 1840-1915 [database on-line].
    Provo, UT, USA: Ancestry.com Operations, Inc., 2013. Original data: Massachusetts Vital Records, 1840–1911. New England Historic Genealogical Society, Boston, Massachusetts. Massachusetts Vital Records, 1911–1915. New England Historic Genealogical Society, Boston, Massachusetts.(for Mary McHale) http://interactive.ancestry.com/2511/41262_b132082-00300?pid=8861316&backurl=http%3a%2f%2fsearch.ancestry.com%2f%2fcgi-bin%2fsse.dll%3fgss%3dangs-c%26new%3d1%26rank%3d1%26gsfn%3dmary%2ba%2b%26gsfn_x%3d0%26gsln%3dmchale%26gsln_x%3d0%26msbdy%3d1895%26msgdd%3d6%26msgdm%3d11%263d Boston%252c%2bSuffolk%252c%2bMassachusetts%252c%2bUSA%26msgpn%3d4668%26msgpn_PInfo%3d8-%257c0%257c1652393%257c0%257c2%257c3242%257c24%257c0%257c2812%257c4668%257c0%257c%26msypn__p%3dPawtucket%252c%2bProvidence%252c%2bRhode%2bIsland%252c%2bUSA%26msypn%3d5530%26msypn_PInfo%3d8-%257c0%257c1652393%257c0%257c2%257c3242%257c42%257c0%257c2441%257c5530%257c0%257c%26mssng%3dseth%26mssns%3dnichols%26cp%3d0%26MSAV%3d0%-6h%3d8861316%26recoff%3d5%2b6%2b7%26db%3dMAMarriageRecords%26indiv%3d1%26ml_rpos%3d1&treeid=&personid=&hintid=&usePUB=true
246. The Day Book. (2 April 1912). Man Confesses Murder of Dr. Helene Knabe. The Day Book. p7-8.
247. Indianapolis News. (4 April 1912). Nichols Takes it Back; Did not Kill Dr. Knabe. Indianapolis News. p.2.
248. The Scranton Truth (3 April 1912). Nichols, Alleged Murderer, is Said Not To Be Sane. The Scranton Truth. p8.
249. Indianapolis News. (2 April 1912). Relatives Declare Nichols is Insane. Indianapolis News. p.1.
250. Indianapolis Star. (7 April 1912).Refutes Nichols' Story. Indianapolis Star. p.28.
251. San Antonio Press (4 April 1912). Murder Confession Hoax. San Antonio Press. p3
252. Indianapolis Star. (23 April 1912).Knabe "Slayer" Sentenced. .Indianapolis Star. p. 2.
253. Lincoln Daily News. (4 April 1912). Admits His Mentality is Out of Gear. Lincoln Daily News. p.5.
254. Wichita Beacon. (6 April 1912). Editorial. Wichita Beacon. p.2.
255. Indianapolis Star. (20 May 1912). "Confession" Amuses Police. .Indianapolis Star. p. 4.
256. Indianapolis Sun. (11 November 1911). Was Street Light OUt Fatal Night?. Indianapolis Sun. p.3.
257. Indianapolis Star. (1 November 1911). Girl, Incited by Knabe Case, "Fakes" Holdup. Indianapolis

Star. p. 8.
258. January, A. (2016 February 19). Email correspondence.
259. Indianapolis Star. (30 October 1911). Woman Cuts Own Throat; Note Blames Ill Health. Indianapolis Star. p. 1.
260. Goodspeed Brothers, Publishers. (1893). Pictorial and Biographical Memoirs of Indianapolis and Marion County. Goodspeed Brothers, Publishers. Chicago: Goodspeed Brothers Publishers
261. Indianapolis Star. (7 December 1911). Editorial. *Indianapolis Star*. p. 8.
262. Indianapolis Star. (2 February 1912). Concert to Aid Teachers' Fund. .Indianapolis Star. p. 52.
263. Indianapolis Star. (13 October 1911). School Notes. Indianapolis Star. p. 14.
264. Indianapolis Star. (25 April 1912). Editorial. .Indianapolis Star. p. 9.
265. Findagrave.com. (n.d.) Katherine Agnes Fleming. Findagrave.com. Retrieved from http://www.findagrave.com/cgi-bin/fg.cgi?page=gr&GRid=54404314
266. Aldridge, B. (1971, November). Who Killed Dr. Helene Knabe, Part 1. Indianapolis Magazine. 16-21.
Aldridge, B. (1971, December). Who Killed Dr. Helene Knabe, Part 2. Indianapolis Magazine. 18-21.
Aldridge, B. (1972, January). Who Killed Dr. Helene Knabe, Part 3. Indianapolis Magazine. 22-23, 34-38.
Ancestry.com. (n.d.) Fact Tree. Ancestry.com Retrieved from http://person.ancestry.com/tree/6385269/person/25344727799/facts
267. Indianapolis News. (3 July 1912). Grand Jurors Complain. Indianapolis News. p.14.
268. Indianapolis Star. (23 December 1912).Editorial. Indianapolis Star. p. 6
269. Indianapolis Star. (25 December 1912).View of the People. Indianapolis Star. p. 8
270. Indianapolis News. (31 December 1912). Webster Believes he Grand Jury Did Duty. Indianapolis News. p.3.

INDICTMENTS AND TRIAL

271. Indianapolis Star. (1 January 1913). Dr. Knabe's Philosophy of Life. *Indianapolis Star*. p. 10
272. Baker, T. (9 December 1911). Who Killed Dr. Helene Knabe?. Colliers Magazine. 63(12). pp.15-16, 27.
273. Indianapolis News. (25 December 1915). From Log Cabin to Big "Movie" Theater.. Indianapolis News. p7.
274. R.L. Polk & Company. (1910). Indianapolis City Directory. R.L. Polk & Company.
275. Indianapolis Star. (1 January 1913). Accused in Dr. Knabe Mystery Give Bonds.*Indianapolis Star*. p. 1,3
276. Indianapolis Star. (15 January 1913). Long Delay Possible in Knabe Hearings. .Indianapolis Star. p.
277. Indianapolis News. (1 November 1911). To Take Last Look at the Knabe Flat. Indianapolis News. pp.1, 17.
278. Ancestry.com. U.S. City Directories, 1822-1995 [database on-line] (Frieda Sondermann). Provo, UT, USA: Ancestry.com Operations, Inc., 2011. Retrieved from http://search.ancestry.com/cgi-bin/sse.dll?gss=angs-g&new=1&rank=1

&msT=1&gsfn=Freda+&gsfn_x=0&gsln=Sondermann&gsln_x=0&msypn__ftp=Indianapolis%2c+Marion%2c+Indiana%2c+USA&msypn=40138&msypn_PInfo=8-%7c0%7c1652393%7c0%7c2%7c3247%7c17%7c0%7c1893%7c40138%7c0%7c&MSAV=0&cp=0&catbucket=rstp&pcat=ROOT_CATEGORY&h=652528113&db=USDirectories&indiv=1&ml_rpos=10

279. Marion County, Indiana. (n.d.) General Entry, Claim and Allowance Docket of Estates, Marion County, Indiana: Dr. Helene Knabe. Marion County, Indiana. Book 39, Estate 10744.
Marion County, Indiana. (n.d.) Report on the State of Dr. Helene Knabe's Estate. Marion County, Indiana. Book 20 pp. 575 a, b.
Marion County, Indiana. (n.d.) Report on the State of Dr. Helene Knabe's Estate. Marion County, Indiana. Book 22 p. 588.
Marion County, Indiana. (n.d.) Report on the State of Dr. Helene Knabe's Estate. Marion County, Indiana. p. Book 20 pp. 532-33.
280. Indianapolis Star. (22 December 1912). Kimono Figures in Knabe Probe. Indianapolis Star. pp. 1,3
281. Marion County, Indiana. (n.d.) General Entry, Claim and Allowance Docket of Estates, Marion County, Indiana: Dr. Helene Knabe. Marion County, Indiana. Book 39, Estate 10744.
Marion County, Indiana. (n.d.) Report on the State of Dr. Helene Knabe's Estate. Marion County, Indiana. Book 20 pp. 575 a, b.
Marion County, Indiana. (n.d.) Report on the State of Dr. Helene Knabe's Estate. Marion County, Indiana. Book 22 p. 588.
Marion County, Indiana. (n.d.) Report on the State of Dr. Helene Knabe's Estate. Marion County, Indiana. p. Book 20 pp. 532-33.
282. Indianapolis Star. (4 January 1913). Baker to Take Active Charge of Knabe Case.Indianapolis Star. pp.1, 3.
283. Indianapolis Star. (3 January 1913). Editorial.Indianapolis Star. p.8.
284. Indianapolis Star. (4 December 1913).Point is Scored by Defense at Dr. Craig Trial. Indianapolis Star. pp. 1, 9.
285. Chanute Daily Tribune (9 December 1913).Judge Orders Jury to Dismiss Case. Chanute Daily Tribune. p. 1.
286. Indianapolis Star. (31 December 1912). Grand Jury Reports Today. .Indianapolis Star. p. 13.
287. Indianapolis Star. (11 January 1913). Editorial.Indianapolis Star. p. 8.
Indianapolis Star. (3 January 1913). Leaders of Bar May be Called to knabe Case.Indianapolis Star. pp.1,3
288. Indianapolis Star. (3 January 1913). Dr. Craig's Former Assistant Offers Explanation of Phone Call to Flat.Indianapolis Star. p.5
289. Indianapolis News. (4 January 1913). Names of Drs. Knabe and Craig on Flyleaf. Indianapolis News. p.3.
290. Indianapolis Star. (3 January 1913). Dr. Craig's Former Assistant Offers Explanation of Phone Call to Flat.Indianapolis Star. p.5
291. This consisted of a vaccine made from the dried rabies virus.
292. Indianapolis Star. (13 January 1913). Strengthen Council For Dr. Knabe Case. p. 14.
293. Indianapolis Star. (1 January 1913). Reward Tendered By Women Stands Alone. Indianapolis Star. p. 12.
Indianapolis Star. (5 January 1913). Ask Physicians to Raise Fund for Knabe Case.Indianapolis

Star. pp. 1,8.
294. Indianapolis Star. (1 January 1913). Reward Tendered By Women Stands Alone. Indianapolis Star. p. 12.
Indianapolis Star. (5 January 1913). Ask Physicians to Raise Fund for Knabe Case.Indianapolis Star. pp. 1,8.
295. Indianapolis Star. (9 January 1913). Kokomo Physician Who Knew Dr. Knabe Scouts Theory She Committed Suicide.Indianapolis Star. p. 9.
296. Watson, F. (2016, April 15). Phone Interview.
297. Watson, F. (2016, April 15). Phone Interview.
298. Indianapolis Star. (26 April 1913).Knabe Trial May not Begin Until Fall. .Indianapolis Star. p. 17.
299. Indianapolis Star. (22 June 1913). Knabe Case Rumors Denied. Indianapolis Star. p. 20.
300. Indianapolis Star. (5 September 1913). Craig-Ragsdale Trial Scheduled to Begin Oct 23. .Indianapolis Star. p. 1.
301. Indianapolis Star. (23 March 1913). Missing Knabe Document Found Wrapped in Kimono. Indianapolis Star. p. 52.
Indianapolis News. (24 March 1913). Coroner's Report Found. Indianapolis News. p.3.
302. By 1920 with the womens' right to vote, Indiana was considered an emancipatory state and women could be on juries.
303. Ft. Wayne News. (28 November 1913). The Knabe Trial is on at Shelbyville. Ft. Wayne News. pp. 1, 11.
304. Ft. Wayne Journal-Gazette. (1 January 1913). Two Indicted for Murder of Doctor. Ft. Wayne Journal-Gazette. P1, 10
305. Watson, F. (2016, April 15). Phone Interview.
306. Shelbyville Democrat. (2 December 1913). Defense to Reply on Suicide and Alibi. Shelbyville Democrat. p.1.
307. It is unknown what Spaan meant by this.
308. Shelbyville Democrat. (2 December 1913). Defense to Reply on Suicide and Alibi. Shelbyville Democrat. p.1.
309. Davis, G.C. (2 December 1913). Spann Brings Spirits into Murder Trial. Indianapolis Evening Sun. pp.1, 9.
310. Indianapolis Star. (3 December 1913). Defense Seeks to Prove Knabe Death a Suicide.. Indianapolis Star. p. 1,4
311. The Day Book. (3 December 1913). Dr. Knabe "Sweet and Pure". The Day Book. p6.
312. Indianapolis Star. (4 December 1913).Point is Scored by Defense at Dr. Craig Trial. Indianapolis Star. pp 1,9.
313. Shelbyville Democrat. (6 December 1913). Touching Description of Dr. Helene Knabe. Shelbyville Democrat. p.1.
314. Indianapolis Star. (7 December 1913). Thrills Scarce in Craig Trial . Indianapolis Star. pp. 1, 9.
315. Indianapolis Star. (7 December 1913). Thrills Scarce in Craig Trial . Indianapolis Star. pp. 1, 9.
316. Indianapolis News. (8 December 1913).Acquittal of Craig is Asked by Spaan. Indianapolis News. pp.1, 12.
317. Indianapolis News. (8 December 1913).Acquittal of Craig is Asked by Spaan. Indianapolis News. pp.1, 12.

318. Indianapolis Star. (9 December 1913). Court Reserves Ruling on Plea to Acquit Craig . Indianapolis Star. p. 1, 11.
319. Watson, F. (2016, April 15). Phone Interview.
Indianapolis News. (9 December 1913). Craig Innocent of the Charge. Indianapolis News. p.1, 12.
Shelbyville Democrat. (9 December 1913). Important Decision Ending Craig Trial. Shelbyville Democrat. pp.1.
Shelbyville Democrat. (9 December 1913). Dr. Craig is Freed by Action of Judge Blair. Shelbyville Democrat. pp.1.
320. Shelbyville Republican. (9 December 1913). Dr. Wm. B. Craig was Dismissed. Shelbyville Republican. Pp.1
321. Indianapolis News. (9 December 1913). Full Text of Judge Blair's Decision Ordering the Acquittal of Dr. Craig. *Indianapolis News*. p.12.
322. Indianapolis Star. (10 December 1913). Court Shatters State's Charge and Frees Craig . Indianapolis Star. p.1,6.
323. Shelbyville Republican. (9 December 1913). Dr. Wm. B. Craig was Dismissed. Shelbyville Republican. pp.1
324. Indianapolis Star. (10 December 1913). Editorial. Indianapolis Star. p.8.
325. Indianapolis News. (18 December 1913). Who Put the Stains on the Knabe Kimono. Indianapolis News. p.1.
326. Indianapolis Star. (19 December 1913). Deny Seeing Blood on Kimono at First. Indianapolis Star. p.15.
327. When the author originally wrote this, she wondered why the judge wasn't more up on the case and asking more questions. After all, he should have had access to the Grand Jury testimony and actions. However, it is not the place of the judge to question what a prosecutor does. The judge needs to decide if it is a sound idea. If anyone should have been making objections, it should have been the State, but since the State was the party making the Statement, there was no one to advocate for Dr. Knabe.
328. Indianapolis Star. (19 December 1913). Deny Seeing Blood on Kimono at First. Indianapolis Star. p.15.
329. Indianapolis News. (1 November 1911). To Take Last Look at the Knabe Flat. Indianapolis News. pp.1, 17.
330. Indianapolis Sun. (10 February 1912). Women Place Knabe Case in Sleuth's Hand. Indianapolis Sun. pp.1, 9.
331. Sadly, Craig would never be able to be retried in a criminal case, but a civil suit wouldn't have been out of the question.

Where are they Now?

The following materials were used, among other reference material in the Bibliography, in creating the biographies of each person. There are also a few notes about the people included.

Augusta Knabe
Indianapolis Star (15 August 1954). Miss Knabe Dies; Former Teacher. Indianapolis Star. p. 50.

Some undocumented sources, state she arrived in 1884 but this is not true. There was an Augusta Knabe who did arrive in 1884 but it is not the same one.
State of Indiana. (n.d.). Marion County Naturalizations (Augusta Knabe). State of Indiana. Retrieved from https://secure.in.gov/apps/iara/search/Home/Detail?rId=915590

Katherine McPhereson
Aldridge, B. (1971, November). Who Killed Dr. Helene Knabe, Part 1. Indianapolis Magazine. 16-21.
Aldridge, B. (1971, December). Who Killed Dr. Helene Knabe, Part 2. Indianapolis Magazine. 18-21.
Aldridge, B. (1972, January). Who Killed Dr. Helene Knabe, Part 3. Indianapolis Magazine. 22-23, 34-38.

Franz Kropp
An article written online states he immigrated in 1867 but this is a different Franz Kropp. His son Karl was born in Germany in 1877. In the 1900 census and others, it states he immigrated in 1879.
Indianapolis News. (28 April 1915). Witness In Knabe Case Found Dead in Hotel.. Indianapolis News. p1.

Dr. William B. Craig
State standards for education were getting stronger and affliation with a university due to Flexnor's Report in 1910 was becoming more attractive. The records for the school, its students and its staff seem to be lost to time, unless a individual has them in a private collection. After the school closed the Indianapolis College of Pharmacy bought the grounds where it stayed for 25 years.

Dr. T. Victor Keene
Findagrave.com. (n.d.) T. Victor Keene Memorial. Findagrave.com. Retrieved from http://www.findagrave.com/cgi-bin/g.i?page=gr&GSln=keene&GSiman=1&GScid=84781&GRid=45928899&

Katherine Fleming
Carroll, S. (2016, March 6). Email correspondence.

Alonzo M. Ragsdale
Marion County, Indiana; Index to Marriage Record 1901 - 1905 Inclusive Vol, Original Record Located: County Clerk's Office Ind; Book:37; Page: 193.

Dr. John W. Sluss
Indianapolis Daily Star. (21 December 1961). Dr. John W. Sluss Dies; Physician Since 1890s. Indianapolis Star. p. 26.

Dr. W.T.S. Dodds
Indianapolis Medical Journal. (1916 January-December). Death of Dr. W.T.S. Dodds.. Indianapolis Medical Journal. 19 (261).
Indianapolis News. (23 May 1916). Dr. W.T.S. Dodds Dead of Acute Heart Disease. Indianapolis News. p19.

Frank Flanner
Indianapolis News. (17 February 1912). F.W. Flanner Drinks Poison; Dies in Chapel Indianapolis News. p.1.
Findagrave.com. (n.d.) Frank Flanner Memorial. Findagrave.com. Retrieved from http://www.findagrave.com/cgi-bin/fg.cgi?page=gr&GRid=31619183

Detective Harry C. Webster
Apparently he did well in 1900 that his wife's father was their bookkeeper and they had a housekeeper, Frances Bybee, a negro
Ancestry.com. Indiana, Select Marriages Index, 1748-1993 [database on-line]. Provo, UT, USA: Ancestry.com Operations, Inc., 2014. Retrieved from http://search.ancestry.com/cgi-bin/sse.dll?gss=angs-g&new=1&rank=1&msT=1&gsfn=Harry+C&gsfn_x=0&gsln=Webster&gsln_x=0&msypn__ftp=Philadelphia%2c+Philadelphia%2c+Pennsylvania%2c+USA&msypn=15153&msypn_PInfo=8-%7c0%7c1652393%7c0%7c2%7c3244%7c41%7c0%7c2341%7c15153%7c0%7c&MSAV=0&msbdy=1858&cp=0&catbucket=rstp&pcat=ROOT_CATEGORY&h=3487910&db=FS1INMarriages1780to1992&indiv=1&ml_rpos=1

Harry Tutewiler
Indianapolis Daily Star. (2 December 1931). Suspended Fine of $10 on Tutewiler. Indianapolis Star. p. 22.
Ancestry.com. U.S., Social Security Applications and Claims Index, 1936-2007 [database on-line]. Provo, UT, USA: Ancestry.com Operations, Inc., 2015. Retrieved from http://search.ancestry.com/cgi-bin/sse.dll?gss=angs-c&new=1&rank=1&msT=1&gsfn=harry+dunn&gsfn_x=0&gsln=tutewiler&gsln_x=0&mswpn__ftp=Indianapolis%2c+Marion%2c+Indiana%2c+USA&mswpn=40138&mswpn_PInfo=8-%7c0%7c1652393%7c0%7c2%7c3247%7c17%7c0%7c1893%7c40138%7c0%7c&MSAV=0&cp=0&catbucket=rstp&pcat=34&h=4328082&recoff=5+6+7&db=Numident&indiv=1&ml_rpos=3

Dr. Lillian Crockett-Lowder
Aldridge, B. (1971, November). Who Killed Dr. Helene Knabe, Part 1. Indianapolis Magazine. 16-21.
Aldridge, B. (1971, December). Who Killed Dr. Helene Knabe, Part 2. Indianapolis Magazine. 18-21.
Aldridge, B. (1972, January). Who Killed Dr. Helene Knabe, Part 3. Indianapolis Magazine. 22-23, 34-38.
Official Gazette of the United States Patent Office (20 August 1918) Hygienic Garment Supporter. United States Patent Office. Volume 253(586)
United States. (26 June 1922)Toy Patent (LC Lowder). United States. US2001/0028505 Retrieved from https://www.google.ch/patents/USD63652
Catalogue of Copyright Entries (1918). White (The) Flame. Washington, DC: Government Printing Office. vol. 15 2(1113)

John Milo Maxwell
Aldridge, B. (1971, November). Who Killed Dr. Helene Knabe, Part 1. Indianapolis Magazine. 16-21.
Aldridge, B. (1971, December). Who Killed Dr. Helene Knabe, Part 2. Indianapolis Magazine. 18-21.

Aldridge, B. (1972, January). Who Killed Dr. Helene Knabe, Part 3. Indianapolis Magazine. 22-23, 34-38.

Northwestern University Library. (n.d.). Guide to the John M. Maxwell Papers. Northwestern University Library. Retrieved from http://findingaids.library.northwestern.edu/catalog/inu-ead-spec-archon-101

Nancy Tenant

Ancestry.com. 1920 United States Federal Census [database on-line] for Nancy Tenant. Provo, UT, USA: Ancestry.com Operations Inc, 2010. Images reproduced by FamilySearch. Retrieved from http://interactive.ancestry.com/6061/4300651_00628?pid=67694018&backurl=http%3a%2f%2fsearch.ancestry.com%2f%2fcgi-bin%2fsse.l%3fdb%3d1920usfedcen%26indiv%3dtry%26h%3d67694018&treeid=&personid=&hintid=&usePUB=true

Congressional Series of United States Public Documents. (1 February 1895). Report No. 864. 53rd COngress. Volume 3289(0). Retrieved from https://books.google.com/s?id=KTNHAQAAIAAJ&pg=PR115&lpg=PR115&dq=%22samuel+f.+tenant%22&source=bl&ots=xKfRFS5b1a&sig=q1XL5fDN05iBGRDq4PR6ZkS-

United States Congress. (1895). United States at Large: Chapter 21- An Act to Pension Samuel F. Tenant. United States Congress. 28 (1034) Retrieved from https://books.google.com/s?id=AWM2AQAAMAAJ&pg=PA1034&lpg=PA1034&dq=%22samuel+f.+tenant%22&source=bl&ots=4jQFVysFC7&sig=1FSzGJ42v8PizE9DHMBSgfOMgfs&hl=en&sa=X&ved=0ahUKEwj067jW2pXMAhVBvIMKHcIfADkQ6AEINTAH#v=onepage&q=%22samuel%20f.%20nt%22&f=falseEwj067jW2pXMAhVBvIMKHcIfADkQ6AEILjAE#v=onepage&q=%22samuel%20f.%20tenant%22&f=false

National Archives and Records Administration. U.S., Civil War Pension Index: General Index to Pension Files, 1861-1934 [database on-line] for Samuel F. Tenant. Provo, UT, USA: Ancestry.com Operations Inc, 2000. Retrieve from http://search.ancestry.com/cgi-bin/sse.dll?gss=angs-c&new=1&rank=1&gsfn=samuel+f.&gsfn_x=0&gsln=tenant&gsln_x=0&msbpn__hio&msddy=1899&pcat=39&h=1678034&recoff=4+5+6+20&db=civilwarpension&indiv=1&ml_rpos=3

National Archives and Records Administration. U.S., Civil War Pension Index: General Index to Pension Files, 1861-1934 [database on-line] for Samuel F. Tenant. Provo, UT, USA: Ancestry.com Operations Inc, 2000. Retrived from http://search.ancestry.com/cgi-bin/sse.dll?gss=angs-c&new=1&rank=1&gsfn=samuel+f.&gsfn_x=0&gsln=tenant&gsln_x=0&msbpn__p=ohio&msddy=1899&pcat=39&h=1678035&recoff=4+5+6&db=civilwarpension&indiv=1&ml_rpos=4

Spencer County, Indiana; Index to Supplemental Record Marriage Transcript 1, W. P. A. Original Record Located: County Clerk's O; Book: C-1; (Bettie Tenant)retrieved from Page: 91http://search.ancestry.com/cgi-bin/sse.dll?indiv=1&db=inmarr1880&h=2861997&tid=&pid=&usePUB=true&rhSource=60281

Dr. Loy McAfee (Inghram)

New York Times. (16 November 1913). Wife to Use Maiden Name. New York Times. P15. http://www.newspapers.com/image/26042509/?terms=Loy%2BMcAfee%2BInghram

National Library of Medicine (n.d.) Dr. Loy McAfee. National Library of Medicine. Retrieved from https://www.nlm.nih.gov/changingthefaceofmedicine/physicians/biography_356.html

Jerimiah "Jerry" Kinney
Findagrave.com. (n.d.) Jeremiah E. KinneyMemorial. Findagrave.com. Retrieved from http://www.findagrave.com/cgi-bin/g.i?page=gr&GSln=Kinney&GSbyrel=all&GSdy=1931&GSdyrel=in&GScntry=4&GSob=n&GSsr=41&GRid=134394091&df=all&
Findagrave.com. (n.d.) Jeremiah E. Kinney Memorial. Findagrave.com. Retrieved from http://www.findagrave.com/cgi-bin/g.i?page=gr&GSln=Kinney&GSbyrel=all&GSdy=1931&GSdyrel=in&GScntry=4&GSob=n&GSsr=41&GRid=134394091&df=all&
Indianapolis Daily Star. (11 June 1931). Kinney Obituary. Indianapolis Star. p. 18.
Aldridge, B. (1971, November). Who Killed Dr. Helene Knabe, Part 1. Indianapolis Magazine. 16-21.
Aldridge, B. (1971, December). Who Killed Dr. Helene Knabe, Part 2. Indianapolis Magazine. 18-21.
Aldridge, B. (1972, January). Who Killed Dr. Helene Knabe, Part 3. Indianapolis Magazine. 22-23, 34-38.
Indianapolis Star. (10 June 1931). Persons from all Walks of Life Praise Kinney-Man and Policeman. Indianapolis Star. p. 10.

John Mullin
Indianapolis Star. (13 October 1958). John Mullin Noted Police Officer Dies. Indianapolis Star. p. 11.
Indianapolis Star. (13 January 1957). Bulldog Mullin is a Living Legend. Indianapolis Star. p. 21.

William A. Holtz
Indianapolis Star. (11 June 1931). W.A. Holtz Former Police Captain Dies; Noted as Outstanding Detective. Indianapolis Star. p. 13.

William M. Morgan
Indianapolis Mayor. (1903). Second Annual Message: Report of Bicycle Corps. Indianapolis Mayor. Indianapolis, IN: Sentinel Publishing Co. Retrieved from https://books.google.com/books?id=uTlEAQAAMAAJ&pg=PA210&lpg=PA210&dq=indianapolis+police+Otto+Simon&source=bl&ots=u-8pvDVPd-&sig=xz8_4WxUvD4RSBVfotUq6EJ8d18&hl=en&sa=X&ved=0ahUKEwiS14Gx77vLAhUKRCYKHafBDtQQ6AEIHDAA#v=onepage&q=indianapolis%20police%20Otto%20Simon&f=false
United States Census. (1920). United States Census 1920.Retrieved from http://interactive.ancestry.com/6061/4300653_00302?pid=73654958&backurl=http%3a%2f%2fsearch.ancestry.com%2f%2fcgi-bin%2fsse.dll%3fgss%3dangs-c%26new%3d1%26rank%3d1%26gsfn%3dWilliam%26gsfn_x%3d0%26gsln%3dmorgan%26gsln_x%3d0%26msrpn__p%3dIndianapolis%252c%2bMarion%252c%2bIndiana%252c%2bUSA%26msrpn%3d40138%26msrpn_PInfo%3d8-%257c0%257c1652393%257c0%257c2%257c3247%257c17%257c0%257c1893%257c40138%257c0%257c%26gskw%3dpolice%252c%2bpatrolman%26cp%3d0%26MSAV%3d06uidh%3dvx3%26pcat%3d35%26h%3d73654958%26db%3d1920usfedcen%26indiv%3d1%26ml_rpos%3d1&treeid=&personid=&hintid=&usePUB=true
United States Census. (1930). United States Census 1930.Retrieved from http://interactive.ancestry.

com/6224/4584360_00249?pid=116355296&backurl=http%3a%2f%2fsearch.ancestry.com%2f%2fcgi-bin%2fsse.dll%3fgss%3dangs-g%26new%3d1%26rank%3d1%26gsfn%3dWilliam%2bM%26gsfn_x%3d0%26gsln%3dmorgan%26gsln_x%3d0%26MSAV%3d0%26msbdy%3d1869%26msbpn__ftp%3dEngland%26msbpn%3d3251%26msbpn_PInfo%3d3-%257c0%257c0%257c3257%257c3251%257c0%257c0%257c0%257c0%257c0%257c0%257c0%257c%26msrpn__p%3dIndianapolis%252c%2bMarion%252c%2bIndiana%252c%2bUSA%26msrpn%3d40138%26msrpn_PInfo%3d8-%257c0%257c1652393%257c0%257c2%257c3247%257c17%257c0%257c1893%257c40138%257c0%257c%26gskw%3dpolice%252c%2bpatrolman%26cp%3d0%26catbucket%3drstp%26uidh%3dvx3%26pcat%3dROOT_CATEGORY%26h%3d116355296%26db%3d1930usfedcen%26indiv%3d1%26ml_rpos%3d3&treeid=&personid=&hintid=&usePUB=true

William A. Larsch
Indianapolis Star (9 July 1923)Detectives May Quit Following Shakeup. Indianapolis Star. p13.
Year: 1920; Census Place: Indianapolis Ward 14, Marion, Indiana; Roll: T625_455; Page: 8A; Enumeration District: 240; Image: 806 (William Larsh)
Year: 1930; Census Place: Indianapolis, Marion, Indiana; Roll: 615; Page: 10A; Enumeration District: 0198; Image: 417.0; FHL microfilm: 2340350 (William Larsh)
Year: 1940; Census Place: Franklin, Montgomery, Indiana; Roll: T627_1080; Page: 5A; Enumeration District:54-11(William Larsh)
Findagrave.com. (n.d.) William A. Larsh Memorial. Findagrave.com. Retrieved from http://www.findagrave.com/cgi-bin/g.i?page=gr&GSln=Larsh+&GSfn=William+&GSbyrel=all&GSdyrel=in&GScntry=4&GSob=n&GRid=42122204&df=all&

Elmer F. Hall
Findagrave.com. (n.d.) Fredrick E. Hall Memorial. Findagrave.com. Retrieved from http://www.findagrave.com/cgi-bin/fg.cgi?page=gr&GRid=29288626
Findagrave.com. (n.d.) Eva Powell Hall Memorial. Findagrave.com. Retrieved from http://www.findagrave.com/cgi-bin/g.i?page=gr&GSln=hall&GSfn=Eva&GSbyrel=in&GSdyrel=in&GSst=24&GScntry=4&GSob=n&GRid=24879417&df=all&
Indianapolis Star. (14 January 1946). F. Elmer Hall Obituary. *Indianapolis Star*. p. 24

Adolph Asch
Findagrave.com. (n.d.) Adolph Asch Memorial. Findagrave.com. Retrieved from http://www.findagrave.com/cgi-bin/g.i?page=gr&GSln=asch&GSfn=adolph&GSbyrel=all&GSdyrel=all&GSst=17&GScntry=4&GSob=n&GRid=101060375&df=all&
Indianapolis Star. (30 December 1914). Funeral For Detective Asch Set for Tomorrow. Indianapolis Star. p14.
Indianapolis Star. (1 January 1915). Crowd Attend Funeral Of City Detective Asch. Indianapolis Star. p13

Otto Henry Simon
Indianapolis Mayor. (1903). Second Annual Message: Report of Bicycle Corps. Indianapolis Mayor. Indianapolis, IN: Sentinel Publishing Co. Retrieved from https://books.google.com/books?id=uTlEAQAAMAAJ&pg=PA210&lpg=PA210&dq=indianapolis+police+Otto+Simo

n&source=bl&ots=u-8pvDVPd-&sig=xz8_4WxUvD4RSBVfotUq6EJ8d18&hl=en&sa=X&v-ed=0ahUKEwiS14Gx77vLAhUKRCYKHafBDtQQ6AEIHDAA#v=onepage&q=indianapolis%20police%20Otto%20Simon&f=false
Indianapolis Star. (28 October 1928). Otto Simon Obituary. Indianapolis Star. p23
Findagrave.com. (n.d.) Otto Simon Memorial. Findagrave.com. Retrieved from http://www.findagrave.com/cgi-bin/g.i?page=gr&GSln=simon&GSfn=otto&GSbyrel=all&GSdyrel=all&GSst=17&GScntry=4&GSob=n&GRid=110223659&df=all&

George M. Stewart
Indianapolis Star. (5 March 1928). Takes Own Life in Hotel Room. Indianapolis Star. p11
Findagrave.com. (n.d.) George V. Stewart. Findagrave.com. Retrieved from http://www.findagrave.com/cgi-bin/g.i?page=gr&GSln=stewart&GSfn=george&GSmn=M&GSbyrel=all&GSdyrel=all&GSst=17&GScntry=4&GSob=n&GRid=129006374&df=all&

John W. Morgan
Indianapolis Star. (24 December 1919). J.W. Morgan, Veteran City Detective Dead.. Indianapolis Star. p8.

Mayor Samuel Lewis Shank
Findagrave.com. (n.d.) Samuel Lewis Shank. Findagrave.com. Retrieved from http://www.findagrave.com/cgi-bin/g.i?page=gr&GSln=Shank&GSfn=Samuel+&GSmn=Lewis+&GSbyrel=in&GSdyrel=in&GSst=17&GScntry=4&GSob=n&GRid=34807536&df=all&
Indianpolis Star. (25 September 1927). Lew Shank, Colorful Public Leader, Dies. Indianapolis Star. p 1, 7.

Otto von Tesmar
Indianapolis Star. (1 September 1907). Local Scientist Who KnowsHuman Body.. Indianapolis Star. p.4.
Indianapolis News. (28 March 1898). Illegal Sales at Paragon. Indianapolis News. p.7
Indianapolis Star. (11 May 1904). Indiana Deaths: Mrs. Otto von Tesmar Obituary. Indianapolis Star. p.3.
Indianapolis News. (3 November 1894). Smoldering Ruins. Indianapolis News. p.1.
Indianapolis News. (2 November 1896). A Grotesque Election Bet. Indianapolis News. p.5.
Indianapolis News. (14 December 1906). Attorney Sues College.. Indianapolis News. p.25.
Indianapolis Star. (14 December 1906). Wants $3.571.43 a Day.. Indianapolis Star. p.1.
Indianapolis News. (10 January 1908). Houren Loses His Case.. Indianapolis News. p13.
Indianapolis Star. (18 October 1907). Editorial by Otto von Tesmar.. Indianapolis Star. p.6
Indianapolis News. (7 January 1910). Bear's Head is Mounted.. Indianapolis News. p. 18.

Dr. Charles O. Durham
Indianapolis Star. (19 December 1924). Apoplexy Stroke fatal to Charles Durham. Indianapolis Star. p1, 3

Dr. Frank B. Wynn
Indianapolis Medical Journal. (1922 January). Death of Dr. Frank B. Wynn.. Indianapolis Medical Journal. 25 (203).
Indianapolis Star. (28 July 1922). Dr. Wynn Killed in Fall From Cliff on Mt. Siyeh. Indianapolis Star. p.1,3.
Walters, David Clyde, "EXPLORING A DEFINITION OF LEADERSHIP AND THE BIOGRAPHY OF DR. FRANK B. WYNN" (2009). Theses, Dissertations, Professional Papers. Paper 1299. Retrieved from http://scholarworks.umt.edu/cgi/viewcontent.cgi?article=2318&context=etd

Dr. Charles E. Ferguson
Findagrave.com. (n.d.) Dr. Charles Euguene Ferguson Memorial. Findagrave.com. Retrieved from http://www.findagrave.com/cgi-bin/fg.cgi?page=gr&GRid=45937019
Kritsky, G. (1995). Charles Darwin's Hoosier Correspondent. Proceedings of the Indiana Academy of Science. 104 (81-84)

Dr. John N. Hurty
Purdue University. (n.d.). John N. Hurty Papers. Purdue University. Retreived from http://www4.lib.purdue.edu/archon/?p=collections/findingaid&id=498&q=&rootcontentid=8509

Dr. John J. Kyle
Indiana Medical Journal. (July 1899- June 1900). Dr. Ernest C. Reyer. Indiana Medical Journal. 18(45) .

Dr. Ernest C. Reyer
American Academy of Ophthalmology and Oto-Larynology. (1920). Dr. John J. Kyle. American Academy of Ophthalmology and Oto-Larynology.Volume 25(364)
Indianapolis News. (25 March 1918). Dr. Ernest Reyer Dies of Injuries at Home. Indianapolis News. p.9
Indiana Medical Journal. (July 1899- June 1900). Dr. Ernest C. Reyer. Indiana Medical Journal. 18(45)
"Indiana Marriages, 1780-1992," database, FamilySearch(https://familysearch.org/ark:/61903/1:1:XFZ5-WMT : accessed 24 April 2016), Ernest C. Reyer and Laura May Carothers, 14 Jun 1899; citing reference p 500; FHL microfilm 499,380.

Dr. Thomas and Ella Hitt
Columbus Dispatch. (27 July 1934). Ella Hitt Obituary. Columbus Dispatch. Pp 6A

Dr. Marie Rimmelin
Indianapolis News. (13 September 1919). Twenty Persons Take Oaths For Citizenship. Indianapolis News. p.2.
Indianapolis News. (6 September 1919). Engagements and Weddings. Indianapolis News. p.18.

Dr. Hannah Graham
United Mine Workers of America. (1912). Proceedings of the United Mine Workers of America. United Mine Workers of America. Indianapolis, IN: The Cheltenham-Aetna Press.

White, E.G. (24 June 1916). Rule or Ruin. The Little Paper. p.2

Dr. Etta Charles
Forkner, J. L. History of Madison County, Indiana ; a narrative account of its historical progress, its people and its principal interests (Volume 1) Etta Charles. Chicago: The Lewis Publishing Company. .p691
Ancestry.com. U.S., Quaker Meeting Records, 1681-1935 [database on-line]. Provo, UT, USA: Ancestry.com Operations, Inc., 2014.Etta Charles. Retrieved from http://interactive.ancestry.com/2189/40780_1821100519_1676-00107?pid=575192&backurl=http%3a%2f%2fsearch.ancestry.com%2f%2fcgi-bin%2fsse.dll%3fgss%3dangs-g%26new%3d1%26rank%3d1%26msT%3d1%26gsfn%3detta%26gsfn_x%3d0%26gsln%3dcharles%26gsln_x%3d0%26msypn__p%3dAnderson%252c%2bMadison%252c%2bIndiana%252c%2bUSA%26msypn%3d40102%26msypn_PInfo%3d8-%257c0%257c1652393%257c0%257c2%257c3247%257c17%257c0%257c1857%257c40102%257c0%257c%26MSAV%3d0%26cp%3d0%26catbucket%3drstp%26pcat%3dROOT3d575192%26recoff%3d3%2b4%2b27%2b39%26db%3dQuakerMeetMins%26indiv%3d1%26ml_rpos%3d30&treeid=&personid=&hintid=&usePUB=true
Indiana Department of Public Welfare. (1920). Indianapolis, IN: Statehouse.120-131(335)
<u>Netterville, J. J.</u> (1925). Centennial History of Madison County Indiana, Volumes I and II. Anderson, IN: Historians' Association.
United States Census. (1900). United States Census Etta Charles 1900.Retrieved from http://interactive.ancestry.com/7602/004118637_01107?pid=13631305&backurl=http%3a%2f%2fsearch.ancestry.com%2f%2fcgi-bin%2fsse.dll%3fgss%3dangs-g%26new%3d1%26rank%3d1%26msT%3d1%26gsfn%3detta%26gsfn_x%3d0%26gsln%3dcharles%26gsln_x%3d0%26msypn__p%3dAnderson%252c%2bMadison%252c%2bIndiana%252c%2bUSA%26msypn%3d40102%26msypn_PInfo%3d8-%257c0%257c1652393%257c0%257c2%257c3247%257c17%257c0%257c1857%257c40102%257c0%257c%26MSAV%3d0%26cp%3d0%26catbucket%3drstp%26pcat%3dROOT_CATEGORY%26h%3d13631305%26db%3d1900usfedcen%26indiv%3d1%26ml_rpos%3d25&treeid=&personid=&hintid=&usePUB=true
Baldwin and Hudson. (1939). Anderson City Directory.Baldwin and Hudson. Retrieved from http://interactive.ancestry.com/2469/10806359?pid=1142309534&backurl=http%3a%2f%2fsearch.ancestry.com%2f%2fcgi-bin%2fsse.dll%3fgss%3dangs-g%26new%3d1%26rank%3d1%26msT%3d1%26gsfn%3detta%26gsfn_x%3d0%26gsln%3dcharles%26gsln_x%3d0%26msypn__p%3dAnderson%252c%2bMadison%252c%2bIndiana%252c%2bUSA%26msypn%3d40102%26msypn_PInfo%3d8-%257c0%257c1652393%257c0%257c2%257c3247%257c17%257c0%257c1857%257c40102%257c0%257c%26MSAV%3d0%26cp%3d0%26catbucket%3drstp%26pcat%3dROOT_CATEGORY%26h%3d1142309534%26db%3dUSDirectories%26indiv%3d1%26ml_rpos%3d14&treeid=&personid=&hintid=&usePUB=true#?imageId=10806520
Terre Haute Tribune. (17 July 1949). Doctor Dies. Terre Haute Tribune. p. 12.

Dr. Jane Ketcham
University Library (2015). Jane Merrill Ketcham, M.D. University Library. Retrieved from http://www2.ulib.iupui.edu/womencreatingexcellence/ketcham

Dr. Amelia Keller
University Library (2015). Amelia Keller, M.D. University Library. Retrieved from http://www2.ulib.iupui.edu/womencreatingexcellence/ameliakeller
Findagrave.com. (n.d.) Amelia Keller Memorial. Findagrave.com. Retrieved from http://www.findagrave.com/cgi-bin/g.i?page=gr&GSln=Keller&GSfn=amelia&GSbyrel=in&GSdyrel=in&GSst=17&GScntry=4&GSob=n&GRid=45929135&df=all&

Dr. Nettie Bainbridge Powell
Whitson, R.L., Campbell, J.P. & Goldthwait, E.L. (1914). Centennial History of Grant County, Indiana, 1812 to 1912 . Chicago: The Lewis Publishing Co. Volume 2 (1024-25)

Dr. John Freeland
Indianapolis Star. (7 April 1943). Dr. Freeland Obituary. Indianapolis Star. p5.
Indianapolis News. (16 May 1912).Vote of Confidence in Dr. John L. Freeland. pp. 12.
Indianapolis Star. (6 April 1943). Dr. Freeland Dies; Headed to Hospital. Indianapolis Star. p. 11.

Dr. John Kolmer
Findagrave.com. (n.d.) Dr. John Kolmer Memorial. Findagrave.com. Retrieved from http://www.findagrave.com/cgi-bin/g.i?page=gr&GSln=kolmer&GSfn=john&GSbyrel=in&GSdyrel=in&GSst=17&GScntry=4&GSob=n&GRid=45934062&df=all&
Indianapolis News. (22 October 1917).Funeral of Dr. Kolmer to be Held Wednesday. p. 22.
Indianapolis News. (20 April 1898).Dr. John Kolmer. P 16.
Gross, C. G. (1999) A Hole in the Head. History of Neuroscience.Vol5 4(263-269). Retreived fromhttps://www.princeton.edu/~cggross/neuroscientist_99_hole.pdf
Indianapolis News. (22 February 1918).Dr. John Kolmer Estate Ad. p. 34.
Indianapolis News. (30 June 1914).Brass band can play at this sound-proof flat and not disturb the neighbors, architect say. P 4
Indianapolis News. (1 November 1917).Bequests of Dr. Kolmer. p. 5.

Blanche Lindley
Unknown. (n.d.). Decisions of National Labor Relations Board. Vol67 161(p1233).
Paper. (29 July 1914). Paper Plant to be Operated in Dayton. Paper. p. 32/

Seth Nichols
Wichita Beacon. (2 April 1912). Deserter Says He Killed Woman. Wichita Beacon. P.1
The Scranton Truth (3 April 1912). Nichols, Alleged Murderer, is Said Not To Be Sane. The Scranton Truth. p. 8.

Judge Joseph T. Markey
Ancestry.com. U.S., World War I Draft Registration Cards, 1917-1918 [database on-line]. Provo, UT, USA: Ancestry.com Operations Inc, 2005. Seth Nichols Retrieved from http://interactive.ancestry.com/6482/005253664_05427?pid=34111700&backurl=http%3a%2f%2fsearch.ancestry.com%2f%2fcgi-bin%2fsse.dll%3fgss%3dangs-c%26new%3d1%26rank%3d1%26msT%3d1%26gsfn%3dseth%2bt.

%26gsfn_x%3d0%26gsln%3dnichols%26gsln_x%3d0%26msbdy%3d1890%26msbpn__p%3dInd
ia%26uidh%3dvx3%26pcat%3d39%26h%3d34111700%26db%3dWW1draft%26indiv%3d1%26ml_
rpos%3d1&treeid=&personid=&hintid=&usePUB=true
The Indianapolis News (19 October 1952). Joseph Thomas Markey Obituary. Indianapolis News. p.19.
The Indianapolis Star (19 October 1952). Judge Joseph Markey Dies, Rites Tomorrow. Indianapolis Star. p.32.

Fred McAllister
The Indianapolis Star (29 December 1927). Municipal Judge Takes Own Life. Indianapolis Star. p.9
The Indianapolis Star (30 December 1927). Bar Association Plans to Honor M'Allister. Indianapolis Star. p.8.

Frank Baker
The Indianapolis Star (19 July 1948). Frank Baker, Ex-Judge Dies. Indianapolis Star. pp.1, 4.
The Indianapolis Star (20 July 1948). Good Jurist, Good Citizen. Indianapolis Star. p.12.
Findagrave.com. (n.d.)Frank Pierce Baker Memorial. Findagrave.com. Retrieved from http://www.findagrave.com/cgi-bin/g.i?page=gr&GSln=baker&GSfn=frank&GSmn=p&GSbyrel=all&GSdy=1939&GSdyrel=after&GSst=17&GScntry=4&GSob=n&GRid=15715057&df=all&
Indianapolis Stat (25 July 1948).Frank P. Baker Burial Permit. Indianapolis Star. p. 21.

Eph Inman
Smithsonian Magazline. (30 August 1912). "Murder Wasn't Very Pretty": The Rise and Fall of D.C. Stephenson. Smithsonian Magazine. Retrieved from http://www.smithsonianmag.com/history/murder-wasnt-very-pretty-the-rise-and-fall-of-dc-stephenson-18935042/#8Ba5mQ3MbyleWf9f.99
Findagrave.com. (n.d.) Ephriam Inman Memorial. Findagrave.com. Retrieved from http://www.findagrave.com/cgi-bin/g.i?page=gr&GSln=+Inman&GSfn=Eph&GSbyrel=all&GSdyrel=after&GScntry=4&GSob=n&GRid=45927479&df=all&
Indianapolis Star. (9 February 1935). Ephriam Inman, 69 Noted Lawyer, Dies. Indinianapolis Star. p. 1.
Indianapolis Star. (13 January 1913). Strengthen Council For Dr. Knabe Case. p. 14.

Judge Alonz Blair
Findagrave.com. (n.d.) Alonzo Blair Memorial. Findagrave.com. Retrieved from http://www.findagrave.com/cgi-bin/g.i?page=gr&GSln=blair&GSfn=alonzo&GSbyrel=all&GSdyrel=all&GSst=17&GScntry=4&GSob=n&GRid=14105480&df=all&

Henry Spaan
He is SPAAN but everyone spells it Spann.
Indianapolis Star. (19 May 1935). Henry N. Spaan,Attorney, is Dead. Indianapolis Star. p8
Indianapolis Star. (20 May 1935). Henry Spaan Loved Nature, Friend Said. Indianapolis Star. p10
Ancestry.com. U.S. Naturalization Record Indexes, 1791-1992 (Indexed in World Archives Project) [database on-line]. Provo, UT, USA: Ancestry.com Operations, Inc., 2010. Hendrik Spaan. Retrieved from http://interactive.ancestry.com/1629/31192_118251-08908?pid=4955089&backurl=http%3a%2f%2fsearch.ancestry.com%2f%2fcgi-bin%2fsse.dll%3fgss%3dangs-c%26new%3d1%26rank%3d1%26gsfn%3dhenry%2bn%26gsfn_x%3d0%26gsln%3dspaan%26gsln_x%3d0%26msbdy%3

d1851%26msbpn__ftp%3dholland%26cp%3d0%26MSAV%3d1%26uidh%3dvx3%26pcat%3dIMG_CITIZENSHIP%26h%3d4955089%26recoff%3d5%2b6%26db%3dUSnatindex_awap%26indiv%3d1%26ml_rpos%3d1&treeid=&personid=&hintid=&usePUB=true#?imageId=31192_118251-08908
Findagrave.com. (n.d.) Henry Spaan Memorial. Findagrave.com. Retrieved from http://www.findagrave.com/cgi-bin/fg.cgi?page=gr&GRid=46015388&ref=acom
Ancestry.com. Indiana, Select Marriages Index, 1748-1993 [database on-line]. Provo, UT, USA: Ancestry.com Operations, Inc., 2014. Henry Spaan Retrieved from http://search.ancestry.com/cgi-bin/sse.dll?gss=angs-c&new=1&rank=1&gsfn=henry+n&gsfn_x=0&gsln=spaan&gsln_x=0&msypn__ftp=Indianapolis%2c+Marion%2c+Indiana%2c+USA&msypn=40138&msypn_PInfo=8-%7c0%7c1652393%7c0%7c2%7c3247%7c17%7c0%7c1893%7c40138%7c0%7c&mssng=cornelia&mssns=spann&cp=0&MSAV=1&uidh=vx3&pcat=34&h=859649&db=FS1INMarriages1780to1992&indiv=1&ml_rpos=3

William Ketcham
Findagrave.com. (n.d.Capt William A. Ketchamr Memorial. Findagrave.com. Retrieved from http://www.findagrave.com/cgi-bin/g.i?page=gr&GSln=baker&GSfn=frank&GSmn=p&GSbyrel=all&GSdy=1939&GSdyrel=after&GSst=17&GScntry=4&GSob=n&GRid=15715057&df=all&
Ft. Wayne Sentinel. (27 December 1921). Ex-Commander in Chief of G.A.R. Passes Away. Ft. Wayne Sentinel. p.3.

Epilogue

Kozinski, A. (2015). Criminal Law 2.0. Georgetown Law Journal 44th Annual Review of Criminal Procedure. Retreived from http://georgetownlawjournal.org/files/2015/06/Kozinski_Preface.pdf

Photograph Credits

Page	Source
13	Dunn, J.P. (1910). *Greater Indianapolis: The History, the Industries, the Institutions, and the People of a City of Homes (Vols 1-2)*. Chicago: The Lewis Publishing Company.
17, 18, 20-23, 25-32	Nicole and Michael Kobrowski's collection
33	*Both:* The Medical Student. (1907). A Parting Word to the Class of I.M.C 1907. The Medical Student. *Vol 5 8(10)*.
35	Cumback, W. & Maynard, J.B. (1899). *Men of progress, Indiana : a selected list of biographical sketches and portraits of the leaders in business, professional and official life, together with brief notes of the history and character of Indiana*. Indianapolis, IN: The Indianapolis Sentinel Company.
37	*Both:* The Medical Student. (1907). A Parting Word to the Class of I.M.C 1907. The Medical Student. *Vol 5 8(23-24)*
39	*Top:* The Medical Student. (1907). A Parting Word to the Class of I.M.C 1907. The Medical Student. *Vol 5 8(39)*. *Bottom:* Nicole and Michael Kobrowski's personal collection
41-42	The Medical Student. (1907). A Parting Word to the Class of I.M.C 1907. The Medical Student. *Vol 5 8(37,41,63)*.
44	Nicole and Michael Kobrowski's personal collection
46	Baines News Service. (n.d.) Frank B. Wynn at Desk. Library of Congress.
47	The Medical Student. (1907). A Parting Word to the Class of I.M.C 1907. The Medical Student. *Vol 5 8(36)*.
48	Medical College of Indiana. (1904). Dr. Knabe's Graduation Portrait. Indiana University School of Medicine Ruth Lilly Special Collections.
49	Rice, T.B. (1946). *Hoosier Health Officer: A Biography of Dr. J. N. Hurty and The History of The Indiana State Board of Health to 1925*. Indianapolis, IN: Indiana State Board of Health.
51	Indianapolis News. (22 January 1907). Bacteriological Division of the Indiana Laboratory of Hygiene at the State House. Indianapolis News. p.11.
55	Indianapolis Star. (25 October 1911). Dr. Knabe in the Laboratory. *Indinaapolis Star*. p.4.
60	Rice, T.B. (1946). *Hoosier Health Officer: A Biography of Dr. J. N. Hurty and The History of The Indiana State Board of Health to 1925*. Indianapolis, IN: Indiana State Board of Health.
63,65	Nicole and Michael Kobrowski's personal collection
67	Nicole and Michael Kobrowski's personal collection

Page	Source
68	The Medical Student. (1907). A Parting Word to the Class of I.M.C 1907. The Medical Student. *Vol 5 8(19. 21-25).*
69	Top right and bottom: The Medical Student. (1907). *Vol 5 8(11, 17)* Top left: The Medical Student (1903). *Vol 2 6(12).*
70	Nicole and Michael Kobrowski's personal collection
71-72	Sluss, J.W. (1908). *Emergency Surgery.* Philadelphia, PA: P. Blakiston Son & Company.
73	Hurty, J. N. (1906). *Life with Health.* Indianapolis, IN: Indiana State Board of Health.
74-75	American Medical Association. (1911). Knabe Art Contest Entries. American Medical Association.
79-82	Normal College of the North American Gymnastic Union. (1911). Catalogue. Indianapolis, IN: Normal College of the North American Gymnastic Union.
84-86	Nicole and Michael Kobrowski's personal collection
88-89	Nicole and Michael Kobrowski's personal collection (1921 Indiana Veterinary College Graduation portrait)
91	Nicole and Michael Kobrowski's personal collection
96	Indianapolis News. (15 December 1913). Woman to be Secretary of the Marion Health Board. *Indianapolis News.*
100	Indianapolis Sun. (26 October 1911). Premeditated Murder is Now Held as Most Plausible Theory. Indianapolis Sun. p. 3.
101	Indianapolis News. (6 December 1913). State's Most Important Witnesses in Knabe Case. *Indianapolis News.* p. 1.
103	Indianapolis News. (24 October 1911). Delaware Flats Where Dr. Knabe Lived. *Indianapolis News..* p. 17.
106	Indianapolis News. (24 October 1911). Scene of Knabe Murder in Delaware Flats. *Indianapolis News.* p. 17.
107	*Top:* Closeup of Indianapolis News. (24 October 1911). Scene of Knabe Murder in Delaware Flats. Indianapolis News. p. 17. *Bottom:* The Medical Student. (1907). A Parting Word to the Class of I.M.C 1907. The Medical Student. *Vol 5 8(19. 21-25).*
110	Military: U.S. National Library of Medicine. (n.d.) Dr. Loy McAfee. U.S. National Library of Medicine. Inset: Medical College of Indiana. (1904). Dr. Knabe's Graduation Portrait. Indiana University School of Medicine Ruth Lilly Special Collections.
114	Indiana University. (1907). Yearbook. Indiana University.

Page	Source
115	Indiana Commission on Public Records, State Archives, (1911) Coroner Inquest Ruling for Dr. Knabe.. Indiana Commission on Public Records, State Archives.
126	Associated Indiana Cartoonists. (1913). *Club men of Indianapolis in caricature 1913*. Associated Indiana Cartoonists. Aurora, NY: The Roycrofters.
127	Indianapolis News. (11 January 1912). Dr. Hannah Graham Eats Soup in Bread Line at Tomlinson Hall; Contributes to Food Fund. *Indianapolis News*. p.3.
129	Baines News Service. (n.d.) William J. Burns. Library of Congress.
132	Wikimedia Commons. (1920). Janet Flanner. Wikimedia Commons.
135	Summitville-Van Buren Township Historical Society (n.d). Summitville Library.
137	Cumback, W. & Maynard, J.B. (1899). *Men of progress, Indiana : a selected list of biographical sketches and portraits of the leaders in business, professional and official life, together with brief notes of the history and character of Indiana*. Indianapolis, IN: The Indianapolis Sentinel Company.
142	Top: Benesch, A.B. (1901). *Men of Indiana in Nineteen Hundred and One*. Indianapolis, IN: The Benesch Publishing Company. Bottom: Indianapolis Sun. (20 June 1912). Funfest Committee is Indignant About Report of Bar on Fairbank's Lawn. *Indianapolis Sun*.
145	Nicole and Michael Kobrowski's personal collection
147	Top: City of Indianapolis.(1910-1912) Annual Report of the City Court of Indianapolis, City of Indianapolis.Vols. 1-3. Bottom: Indiana Commission on Public Records, State Archives, (n.d.) Marion County Employee Records and Photos. Indiana Commission on Public Records, State Archives.
148	Indiana Commission on Public Records, State Archives, (n.d.) Marion County Employee Records and Photos. Indiana Commission on Public Records, State Archives.
149	*Top and bottom left:* Indiana Commission on Public Records, State Archives, (n.d.) Marion County Employee Records and Photos. Indiana Commission on Public Records, State Archives. *Bottom right:* Indianapolis News. (30 April 1910). Police Tragedies and Battles Recalled in Other Years By Killing of Patrolman Joseph Krupp. Indianapolis News.p.15.
153	Associated Indiana Cartoonists. (1913) *Club men of Indianapolis in caricature 1913*. Associated Indiana Cartoonists. Aurora, NY: The Roycrofters.
154	Indianapolis News. (4 April 1912). Nichols Takes it Back; Did not Kill Dr. Knabe. *Indianapolis News*. p.2.
162	Benesch, A.B. (1901). *Men of Indiana in Nineteen Hundred and One*. Indianapolis, IN: The Benesch Publishing Company.

Page	Source
168	Top: Nicole and Michael Kobrowski's personal collection Bottom: Indianapolis News. (31 December 1912). Dr. W.B. Craig and A.M. Ragsdale Indicted in Helene Knabe Case. *Indianapolis News*.
169	Marion County Courts. (1912). Indictment of Dr. William B. Craig and Alonzo Ragsdale. Marion County Courts.
181	Sluss, J.W. (1908). *Emergency Surgery*. Philadelphia, PA: P. Blakiston Son & Company.
186-187	Shelbyville Republican. (4 December 1913). Dr. Wm. B. Craig is Now on Trial. *Shelbyville Republican*. p.1.
191	Boetcker, W. J. H. (1902). *Picturesque Shelbyville : representing the official, business and social relations of Shelbyville, Indiana*. Shelbyville, IN: Reverend William J. H. Boetcker.
192	Indianapolis News. (3 December 1913). Guards the Knabe Case Jury. *Indianapolis News*. p. 6.
193	Indianapolis News. (29 November 1913). Defendant, Daughter, and One of His Lawyers. *Indianapolis News*.
194	Indianapolis News. (8 December 1913). Jurors in the Knabe Case at Shelbyville Taking an Early Morning Stroll.. *Indianapolis News*.
200	Indianapolis Sun (30 November 1913). Slain Doctor's Cousin. *Indianapolis Sun*. p.1.
203	Indianapolis Sun. (31 October 1911). Harry W. Haskett. *Indianapolis Sun*.
207	Katherine A. Fleming courtesy of the Steve Carroll Family
209	Both: Boetcker, W. J. H. (1902). *Picturesque Shelbyville : representing the official, business and social relations of Shelbyville, Indiana*. Shelbyville, IN: Reverend William J. H. Boetcker.
211	Indianapolis News. (29 November 1913). Defendant, Daughter, and One of His Lawyers. *Indianapolis News*.
219	Shelbyville County Courts. (1913). Dr. Craig Not Guilty Jury Decision. Shelbyville County Courts.
222, 224, 247, 253-260	Nicole and Michael Kobrowski's personal collection

Bibliography

This book was a massive research undertaking. It is no surprise the bibliography is so rich and full. Many of these resources were used in a general way to triangulate information. Others were specifically used in the chapter notes section for direct quotes or information that would be easier to find with this information.

Abram, R. J (Ed.). (1985). *Send Us a Lady Physician: Women Doctors in America 1835-1920*. New York: W.W. Norton & Company.

Aldridge, B. (1971, November). Who Killed Dr. Helene Knabe, Part 1. *Indianapolis Magazine. 16-21.*

Aldridge, B. (1971, December). Who Killed Dr. Helene Knabe, Part 2. *Indianapolis Magazine. 18-21.*

Aldridge, B. (1972, January). Who Killed Dr. Helene Knabe, Part 3. *Indianapolis Magazine. 22-23, 34-38.*

American Academy of Ophthalmology and Oto-Larynology. (1920). Dr. John J. Kyle. *American Academy of Ophthalmology and Oto-Larynology. Volume 25(364).*

American Medical Association. (1906 January-June). Society Proceedings. American Medical Association.

American Medical Association. (1910). Public Health Education Committee Report of Work for the Year 1909-1910. American Medical Association.

American Medical Association. (1910). Society Proceedings. American Medical Association. 21 (1833-1837)

Ancestry.com. *1871 Scotland Census* [database on-line]. Provo, UT, USA: Ancestry.com Operations Inc, 2007. Parish: *Maybole*; ED: *15*; Page: *5*; Line: *7*; Roll: *CSSCT1871_113*

Ancestry.com. *1881 Scotland Census* [database on-line]. Provo, UT, USA: Ancestry.com Operations Inc, 2007. Parish: *Maybole*; ED: *15*; Page: *12*; Line: *22*; Roll: *cssct1881_193*

Ancestry.com. *1920 United States Federal Census* [database on-line] for Nancy Tenant. Provo, UT, USA: Ancestry.com Operations Inc, 2010. Images reproduced by FamilySearch. Retrieved from http://interactive.ancestry.com/6061/4300651_00628?pid=67694018&backurl=http%3a%2f%2fsearch.ancestry.com%2f%2fcgi-bin%2fsse.b%3d1920usfedcen%26indiv%3dtry%26h%3d67694018&treeid=&personid=&hintid=&usePUB=true

Ancestry.com. *Berlin, Germany, Marriages, 1874-1920* [database on-line] (Otto Windschild). Provo, UT, USA: Ancestry.com Operations, Inc., 2014.

Ancestry.com. *Canadian Passenger Lists, 1865-1935* [database on-line]. Provo, UT, USA: Ancestry.com Operations Inc, 2010.

Ancestry.com. *Cook County, Illinois Death Index, 1908-1988* [database on-line] (Otto von Tesmar). Provo, UT, USA: Ancestry.com Operations Inc, 2008.

Ancestry.com. *California, Death Index, 1940-1997* [database on-line]. Provo, UT, USA: Ancestry.com Operations Inc, 2000.

Ancestry.com. (n.d.) Fact Tree. Ancestry.com Retrieved from http://person.ancestry.com/tree/6385269/person/25344727799/facts

Ancestry.com. *Illinois, Deaths and Stillbirths Index, 1916-1947* [database on-line] (Otto von Tesmar). Provo, UT, USA: Ancestry.com Operations, Inc., 2011.

Ancestry.com. *Indiana, Select Marriages Index, 1748-1993* [database on-line]. Provo, UT, USA: Ancestry.com Operations, Inc., 2014. Henry Spaan Retrieved from http://search.ancestry.com/cgi-bin/sse.dll?gss=angs-c&new=1&rank=1&gsfn=henry+n&gsfn_x=0&gsln=spaan&gsln_x=0&msypn__ftp=Indianapolis%2c+Marion%2c+Indiana%2c+USA&msypn=40138&msypn_PInfo=8-%7c0%7c1652393%7c0%7c2%7c3247%7c17%7c0%7c1893%7c40138%7c0%7c&mssng=cornelia&mssns=spann&cp=0&MSAV=1&uidh=vx3&pcat=34&h=859649&db=FS1INMarriages1780to1992&indiv=1&ml_rpos=3

Ancestry.com. *Indiana, Select Marriages Index, 1748-1993* [database on-line]. Provo, UT, USA: Ancestry.com Operations, Inc., 2014. Retrieved from http://search.ancestry.com/cgi-bin/sse.dll?gss=angs-g&new=1&rank=1&msT=1&gsfn=Harry+C&gsfn_x=0&gsln=Webster&gsln_x=0&msypn__ftp=Philadelphia%2c+Philadelphia%2c+Pennsylvania%2c+USA&msypn=15153&msypn_PInfo=8-%7c0%7c1652393%7c0%7c2%7c3244%7c41%7c0%7c2341%7c15153%7c0%7c&MSAV=0&msbdy=1858&cp=0&catbucket=rstp&pcat=ROOT_CATEGORY&h=3487910&db=FS1INMarriages1780to1992&indiv=1&ml_rpos=1

Ancestry.com. *Kentucky Death Index, 1911-2000* [database on-line] (Seth Nichols). Provo, UT, USA: Ancestry.com Operations Inc, 2000.

Ancestry.com. *Kentucky, Death Records, 1852-1963* [database on-line] (Seth Nichols). Provo, UT, USA: Ancestry.com Operations Inc, 2007.

Registration State: *Ohio*; Registration County: *Hamilton*; Roll: *1819889*; Draft Board: *09*

Ancestry.com. *Massachusetts, Marriage Records, 1840-1915* [database on-line]. Provo, UT, USA: Ancestry.com Operations, Inc., 2013.(for Mary McHale) Retrieved from http://interactive.ancestry.com/2511/41262_b132082-00300?pid=8861316&backurl=http%3a%2f%2fsearch.ancestry.com%2f%2fcgi-bin%2fsse.dll%3fgss%3dangs-c%26new%3d1%26rank%3d1%26gsfn%3dmary%2ba%2b%26gsfn_x%3d0%26gsln%3dmchale%26gsln_x%3d0%26msbdy%3d1895%26msgdd%3d6%26msgdm%3d11%26msgdy%3d1911%26msgpn__dBoston%252c%2bSuffolk%252c%2bMassachusetts%252c%2bUSA%26msgpn%3d4668%26msgpn_PInfo%3d8-%257c0%257c1652393%257c0%257c2%257c3242%257c24%257c0%257c2812%257c4668%257c0%257c%26msypn__p%3dPawtucket%252c%2bProvidence%252c%2bRhode%2bIsland%252c%2bUSA%26msypn%3d5530%26msypn_PInfo%3d8-%257c0%257c1652393%257c0%257c2%257c3242%257c42%257c0%257c2441%257c5530%257c0%257c%26mssng%3dseth%26mssns%3dnichols%26cp%3d0%26MSAV%3d0%26uidh%3dvx3%26pcat%3dBMD_d8861316%26recoff%3d5%2b6%2b7%26db%3dMAMarriageRecords%26indiv%3d1%26ml_rpos%3d1&treeid=&personid=&hintid=&usePUB=true

Ancestry.com. *Registers of Patients at Naval Hospitals, 1812 - 1934* [database on-line] (Seth Nichols). Provo, UT, USA: Ancestry.com Operations, Inc., 2014.

Ancestry.com. *U.S., Adjutant General Military Records, 1631-1976* [database on-line]. Provo, UT, USA: Ancestry.com Operations, Inc., 2011.

Ancestry.com. *U.S. and Canada, Passenger and Immigration Lists Index, 1500s-1900s* [database on-line]. Place: *Indiana*; Page Number: *29*. Provo, UT, USA: Ancestry.com Operations, Inc, 2010.

Ancestry.com. *U.S. Naturalization Record Indexes, 1791-1992 (Indexed in World Archives Project)* [database on-line]. Provo, UT, USA: Ancestry.com Operations, Inc., 2010. Hendrik Spaan. Retrieved from http://interactive.ancestry.com/1629/31192_118251-08908?pid=4955089&backurl=http%3a%2f%2fsearch.ancestry.com%2f%2fcgi-bin%2fsse.dll%3fgss%3dangs-c%26new%3d1%26rank%3d1%26gsfn%3dhenry%2bn%26gsfn_x%3d0%26gsln%3dspaan%26gsln_x%3d0%26msbdy%3d1851%26msbpn__ftp%3dholland%26cp%3d0%26MSAV%3d1%26uidh%3dvx3%26pcat%3dIMG_

CITIZENSHIP%26h%3d4955089%26recoff%3d5%2b6%26db%3dUSnatindex_awap%26indiv%3d1%26ml_rpos%3d1&treeid=&personid=&hintid=&usePUB=true#?imageId=31192_118251-08908

Ancestry.com. *U.S., Quaker Meeting Records, 1681-1935* [database on-line]. Provo, UT, USA: Ancestry.com Operations, Inc., 2014.Etta Charles. Retrieved from http://interactive.ancestry.com/2189/40780_1821100519_1676-00107?pid=575192&backurl=http%3a%2f%2fsearch.ancestry.com%2f%2fcgi-bin%2fsse.dll%3fgss%3dangs-g%26new%3d1%26rank%3d1%26msT%3d1%26gsfn%3detta%26gsfn_x%3d0%26gsln%3dcharles%26gsln_x%3d0%26msypn__p%3dAnderson%252c%2bMadison%252c%2bIndiana%252c%2bUSA%26msypn%3d40102%26msypn_PInfo%3d8-%257c0%257c1652393%257c0%257c2%257c3247%257c17%257c0%257c1857%257c40102%257c0%257c%26MSAV%3d0%26cp%3d0%26catbucket%3drstp%26pcat%3dROOT-_6h%3d575192%26recoff%3d3%2b4%2b27%2b39%26db%3dQuakerMeetMins%26indiv%3d1%26ml_rpos%3d30&treeid=&personid=&hintid=&usePUB=true

Ancestry.com. *U.S., Social Security Applications and Claims Index, 1936-2007* [database on-line]. Provo, UT, USA: Ancestry.com Operations, Inc., 2015. Retrieved from http://search.ancestry.com/cgi-bin/sse.dll?gss=angs-c&new=1&rank=1&msT=1&gsfn=harry+dunn&gsfn_x=0&gsln=tutewiler&gsln_x=0&mswpn__ftp=Indianapolis%2c+Marion%2c+Indiana%2c+USA&mswpn=40138&mswpn_PInfo=8-%7c0%7c1652393%7c0%7c2%7c3247%7c17%7c0%7c1893%7c40138%7c0%7c&MSAV=0&cp=0&catbucket=rstp&pcat=34&h=4328082&recoff=5+6+7&db=Numident&indiv=1&ml_rpos=3

Ancestry.com. *U.S., World War I Draft Registration Cards, 1917-1918* [database on-line]. Provo, UT, USA: Ancestry.com Operations Inc, 2005. Seth Nichols Retrieved from http://interactive.ancestry.com/6482/005253664_05427?pid=34111700&backurl=http%3a%2f%2fsearch.ancestry.com%2f%2fcgi-bin%2fsse.dll%3fgss%3dangs-c%26new%3d1%26rank%3d1%26msT%3d1%26gsfn%3dseth%2bt.%26gsfn_x%3d0%26gsln%3dnichols%26gsln_x%3d0%26msbdy%3d1890%26msbpn__p%3dIndia-3d0%26uidh%3dvx3%26pcat%3d39%26h%3d34111700%26db%3dWW1draft%26indiv%3d1%26ml_rpos%3d1&treeid=&personid=&hintid=&usePUB=true

Baker, T. (9 December 1911). Who Killed Dr. Helene Knabe?. *Colliers Magazine. 63(12)*. p.15-16, 27.

Baldwin and Hudson. (1939). Anderson City Directory. Baldwin and Hudson. Retrieved from http://interactive.ancestry.com/2469/10806359?pid=1142309534&backurl=http%3a%2f%2fsearch.ancestry.com%2f%2fcgi-bin%2fsse.dll%3fgss%3dangs-g%26new%3d1%26rank%3d1%26msT%3d1%26gsfn%3detta%26gsfn_x%3d0%26gsln%3dcharles%26gsln_x%3d0%26msypn__p%3dAnderson%252c%2bMadison%252c%2bIndiana%252c%2bUSA%26msypn%3d40102%26msypn_PInfo%3d8-%257c0%257c1652393%257c0%257c2%257c3247%257c17%257c0%257c1857%257c40102%257c0%257c%26MSAV%3d0%26cp%3d0%26catbucket%3drstp%26pcat%3dROOT_CATEGORY%26h%3d1142309534%26db%3dUSDirectories%26indiv%3d1%26ml_rpos%3d14&treeid=&personid=&hintid=&usePUB=true#?imageId=10806520

Barnard, H.E. (8 October 1905). Unpublished correspondence. W.H. Smith Memorial Library, Indiana Historical Society.

Barnard, H.E. (20 March 1906). Unpublished correspondence. W.H. Smith Memorial Library, Indiana Historical Society.

Barnard, H.E. (30 March 1906). Unpublished correspondence. W.H. Smith Memorial Library, Indiana Historical Society.

Benesch, A.B. (1901). *Men of Indiana in Nineteen Hundred and One.* Indianapolis, IN: The Benesch Publishing Company.

Blackie & Sons. (1882). Pommern (Pomerania), Prussia 1882. Edinburgh, Scotland: Blackie & Sons. Retrieved from http://feefhs.org/maplibrary/german/ge-pomer.html

Boetcker, W. J. H. (1902). *Picturesque Shelbyville : representing the official, business and social relations of Shelbyville, Indiana.* Shelbyville, IN: Reverend William J. H. Boetcker.

Bogart, G.H. (1909 March). Report of a peculiar case of walking Typhoid. *The Medical Summary.* 31(139).

Bonner, T. N. (1995). *Becoming a Physician: Medical Education in Britain, France, Germany, and the United States, 1750-1945.* Baltimore, MD: Johns Hopkins.

Bonsett, C.A. (1984 October). Medical Museum Notes. *Indiana Medicine.* 77(754).

Burke, Bernard (1858). *The book of orders of knighthood and decorations of honour of all nations.* London: Hurst and Blackett.

Carroll, S. (2016, March 6). Email correspondence.

Catalogue of Copyright Entries (1918). White (The) Flame. Washington, DC: Government Printing Office. *Vol. 15 2(1113).*

Centers for Disease Control. WISQARS. Data compiled by searching http://www.cdc.gov/injury/wisqars/leadingcauses.html

Chanute Daily Tribune (3 November 1911). Hers was a Life of Mystery. *Chanute Daily Tribune.* p. 3.

Chanute Daily Tribune (9 December 1913).Judge Orders Jury to Dismiss Case. *Chanute Daily Tribune.* p. 1.

Clark, C.A. (2008). *God - or Gorilla: Images of Evolution in the Jazz Age (Medicine, Science, and Religion in Historical Context).* Baltimore, MD: Johns Hopkins University Press

Cliff Notes. (n.d.) *Progressive Police Reform.* Cliff Notes. Retrieved from http://www.cliffsnotes.com/study-guides/criminal-justice/development-of-the-american-police/progressive-police-reform

Columbus Dispatch. (27 July 1934). Ella Hitt Obituary. *Columbus Dispatch.* p. 6A.

Congressional Series of United States Public Documents. (1 February 1895). Report No. 864. 53rd Congress. *Volume 3289(0).* Retrieved from https://books.google.com/s?id=KTNHAQAAIAAJ&pg=PR115&lpg=PR115&dq=%22samuel+f.+tenant%22&source=bl&ots=xKfRFS5b1a&sig=q1XL5fDN05iBGRDq4PR6ZkS

Crown Hill Cemetery. (1921). Burial Record Franz F.W. Kropp. Crown Hill Cemetery.

Crown Hill Cemetery. (1896). Burial Record Karoline Kropp. Crown Hill Cemetery.

Cumback, W. & Maynard, J.B. (1899). *Men of progress, Indiana : a selected list of biographical sketches and portraits of the leaders in business, professional and official life, together with brief notes of the history and character of Indiana.* Indianapolis, IN: The Indianapolis Sentinel Company.

Daily Journal. (23 June 1913). Craig Murder Case Opens. *Daily Journal.* p.1.

Daly, W. J. (1993). *Indiana University Medical Center 1903-1993.* New York: The Newcomen Society of the United States.

Davis, G.C. (28 November 1913). Craig Fears "Spirits" in Murder Trial. *Indianapolis Sun.* p.1, 9.

Davis, G.C. (29 November 1913). Knabe Jury is not Filled as Court Closes. *Indianapolis Evening Sun.* p.1,2.

Davis, G.C. (29 November 1913). Knabe Jury is not Filled as Court Closes. *Indianapolis Sun.* p.1.

Davis, G.C. (30 November 1913). State Ready to Begin Craig Trial. *Indianapolis Sunday Sun.* p.1.

Davis, G.C. (1 December 1913). Charges Craig Betrayed Two School Girls. *Indianapolis Sun.* p.1, 3.

Davis, G.C. (2 December 1913). Spann Brings Spirits into Murder Trial. *Indianapolis Evening Sun.* pp.1, 9.

Davis, G.C. (3 December 1913). Durham Says He Found Two Gashes on Neck. *Indianapolis Evening Sun.* p.1, 9.

Davis, G.C. (4 December 1913). Woman in the Case is Craig Trial Witness. *Indianapolis Evening Sun*. p.1, 2.

Davis, G.C. (5 December 1913). Points Finger of Accusation Toward Craig. *Indianapolis Evening Sun*. p.1, 2.

Davis, G.C. (6 December 1913). Cousin Weeps in Court Over Knabe Kimono. *Indianapolis Evening Sun*. p.1, 2.

Davis, G.C. (7 December 1913). State Awaits New Evidence in Knabe Case. *Indianapolis Evening Sun*. p.1, 2.

Davis, G.C. (8 December 1913). State Rests Case in Craig Trial. *Indianapolis Evening Sun*. p.1, 2.

Denning D.G., Conwell, Y,. King, D., and Cox, C. (2000 Fall). Method Choice, Intent and Gender in Completed Suicide. *Suicide Life Threat Behavior*. 30(3):282-8. Retrieved from http://www.ncbi.nlm.nih.gov/pubmed/11079640

Department of Commerce and Labor Immigration Service. (8 September 1906). List of Manifest of Alien Passengers for the U.S. Immigration Officer at the Port of Arrival. Department of Commerce Bureau of the Census. (1911). Mortality Statistics. Department of Commerce Bureau of the Census Retrieved from http://www.cdc.gov/nchs/data/vsushistorical/mortstatbl_1911.pdf

Department of Commerce and Labor Immigration Service (Daniel and Clara Ehmke). p.81

Deutsche Bauzeitung. (28 July 1870). Hülfskomité für die Feld stehenden Architekten und Bau-Ingenieure. Deutsche Bauzeitung. p. 245.

Deutsche Bauzeitung. (29 November 1873). Das preussiche Staats-Bauwesen. Deutsche Bauzeitung. p. 371-379.

Deutsche Bauzeitung. (2 July 1890). Besuchstafel der Technischen Hochschule Berlin, bezw. Ihrer Vorläufer. Deutsche Bauzeitung. p. 317-368.

Deutsche Bauzeitung. (9 July 1890). Personal-nachrichten. Deutsche Bauzeitung. p. 332.

Drumshang Farmhouse. (n.d.) rightmove. Retrieved from http://www.rightmove.co.uk/property-for-sale/property-10946964.html

Dunn, J.P. (1910). Greater Indianapolis: The History, the Industries, the Institutions, and the People of a City of Homes (Vols 1-2). Chicago: The Lewis Publishing Company.

Ellis Island. (1894). Customer List of Passengers (Augusta Knabe). Ellis Island.

Ellis Island. (1896). Passenger Record (Helene Knabe). Ellis Island.

Ernestinoff, H. (1 January 1913). Cousin of Dr. Knabe FIlled With Gratitude to Women for Indictments. *Indianapolis Star*. p. 12.

Evans, R.J. (1976). *The Feminist Movement in Germany 1894-1933*. London: Sage Publications.

Evening Telegraph. (19 November 1913). Physician Fights Murder Charge by Indiana Coroner. *Evening Telegraph*. p.1.

Earlham College; Richmond, Indiana; *Memberships*; Collection: *Indiana Yearly Meeting Minutes*.

Earlham College; Richmond, Indiana; *The Record of the Members of Fairmount Monthly Meeting of Friends, 1869*; Collection: *Indiana Yearly Meeting Minutes*.

Earlham College; Richmond, Indiana; *Record Book, 1842*; Collection: *Indiana Yearly Meeting Minutes*.

Earlham College; Richmond, Indiana; *Women's Minutes, 1850-1869*; Collection: *Indiana Yearly Meeting Minutes*

Earlham College; Richmond, Indiana; *Records of the Society of Friends in Indiana*; Collection: *Indiana Yearly Meeting Minutes*. Collection: *Indiana Yearly Meeting Minutes*

FamilySearch. (1920). United States Census 1920. Retrieved from https://familysearch.org/

ark:/61903/3:1:33SQ-GR66-DSY?mode=g&i=7&wc=QZJP-8Y1%3A1036470701%2C1036668101%2C1038501501%2C1589332834%3Fcc%3D1488411&cc=1488411

Findagrave.com. (n.d.) Adolph Asch Memorial. Findagrave.com. Retrieved from http://www.findagrave.com/cgi-bin/i?page=gr&GSln=asch&GSfn=adolph&GSbyrel=all&GSdyrel=all&GSst=17&GScntry=4&GSob=n&GRid=101060375&df=all&

Findagrave.com. (n.d.)Frank Pierce Baker Memorial. Findagrave.com. Retrieved from http://www.findagrave.com/cgi-bin/i?page=gr&GSln=Ketcham&GSfn=william&GSbyrel=all&GSdyrel=in&GSst=17&GScntry=4&GSob=n&GRid=19615974&df=all&

Findagrave.com. (n.d.) Alonzo Blair Memorial. Findagrave.com. Retrieved from http://www.findagrave.com/cgi-bin/i?page=gr&GSln=blair&GSfn=alonzo&GSbyrel=all&GSdyrel=all&GSst=17&GScntry=4&GSob=n&GRid=14105480&df=all&

Findagrave.com. (n.d.) Dr. Charles Euguene Ferguson Memorial. Findagrave.com. Retrieved from http://www.findagrave.com/cgi-bin/fg.cgi?page=gr&GRid=45937019

Findagrave.com. (n.d.) Frank Flanner Memorial. Findagrave.com. Retrieved from http://www.findagrave.com/cgi-bin/fg.cgi?page=gr&GRid=31619183

Findagrave.com. (n.d.) Katherine Agnes Fleming. Findagrave.com. Retrieved from http://www.findagrave.com/cgi-bin/fg.cgi?page=gr&GRid=54404314

Findagrave.com. (n.d.) Eva Powell Hall Memorial. Findagrave.com. Retrieved from http://www.findagrave.com/cgi-bin/i?page=gr&GSln=hall&GSfn=Eva&GSbyrel=in&GSdyrel=in&GSst=24&GScntry=4&GSob=n&GRid=24879417&df=all&

Findagrave.com. (n.d.) Fredrick E. Hall Memorial. Findagrave.com. Retrieved from http://www.findagrave.com/cgi-bin/fg.cgi?page=gr&GRid=29288626

Findagrave.com. (n.d.) Ephriam Inman Memorial. Findagrave.com. Retrieved from http://www.findagrave.com/cgi-bin/i?page=gr&GSln=+Inman&GSfn=Eph&GSbyrel=all&GSdyrel=after&GScntry=4&GSob=n&GRid=45927479&df=all&

Findagrave.com. (n.d.) T. Victor Keene Memorial. Findagrave.com. Retrieved from http://www.findagrave.com/cgi-bin/fg.cgi?page=gr&GSln=keene&GSiman=1&GScid=84781&GRid=45928899&

Findagrave.com. (n.d.) Amelia Keller Memorial. Findagrave.com. Retrieved from http://www.findagrave.com/cgi-bin/i?page=gr&GSln=Keller&GSfn=amelia&GSbyrel=in&GSdyrel=in&GSst=17&GScntry=4&GSob=n&GRid=45929135&df=all&

Findagrave.com. (n.d.) Capt William A. Ketcham Memorial. Findagrave.com. Retrieved from http://www.findagrave.com/cgi-bin/i?page=gr&GSln=baker&GSfn=frank&GSmn=p&GSbyrel=all&GSdy=1939&GSdyrel=after&GSst=17&GScntry=4&GSob=n&GRid=15715057&df=all&

Findagrave.com. (n.d.) Jeremiah E. Kinney Memorial. Findagrave.com. Retrieved from http://www.findagrave.com/cgi-bin/i?page=gr&GSln=Kinney&GSbyrel=all&GSdy=1931&GSdyrel=in&GScntry=4&GSob=n&GSsr=41&GRid=134394091&df=all&

Findagrave.com. (n.d.) Dr. John Kolmer Memorial. Findagrave.com. Retrieved from http://www.findagrave.com/cgi-bin/i?page=gr&GSln=kolmer&GSfn=john&GSbyrel=in&GSdyrel=in&GSst=17&GScntry=4&GSob=n&GRid=45934062&df=all&

Findagrave.com. (n.d.) William A. Larsh Memorial. Findagrave.com. Retrieved from http://www.findagrave.com/cgi-bin/i?page=gr&GSln=Larsh+&GSfn=William+&GSbyrel=all&GSdyrel=in&GScntry=4&GSob=n&GRid=42122204&df=all&

Findagrave.com. (n.d.) Lillian Crockett-Lowder Memorial. Findagrave.com. Retrieved from http://www.findagrave.com/cgi-bin/fg.cgi?page=pv&GRid=17180071&PIpi=105791721

Findagrave.com. (n.d.) Samuel Lewis Shank Memorial. Findagrave.com. Retrieved from http://www.findagrave.com/cgi-bin/i?page=gr&GSln=Shank&GSfn=Samuel+&GSmn=Lewis+&GSbyrel=in&GSdyrel=in&GSst=17&GScntry=4&GSob=n&GRid=34807536&df=all&

Findagrave.com. (n.d.) Otto Simon Memorial. Findagrave.com. Retrieved from http://www.findagrave.com/cgi-bin/i?page=gr&GSln=simon&GSfn=otto&GSbyrel=all&GSdyrel=all&GSst=17&GScntry=4&GSob=n&GRid=110223659&df=all&

Findagrave.com. (n.d.) Henry Spaan Memorial. Findagrave.com. Retrieved from http://www.findagrave.com/cgi-bin/fg.cgi?page=gr&GRid=46015388&ref=acom

Findagrave.com. (n.d.) George V. Stewart. Findagrave.com. Retrieved from http://www.findagrave.com/cgi-bin/i?page=gr&GSln=stewart&GSfn=george&GSmn=M&GSbyrel=all&GSdyrel=all&GSst=17&GScntry=4&GSob=n&GRid=129006374&df=all&

Findagrave.com. (n.d.) Harry Dunn Tutewiler Memorial. Findagrave.com. Retrieved from http://www.findagrave.com/cgi-bin/i?page=gr&GSln=Tutewiler&GSfn=Harry+&GSmn=d&GSbyrel=all&GSdyrel=all&GSst=17&GScntry=4&GSob=n&GRid=46036952&df=all&

Flexnor, A. (1910). Medical Education in the United States and Canada. New York: The Carnegie Foundation for the Advancement of Teaching.

Forkner, J. L. *History of Madison County, Indiana : A narrative account of its historical progress, its people and its principal interests (Volume 1).* (Etta Charles). Chicago: The Lewis Publishing Company. p. 691.

Ft. Wayne Journal Gazette. (2 November 1911). Turn to Suicide Theory in Knabe Death Mystery. *Ft. Wayne Journal Gazette.* p.6.

Ft. Wayne Journal-Gazette. (1 January 1913). Two Indicted for Murder of Doctor. Ft. Wayne Journal-Gazette. p.1, 10.

Ft. Wayne News. (11 November 1913). Knabe Murder Case Goes to Trial Friday. *Ft. Wayne News.* p.3.

Ft. Wayne News. (28 November 1913). The Knabe Trial is on at Shelbyville. *Ft. Wayne News.* pp. 1, 11.

Ft. Wayne News. (01 December 1913). Kate Fleming to be Witness. *Ft. Wayne News.* pp. 1, 12.

Ft. Wayne News. (3 December 1913). The Suicide Theory Rapped. *Ft. Wayne News.* pp. 1, 12.

Ft. Wayne News. (6 December 1913). Knabe Case Adjournment.. *Ft. Wayne News.* pp. 1, 14.

Ft. Wayne News. (8 December 1913). Knabe Case Nearing End. *Ft. Wayne News.* pp. 1, 12.

Ft. Wayne News. (9 December 1913). Who Killed Doctor Knabe?. *Ft. Wayne News.* pp. 1, 13.

Ft. Wayne News. (31 December 1912). The Knabe Murder Case. *Ft. Wayne News.* pp. 1-2.

Ft. Wayne Sentinel. (27 December 1921). Ex-Commander in Chief of G.A.R. Passes Away. *Ft. Wayne Sentinel.* p.3.

Forensic Science Ireland (Eolaíocht Fhóiréinseach Éireann) n.d.) The History of Forensic Science. Forensic Science Ireland (Eolaíocht Fhóiréinseach Éireann) . Retrieved from http://www.forensicscience.ie/Services/History-of-Forensic-Science/

Fuller, G.W., Ferguson, C.E., Jeup. B.J.T. (1904). Report upon the Water Supply and Sanitary Conditions of the City of Indianapolis. City of Indianapolis.

Familienforschung in Westpreußen. (n.d.). Verzeichnis westpreußischer Standesamtsregister, Zivilstandsregister, Dissidentenregister und Kirchenbuchzweitschriften. Retrieved from http://www.westpreussen.de/cms/ct/standesamtsregister.php

Friedman, G.A. (1910). Supperative Perigastritis: A Case with Tumor formation following perforated gastric ulcer of the greater curature. *JAMA*. 1910;LIV(8):611-613 Retrieved from http://jama.jamanetwork.com/article.aspx?articleid=431320

The Gazette. (10 April 1912). No title. *The Gazette* (Stevens Point, WI). p9.

Geis, J.F. (1903). *Manual of Physiological and Clinical Chemistry*. Indianapolis, IN: John F. Geis.

Gray, R.D. (2003). *IUPUI- The Making of an Urban University*. Bloomington, IN: Indiana University Press.

Gross, C. G. (1999) A Hole in the Head. *History of Neuroscience*.Vol5 4(263-269). Retrieved from https://www.princeton.edu/~cggross/neuroscientist_99_hole.pdf

Genealoger.com (2012). Pomeranian Genealogy: Kreis Schlawe. Retrieved from http://www.genealoger.com/german/pommern/kreis/schlawe.htm

Goodspeed Brothers, Publishers. (1893). *Pictorial and Biographical Memoirs of Indianapolis and Marion County*. Goodspeed Brothers, Publishers. Chicago: Goodspeed Brothers Publishers.

Greencastle Herald. (4 December 1908). New Emblem for Eagles. *Greencastle Herald*. p.1

Hammond Times. (16 February 1938). Veterinarian Dies. *Hammond Times*. p.1.

Hepworth, T. C. (1905). *The Book of the Lantern*. London: Wyman and Sons.

Hurty, J. N. (1906). *Life with Health*. Indianapolis, IN: Indiana State Board of Health.

Hyman, M.R. (1897). *Hyman's Handbook of Indianapolis*. Indianapolis, IN: M.R. Hyman Company.

Hyman, M.R. (1907). *Hyman's Handbook of Indianapolis*. Indianapolis, IN: M.R. Hyman Company.

Hyman, M.R. (1909). *Hyman's Handbook of Indianapolis*. Indianapolis, IN: M.R. Hyman Company.

Hyman, M.R. (1910). *Hyman's Handbook of Indianapolis*. Indianapolis, IN: M.R. Hyman Company.

Indiana Department of Public Welfare. (1920). Indianapolis, IN: Statehouse.*120-131(335)*.

Indianapolis Daily Star. (4 May 1923). Veterinarians' Body to Incorporate. *Indianapolis Star*. p.11.

Indianapolis Daily Star. (29 July 1924). Pharmacy College to Move Quarters Opens Sept. 15. *Indianapolis Star*. p. 8.

Indianapolis Daily Star. (2 December 1931). Suspended Fine of $10 on Tutewiler. *Indianapolis Star*. p. 22.

Indianapolis Daily Star. (21 December 1961). Dr. John W. Sluss Dies; Physician Since 1890s. *Indianapolis Star*. p. 26.

Indianapolis Magazine. (1975, July). Editor's Note: Farewell, Bruce- The Magazine Won't be the Same Without You. *Indianapolis Magazine*. 6-7.

Indianapolis Mayor. (1903). Second Annual Message: Report of Bicycle Corps. Indianapolis Mayor. Indianapolis, IN: Sentinel Publishing Co. Retrieved from https://books.google.com/books?id=uTlEAQAAMAAJ&pg=PA210&lpg=PA210&dq=indianapolis+police+Otto+Simon&source=bl&ots=u-8pvDVPd-&sig=xz8_4WxUvD4RSBVfotUq6EJ8d18&hl=en&sa=X&ved=0ahUKEwiS14Gx77vLAhUKRCYKHafBDtQQ6AEIHDAA#v=onepage&q=indianapolis%20police%20Otto%20Simon&f=false

Indianapolis Evening Sun. (4 December 1913). Scene of The Craig Trial. *Indianapolis Evening Sun*. p.1.

Indiana Medical College. (1906). *First Annual Catalogue and Announcement*. Bloomington: Indiana Medical College, The School of Medicine of Purdue University.

Indiana Medical College. (1907). *Second Annual Catalogue and Announcement*. Bloomington: Indiana Medical College, The School of Medicine of Purdue University.

Indianapolis Medical Journal. (1910).   Book and Journal Reviews. *Indianapolis Medical Journal.* 7 (199).

Indianapolis Medical Journal. (1910).   The Indianapolis Medical Society. *Indianapolis Medical*

Journal. 13 (188).

Indianapolis Medical Journal. (1916 January-December). Death of Dr. W.T.S. Dodds. *Indianapolis Medical Journal.* 19 (261).

Indianapolis Medical Journal. (1922 January). Death of Dr. Frank B. Wynn.. *Indianapolis Medical Journal.* 25 (203).

Indiana Medical Journal. (July 1899- June 1900). Dr. Ernest C. Reyer. Indiana Medical Journal. 18(45).

Indiana Medical Journal. (1904). Thirty-fourth Annual Commencement of the Medical College of Indiana. Indiana Medical Journal. p. 463.

Indiana Medical Journal. (1908). Physicians Registers at French Lick Meeting, Indiana State Medical Association, June 18 and 19, 1908. Indiana Medical Journal. p. 16-17.

Indianapolis News. (3 November 1894). Smoldering Ruins. *Indianapolis News.* p.1.

Indianapolis News. (2 November 1896). A Grotesque Election Bet. Indianapolis News. p.5

Indianapolis News. (23 December 1896).Wants a Divorce from Lorraine. *Indianapolis News.* p.5.

Indianapolis News. (28 March 1898). Illegal Sales at Paragon. Indianapolis News. p.7.

Indianapolis News. (6 April 1897). Lorraine Divorce Case. *Indianapolis News.* p.7.

Indianapolis News. (20 April 1898).Dr. John Kolmer. *Indianapolis News.* p. 16.

Indianapolis News. (4 January 1905). Dr. Ferguson Renders Bill. Indianapolis News. p3.

Indianapolis News. (2 October 1905). The State's Typhoid Fever. *Indianapolis News.* p.12.

Indianapolis News. (7 October 1905). Bad Water Causes Typhoid. *Indianapolis News.* p.5.

Indianapolis News. (11 October 1905). Farmer's Pride in Wells Handicap Typhoid Inquiry. *Indianapolis News.* p.18.

Indianapolis News. (16 November 1905). Two Deaths from Typhoid Fever. *Indianapolis News.* p.14.

Indianapolis News. (14 December 1905). Flies Worst Insect as Disease Carrier. *Indianapolis News.* p.3.

Indianapolis News. (29 December 1905). Learned His Disease at State Laboratory. *Indianapolis News.* p.8.

Indianapolis News. (16 May 1906). Microbe That Causes Everlasting Sleep. *Indianapolis News.* p.1.

Indianapolis News. (13 August 1906). Dogs Infected with Rabies. *Indianapolis News.* p.11.

Indianapolis News. (19 October 1906). Class in Home Nursing. *Indianapolis News.* p.25.

Indianapolis News. (26 October 1906). Home Nursing Class. *Indianapolis News.* p.7.

Indianapolis News. (14 December 1906). Attorney Sues College.. *Indianapolis News.* p.25.

Indianapolis News. (15 January 1907). Students Write for Paper. *Indianapolis News.* p.16.

Indianapolis News. (13 April 1907). Dr. Knabe Injured. *Indianapolis News.* p.3.

Indianapolis News. (17 May 1907). Ready to Leave Hospital. *Indianapolis News.* p.2.

Indianapolis News. (6 June 1907). Baseball Game. *Indianapolis News.* p.7.

Indianapolis News. (5 November 1907). Y.W.C.A. Classes. *Indianapolis News.* p.8.

Indianapolis News. (9 November 1907). Y.W.C.A. Notes. *Indianapolis News.* p.23.

Indianapolis News. (23 November 1907). Y.W.C.A. Notes. *Indianapolis News.* p.14.

Indianapolis News. (14 November 1907). Tuberculosis Killed 325 Last September. *Indianapolis News.* p.11.

Indianapolis News. (14 December 1907). Physicians Careless with Deadly Microbe. *Indianapolis News.* p.16.

Indianapolis News. (27 December 1907). Fight for the Head of the Dog That Had the Rabies.

Indianapolis News. p.2.

Indianapolis News. (10 January 1908). Houren Loses His Case.. *Indianapolis News*. p.13.

Indianapolis News. (11 January 1908). YWCA Notes. *Indianapolis News*. p.21.

Indianapolis News. (13 January 1908). YWCA to Build Girls' Boarding School. *Indianapolis News*. p.3.

Indianapolis News. (13 January 1908). Will Begin a Crusade Against Tuberculosis. *Indianapolis News*. p.10.

Indianapolis News. (18 January 1908). YWCA Class Schedule. *Indianapolis News*. p.24.

Indianapolis News. (27 January 1908). Wishes $5,000 for Sprained Ankle. *Indianapolis News*. p.3.

Indianapolis News. (12 March 1908). Spencer May Soon Be Made a Dogless Town. *Indianapolis News*. p.9.

Indianapolis News. (25 April 1908). Puro Water Analyzed. *Indianapolis News*. p.3.

Indianapolis News. (12 May 1908). Wish Calf's Head Examined. *Indianapolis News*. p.8.

Indianapolis News. (9 June 1908). Medics' Meeting Pleased. *Indianapolis News*. p.16.

Indianapolis News. (17 June 1908). Dog Died of Rabies. *Indianapolis News*. p.10.

Indianapolis News. (23 June 1908). Dog Had Rabies. *Indianapolis News*. p.3.

Indianapolis News. (20 July 1908). Dogs With Rabies Are at Large in Indianapolis. *Indianapolis News*. p.1.

Indianapolis News. (23 July 1908). Several Victims in Danger of Rabies. *Indianapolis News*. p.4.

Indianapolis News. (27 July 1908). On the Trail of the Mad Dog. *Indianapolis News*. p.13.

Indianapolis News. (29 July 1908). Cases of Hydrophobia Among Dogs Increase. *Indianapolis News*. p.3.

Indianapolis News. (2 September 1908). Nurses of Indiana to Hold Annual Meeting. *Indianapolis News*. p.5.

Indianapolis News. (9 September 1908). Dr. Knabe Gives Demonstrations. *Indianapolis News*. p.4.

Indianapolis News. (7 November 1908). Resigns from the State Laboratory of Hygiene. *Indianapolis News*. p.20.

Indianapolis News. (6 October 1909). Women's Local Council Hears of Many Things. *Indianapolis News*. p.8.

Indianapolis News. (28 October 1909). YWCA Notes. *Indianapolis News*. p.8.

Indianapolis News. (7 January 1910). Bear's Head is Mounted.. Indianapolis News. p. 18.

Indianapolis News. (1 July 1911). Notes of Colored People. *Indianapolis News*. p.14.

Indianapolis News. (25 April 1911). YWCA Holds Session. *Indianapolis News*. p.5.

Indianapolis News. (26 July 1911). No Action Taken on Kendall's Resignation. *Indianapolis News*. p.8.

Indianapolis News. (7 October 1911). News of Colored Folk. *Indianapolis News*. p.27.

Indianapolis News. (30 September 1911). YWCA Notes. *Indianapolis News*. p.28.

Indianapolis News. (7 October 1911). Indianapolis School Notes. *Indianapolis News*. p.19.

Indianapolis News. (20 October 1911). Indianapolis School Notes. *Indianapolis News*. p.22.

Indianapolis News. (24 October 1911). Negro Held in Mysterious Murder of Dr. Helene Knabe. *Indianapolis News*. pp.1, 17.

Indianapolis News. (24 October 1911). Delaware Flats Where Dr. Knabe Lived. *Indianapolis News*. p.1.

Indianapolis News. (24 October 1911). Scene of Dr. Knabe Murder in Delaware Flats. *Indianapolis News*. p.1.

Indianapolis News. (25 October 1911). Police Start Anew in Knabe Mystery. *Indianapolis News*. pp.1, 15.

Indianapolis News. (26 October 1911). Strange Man Rear Room of Dr. Knabe. *Indianapolis News*. pp.1, 8.

Indianapolis News. (27 October 1911). Mayor Plans to Assign Knabe Case to Kinney. *Indianapolis News*. p.1.

Indianapolis News. (27 October 1911). Ignore Carr Clew in Knabe Mystery. *Indianapolis News*. pp.1, 30.

Indianapolis News. (28 October 1911). May Find a Clew in Knabe Letter. *Indianapolis News*. pp.1, 2, 6.

Indianapolis News. (30 October 1911). Window Shade up in Knabe Bedroom. *Indianapolis News*. pp.1, 18.

Indianapolis News. (31 October 1911). Miss Knabe Breaks Down in Her Story. *Indianapolis News*. pp.1, 3.

Indianapolis News. (1 November 1911). To Take Last Look at the Knabe Flat. *Indianapolis News*. pp.1, 17.

Indianapolis News. (2 November 1911). Prosecutor Baker Warns Detectives. *Indianapolis News*. p.1.

Indianapolis News. (2 November 1911). Missing Key Found In Knabe Bedroom. *Indianapolis News*. pp.1, 3.

Indianapolis News. (3 November 1911). Police Will Call Miss Knabe Again. *Indianapolis News*. pp.1, 4.

Indianapolis News. (3 November 1911). Voice of the People. *Indianapolis News*. p.2.

Indianapolis News. (4 November 1911). Custodian Called in Knabe Inquiry. *Indianapolis News*. pp.1, 4.

Indianapolis News. (6 November 1911). Police Search Abroad for Knabe Case Clew. *Indianapolis News*. pp.1, 3.

Indianapolis News. (6 November 1911). Coroner Grills Carr in the Knabe Inquiry. *Indianapolis News*. pp.1, 4.

Indianapolis News. (6 November 1911). Dodds Statement Condemned. *Indianapolis News*. p.3.

Indianapolis News. (8 November 1911). Mrs. Wynn Tells of Visit to Knabe Flat. *Indianapolis News*. pp.1, 3.

Indianapolis News. (9 November 1911).Still Running Down Knabe Murder "Tips". *Indianapolis News*. p.2.

Indianapolis News. (10 November 1911). Mysterious Hand Seen by Dr. Knabe. *Indianapolis News*. p.1.

Indianapolis News. (11 November 1911). No Light at Night in the Knabe Apartment. *Indianapolis News*. p.8.

Indianapolis News. (13 November 1911). Says Dr. Knabe was a Martyr to Science. *Indianapolis News*. pp.1, 7.

Indianapolis News. (14 November 1911). New Tenants Pleased with Knabe Apartment. *Indianapolis News*. pp.1,14.

Indianapolis News. (15 November 1911). Grand Jury will take up the Dr. Knabe Case. *Indianapolis News*. pp.1, 17.

Indianapolis News. (15 November 1911). Women, young and Old Wish to be Detectives. *Indianapolis News*. p.1.

Indianapolis News. (16 November 1911). Everyman at City Hall Dodgers Everywoman. *Indianapolis News*. pp.1, 11.

Indianapolis News. (17 November 1911). Promising Evidence in Knabe Investigation. *Indianapolis News*. p.1.

Indianapolis News. (18 November 1911). Grand Jury May Solve the Dr. Knabe Mystery. *Indianapolis News*. pp.1-2.

Indianapolis News. (21 November 1911). Knabe Case Ties Up Report. *Indianapolis News*. p.2.

Indianapolis News. (23 November 1911). Repeats Story of Scream. *Indianapolis News*. p.4.

Indianapolis News. (24 November 1911). No Word From Germany in the Knabe Mystery. *Indianapolis News*. pp.1, 6.

Indianapolis News. (3 December 1911). Tells of Loiterers at Delaware Apartments. *Indianapolis News*. p.5.

Indianapolis News. (6 December 1911). Women Would Solve Knabe Death Mystery. *Indianapolis News*. p.8.

Indianapolis News. (16 December 1911). For Knabe Investigating Fund. *Indianapolis News*. p.17.

Indianapolis News. (29 December 1911). Murder is Verdict in Dr. Knabe Case. *Indianapolis News*. pp.1, 5.

Indianapolis News. (30 December 1911). The Knabe Case Verdict. *Indianapolis News*. p.6.

Indianapolis News. (4 January 1912). The Knabe Murder. *Indianapolis News*. p.6.

Indianapolis News. (12 January 1912). Knabe Case Taken Up by Grand Jury. *Indianapolis News*. p.9.

Indianapolis News. (17 February 1912). F.W. Flanner Drinks Poison; Dies in Chapel *Indianapolis News*. p.1.

Indianapolis News. (2 April 1912). Relatives Declare Nichols is Insane. *Indianapolis News*. p.1.

Indianapolis News. (4 April 1912). Nichols Takes it Back; Did not Kill Dr. Knabe. *Indianapolis News*. p.7.

Indianapolis News. (20 April 1912). Indignant at Refusal to Give Knabe Reward. *Indianapolis News*. p.2.

Indianapolis News. (16 May 1912).Vote of Confidence in Dr. John L. Freeland. p. 12.

Indianapolis News. (3 July 1912). Grand Jurors Complain. *Indianapolis News*. p.14.

Indianapolis News. (11 July 1912). Knows Knabe Murderer. *Indianapolis News*. p.4.

Indianapolis News. (16 July 1912). Echo of Knabe Murder. *Indianapolis News*. p.14.

Indianapolis News. (31 December 1912). Woman Whose Death Resulted in Indictments by Grand Jury. *Indianapolis News*. p.3.

Indianapolis News. (31 December 1912). Ragsdale is Silent. *Indianapolis News*. p.3.

Indianapolis News. (31 December 1912). Webster Believes he Grand Jury Did Duty. *Indianapolis News*. p.3.

Indianapolis News. (31 December 1912). In Charge of Investigation. *Indianapolis News*. p.3.

Indianapolis News. (31 December 1912). Dr. W.B. Craig and A.M. Ragsdale Indicted in Helene Knabe Case. *Indianapolis News*. p.1, Third Extra.

Indianapolis News. (4 January 1913). Names of Drs. Knabe and Craig on Flyleaf. *Indianapolis News*. p.3.

Indianapolis News. (24 March 1913). Coroner's Report Found. *Indianapolis News*. p.3.

Indianapolis News. (21 November 1913). The Knabe Case. *Indianapolis News*. p.1.

Indianapolis News. (28 November 1913). Craig to Testify in the Knabe Case. *Indianapolis News*. pp.1, 3.

Indianapolis News. (29 November 1913). Knabe Case Goes over Without Jury. *Indianapolis News*. pp.1, 3.

Indianapolis News. (1 December 1913). No Spirit Evidence in the Knabe Case. *Indianapolis News*. pp.1, 14.

Indianapolis News. (2 December 1913). Tells What He Saw in the Death Room. *Indianapolis News*. pp.1, 14.

Indianapolis News. (3 December 1913). Dr. Knabe's Death Wounds Described. *Indianapolis News*. pp.1, 8.

Indianapolis News. (4 December 1913). Not the Fiancée of Dr. Craig, She Says. *Indianapolis News*. pp.1, 8.

Indianapolis News. (5 December 1913). Craig to Tell Own Story to the Court. *Indianapolis News*. p.1, 19.

Indianapolis News. (6 December 1913). Sobs When Kimono is Shown in Court. *Indianapolis News*. pp.1, 20.

Indianapolis News. (8 December 1913).Acquittal of Craig is Asked by Spaan. *Indianapolis News*. pp.1, 12.

Indianapolis News. (9 December 1913). Full Text of Judge Blair's Decision Ordering the Acquittal of Dr. Craig. *Indianapolis News*. p.12.

Indianapolis News. (18 December 1913). Who Put the Stains on the Knabe Kimono. *Indianapolis News*. p.1.

Indianapolis News. (29 November 1913). Defendant, Daughter and one of his Lawyers. *Indianapolis News*. p.2.

Indianapolis News. (29 November 1913). Knabe Case Goes Over Till Monday. *Indianapolis News*. pp.1. 2.

Indianapolis News. (30 June 1914).Brass band can play at this sound-proof flat and not disturb the neighbors, architect say. p. 4.

Indianapolis News. (28 April 1915). Witness In Knabe Case Found Dead in Hotel.. Indianapolis News. p.1.

Indianapolis News. (25 December 1915). From Log Cabin to Big "Movie" Theater. Indianapolis News. p. 7.

Indianapolis News. (23 May 1916). Dr. W.T.S. Dodds Dead of Acute Heart Disease. Indianapolis News. p.19.

Indianapolis News. (22 October 1917).Funeral of Dr. Kolmer to be Held Wednesday. p. 22.

Indianapolis News. (1 November 1917).Bequests of Dr. Kolmer. p. 5.

Indianapolis News. (22 February 1918).Dr. John Kolmer Estate Ad. p.34.

Indianapolis News. (25 March 1918). Dr. Ernest Reyer Dies of Injuries at Home. Indianapolis News. p.9.

Indianapolis News. (6 September 1919). Engagements and Weddings. Indianapolis News. p.18.

Indianapolis News. (13 September 1919). Twenty Persons Take Oaths For Citizenship. Indianapolis News. p.2.

Indianapolis News. (24 December 1919). J.W. Morgan, Veteran City Detective Dead. *Indianapolis Star*. p.8.

Indianapolis News (19 October 1952). Joseph Thomas Markey Obituary. Indianapolis News. p.19

Indianapolis Recorder. (24 June 1911). No title. *Indianapolis Recorder*. p.1.

Indianapolis Recorder. (24 June 1911). Simpson Chapel Church. *Indianapolis Recorder.* p.2.
Indianapolis Recorder. (1 July 1911). Simpson Chapel Church. *Indianapolis Recorder.* p.2.
Indianapolis Recorder. (5 August 1911). In Club Circles. *Indianapolis Recorder.* p.1.
Indianapolis Recorder. (7 October 1911). Flanner Guild Notes. *Indianapolis Recorder.* p.1.
Indianapolis Recorder. (1 November 1911). Women's Civic Club Notes. *Indianapolis Recorder.* p.1.
Indianapolis Star. (13 July 1903). King of Ghouls Writing a Book. *Indianapolis Star.* p.1.
Indianapolis Star. (1 November 1903). Speed to Scene of Wreck Like Madmen. *Indianapolis Star.* p. 7.
Indianapolis Star. (10 March 1904). John F. Geis Funeral Notice. *Indianapolis Star.* p. 1.
Indianapolis Star. (11 May 1904). Indiana Deaths: Mrs. Otto von Tesmar Obituary. *Indianapolis Star.* p.3.
Indianapolis Star. (4 January 1906). State Laboratory Work. *Indianapolis Star.* p. 7.
Indianapolis Star. (6 October 1906). Class to meeting this evening. *Indianapolis Star.* p. 3.
Indianapolis Star. (2 December 1906). Y.W.C.A. Notes. *Indianapolis Star.* p. 26.
Indianapolis Star. (14 December 1906). Wants $3.571.43 a Day. *Indianapolis Star.* p.1.
Indianapolis Star. (13 April 1907). Weather Makes Sad. *Indianapolis Star.* p. 1.
Indianapolis Star. (12 May 1907). Olga Tetley Beauty Shop Ad. *Indianapolis Star.* p. 18.
Indianapolis Star. (1 September 1907). Local Scientist Who Knows Human Body.. Indianapolis Star. p.4.
Indianapolis Star. (18 October 1907). Editorial by Otto von Tesmar.. Indianapolis Star. p.6.
Indianapolis Star. (20 October 1907). Weather Makes Sad. *Indianapolis Star.* p. 1.
Indianapolis Star. (28 January 1908). Presents Picture of Ankle. *Indianapolis Star.* p. 12.
Indianapolis Star. (30 January 1908). Ankle Picture Fails to Win. *Indianapolis Star.* p. 14.
Indianapolis Star. (09 February 1908). Dog Had Rabies. *Indianapolis Star.* p. 17.
Indianapolis Star. (12 February 1908). Finds Spaniel Had Rabies. *Indianapolis Star.* p. 3.
Indianapolis Star. (6 March 1908). Friend of Homeless Curs Bitten by Mad Dog. *Indianapolis Star.* p. 1.
Indianapolis Star. (26 July 1908). The Fight Against Hydrophobia in Indiana. *Indianapolis Star.* p. 39.
Indianapolis Star. (09 September 1908). Holds Statistics Aid Public Health. *Indianapolis Star.* p. 6.
Indianapolis Star. (15 October 1908). City Physician Named. *Indianapolis Star.* p. 14.
Indianapolis Star. (8 November 1908). State Loses Dr. Knabe. Indianapolis Star. p. 28.
Indianapolis Star. (29 July 1909). Takes State Position in Health Movement. *Indianapolis Star.* p. 7.
Indianapolis Star. (9 September 1909). Five Women Initiated into Medical Sorority. *Indianapolis Star.* p. 22.
Indianapolis Star. (19 September 1909). Local School Heads List. *Indianapolis Star.* p. 3.
Indianapolis Star. (3 April 1910). Veterinaries Get Degrees. *Indianapolis Star.* p. 12.
Indianapolis Star. (18 June 1910). Parties and Meetings. *Indianapolis Star.* p. 22.
Indianapolis Star. (3 January 1911). Loom Ends Ad. Indianapolis Star. p. 4.
Indianapolis Star. (26 April 1911). Holds Leadership Day's Crying Need. *Indianapolis Star.* p. 6.
Indianapolis Star. (30 July 1911). News of Colored Folk. *Indianapolis Star.* p. 48.
Indianapolis Star. (17 September 1911). Normal College Roster Shows 65 Per Cent Gain. *Indianapolis Star.* p. 32.
Indianapolis Star. (23 September 1911). Booths Depict Y.W.C.A. Work. *Indianapolis Star.* p. 7.
Indianapolis Star. (29 September 1911). Gives Beauty Hint in Back Yard Art . Indianapolis Star. p.3.

Indianapolis Star. (13 October 1911). School Notes. *Indianapolis Star*. p. 14.

Indianapolis Star. (24 October 1911). Dr. Knabe in Laboratory. *Indianapolis Star*. p. 1.

Indianapolis Star. (24 October 1911). Murder Victim was Self-Made. *Indianapolis Star*. pp. 1, 4.

Indianapolis Star. (25 October 1911). State Officials Pay Tributes to Dr. Knabe as Woman and Scientist. *Indianapolis Star*. p. 1.

Indianapolis Star. (25 October 1911). Find No Clue to Murderer of Dr. Knabe. *Indianapolis Star*. p. 1.

Indianapolis Star. (26 October 1911). Hunt in Vain for Clews in Murder Case. *Indianapolis Star*. p. 3.

Indianapolis Star. (26 October 1911). Many Weep at Bier of Murdered Doctor. *Indianapolis Star*. p. 3.

Indianapolis Star. (26 October 1911). Any Clew May Be Right. *Indianapolis Star*. p. 16.

Indianapolis Star. (27 October 1911). Murder Clew Given by Carr is Abandoned. *Indianapolis Star*. pp 1,13.

Indianapolis Star. (28 October 1911). Prowler was Heard at Flat Before Crime. *Indianapolis Star*. pp. 1,6.

Indianapolis Star. (28 October 1911). Dr. Knabe's Charity Praised at Funeral. *Indianapolis Star*. pp. 1,6.

Indianapolis Star. (29 October 1911). Second Clew in Knabe Case is Cast Aside. *Indianapolis Star*. pp. 1,7.

Indianapolis Star. (29 October 1911). Card of Thanks from Augusta Knabe and Family. *Indianapolis Star*. p. 43.

Indianapolis Star. (30 October 1911). Murder Case Letter Clew is Abandoned. *Indianapolis Star*. pp. 1,3.

Indianapolis Star. (30 October 1911). Woman Cuts Own Throat; Note Blames Ill Health. *Indianapolis Star*. p. 1.

Indianapolis Star. (31 October 1911). Council Votes $1000 Reward in Knabe Case. *Indianapolis Star*. pp. 1,4.

Indianapolis Star. (29 September 1911). Gives Beauty Hint in Back Yard Art. *Indianapolis Star*. p. 3.

Indianapolis Star. (1 November 1911). Assured That Women Keep Back No Clew. *Indianapolis Star*. pp. 1,7.

Indianapolis Star. (1 November 1911). Girl, Incited by Knabe Case, "Fakes" Holdup. *Indianapolis Star*. p. 8.

Indianapolis Star. (2 November 1911). Hyland Holds Suicide More Likely Theory. *Indianapolis Star*. pp. 1,8.

Indianapolis Star. (3 November 1911). Missing Knife is Found in Flat. *Indianapolis Star*. pp. 1,8.

Indianapolis Star. (3 November 1911). Respect for the Dead *Indianapolis Star*. p. 8.

Indianapolis Star. (3 November 1911). Burns Favors Suicide Stand in Knabe Case. *Indianapolis Star*. pp. 1,3.

Indianapolis Star. (4 November 1911). Bend Efforts for Solution of Key Tangle. *Indianapolis Star*. pp. 1,6

Indianapolis Star. (4 November 1911). Sketches by Late Dr. Knabe in Medical Cartoon Contest. *Indianapolis Star*. p.29.

Indianapolis Star. (6 November 1911). Shank Trails Tip in Knabe Inquiry. *Indianapolis Star*. p. 1.

Indianapolis Star. (6 November 1911). Decries Course in Murder Case. *Indianapolis Star*. p. 1.

Indianapolis Star. (7 November 1911). Tells of Voices in Doctor's Fat. *Indianapolis Star*. p. 1.

Indianapolis Star. (8 November 1911). Mystery Story Retold By Carr. *Indianapolis Star*. p. 14.

Indianapolis Star. (9 November 1911). Fails to Glean Mystery Clew. *Indianapolis Star*. p. 10.

Indianapolis Star. (10 November 1911). Wild Theories Given in Knabe Case Tips. *Indianapolis Star*. p. 6.

Indianapolis Star. (11 November 1911). New Witness Heard Scream in Knabe Flat. *Indianapolis Star*. pp. 1,7.

Indianapolis Star. (12 November 1911). Phone Alarm Newest Clew in Knabe Case. *Indianapolis Star*. pp. 1. 4.

Indianapolis Star. (12 November 1911). Editorial. *Indianapolis Star*. p. 10.

Indianapolis Star. (13 November 1911). Negress offers no Clew in Knabe Case. *Indianapolis Star*. p. 12.

Indianapolis Star. (13 November 1911). Editorial. *Indianapolis Star*. p. 14.

Indianapolis Star. (14 November 1911). Next Step Undecided in Mystery Inquiry. *Indianapolis Star*. pp. 1,5.

Indianapolis Star. (15 November 1911). Editorial. *Indianapolis Star*. p. 6.

Indianapolis Star. (15 November 1911). Ouija Board Solves Dr. Knabe Mystery. *Indianapolis Star*. p. 5.

Indianapolis Star. (15 November 1911). Bares Lite to Cast Light on Knabe Death. *Indianapolis Star*. pp. 1,6.

Indianapolis Star. (16 November 1911). Would have Detained women in Knabe Case. *Indianapolis Star*. p. 1

Indianapolis Star. (17 November 1911). Prowler Sought in Knabe Inquiry. *Indianapolis Star*. p. 1

Indianapolis Star. (18 November 1911). Secrecy Marks Knabe Case Quiz. *Indianapolis Star*. p. 1.

Indianapolis Star. (18 November 1911). Editorial. *Indianapolis Star*. p. 8.

Indianapolis Star. (21 November 1911). Coroner and Police Rest in Knabe Case Inquiry. *Indianapolis Star*. p.3.

Indianapolis Star. (21 November 1911). More from Dr. Charles. *Indianapolis Star*. p.6

Indianapolis Star. (22 November 1911). Colored Janitor Finishes Testimony in Knabe Case. *Indianapolis Star*. p. 14.

Indianapolis Star. (23 November 1911). Story of Knabe Case Retold By Mrs. Hitt. *Indianapolis Star*. p. 16.

Indianapolis Star. (25 November 1911). Halts Knabe Case Inquiry. *Indianapolis Star*. p. 13.

Indianapolis Star. (30 November 1911). Editorial. *Indianapolis Star*. p. 8.

Indianapolis Star. (3 December 1911). Gives Light on Dr. Knabe's Life. *Indianapolis Star*. p. 12.

Indianapolis Star. (4 December 1911). Editorial. *Indianapolis Star*. p. 8.

Indianapolis Star. (5 December 1911). Offers to Solve Mystery. *Indianapolis Star*. p. 5.

Indianapolis Star. (5 December 1911). Confirm Prowler Story. *Indianapolis Star*. p. 3.

Indianapolis Star. (6 December 1911). Votes to Aid in Knabe Inquiry. *Indianapolis Star*. p. 16.

Indianapolis Star. (6 December 1911). Editorial. *Indianapolis Star*. p. 8.

Indianapolis Star. (7 December 1911). Seeks Ring Given Dr. Knabe. *Indianapolis Star*. p. 5.

Indianapolis Star. (7 December 1911). Editorial. *Indianapolis Star*. p. 8.

Indianapolis Star. (8 December 1911). Editorial. *Indianapolis Star*. p. 8.

Indianapolis Star. (11 December 1911). Editorial. *Indianapolis Star*. p. 12.

Indianapolis Star. (11 December 1911). Editorial. *Indianapolis Star*. p. 6.

Indianapolis Star. (30 December 1911). The Knabe Murder Verdict. *Indianapolis Star*. p. 8.

Indianapolis Star. (30 December 1911). Knabe Murder Verdict Ridiculed by Hyland. *Indianapolis Star.* p. 1.

Indianapolis Star. (31 December 1911). Editorial. *Indianapolis Star.* p. 12.

Indianapolis Star. (31 December 1911). Gives Light on Dr. Knabe's Life. *Indianapolis Star.* p. 1.

Indianapolis Star. (2 February 1912). Concert to Aid Teachers' Fund. *Indianapolis Star.* p.5.

Indianapolis Star. (11 February 1912). Knabe Mystery Inquiry Started. *Indianapolis Star.* p. 4.

Indianapolis Star. (16 February 1912). Propose Reward in Knabe Puzzle. *Indianapolis Star.* p. 1.

Indianapolis Star. (25 February 1912). Reward Offer Renewal Asked in Knabe Case. *Indianapolis Star.* pp. 1, 23.

Indianapolis Star. (12 April 1912). Sailor Held in the East Admits Knabe Murder. *Indianapolis Star.* p. 1.

Indianapolis Star. (5 April 1912). Admits he Imagined Confession of Crime. *Indianapolis Star.* p.1.

Indianapolis Star. (7 April 1912). Refutes Nichols' Story. *Indianapolis Star.* p.28.

Indianapolis Star. (11 April 1912). Nichols Says He Will Tell More. *Indianapolis Star.* p. 1.

Indianapolis Star. (23 April 1912). Knabe "Slayer" Sentenced. *Indianapolis Star.* p. 2.

Indianapolis Star. (25 April 1912). Editorial. *Indianapolis Star.* p. 9.

Indianapolis Star. (20 May 1912). "Confession" Amuses Police. *Indianapolis Star.* p. 4.

Indianapolis Star. (12 July 1912). Would Name Knabe Murderer. *Indianapolis Star.* p. 10.

Indianapolis Star. (23 October 1912). Knabe Mystery Year Old Today. *Indianapolis Star.* pp. 1,3

Indianapolis Star. (27 December 1912). Knabe Inquiry Deferred. *Indianapolis Star.* p. 3.

Indianapolis Star. (21 December 1912). New Knabe Quiz Will End Today. *Indianapolis Star.* p. 7.

Indianapolis Star. (22 December 1912). Kimono Figures in Knabe Probe. *Indianapolis Star.* pp. 1,3.

Indianapolis Star. (23 December 1912). Editorial. *Indianapolis Star.* p. 6.

Indianapolis Star. (25 December 1912). View of the People. *Indianapolis Star.* p. 8.

Indianapolis Star. (27 December 1912). Knabe Inquiry Takes New Turn. *Indianapolis Star.* p. 1.

Indianapolis Star. (31 December 1912). Grand Jury Reports Today. *Indianapolis Star.* p. 13.

Indianapolis Star. (1 January 1913). Accused in Dr. Knabe Mystery Give Bonds. *Indianapolis Star.* pp. 1,3.

Indianapolis Star. (1 January 1913). Chronology of the Knabe Mystery. *Indianapolis Star.* p. 1.

Indianapolis Star. (1 January 1913). Police Baffled in Long Search. *Indianapolis Star.* p. 10.

Indianapolis Star. (1 January 1913). Dr. Knabe's Philosophy of Life. *Indianapolis Star.* p. 10.

Indianapolis Star. (1 January 1913). Durham Feels Justified; Hyland Still Skeptical. *Indianapolis Star.* p.3.

Indianapolis Star. (1 January 1913). Editorial. *Indianapolis Star.* p. 4.

Indianapolis Star. (1 January 1913). Reward Tendered By Women Stands Alone. *Indianapolis Star.* p. 12.

Indianapolis Star. (2 January 1913). Arguments Advanced by Supports of Two Knabe Death Case Theories. *Indianapolis Star.* p.1.

Indianapolis Star. (2 January 1913). Editorial. *Indianapolis Star.* p.6.

Indianapolis Star. (2 January 1913). Baker Proposes Early Trial in Dr. Knabe Case. *Indianapolis Star.* pp.1,5.

Indianapolis Star. (3 January 1913). Leaders of Bar May be Called to Knabe Case. *Indianapolis Star.*

pp.1,3.

Indianapolis Star. (3 January 1913). Dr. Craig's Former Assistant Offers Explanation of Phone Call to Flat. *Indianapolis Star*. p.5

Indianapolis Star. (3 January 1913). Editorial. *Indianapolis Star*. p.8.

Indianapolis Star. (4 January 1913). Baker to Take Active Charge of Knabe Case. *Indianapolis Star*. pp.1, 3.

Indianapolis Star. (4 January 1913). Chosen to Assist in Knabe Case Prosecution. *Indianapolis Star*. p.3.

Indianapolis Star. (5 January 1913). Ask Physicians to Raise Fund for Knabe Case. *Indianapolis Star*. pp. 1,8.

Indianapolis Star. (8 January 1913). Doctors Table Knabe Request. *Indianapolis Star*. p. 1, 3.

Indianapolis Star. (9 January 1913). Kokomo Physician Who Knew Dr. Knabe Scouts Theory She Committed Suicide. *Indianapolis Star*. p. 9.

Indianapolis Star. (10 January 1913). Editorial. *Indianapolis Star*. p. 8.

Indianapolis Star. (11 January 1913). Editorial. *Indianapolis Star*. p. 8.

Indianapolis Star. (12 January 1913). Editorial. *Indianapolis Star*. p. 16.

Indianapolis Star. (13 January 1913). Dream Deepens Knabe Mystery. *Indianapolis Star*. p. 12.

Indianapolis Star. (13 January 1913). Strengthen Council For Dr. Knabe Case. p. 14.

Indianapolis Star. (13 January 1913). Editorial. *Indianapolis Star*. p. 6.

Indianapolis Star. (14 January 1913). Equal Suffrage Meeting. *Indianapolis Star*. p. 11.

Indianapolis Star. (15 January 1913). Long Delay Possible in Knabe Hearings. *Indianapolis Star*. p. 3.

Indianapolis Star. (23 March 1913). Missing Knabe Document Found Wrapped in Kimono. .*Indianapolis Star*. p. 52

Indianapolis Star. (26 April 1913).Knabe Trial May not Begin Until Fall. *Indianapolis Star*. p. 17.

Indianapolis Star. (14 June 1913). Editorial. .*Indianapolis Star*. p. 7.

Indianapolis Star. (22 June 1913). Knabe Case Rumors Denied. *Indianapolis Star*. p. 20.

Indianapolis Star. (5 September 1913). Craig-Ragsdale Trial Scheduled to Begin Oct 23. *Indianapolis Star*. p. 1.

Indianapolis Star. (3 October 1913). Knabe Case Plea Adds New Delay. *Indianapolis Star*. p. 1,15.

Indianapolis Star. (4 October 1913). Date for Craig Trial Not Yet Determined. *Indianapolis Star*. p. 4.

Indianapolis Star. (13 October 1913). Dream Deepens Knabe Mystery. .*Indianapolis Star*. p. 12.

Indianapolis Star. (28 October 1913). Dr. Craig Trial at Shelbyville to Open Today. *Indianapolis Star*. p. 1,3.

Indianapolis Star. (29 October 1913). 11 Jurors in Box as First Day of Craig Trial Ends. .*Indianapolis Star*. p. 1.

Indianapolis Star. (29 October 1913). Trial Judge in Knabe Murder Case. *Indianapolis Star*. p. 5.

Indianapolis Star. (24 November 1913). Craig Ready to Face Court in Knabe Case. *Indianapolis Star*. pp. 1, 3.

Indianapolis Star. (30 November 1913). First Evidence in Craig Trial is Due Monday. *Indianapolis Star*. pp. 1.8

Indianapolis Star. (1 December 1913). Craig Jury May Be Seated Today. .*Indianapolis Star*. p. 7.

Indianapolis Star. (2 December 1913). Lawyers Clash at Craig Trial; Jury is Seated. *Indianapolis Star*. pp. 1.6.

Indianapolis Star. (2 December 1913). Lawyers Interested in Craig Trial. *Indianapolis Star.* p. 6.

Indianapolis Star. (2 December 1913). Lawyers Clash at Craig Trial; Jury is Seated. *Indianapolis Star.* pp. 1, 6.

Indianapolis Star. (3 December 1913). Defense Seeks to Prove Knabe Death a Suicide. *Indianapolis Star.* pp. 1,4.

Indianapolis Star. (3 December 1913). Important Witnesses "Dodging" Camera. *Indianapolis Star.* p. 4.

Indianapolis Star. (4 December 1913). Point is Scored by Defense at Dr. Craig Trial. *Indianapolis Star.* pp. 1, 9.

Indianapolis Star. (5 December 1913). Three Tell of Hearing Cries at Knabe Flat. *Indianapolis Star.* pp. 1.5.

Indianapolis Star. (6 December 1913). Miss M'Pherson Recounts Story of Knabe Death. *Indianapolis Star.* p.1, 4.

Indianapolis Star. (7 December 1913). Thrills Scarce in Craig Trial . *Indianapolis Star.* pp. 1, 9.

Indianapolis Star. (8 December 1913). Knabe Evidence May End Today . *Indianapolis Star.* pp.1, 5.

Indianapolis Star. (9 December 1913). Court Reserves Ruling on Plea to Acquit Craig . *Indianapolis Star.* pp. 1, 11.

Indianapolis Star. (10 December 1913). Court Shatters State's Charge and Frees Craig . *Indianapolis Star.* pp.1,6.

Indianapolis Star. (10 December 1913). Veterinarian Freed of Murder Charge. *Indianapolis Star.* p.6.

Indianapolis Star. (10 December 1913). Chronology of Knabe Mystery. *Indianapolis Star.* p.6.

Indianapolis Star. (10 December 1913). Editorial. *Indianapolis Star.* p.8.

Indianapolis Star. (19 December 1913). Deny Seeing Blood on Kimono at First. *Indianapolis Star.* p.15.

Indianapolis Star. (30 December 1914). Funeral For Detective Asch Set for Tomorrow. *Indianapolis Star.* p.14.

Indianapolis Star. (1 January 1915). Crowd Attend Funeral Of City Detective Asch. *Indianapolis Star.* p.13.

Indianapolis Star. (26 January 1915). Editorial. *Indianapolis Star.* p6.

Indianapolis Star. (20 April 1915). Jefferson Haynes Obituary . *Indianapolis Star.* p. 2.

Indianapolis Star. (9 February 1935). Ephriam Inman, 69 Noted Lawyer, Dies. *Indianapolis Star.* p1.

Indianapolis Star. (26 June 1915). Local School Growing Fast. *Indianapolis Star.* p. 4.

Indianapolis Star. (24 December 1919). Death Comes to Police Veteran. *Indianapolis Star.* p.9.

Indianapolis Star. (28 July 1922). Dr. Wynn Killed in Fall From Cliff on Mt. Siyeh. *Indianapolis Star.* pp.1,3.

Indianapolis Star. (3 January 1923). Veterinarians of State Reinstate Ousted Members. Indianapolis Star. pp. 1, 10.

Indianapolis Star (9 July 1923). Detectives May Quit Following Shakeup. *Indianapolis Star.* p.13.

Indianapolis Star. (19 December 1924). Apoplexy Stroke fatal to Charles Durham. *Indianapolis Star.* pp. 1, 3.

Indianapolis Star. (25 September 1927). Lew Shank, Colorful Public Leader, Dies. *Indianapolis Star.* pp.1, 7.

Indianapolis Star (29 December 1927). Municipal Judge Takes Own Life. *Indianapolis Star.* p.9.

Indianapolis Star (30 December 1927). Bar Association Plans to Honor M'Allister. *Indianapolis Star.* p.8.

Indianapolis Star. (5 March 1928). Takes Own Life in Hotel Room. *Indianapolis Star.* p.11.

Indianapolis Star. (28 October 1928). Otto Simon Obituary. *Indianapolis Star.* p.23.

Indianapolis Star. (10 June 1931). Persons from all Walks of Life Praise Kinney-Man and Policeman. *Indianapolis Star.* p. 10.

Indianapolis Star. (19 February 1932). Former Mayor of Kokomo Dies. *Indianapolis Star.* p.4.

Indianapolis Star. (19 May 1935). Henry N. Spaan, Attorney, is Dead. *Indianapolis Star.* p.8.

Indianapolis Star. (20 May 1935). Henry Spaan Loved Nature, Friend Said. *Indianapolis Star.* p.10.

Indianapolis Star. (6 April 1943). Dr. Freeland Dies; Headed to Hospital. *Indianapolis Star.* p.11.

Indianapolis Star. (7 April 1943). Dr. Freeland Obituary. Indianapolis Star. p.5.

Indianapolis Star. (21 November 1943). W.A. Holtz Former Police Captain Dies; Noted as Outstanding Detective. *Indianapolis Star.* p. 13.

Indianapolis Star. (25 July 1945). Mrs. Olga Tetley Obituary. *Indianapolis Star.* p. 22.

Indianapolis Star. (14 January 1946). F. Elmer Hall Obituary. *Indianapolis Star.* p. 24.

Indianapolis Star (19 July 1948). Frank Baker, Ex-Judge Dies. *Indianapolis Star.* pp.1, 4.

Indianapolis Star (20 July 1948). Good Jurist, Good Citizen. *Indianapolis Star.* p.12.

Indianapolis Star (25 July 1948).Frank P. Baker Burial Permit. *Indianapolis Star.* p.21.

Indianapolis Star (19 October 1952). Judge Joseph Markey Dies, Rites Tomorrow. *Indianapolis Star.* p.32.

Indianapolis Star (15 August 1954). Miss Knabe Dies; Former Teacher. Indianapolis Star. p.50.

Indianapolis Star (20 September 1955). Pioneer Doctor, Lillian C. Lowder, Dies. Indianapolis Star p13.

Indianapolis Star. (13 January 1957). Bulldog Mullin is a Living Legend. *Indianapolis Star.* p. 21.

Indianapolis Star. (13 October 1958). John Mullin Noted Police Officer Dies. *Indianapolis Star.* p. 11.

Indianapolis Star. (28 June 1968). Woman Doctor's Murder in 1911 Baffled Police, Private Probes. *Indianapolis Star.* p. 6.

Indianapolis Star. (1 November 1971). Determined Women Helped Build City. *Indianapolis Star.* p. 19.

Indianapolis Star. (7 November 1971). Bizarre Slaying of Doctor in 1911 Still Unsolved. *Indianapolis Star.* p. 14.

Indianapolis Star. (30 April 1975).Bruce Aldridge Obituary. *Indianapolis Star.* p.17.

Indiana State Board of Charities. (1907 September). The Indiana Bulletin of Charities and Correction. Indiana State Board of Charities.Vol *7 0-74(36)*.

Indiana State Board of Health. (1905) Report of Indiana State Board of Health: Twenty-Fourth Annual Report. State of Indiana. *Indiana State Archives Indiana Commission on Public Records. 5(1)*.

Indiana State Board of Health. (1906) Report of Indiana State Board of Health: Twenty-Fourth Annual Report. State of Indiana. *Indiana State Archives Indiana Commission on Public Records. 8 (1-12)*.

Indiana State Board of Health. (1907) Report of Indiana State Board of Health: Twenty-Fourth Annual Report. State of Indiana. *Indiana State Archives Indiana Commission on Public Records. 9 (1-12)*.

Indiana State Board of Health. (1908) Dr. J.N. Hurty Correspondence. State of Indiana. *Indiana State Archives Indiana Commission on Public Records. Pp. 6, 20, 48, 57, 62, 66,87, 88, 95-96, 334, 374, 449*.

Indiana State Board of Health. (1908) Report of Indiana State Board of Health: Twenty-Fourth Annual Report. State of Indiana. *Indiana State Archives Indiana Commission on Public Records. 10 (1-12)*.

Indiana State Medical Association. (15 December 1908). News, Notes and Comments. *Journal of the Indiana State Medical Association.* p.479.

Indiana State Medical Association. (1911). *Journal of the Indiana State Medical Association.*

Indianapolis, IN: Indiana State Medical Association. 4 (495).

Indiana State Medical Association. (15 November 1911). News, Notes and Comments. *Journal of the Indiana State Medical Association.* p.495.

Indiana State Medical Society. (1905). Members Registered at the West Baden Meeting. Indiana State Medical Society. pp..3, 528. Indianapolis; Wm. B. Buford, Printer and Binder.

Indiana State Medical Society. (1906). Members Registered at the Winona Lake Meeting. Indiana State Medical Society. pp.vii, 572. Indianapolis; Wm. B. Buford, Printer and Binder.

Indiana State Medical Society. (1907). Members Registered at the Indianapolis Meeting. Indiana State Medical Society. pp.vii, 570. Indianapolis; Wm. B. Buford, Printer and Binder.

Indianapolis Sun. (24 October 1911). Dr. Helene Knabe Killed in Night, Janitor is Held. *Indianapolis Sun.* pp. 1-2.

Indianapolis Sun. (24 October 1911). Sketch of Room Where Body of Woman was Found by Girl. *Indianapolis Sun.* p. 2.

Indianapolis Sun. (25 October 1911). Crime Chronology as Told in Hours. *Indianapolis Sun.* p.2.

Indianapolis Sun. (25 October 1911). Says Women Should Know How to Shoot. *Indianapolis Sun.* p.2.

Indianapolis Sun. (25 October 1911). Murderers of Women in This City Shrouded in Mystery. *Indianapolis Sun.* p.2.

Indianapolis Sun. (25 October 1911). Women Physicians of City Laud Life Work of Victim. *Indianapolis Sun.* p.2.

Indianapolis Sun. (25 October 1911). Women in Face of Fierce Quiz by Detectives. *Indianapolis Sun.* pp.1,12.

Indianapolis Sun. (25 October 1911). Why the Police?. *Indianapolis Sun.* p.2.

Indianapolis Sun. (25 October 1911). Unconscious Before Her Throat Cut. *Indianapolis Sun..*

Indianapolis Sun. (25 October 1911). State Officers Laud Her. *Indianapolis Sun.*

Indianapolis Sun. (25 October 1911). Emergency Call for Council Reward. *Indianapolis Sun.*

Indianapolis Sun. (25 October 1911). Developments in the Knabe Murder Case. *Indianapolis Sun.*

Indianapolis Sun. (26 October 1911). Premeditated Murder is Now Held as Most Plausible Theory. *Indianapolis Sun.* pp.1,3.

Indianapolis Sun. (26 October 1911). Analysis of Doctor's Mind is Side Light on Mystery. *Indianapolis Sun.* p.3.

Indianapolis Sun. (26 October 1911). First Physician at Bedside of Victim. *Indianapolis Sun.* p.3.

Indianapolis Sun. (26 October 1911). Things Known by Doctor in Work may be Murder Cause. *Indianapolis Sun.* p.3.

Indianapolis Sun. (26 October 1911). Hears Screams; Later Sees Man Walk Out Alley. *Indianapolis Sun.* pp.1, 3.

Indianapolis Sun. (26 October 1911). Cousin's Coolness Attracts Attention. *Indianapolis Sun.* p.1.

Indianapolis Sun. (26 October 1911). Victim Buried Friday. *Indianapolis Sun.* p.3.

Indianapolis Sun. (26 October 1911). City Reward Delayed. *Indianapolis Sun.* p.3.

Indianapolis Sun. (26 October 1911). Once Childhood Playmate; Says Doctor Acted Queerly. *Indianapolis Sun.* p.16.

Indianapolis Sun. (27 October 1911). Augusta Knabe Denies She Ever Loaned Doctor $500. *Indianapolis Sun.* p.1.

Indianapolis Sun. (27 October 1911). Miss Knabe to Bare Detailed Murder Facts. *Indianapolis Sun.* p.1.

Indianapolis Sun. (27 October 1911). Many Friends Follow body of Murder Victim to Grave. *Indianapolis Sun*. p.1.

Indianapolis Sun. (28 October 1911). Miss Knabe is Now on Verge of Collapsing. *Indianapolis Sun*. pp.1-2.

Indianapolis Sun. (29 October 1911). Letter shows Suicide Was Not Intended. *Indianapolis Sun*. pp.1-2.

Indianapolis Sun. (29 October 1911). Women at Highest Pitch in Years over Knabe Mystery. *Indianapolis Sun*. p.2.

Indianapolis Sun. (30 October 1911). Saw Tall Man Dodge Out of Passage Way. *Indianapolis Sun*. pp.1, 10.

Indianapolis Sun. (30 October 1911). Is Murder of Knabe to be Fourteenth Unsolved?. *Indianapolis Sun*. p.2.

Indianapolis Sun. (30 October 1911). Offered Prayer over Body of Her Murdered Cousin. *Indianapolis Sun*. p.1.

Indianapolis Sun. (30 October 1911). Dr. Knabe Mystery Blamed for Suicide. *Indianapolis Sun*. p.12.

Indianapolis Sun. (31 October 1911). Dreamt Snake Crushing Her and Dr. Knabe. *Indianapolis Sun*. pp.1, 5.

Indianapolis Sun. (31 October 1911). Medical Men and Women Take Cross Views of Crime. *Indianapolis Sun*. p.1.

Indianapolis Sun. (31 October 1911). None Will Don Suit Dr. Knabe Ordered. Indianapolis Sun. p1.

Indianapolis Sun. (1 November 1911). Harry W. Haskett. *Indianapolis Sun*. p.1.

Indianapolis Sun. (1 November 1911). Doctor's Property will be Searched for Minute Clews. *Indianapolis Sun*. pp.1, 3.

Indianapolis Sun. (1 November 1911). Mental Telepathy Focus Told of Dr. Knabe Tragedy. *Indianapolis Sun*. p.3.

Indianapolis Sun. (1 November 1911). Psychologist Analyses Snake Dream of Miss Augusta Knabe. *Indianapolis Sun*. p.12.

Indianapolis Sun. (2 November 1911). Dr. Knabe's Key is Discovered on Top of Her Chiffonier. *Indianapolis Sun*. p.1, 8.

Indianapolis Sun. (2 November 1911). Suicide Impossible, Thinks College Chum of Dr. Knabe. *Indianapolis Sun*. p.3.

Indianapolis Sun. (3 November 1911). Is Helene Knabe's Murder Playing Tag with Sleuths?. *Indianapolis Sun*. p.1,22.

Indianapolis Sun. (4 November 1911). Teachers Raising Fund for Sleuths to Clear Mystery. *Indianapolis Sun*. p.1,2.

Indianapolis Sun. (5 November 1911). Hunt Greek Prince Who Saw Man with Dr. Knabe in Flat. *Indianapolis Sun*. pp.1, 11.

Indianapolis Sun. (6 November 1911). Police and Coroner Compile Knabe Data. *Indianapolis Sun*. p.1.

Indianapolis Sun. (7 November 1911). Stories of Haskett and Carr Tally Up. *Indianapolis Sun*. p.14.

Indianapolis Sun. (8 November 1911). Coroner Questions Mrs. Frank B. Wynn. *Indianapolis Sun*. p.3.

Indianapolis Sun. (9 November 1911). Woman Testifies In Knabe Case of Fear. *Indianapolis Sun*. p.3.

Indianapolis Sun. (10 November 1911). Fancy Crazy Quilt missing From Flat Lest Murder Find. *Indianapolis Sun*. p.1.

Indianapolis Sun. (11 November 1911). Was Street Light Out Fatal Night?. *Indianapolis Sun*. p.3.

Indianapolis Sun. (12 November 1911). Dr. Knabe at German House Night Just Before Her Death.

Indianapolis Sun. p.1.

Indianapolis Sun. (14 November 1911). No "Horrors" Deter Couple from Renting Knabe Flat. *Indianapolis Sun*. p.1.

Indianapolis Sun. (15 November 1911). Dr. Knabe Case is Without New Facts. *Indianapolis Sun*. p.3.

Indianapolis Sun. (16 November 1911). Dr. Knabe Relics Attract Stream of Morbidly Curious. *Indianapolis Sun*. p.1.

Indianapolis Sun. (17 November 1911). The Knabe Case. *Indianapolis Sun*. p.3.

Indianapolis Sun. (29 November 1911). Dr. Knabe was Murdered is Durham Edict. *Indianapolis Sun*. p.1.

Indianapolis Sun. (10 February 1912). Women Place Knabe Case in Sleuth's Hand. *Indianapolis Sun*. pp.1, 9.

Indianapolis Sun. (2 April 1912). Murder Confessor Thought Insane by Portsmouth Police. *Indianapolis Sun*. pp.1-2.

Indianapolis Sun. (4 April 1912). Lieut. Kinney to Question Nichols. *Indianapolis Sun*. p.1.

Indianapolis Sun. (15 April 1912). Shank Hedging Upon Vice; Police Power is Refused Women. *Indianapolis Sun*. p.1.

Indianapolis Sun. (6 June 1912). Suffrage Campaign Spreads by Trolley. *Indianapolis Sun*. p.1.

Indianapolis Sun. (6 June 1912). Requests for Powers Makes Hyland Swear. *Indianapolis Sun*. p.1.

Indianapolis Sun. (20 June 1912). Dr. Craig is Prepared to Meet Charge. *Indianapolis Sun*. p.1, 3.

Indianapolis Sun. (21 June 1912). Women on Stand for Hours in Knabe Pry. *Indianapolis Sun*. p.1.

Indianapolis Sun. (22 June 1912). Grand Jury Closes its Knabe Inquiry. *Indianapolis Sun*. p.2.

Indianapolis Sun. (11 July 1912). Thinks he's solved Knabe Murder Case. *Indianapolis Sun*. p.1.

Indianapolis Sun. (19 December 1912). Grand Jury Reopens Knabe Case; Leading Witnesses Testify. *Indianapolis Sun*. p.1.

Indianapolis Sun. (22 December 1912). Holtz Before Jury in Knabe Inquiry. *Indianapolis Sun*. p.1.

Indianapolis Sun. (26 December 1912). Sleuth Before Grand Jury in Knabe Inquiry. *Indianapolis Sun*. p.1.

Indianapolis Sun. (28 December 1912). Durham Before Jury. *Indianapolis Sun*. p.1.

Indianapolis Sun. (30 December 1912). Woman Called in Knabe Investigation. *Indianapolis Sun*. p.1.

Indianapolis Sun. (31 December 1912). Grand Jury Returns Indictments in Knabe Murder and the C, H. & D. Catastrophe. *Indianapolis Sun*. p.1, 9.

Indianapolis Sun. (1 January 1913). Knabe Indictments. *Indianapolis Sun*. p.1.

Indianapolis Sun. (2 January 1913). Augusta Knabe editorial. *Indianapolis Sun*. p.1.

Indianapolis Sun. (3 January 1913). Inman Engaged to Help Prosecution in Trial of Craig. *Indianapolis Sun*. p.1.

Indianapolis Sun. (5 January 1913). Physicians Asked to Help Prosecute. *Indianapolis Sun*. p.1.

Indianapolis Sun. (6 February 1913). Spiritual Communication to Local Clubwoman Detailed.

Indianapolis Sun. (8 January 1913). Table Motion to Raise Knabe Fund. *Indianapolis Sun*. p.1.

Indianapolis Sun. (7 May 1913). Knabe Case Delayed; Lawyers Campaigning. *Indianapolis Sun*. p.1.

Indianapolis Sun. (20 October 1913). Craig Trial May Open Nov. 24. *Indianapolis Sun*. p.1.

Indianapolis Sunday Sun. (30 November 1913). Slain Doctor's Cousin. *Indianapolis Sunday Sun*. p.1.

Indianapolis Times. (4 December 1935). Mrs. Kropp Dies; Former Teacher. *Indianapolis Times*. p.10.

Indianapolis Times. (24 May 1950). Brilliant Woman Doctor's Killer Committed A Perfect Crime. *Indianapolis Times*. p. 17.

Indiana University (1906). Yearbook. Indiana University. Bloomington: Indiana University.

Indiana University School of Medicine. (1905). *Register and Announcements*. Bloomington: Indiana University School of Medicine.

Indiana University School of Medicine. (1906). *Register and Announcements*. Bloomington: Indiana University School of Medicine.

Indiana University School of Medicine. (1907). *Register and Announcements*. Bloomington: Indiana University School of Medicine.

Indiana University School of Medicine. (1908). *Register and Announcements*. Bloomington: Indiana University School of Medicine.

Indiana University School of Medicine. (1909). *Register and Announcements*. Bloomington: Indiana University School of Medicine.

Indiana University School of Medicine. (1910). *Register and Announcements*. Bloomington: Indiana University School of Medicine.

Indiana University School of Medicine. (1911). *Register and Announcements*. Bloomington: Indiana University School of Medicine.

Indiana University School of Medicine (n.d.). A Brief History of the Indiana University School of Medicine 1903-1993. Bloomington: Indiana University School of Medicine.

Indiana Veterinary College. (1908). *Corporate Report*. Indiana Veterinary College. Indiana State Archives, Indiana Commission on Public Records.

Indiana Veterinary College. (1910). *Corporate Report*. Indiana Veterinary College. Indiana State Archives, Indiana Commission on Public Records.

Indiana Veterinary College. (1911). *Corporate Report*. Indiana Veterinary College. Indiana State Archives, Indiana Commission on Public Records.

Indiana Veterinary College. (1912). *Corporate Report*. Indiana Veterinary College. Indiana State Archives, Indiana Commission on Public Records.

Indiana Veterinary College. (1913). *Corporate Report*. Indiana Veterinary College. Indiana State Archives, Indiana Commission on Public Records.

Indiana Veterinary College. (1915). *Amendment*. Indiana Veterinary College. Indiana State Archives, Indiana Commission on Public Records.

Indiana Veterinary College. (1915). *Corporate Report*. Indiana Veterinary College. Indiana State Archives, Indiana Commission on Public Records.

Indiana Veterinary College. (1916). *Corporate Report*. Indiana Veterinary College. Indiana State Archives, Indiana Commission on Public Records.

Indiana Veterinary College. (1917). *Corporate Report*. Indiana Veterinary College. Indiana State Archives, Indiana Commission on Public Records.

Indiana Veterinary College. (1919). *Corporate Report*. Indiana Veterinary College. Indiana State Archives, Indiana Commission on Public Records.

Indiana Veterinary College (1918). Catalogue. W.H. Smith Memorial Library, Indiana Historical Society.

Indiana Veterinary College (1921). Catalogue. W.H. Smith Memorial Library, Indiana Historical Society.

Indiana Veterinary College. (1921). *Corporate Report*. Indiana Veterinary College. Indiana State Archives, Indiana Commission on Public Records.

Indiana Veterinary College. (1923). *Corporate Report*. Indiana Veterinary College. Indiana State Archives, Indiana Commission on Public Records.

Indiana Veterinary College. (1924). *Corporate Report*. Indiana Veterinary College. Indiana State Archives, Indiana Commission on Public Records.

Indiana Veterinary College. (1947). *Complaint for Forfeiture of Corporate Franchise*. Indiana Veterinary College. Indiana State Archives, Indiana Commission on Public Records.

Indiana Veterinary College. (1947). *Finding*. Indiana Veterinary College. Indiana State Archives, Indiana Commission on Public Records.

Indiana Veterinary College. (1947). *Notice*. Indiana Veterinary College. Indiana State Archives, Indiana Commission on Public Records.

January, A. (2016 February 19). Email correspondence.

Journal of the American Medical Association. (1905 July-December). Society Proceedings. Journal of the American Medical Association. 45(485).

Journal of the American Medical Association. (1910 January-June). News, Notes and Comments. *Journal of the American Medical Association*. 3(44).

Journal of the American Veterinary Medical Association. (1923). Miscellaneous. *Journal of the American Veterinary Medical Association*. 63 (685).

Journal of the American Veterinary Medical Association. (1924). Another College Closes. *Journal of the American Veterinary Medical Association*. 65 (401-2).

Kartenmeister. (n.d.). Rügenwaldermünde. Retrieved from http://www.kartenmeister.com/preview/City.asp?CitNum=4610

Kozinski, A. (2015). Criminal Law 2.0. *Georgetown Law Journal. Vol. 44 (2015)*.

Kritsky, G. (1995). Charles Darwin's Hoosier Correspondent. *Proceedings of the Indiana Academy of Science*. 104 (81-84).

Kyle, J.J (1906). *Disease of the Ears, Nose and Throat*. Philadelphia, PA: P. Blakiston Son & Company.

Le De Auguste, M. (1909). L'etude experimentale de la Rage. Paris: Octave Doin et Fils.

Lima Daily News. (30 November 1913). Light Upturned will be Turned on Murder Case. *Lima Daily News*. p.1.

Lincoln Evening News. (26 October 1911). Man with Kerchief Tied Across Face. *Lincoln Evening News*. p.2.

Lincoln Daily News. (9 December 1913). State Fails to Make Case Against Accused. *Lincoln Daily News*. p.1.

Lincoln Daily News. (7 December 1913). Helen Knabe is Called a Fighter. *Lincoln Daily News*. p.1.

Lincoln Daily News. (4 April 1912). Admits His Mentality is Out of Gear. *Lincoln Daily News*. p.5.

Lincoln Daily Star. (30 November 1913). Dr. Craig May Go on Stand in Trial. *Lincoln Daily Star*. p.5.

Los Angeles Times. (16 September 1959). Deaths. *Los Angeles Times*. p.B7.

Mansfield News. (24 November 1911). Indianapolis Woman Doctor. Mansfield News. p1.

Marion County Clerk. (1896). Arrival: *New York, New York*; Marion County Clerk, Indiana. Microfilm Serial: *M237, 1820-1897*; Microfilm Roll: *Roll 668*; Line: *1 (Helene Knabe)*.

Marion County, Indiana. (n.d.). *Execution Docket*. Marion County, Indiana. *No. 310*.

Marion County, Indiana. (n.d.) *General Entry, Claim and Allowance Docket of Estates, Marion County, Indiana: Dr. Helene Knabe*. Marion County, Indiana. *Book 39, Estate 10744*.

Marion County Clerk; *Index to Marriage Record 1911 - 1915 Inclusive Vol,* Marion County Clerk, Indiana Book.: *75*; Page: *67*.

Marion County, Indiana; *Index to Marriage Record 1911 - 1915 Inclusive Vol, Original Record Located: County Clerk's Office Ind*; Book: *78*; Page: *387*

Marion County, Indiana; *Index to Marriage Record 1896 - 1900 Inclusive Vol, Original Record Located: County Clerk's Office Ind*; Book: *190*

Marion County, Indiana. *(n.d.) Report on the State of Dr. Helene Knabe's Estate.* Marion County, Indiana. *Book 17 pp. 559.*

Marion County, Indiana. *(n.d.) Report on the State of Dr. Helene Knabe's Estate.* Marion County, Indiana. *Book 18 p. 28.*

Marion County, Indiana. *(1911) Report on the State of Dr. Helene Knabe's Estate.* Marion County, Indiana. *Book 22 p. 588.*

Marion County, Indiana. *(1913) Report on the State of Dr. Helene Knabe's Estate.* Marion County, Indiana. *p. Book 20 pp. 532-33, 575 a, b.*

Marion County, Indiana. (n.d.). *Superior Court Entry Docket Book 94. Superior Court,* Marion County, Indiana. *, No. 74393.*

Marion County, Indiana. (n.d.). *Superior Court Order Book 286, No. 74393. Superior Court,* Marion County, Indiana. *p. 345. 348, 350-352, 430.*

Marion County, Indiana. (n.d.). *Superior Court Order Book 286, No. 74395. Superior Court,* Marion County, Indiana. *p. 70.*

Marion County, Indiana. (n.d.). *Superior Court Order Book 289, No. 74393. Superior Court,* Marion County, Indiana. *p. 368.*

Marion County Superior Court. (1946). *Judgement on Finding regarding the Indiana Veterinary College.* Indiana State Archives, Indiana Commission on Public Records. *No. 1358904.*

Medical College of Indiana. (1898). *Register and Announcements.* Indianapolis, IN: Medical College of Indiana.

Medical College of Indiana. (1899). *Register and Announcements.* Indianapolis, IN: Medical College of Indiana.

Medical College of Indiana. (1900). *Register and Announcements.* Indianapolis, IN: Medical College of Indiana.

Medical College of Indiana. (1901). *Register and Announcements.* Indianapolis, IN: Medical College of Indiana.

Medical College of Indiana. (1902). *Register and Announcements.* Indianapolis, IN: Medical College of Indiana.

Medical College of Indiana. (1903). *Register and Announcements.* Indianapolis, IN: Medical College of Indiana.

Medical College of Indiana. (1904). *Register and Announcements.* Indianapolis, IN: Medical College of Indiana.

Mind and Body (1911 March- 1912 February) Notes from Normal Schools. *Mind and Body.* 18(297).

Ministerium der Öffentlichen Arbeiten. (5 July 1890). Centralblatt der Bauverwaltung. Ministerium der Öffentlichen Arbeiten. Berlin: Verlag von Ernst & Korn. 10 (273).

Ministerium der Öffentlichen Arbeiten. (31 August 1901).Zentralblatt der Bauverwaltung.Ministerium der Öffentlichen Arbeiten. Berlin: Verlag von Ernst & Korn. (422).

Ministerium der Öffentlichen Arbeiten. (14 December 1907). Zentralblatt der Bauverwaltung.

Ministerium der Öffentlichen Arbeiten. Berlin: Verlag von Ernst & Korn. 101 (657).

Ministerium der Öffentlichen Arbeiten. (4 January 1908). Zentralblatt der Bauverwaltung.Ministerium der Öffentlichen Arbeiten. Berlin: Verlag von Ernst & Korn. 1 (1).

Ministerium der Öffentlichen Arbeiten. (20 November 1911). Zentralblatt der Bauverwaltung. Berlin: Verlag von Ernst & Korn. 95 (593)/

Miyamoto, R. (2016, March 28). Personal Interview.

National Archives and Records Administration. *U.S., Civil War Pension Index: General Index to Pension Files, 1861-1934* [database on-line] for Samuel F. Tenant. Provo, UT, USA: Ancestry.com Operations Inc, 2000. Retrieve from http://search.ancestry.com/cgi-bin/sse.dll?gss=angs-c&new=1&rank=1&gsfn=samuel+f.&gsfn_x=0&gsln=tenant&gsln_x=0&msbpn__tp=ohio&msddy=1899&pcat=39&h=1678034&recoff=4+5+6+20&db=civilwarpension&indiv=1&ml_rpos=3

National Archives and Records Administration. *U.S., Civil War Pension Index: General Index to Pension Files, 1861-1934* [database on-line] for Samuel F. Tenant. Provo, UT, USA: Ancestry.com Operations Inc, 2000. Retrieved from http://search.ancestry.com/cgi-bin/sse.dll?gss=angs-c&new=1&rank=1&gsfn=samuel+f.&gsfn_x=0&gsln=tenant&gsln_x=0&msbpn__ftp=ohio&msddy=1899

National Library of Medicine (n.d.) Dr. Loy McAfee. National Library of Medicine. Retrieved from https://www.nlm.nih.gov/changingthefaceofmedicine/physicians/biography_356.html

Netterville, J. J. (1925). Centennial History of Madison County Indiana, Volumes I and II. Anderson, IN: Historians' Association.

New York State. (n.d.) Forensic Science History. New York State. Retrieved from https://www.troopers.ny.gov/Crime_Laboratory_System/History/Forensic_Science_History/

New York Sun. (25 October 1911). Woman Doctor Slain in Bed. *New York Sun*. p.4.

New York Times. (11 February 1912). Sleuths on Knabe Case. *New York Times*. p.11.

New York Times. (3 April 1912).Insists He Killed Dr. Helen Knabe. *New York Times*. p.10.

New York Times. (2 April 1912).Deserter got $1,500 for Killing Woman. *New York Times*. p.1.

New York Times. (1 January 1913).Two Indictments in Knabe Murder. *New York Times*. p.11.

New York Times, (25 October 1911). Find Woman Doctor Slain in her Home. *New York Times*. p.7.

New York Times. (26 October 1911). No Trace of Knife. *New York Times*. p.9.

New York Times. (27 October 1911).Clue to Dr. Knabe's Slayer. *New York Times*. p.11.

New York Times. (29 October 1911). Get Slain Woman's Papers. *New York Times*. p. C12.

New York Times. (28 October 1911). Was Seeking Flats Dr. Knabe Lived In. *New York Times*. p.20.

New York Times. (30 October 1911). Now Think Dr. Knabe Suicide. *New York Times*. p.4.

New York Times. (1 November 1911). Buddhism a Clue in Dr. Knabe Case. *New York Times*. p.2.

New York Times. (8 November 1911). Saw Man in Knabe Flat. *New York Times*. p.6.

New York Times. (11 November 1911).Sure Dr. Knabe Was Suicide. *New York Times*. p.5.

New York Times. (14 November 1911). New Knabe Murder Theory. *New York Times*. p.4.

New York Times. (16 November 1913). Wife to Use Maiden Name. *New York Times*. p. 15.

New York Times. (28 November 1913).At Bar for Knabe Murder. *New York Times*. p.20.

New York Times. (30 November 1913).Won't Ask Death Penalty. *New York Times*. p.14.

New York Times. (4 December 1913).Fails to Identify Craig. *New York Times*. p.2.

New York Times. (5 December 1913). Seek Dr. Craig's Acquittal. New York Times. p. 48.

New York Times. (7 December 1913). Knabe kimono as Evidence. *New York Times*. p.16.

New York Times. (10 December 1913). No title. *New York Times*. p.8.

New York Times. (10 December 1913). Dr. Craig Goes Free. *New York Times*. p.8.

New York Times. (30 December 1911).Knabe Verdict is Murder. *New York Times*. p.2.

Normal College of the North American Gymnastic Union. (n.d.). *Complimentary Tickets Distributed by A.G Herrmann to Members of the Faculty at the Normal College*. IUPUI University Library Ruth Lilly Special Collections and Archives.

Normal College of the North American Gymnastic Union. (n.d.). *Student Alliance Minutes (1909-1918) (Vol. 1)*. IUPUI University Library Ruth Lilly Special Collections and Archives.

Normal College of the North American Gymnastic Union. (1909). *Catalogue*. Indianapolis, IN: Normal College of the North American Gymnastic Union.

Normal College of the North American Gymnastic Union. (1910). *Catalogue*. Indianapolis, IN: Normal College of the North American Gymnastic Union.

Normal College of the North American Gymnastic Union. (1911). *Catalogue*. Indianapolis, IN: Normal College of the North American Gymnastic Union.

Normal College of the North American Gymnastic Union. (1911). *Summer Session Catalogue*. Indianapolis, IN: Normal College of the North American Gymnastic Union.

Normal College of the North American Gymnastic Union. (1912). *Summer Session Catalogue*. Indianapolis, IN: Normal College of the North American Gymnastic Union.

Normal College of the North American Gymnastic Union. (1910). *Faculty Pay Roll for Month Ending April 23, 1910*. IUPUI University Library Ruth Lilly Special Collections and Archives.

Normal College of the North American Gymnastic Union. (1910). *Faculty Pay Roll for Month Ending May 21, 1910*. IUPUI University Library Ruth Lilly Special Collections and Archives.

Normal College of the North American Gymnastic Union. (1910). *Faculty Pay Roll for Month Ending June 18, 1910*. IUPUI University Library Ruth Lilly Special Collections and Archives.

Normal College of the North American Gymnastic Union. (1910). *Faculty Pay Roll for Month Ending February 18, 1911*. IUPUI University Library Ruth Lilly Special Collections and Archives.

Normal College of the North American Gymnastic Union. (1910). *Faculty Pay Roll for Month Ending March 18, 1911*. IUPUI University Library Ruth Lilly Special Collections and Archives.

Normal College of the North American Gymnastic Union. (1910). *Faculty Pay Roll for Month Ending April 22, 1911*. IUPUI University Library Ruth Lilly Special Collections and Archives.

Normal College of the North American Gymnastic Union. (1910). *Faculty Pay Roll for Month Ending May 20, 1911*. IUPUI University Library Ruth Lilly Special Collections and Archives.

Normal College of the North American Gymnastic Union. (1910). *Faculty Pay Roll for Month Ending June 17, 1911*. IUPUI University Library Ruth Lilly Special Collections and Archives.

Normal College of the North American Gymnastic Union. (1910). *Faculty Pay Roll for Month Ending October 14, 1911*. IUPUI University Library Ruth Lilly Special Collections and Archives.

Normal College of the North American Gymnastic Union. (1910). *Faculty Pay Roll for Month Ending November 11, 1911*. IUPUI University Library Ruth Lilly Special Collections and Archives.

Notre Dame Scholastic. (11 March 1876). Personal. Notre Dame Scholastic. 9(441).

Notre Dame Scholastic. (13 May 1876). Personal. Notre Dame Scholastic. 9(586).

Notre Dame Scholastic. (17 June 1876). Personal. Notre Dame Scholastic. 9(669).

Notre Dame Scholastic. (24 June 1876). Personal. Notre Dame Scholastic. 9(685).

Official Gazette of the United States Patent Office (20 August 1918) Hygienic Garment Supporter. United States Patent Office. Volume 253(586)

Paper. (29 July 1914). Paper Plant to be Operated in Dayton. Paper. p.32.
R.L. Polk & Company. (1896). Indianapolis City Directory. R.L. Polk & Company.
R.L. Polk & Company. (1897). Indianapolis City Directory. R.L. Polk & Company
R.L. Polk & Company. (1898). Indianapolis City Directory. R.L. Polk & Company.
R.L. Polk & Company. (1899). Indianapolis City Directory. R.L. Polk & Company.
R.L. Polk & Company. (1900). Indianapolis City Directory. R.L. Polk & Company.
R.L. Polk & Company. (1901). Indianapolis City Directory. R.L. Polk & Company.
R.L. Polk & Company. (1902). Indianapolis City Directory. R.L. Polk & Company.
R.L. Polk & Company. (1903). Indianapolis City Directory. R.L. Polk & Company.
R.L. Polk & Company. (1904). Indianapolis City Directory. R.L. Polk & Company.
R.L. Polk & Company. (1905). Indianapolis City Directory. R.L. Polk & Company.
R.L. Polk & Company. (1906). Indianapolis City Directory. R.L. Polk & Company.
R.L. Polk & Company. (1907). Indianapolis City Directory. R.L. Polk & Company.
R.L. Polk & Company. (1908). Indianapolis City Directory. R.L. Polk & Company.
R.L. Polk & Company. (1909). Indianapolis City Directory. R.L. Polk & Company.
R.L. Polk & Company. (1910). Indianapolis City Directory. R.L. Polk & Company.
R.L. Polk & Company. (1911). Indianapolis City Directory. R.L. Polk & Company.
R.L. Polk & Company. (1912). Indianapolis City Directory. R.L. Polk & Company.
R.L. Polk & Company. (1913). Indianapolis City Directory. R.L. Polk & Company.
R.L. Polk & Company. (1916). Indianapolis City Directory. R.L. Polk & Company.
R.L. Polk & Company. (1921). Indianapolis City Directory. R.L. Polk & Company.
R.L. Polk & Company. (1922). Indianapolis City Directory. R.L. Polk & Company.
R.L. Polk & Company. (1926). Indianapolis City Directory. R.L. Polk & Company.
R.L. Polk & Company. (1929). Indianapolis City Directory. R.L. Polk & Company.
Purdue University. (n.d.). John N. Hurty Papers. Purdue University. Retrieved from http://www4.lib.purdue.edu/archon/?p=collections/findingaid&id=498&q=&rootcontentid=8509
Rennison, M.C. & Dodge, M. (2015). Introduction to Criminal Justice: Systems, Diversity and Changes. Thousand Oaks, CA: Sage Publications. Retrieved from http://www.sagepub.com/sites/default/files/upm-binaries/66074_Renninson_Chapter_4.pdf
Reno Evening Gazette. (24 November 1913). Slain After Quarrel by Old Friend. *Reno Evening Gazette*. p.16.
Rice, T.B. (1946). *Hoosier Health Officer: A Biography of Dr. J. N. Hurty and The History of The Indiana State Board of Health to 1925*. Indianapolis, IN: Indiana State Board of Health.
Rossiter, M. W. (1982). *Women Scientists in America: Struggles and Strategies to 1940*. Baltimore (Vol. 1). Baltimore, MD: Johns Hopkins.
Rouse, W. (2016) Email regarding cold case files.
San Antonio Press (4 April 1912). Murder Confession Hoax. *San Antonio Press*. p.3.
Saloniki-Greek Press. (13 April 1918). Celebration of the Ninety-Seventh Anniversary of Greek Independence Mr. Constantine Mammonas Appeals for Third Liberty Loan. Retrieved from http://flps.newberry.org/article/5422062_5_0789
Sandusky Star. (27 October 1911). Murderer is not Seen at Funeral. *Sandusky Star*. p1.
Smith, C.N. (2009). Nineteenth-Century Emigration of "Old Lutherans" from Eastern Germany

(Mainly Pomerania and Lower Silesia) to Australia, Canada, and the United States. Baltimore, MD: Clearfield Company, Inc.

Smithsonian Magazine. (30 August 1912).Murder Wasn't Very Pretty: The Rise and Fall of D.C. Stephenson. *Smithsonian Magazine.* Retrieved from http://www.smithsonianmag.com/history/murder-wasnt-very-pretty-the-rise-and-fall-of-dc-stephenson-18935042/#8Ba5mQ3MbyleWf9f.99

Spencer County, Indiana; *Index to Supplemental Record Marriage Transcript 1, W. P. A. Original Record Located: County Clerk's O*; Book: *C-1*; (Bettie Tenant0. Retrieved from http://search.ancestry.com/cgi-bin/sse.dll?indiv=1&db=inmarr1880&h=2861997&tid=&pid=&usePUB=true&rhSource=60281

Shelby County. (1913) W.B. Craig and A.M. Ragsdale Indictment. Shelby County, Indiana.

Shelbyville Democrat. (4 October 1913). Shelby County Gets Knabe Murder Case. *Shelbyville Democrat.* p.1.

Shelbyville Democrat. (22 October 1913). Date Agreed Upon for Murder Trial. *Shelbyville Democrat.* p.1.

Shelbyville Democrat. (26 November 1913). Sensational Murder Trial to Begin Friday. *Shelbyville Democrat.* p.1.

Shelbyville Democrat. (27 November 1913). Special Venire of 50 for Murder Trial. *Shelbyville Democrat.* p.1.

Shelbyville Democrat. (28 November 1913). Knabe Murder Case Now on Trial Here. *Shelbyville Democrat.* p.1.

Shelbyville Democrat. (29 November 1913). Only 15 of Special Venire of 50 Left. *Shelbyville Democrat.* p.1.

Shelbyville Democrat. (1 December 1913). Opening Statement Made This Afternoon. *Shelbyville Democrat.* p.1.

Shelbyville Democrat. (2 December 1913). Defense to Reply on Suicide and Alibi. *Shelbyville Democrat.* p.1.

Shelbyville Democrat. (2 December 1913). Defense to Reply on Suicide and Alibi. *Shelbyville Democrat.* p.1.

Shelbyville Democrat. (3 December 1913). Coroner of Marion County Testifies. *Shelbyville Democrat.* p.1.

Shelbyville Democrat. (5 December 1913). "The Other Woman" a Witness. *Shelbyville Democrat.* p.1.

Shelbyville Democrat. (6 December 1913). Touching Description of Dr. Helene Knabe. *Shelbyville Democrat.* p.1.

Shelbyville Democrat. (6 December 1913). Defense to Reply on Suicide and Alibi. *Shelbyville Democrat.* p.1.

Shelbyville Democrat. (8 December 1913). Defense is Demanding Acquittal of Dr. Craig. *Shelbyville Democrat.* p.1.

Shelbyville Democrat. (9 December 1913). Important Decision Ending Craig Trial. *Shelbyville Democrat.* p.1.

Shelbyville Democrat. (9 December 1913). Dr. Craig is Freed by Action of Judge Blair. *Shelbyville Democrat.* p.1.

Shelbyville Republican. (25 October 1911). Murder Mystery Still Unsolved. *Shelbyville Republican.* p.1.

Shelbyville Republican. (4 January 1912). Murder Verdict in Knabe Case. *Shelbyville Republican.* p.2.

Shelbyville Republican. (3 October 1913). Knabe Murder Case Sent Here. *Shelbyville Republican.* p.1.

Shelbyville Republican. (22 October 1913). Craig Murder Case Nob. 28th. *Shelbyville Republican.* p.1.

Shelbyville Republican. (1 December 1913). Craig Case Jury Selected by Noon. *Shelbyville Republican.* p.1.

Shelbyville Republican. (2 December 1913). Attorney Spann Rakes Webster. *Shelbyville Republican.* p.1.

Shelbyville Republican. (3 December 1913). Coroner Durham Used as Witness. *Shelbyville Republican.* p.1.

Shelbyville Republican. (4 December 1913). Janitor Hains told of Screams. *Shelbyville Republican.* p.1.

Shelbyville Republican. (4 December 1913). Dr. Wm. B. Craig is Now on Trial. *Shelbyville Republican.* p.1.

Shelbyville Republican. (4 December 1913). Judge and Attorneys in Knabe-Craig Case. *Shelbyville Republican.* p.1.

Shelbyville Republican. (6 December 1913). Court Adjourned Until Monday. *Shelbyville Republican.* p.1.

Shelbyville Republican. (8 December 1913). Motion Made to Dismiss Charge. *Shelbyville Republican.* p.1.

Shelbyville Republican. (9 December 1913). Dr. Wm. B. Craig was Dismissed. *Shelbyville Republican.* p.1.

Sluss, J.W. (1908). *Emergency Surgery.* Philadelphia, PA: P. Blakiston Son & Company.

Staatsarchiv Hamburg. Passenger list (Daniel and Clara Ehmke).. Auswandererlisten VII A1 Band.

Stanford Veterinary College. (n.d.) *Articles of Incorporation.* Stanford Veterinary College. Indiana State Archives, Indiana Commission on Public Records.

Stanford Veterinary College. (1899). *Name Change.* Stanford Veterinary College. Indiana State Archives, Indiana Commission on Public Records. *Cause No. 6575.*

State of Indiana. (n.d.). Marion County Naturalizations (Karl Kropp). State of Indiana. Retrieved from https://secure.in.gov/apps/iara/search/Home/Detail?rId=908317

State of Indiana. (n.d.). Marion County Naturalizations (Augusta Knabe). State of Indiana. Retrieved from https://secure.in.gov/apps/iara/search/Home/Detail?rId=915590

State of Indiana. (1894). *Secretary of State Biennial Report.* Indianapolis, IN: State of Indiana. Indiana State Library Collection.

State of Indiana. (1911). Officers of State, State of Indiana. State of Indiana. Indianapolis, IN: Wm. Buford.

State of Indiana. (1913) Indictment of William B. Craig and Alonzo M Ragsdale for Murder in the First Degree. *State of Indiana, Marion County. p.236.*

State of Indiana. (1911) Inquest Death Record. *State of Indiana, Marion County. No. 11257, Book 106.*

State of Indiana, Marion County. (n.d.). Marion County Department of Public Safety, Marion County Employee Card: Adolph Asch. *State of Indiana, Marion County. Indiana State Archives Indiana Commission on Public Records.*

State of Indiana, Marion County. (n.d.), Marion County Department of Public Safety, Marion County Employee Card: Elmer F. Hall. *State of Indiana, Marion County. Indiana State Archives Indiana Commission on Public Records.*

State of Indiana, Marion County. (n.d.), Marion County Department of Public Safety, Marion County Employee Card: William Holtz. *State of Indiana, Marion County. Indiana State Archives Indiana Commission on Public Records.*

State of Indiana, Marion County. (n.d.). Marion County Department of Public Safety, Marion County

Employee Card: John W. Morgan. *State of Indiana, Marion County. Indiana State Archives Indiana Commission on Public Records.*

State of Indiana, Marion County. (n.d.). Marion County Department of Public Safety, Marion County Employee Card: William Morgan. *State of Indiana, Marion County. Indiana State Archives Indiana Commission on Public Records.*

State of Indiana, Marion County. (n.d.). Marion County Department of Public Safety, Marion County Employee Card: John Mullin. *State of Indiana, Marion County. Indiana State Archives Indiana Commission on Public Records.*

State of Indiana, Marion County. (n.d.). Marion County Department of Public Safety, Marion County Employee Card: Otto H. Simon. *State of Indiana, Marion County. Indiana State Archives Indiana Commission on Public Records.*

State of Indiana, Marion County. (n.d.). Marion County Department of Public Safety, Marion County Employee Card: George M. Stewart. *State of Indiana, Marion County. Indiana State Archives Indiana Commission on Public Records.*

State of Indiana, Marion County. (1911) Coroner's Summary of Findings in the Death of Dr. Helene Knabe. *State of Indiana, Marion County. Indiana State Archives Indiana Commission on Public Records.* No. 11257.

State of Indiana, Marion County. (1904) License to Practice Medicine, Surgery, and Obstetrics. *State of Indiana, Marion County.* No. 7884.

State of Indiana, Marion County. (1912) Judgement Docket Criminal Court of Marion County for William B. Craig and Alonzo M Ragsdale. *State of Indiana, Marion County.* No. 41234.

State of Indiana Office of the Secretary of State (1923). Indian Veterinary Medical Association By Laws. State of Indiana.

State of Indiana Office of the Secretary of State (1961). Indian Veterinary Medical Association By Laws. State of Indiana.

State of Indiana Office of the Secretary of State (1964). Indian Veterinary Medical Association By Laws. State of Indiana.

State of Indiana Office of the Secretary of State (1973). Indian Veterinary Medical Association By Laws. State of Indiana.

State of Indiana Office of the Secretary of State (1977). Indian Veterinary Medical Association. State of Indiana.

Stockton, J.J. (Ed.). (1984). *A Century of Service: Veterinary medicine in Indiana.* Indianapolis, IN: The Board of Directors, Indiana Veterinary Medical Association.

Susan, C. (2004). Hollywood Fantasies of Miscegenation: Spectacular Narratives of Gender and Race. Princeton, NJ: Princeton University Press

Syracuse Journal. (5 December 1913). Mysterious "Jack the Peeper" was seen by several. Syracuse Journal p.17

Thayer, L. (25 October 1911). Tragic Fate Symbolic of Professional Woman's Life *Indianapolis Sun*. p.2.

Thayer, L. (28 October 1911). Clasps Dead Woman's Hand and Presses Lips to Brow. *Indianapolis Sun*. p.1-2.

The Concord Daily Tribune. (2 April 1912). Says He Received $1500 to Commit Murder. *The Concord Daily Tribune*. p.1.

The Day Book. (2 April 1912). Man Confesses Murder of Dr. Helene Knabe. *The Day Book*. p7-8.

The Day Book. (12 December 1912). The World News in Brief. *The Day Book*. p.31.

The Day Book. (31 December 1912). Doctor Held for Murder of Helen Knabe. *The Day Book*. p.8.

The Day Book. (28 November 1913). Indianapolis College Dean goes to Trial for Murder of Helene Knabe. *The Day Book*. pp. 5-6.

The Day Book. (2 December 1913). Defense to Claim that Love was Unknown to Dr. Knabe. *The Day Book*. p,3.

The Day Book. (3 December 1913). Dr. Knabe "Sweet and Pure". *The Day Book*. p. 6.

The Day Book. (5 December 1913). Didn't Identify Dr. Craig. *The Day Book*. p. 30.

The Day Book. (6 December 1913). Craig May be Freed Before Night By Court Order. *The Day Book*. p. 30.

The Day Book. (8 December 1913). The Craig-Knabe Case. *The Day Book*. p. 4.

The Day Book. (9 December 1913). Dr. Wm. B. Craig is Acquitted of Murder Charge.. *The Day Book*. p. 6.

Dunn, J.P. (1919). *Indiana and Indians (Vol. 2)*. Chicago: Anienian Historical Society.

The Encyclopedia of Arkansas History & Culture. (n.d.). Rabies. Retrieved from: http://www.encyclopediaofarkansas.net/encyclopedia/entry-detail.aspx?entryID=6451

The Huntington Herald. (16 February 1911). Cravenette (Ad). *The Huntington Herald*. P.7.

The Medical Student. (1902). Junior Class. *The Medical Student. Vol 1 3(29)*.

The Medical Student. (1903). Junior Class.. *The Medical Student.Vol. 1 4(20)*.

The Medical Student. (1903).Vaccination Record of 35 Junior Students of the Medical College of Indiana.. *The Medical Student. Vol 1 3(24)*.

The Medical Student. (1903). Dr. John Frank Geis.. *The Medical Student. Vol 2 6(12-13)*.

The Medical Student. (1903).Commencement. *The Medical Student. Vol 2 7(11,21)*.

The Medical Student. (1903). Sydenham Society. *The Medical Student. Vol 2 7(44-45)*.

The Medical Student. (1907). A Parting Word to the Class of I.M.C 1907. *The Medical Student. Vol 5 8(19. 21-25)*.

The National Archives at Washington, D.C.; Washington, D.C.; *Records of the US Customs Service, RG36*; NAI Number: *2655153*; Record Group Title: *Records of the Immigration and Naturalization Service, 1787-2004*; Record Group Number: 85 *(Franz Kropp)*.

The Scranton Truth (3 April 1912). Nichols, Alleged Murderer, is Said Not To Be Sane. *The Scranton Truth*. p. 8.

Tucker, S. (2008). William Blair Craig. Ancestry.com. Retrieved from http://mv.ancestry.com/viewer/bc8b2856-86bd-4832-9f16-f9a1d2600169/1587756/-1915861085

United Mine Workers of America. (1912). Proceedings of the United Mine Workers of America. United Mine Workers of America. Indianapolis, IN: The Cheltenham-Aetna Press.

Archbold, C.A. (2012). Policing. Thousand Oaks, CA: Sage Publications. Retrieved from http://www.sagepub.com/sites/default/files/upm-binaries/50819_ch_1.pdf

United States Census Bureau. (1870). United States Federal Census. Retrieved from http://interactive.ancestry.com/7163/4263382_00116?pid=20411016&backurl=http%3a%2f%2fsearch.ancestry.com%2f%2fcgi-bin%2fsse.dll%3fgss%3dangs-g%26new%3d1%26rank%3d1%26gsfn%3dhenrietta%2b%26gsfn_x%3d0%26gsln%3dcharles%26gsln_x%3d0%26msypn__ftp%3dIndiana%252c%2bUSA%26msypn%3d17%26msypn_PInfo%3d5-%257c0%257c1652393%257c0%257c2%257c3247%257c17%257c0%257c0%257c0%257c0%257c%26MSAV%3d0%26cp%3d0%26catbucket%3drstp%26uidh%3dvx3%26pcat%3dROOT_CATEGORY%26h%3d20411016%26db%3d1870usfedcen%26indiv%3d1%26ml_

rpos%3d2&treeid=&personid=&hintid=&usePUB=true

United States Census Bureau. (1880). United States Federal Census. Retrieved from http://interactive.ancestry.com/6742/4240573-00287/25709492?backurl=http://person.ancestry.com/tree/88674389/person/48572085465/facts/citation/343694010025/edit/record

United States Census Bureau. (1900). United States Federal Census. Retrieved from http://interactive.ancestry.com/7602/004118640_00825/92329824?backurl=http://person.ancestry.com/tree/88422739/person/48567678289/facts

United States Census Bureau. (1900). United States Federal Census. Retrieved from http://interactive.ancestry.com/2442/m-t0627-00376-00034/73699515?backurl=http://person.ancestry.com/tree/88674389/person/48572085465/facts/citation/343694031115/edit/record

United States Census Bureau. (1900). United States Federal Census. Retrieved from http://interactive.ancestry.com/7602/004118640_00770/4061690?backurl=http://person.ancestry.com/tree/51251264/person/13170310177/facts/citation/33779967015/edit/record

United States Census. (1900). United States Census Etta Charles 1900.Retrieved from http://interactive.ancestry.com/7602/004118637_01107?pid=13631305&backurl=http%3a%2f%2fsearch.ancestry.com%2f%2fcgi-bin%2fsse.dll%3fgss%3dangs-g%26new%3d1%26rank%3d1%26msT%3d1%26gsfn%3detta%26gsfn_x%3d0%26gsln%3dcharles%26gsln_x%3d0%26msypn__p%3dAnderson%252c%2bMadison%252c%2bIndiana%252c%2bUSA%26msypn%3d40102%26msypn_PInfo%3d8-%257c0%257c1652393%257c0%257c2%257c3247%257c17%257c0%257c1857%257c40102%257c0%257c%26MSAV%3d0%26cp%3d0%26catbucket%3drstp%26pcat%3dROOT_CATEGORY%26h%3d13631305%26db%3d1900usfedcen%26indiv%3d1%26ml_rpos%3d25&treeid=&personid=&hintid=&usePUB=true

United States Census Bureau. (1910). United States Federal Census. Retrieved from http://interactive.ancestry.com/7884/31111_4328263-01280/145259545?backurl=http://person.ancestry.com/tree/88422739/person/48567678289/facts/citation/343666944949/edit/record

United States Census Bureau. (1920). United States Federal Census. Retrieved from http://interactive.ancestry.com/7884/31111_4328263-01280?pid=145259545&backurl=http%3a%2f%2fsearch.ancestry.com%2f%2fcgi-bin%2fsse.l%3findiv%3d1%26dbid%3d7884%26h%3d145259545%26ssrc%3dpt%26tid%3d88422739%26pid%3d48567678289%26usePUB%3dtrue&ssrc=pt&treeid=88422739&personid=48567678289&hintid=&usePUB=true

United States Census. (1920). United States Census 1920.Retrieved from http://interactive.ancestry.com/6061/4300653_00302?pid=73654958&backurl=http%3a%2f%2fsearch.ancestry.com%2f%2fcgi-bin%2fsse.dll%3fgss%3dangs-c%26new%3d1%26rank%3d1%26gsfn%3dWilliam%26gsfn_x%3d0%26gsln%3dmorgan%26gsln_x%3d0%26msrpn__p%3dIndianapolis%252c%2bMarion%252c%2bIndiana%252c%2bUSA%26msrpn%3d40138%26msrpn_PInfo%3d8-%257c0%257c1652393%257c0%257c2%257c3247%257c17%257c0%257c1893%257c40138%257c0%257c%26gskw%3dpolice%252c%2bpatrolman%26cp%3d0%26MSAV%3d0-%26uidh%3dvx3%26pcat%3d35%26h%3d73654958%26db%3d1920usfedcen%26indiv%3d1%26ml_rpos%3d1&treeid=&personid=&hintid=&usePUB=true

United States Census Bureau. (1920). *Indianapolis Ward 14, Marion, Indiana*; Roll: *T625_455*; Page: *8A*; Enumeration District: *240*; Image: *806 (William Larsh)*

United States Census Bureau. (1930). United States Federal Census. Retrieved from http://interactive.ancestry.com/7602/004118640_00283/4039189?backurl=http://person.ancestry.com/tree/88674389/person/48572085465/facts/citation/343694021304/edit/record

United States Census Bureau. (1930). *Indianapolis, Marion, Indiana*; Roll: *615*; Page: *10A*; Enumeration

District: *0198*; Image: *417.0*; FHL microfilm: *2340350 (William Larsh)*

United States Census. (1930). United States Census 1930.Retrieved from http://interactive.ancestry.com/6224/4584360_00249?pid=116355296&backurl=http%3a%2f%2fsearch.ancestry.com%2f%2fcgi-bin%2fsse.dll%3fgss%3dangs-g%26new%3d1%26rank%3d1%26gsfn%3dWilliam%2bM%26gsfn_x%3d0%26gsln%3dmorgan%26gsln_x%3d0%26MSAV%3d0%26msbdy%3d1869%26msbpn__ftp%3dEngland%26msbpn%3d3251%26msbpn_PInfo%3d3-%257c0%257c0%257c3257%257c3251%257c0%257c0%257c0%257c0%257c0%257c0%257c%26msrpn__p%3dIndianapolis%252c%2bMarion%252c%2bIndiana%252c%2bUSA%26msrpn%3d40138%26msrpn_PInfo%3d8-%257c0%257c1652393%257c0%257c2%257c3247%257c17%257c0%257c1893%257c40138%257c0%257c%26gskw%3dpolice%252c%2bpatrolman%26cp%3d0%26catbucket%3drstp%26uidh%3dvx3%26pcat%3dROOT_CATEGORY%26h%3d116355296%26db%3d1930usfedcen%26indiv%3d1%26ml_rpos%3d3&treeid=&personid=&hintid=&usePUB=true

United States Census Bureau. (1940). Census Place: *Franklin, Montgomery, Indiana*; Roll: *T627_1080*; Page: *5A*; Enumeration District:*54-11(William Larsh)*

United States Census Bureau. (1940). United States Federal Census. Retrieved from http://interactive.ancestry.com/6224/4532466_00149/90722064?backurl=http://person.ancestry.com/tree/88674389/person/48572085465/facts/citation/343694021872/edit/record

United States Census Bureau. (1940). United States Federal Census. Retrieved from http://interactive.ancestry.com/2442/M-T0627-01129-00485/54327865?backurl=http://person.ancestry.com/tree/88422739/person/48567678289/facts/citation/343666942585/edit/record

University Library (2015). Amelia Keller, M.D. University Library. Retrieved from http://www2.ulib.iupui.edu/womencreatingexcellence/ameliakeller

University Library (2015). Jane Merrill Ketcham, M.D. University Library. Retrieved from http://www2.ulib.iupui.edu/womencreatingexcellence/ketcham

United States Congress. (1895). United States at Large: Chapter 21- An Act to Pension Samuel F. Tenant. United States Congress. 28 (1034) Retrieved from https://books.google.com/s?id=AWM2AQAAMAAJ&pg=PA1034&lpg=PA1034&dq=%22samuel+f.+tenant%22&source=bl&ots=4jQFVysFC7&sig=1FSzGJ42v8PizE9DHMBSgfOMgfs&hl=en&sa=X&ved=0ahUKEwj067jW2pXMAhVBvIMKHcIfADkQ6AEINTAH#v=onepage&q=%22samuel%20f.%20sa=X&ved=0ahUKEwj067jW2pXMAhVBvIMKHcIfADkQ6AEILjAE#v=onepage&q=%22samuel%20f.%20tenant%22&f=false

United States Patent Office. (26 June 1922)Toy Patent (LC Lowder). United States. US2001/0028505 Retrieved from https://www.google.ch/patents/USD63652

Unknown .(n.d.). Decisions of National Labor Relations Board. Vol67 161(1233).

Unknown. (n.d.) Police; History- Policing Twentieth-century America. Retrieved from http://law.jrank.org/pages/1643/Police-History-Policing-twentieth-century-America-reform-era.html

Unknown. (n.d.). X-Rays ~ Wilhelm Röntgen. Retrieved from https://archive.org/details/WilhelmCRoentgenXRays

Walters, D.C., (2009). Exploring a Definition of Leadership and the Biography of Dr. Frank B. Wynn. Theses, Dissertations, Professional Papers. Paper 1299. Retrieved from http://scholarworks.umt.edu/cgi/viewcontent.cgi?article=2318&context=etd

Ward, J. (2016, February 28). Electronic chat interview.

Warfel-Hull, K.. (2004 Summer). Path to the Future: History of the Department of Pathology & Laboratory Medicine. Indiana University Department of Pathology and Laboratory Medicine. 1(3-6).

Warfel-Hull, K.. (2005 Summer). Path to the Future: History of the Department of Pathology &

Laboratory Medicine. Indiana University Department of Pathology and Laboratory Medicine. 2(3-6).

Warfel-Hull, K.. (2008 Summer). Path to the Future: History of the Department of Pathology & Laboratory Medicine. Indiana University Department of Pathology and Laboratory Medicine. 2(2-5).

Warfel-Hull, K.. (2009 Summer). Path to the Future: History of the Department of Pathology & Laboratory Medicine. Indiana University Department of Pathology and Laboratory Medicine. 3(4-5).

Warfel-Hull, K.. (2009 Winter). Path to the Future: History of the Department of Pathology & Laboratory Medicine. Indiana University Department of Pathology and Laboratory Medicine. 3(2-3, 6).

Warfel-Hull, K.. (2006 Summer). Path to the Future: History of the Department of Pathology & Laboratory Medicine. Indiana University Department of Pathology and Laboratory Medicine. 1(3-6).

Warfel-Hull, K.. (2006 Winter). Path to the Future: History of the Department of Pathology & Laboratory Medicine. Indiana University Department of Pathology and Laboratory Medicine. 2(3-5).

Warfel-Hull, K.. (2007 Summer). Path to the Future: History of the Department of Pathology & Laboratory Medicine. Indiana University Department of Pathology and Laboratory Medicine. 2(4-5).

Warfel-Hull, K.. (2008 Winter). Path to the Future: History of the Department of Pathology & Laboratory Medicine. Indiana University Department of Pathology and Laboratory Medicine. *4(2-5)*.

Warfel-Hull, K.. (2011 Winter). Path to the Future: History of the Department of Pathology & Laboratory Medicine. Indiana University Department of Pathology and Laboratory Medicine. *4(6-8)*.

Warkel, H. G, Krause, M.F. & Berry, S.L. (2003). The Herron Chronicle. Heron School of Art. p. 254.

Washington Post. (1 January 1913). Held as Her Slayer. *Washington Post*. p.1, 3.

Watson, F. (2016, April 15). Phone Interview.

White, E.G. (24 June 1916). Rule or Ruin. *The Little Paper*. p.2

Whitson, R.L., Campbell, J.P. & Goldthwait, E.L. (1914). Centennial History of Grant County, Indiana, 1812 to 1912 . Chicago: The Lewis Publishing Co. Volume 2 (1024-25).

Wichita Beacon. (2 April 1912). Deserter Says He Killed Woman. *Wichita Beacon*. p.1

Wichita Beacon. (6 April 1912). Editorial. *Wichita Beacon*. p.2.

Williams, A.W. (1906). The Etiology and Diagnosis of Hydrophobia. *The Journal of Infectious* Diseases. 3 (452-483).

World Health Organization (2016). Rabies. World Health Organization. Retrieved from http://www.who.int/mediacentre/factsheets/fs099/en/

Wynn, F. B. & Knabe, H. (1904). Medical College of Indiana, University of Indianapolis. *American Medical Association Transactions of the Section of Pathology and Physiology.* pp. 426-27.

Verlag von Frederich Nagel. (1892). Pommersches Güter-Adressbuch. Verzeichniss sämmtlicher Güter mit Angabe der Guts-Eigenschaft, der Gesämmtfläche und Flächeninhalts, des Grundsteuer-Reintrages, der Besitzer bezw. Stettin: Verlag von Frederich Nagel. Retrieved from http://bibliotekacyfrowa.eu/dlibra/docmetadata?id=oai:bibliotekacyfrowa.eu:582&from=http://fbc.pionier.net.pl

Veterinary Medicine (1923 September). *The Indiana Veterinary College*. p. 814.

YMCA. (2008). About Us: Local History. YMCA. Retrieved from http://www.ywca.org/site/pp.asp?c=qkI3KgMTIrF&b=3841307

INDEX

A

acquittal 215, 218
Aldridge, Bruce 9
American Medical Association 46, 62, 63, 66, 68, 70, 263, 267, 268, 290, 293, 317, 328
American Veterinary Medical Association 85, 317
ankle 70, 76
ape 152, 214
Arlington National Cemetery 234
Art 67, 131, 167, 180, 263, 290, 306, 307, 328
  books 67, 131, 167, 180, 263, 290, 306, 307, 328
  illustrations 67, 131, 167, 180, 263, 290, 306, 307, 328
Asch, Adolph
  Asch 149, 163, 170, 182, 240, 283, 298, 311, 323
Ash, Mary E. Dr. 137
  Ash 137
Athenaeum 79, 80, 94, 157, 263
  Das Deutsche Haus 79, 80, 94, 157, 263
auction 173, 245

B

bailiff 192, 198, 218
Baker, Frank P.
  Baker 146, 185, 220, 243, 287, 312
  Baker, Frank 146, 185, 220, 243, 287, 312
Baltic Sea 11, 15, 23, 25, 27
Barnard, Harry E. Dr. 160
  Barnard, Dr. 160
Barton Center of Hope 225
Barton House 225, 226
Baughmgartner, Ray
  Baumgartner, Ray 167
bed 98, 102, 103, 106, 109, 119, 121, 122, 140, 146, 150, 152, 155, 173, 174, 183, 202, 203, 204, 208, 241, 250, 273
Blair, Alonzo Judge
  Blair, Judge 185, 241
blood 56, 61, 97, 98, 99, 102, 106, 109, 119, 120, 121, 122, 123, 125, 150, 158, 163, 164, 166, 172, 197, 199, 201, 204, 210, 212, 215, 221, 240, 251, 264, 273
Bobb's Free Dispensary 35, 42, 44, 45, 61, 66
bond 78, 150, 170, 172
bonders 172

bondsman 170
Bonsett, Charles 9
Book 66, 174, 263, 270, 274, 276, 277, 279, 281, 297, 300, 306, 317, 318, 322, 323, 324, 325
Brigham, Marry K. 167
Brocking, E.D. 111
Buddhism 102, 319
Bukalowski, Jerzy 9
Burns, William J. 128, 129, 241, 291
  Burns 128, 129, 241, 291
Burske, Heinrica 33
Burton, Alonzo 167
Bush, Louisa 163, 167

C

California
  Inglewood 236
Campbell, Thomas H.
  Campbell 185
Cantrell, Rufus 47, 240
Carper,Florence 57
Carr, Joseph C. 105
  Carr, Joseph 166
Catholic Cemetery 229
cauterizing 54
Central Christian Church 144
Central College of Physicians and Surgeons 62, 189, 232, 234
chalkboard 156
change of venue 190, 195
Chappell, Ralph Dr. 167
Charles, Etta Dr. 10, 134, 135, 285, 295, 299, 326
  Charles, Henrietta 10, 134, 135, 285, 295, 299, 326
Charles Ferguson
  Ferguson, Charles E. 99, 107, 166
Cheney, John C.
  Cheney 185
City Dispensary 44, 76
City Hospital 34, 37, 40, 43, 44, 45, 61, 143, 150, 163, 180, 229, 237, 238, 240
clairvoyant 202, 273
Clark, Edmund D. Dr. 144
Clark, Edumund D. Dr.
  Clark, Dr. 166
Clemens, Lulu 159
clinical 34, 35, 39, 44, 61, 87, 92, 267

Clinton County 58
Cloverdale Cemetery 237
commencement 47, 76
Concordia Cemetery 224, 225
Cook, George J. Dr. 48, 166, 201
Coroner 97, 99, 102, 112, 113, 114, 115, 119, 121, 122, 125, 128, 130, 146, 150, 151, 158, 161, 163, 164, 237, 272, 277, 291, 297, 303, 304, 308, 314, 322, 323, 324
Craig, Marion 60, 83, 228
Craig, William B. Dr.. *See* Craig, William Blair Dr.
Craig, William Blair Dr. 83, 227
  Craig 5, 60, 83, 88, 97, 166, 167, 168, 170, 171, 175, 176, 177, 178, 179, 180, 182, 183, 185, 187, 189, 190, 191, 195, 196, 197, 198, 199, 201, 202, 203, 204, 205, 206, 207, 208, 210, 211, 212, 213, 214, 215, 216, 217, 218, 219, 220, 221, 223, 227, 228, 230, 231, 241, 242, 246, 249, 250, 251, 252, 269, 270, 274, 276, 277, 278, 279, 292, 296, 297, 300, 304, 305, 310, 311, 315, 317, 319, 320, 322, 323, 324, 325
  Craig, Dr. 83, 227
  Craig, William B. Dr. 83, 227
  Craig, William Dr. 83, 227
  Dr. Craig 83, 227
  Dr. William B. Craig 88, 97, 168, 182, 211, 249, 279, 292
creditors 175
Crockett-Lowder, Lillian Dr.
  Crockett-Lowder, Dr. 163, 164, 170, 188, 221, 233, 280
Crown Hill Cemetery 10, 144, 145, 225, 226, 228, 229, 230, 231, 232, 235, 236, 237, 238, 239, 241, 242, 243, 245, 246, 262, 296
Crownland Cemetery 230
cut 61, 112, 113, 116, 119, 120, 121, 122, 125, 150, 159, 172, 180, 182, 197, 199, 201, 203, 204, 250, 251, 273

D

Darlington Odd Fellows Cemetery 244
Darlowko 9, 11, 15, 23, 25, 28, 32
Darlowo 9, 11, 15, 17, 20, 23, 25, 247
Defense
  Hack, Charles 5, 185, 187, 276, 277, 311, 322, 325
  Hack, Oren S. 5, 185, 187, 276, 277, 311, 322, 325
  Hooten, Elliot 5, 185, 187, 276, 277, 311, 322, 325
  Meiks, George H. 5, 185, 187, 276, 277, 311, 322, 325
  Spaan, Henry N. 5, 185, 187, 276, 277, 311, 322, 325
defense fund 188
Delaware Flats 10, 64, 66, 98, 102, 103, 105, 108, 151, 170, 179, 203, 208, 210, 213, 214, 217, 222, 230, 270, 273, 290, 302
  Delaware 10, 64, 66, 98, 102, 103, 105, 108, 151, 170, 179, 203, 208, 210, 213, 214, 217, 222, 230, 270,

273, 290, 302
Deming, George 123
diagnose 53, 54, 61, 64, 70, 134, 159
diphtheria 50, 56, 57, 58, 59, 83
directed verdict 217
Dixon, Frank
  Dixon, B. Frank 167
Dodds, William T.S. Dr. 124, 170, 237
  Dodds 124, 170, 237
Dodge, Ray C. 167, 170
dream 95, 99, 157, 158, 183, 184, 273
Dr. Knabe 7, 9, 10, 11, 12, 16, 19, 35, 44, 45, 49, 50, 51, 52, 53, 54, 55, 56, 57, 58, 59, 60, 61, 62, 63, 64, 65, 66, 67, 68, 69, 70, 71, 72, 74, 76, 78, 80, 82, 83, 84, 86, 90, 91, 92, 93, 94, 95, 96, 97, 98, 99, 100, 101, 102, 103, 104, 105, 107, 108, 109, 111, 112, 113, 114, 116, 117, 118, 119, 120, 121, 122, 123, 124, 125, 126, 127, 128, 129, 130, 131, 132, 133, 134, 135, 136, 137, 138, 139, 140, 141, 142, 143, 144, 145, 146, 147, 150, 151, 152, 154, 155, 156, 157, 158, 159, 160, 161, 162, 163, 164, 165, 166, 167, 168, 170, 171, 172, 173, 174, 175, 176, 177, 178, 179, 180, 181, 182, 183, 188, 189, 190, 195, 196, 197, 198, 199, 201, 202, 203, 204, 205, 206, 208, 210, 212, 213, 214, 215, 216, 217, 218, 220, 221, 223, 225, 226, 227, 228, 229, 230, 232, 233, 234, 235, 237, 240, 241, 242, 243, 244, 245, 246, 249, 251, 252, 255, 256, 257, 258, 259, 261, 262, 263, 268, 270, 271, 272, 273, 274, 275, 276, 277, 287, 289, 290, 291, 297, 301, 302, 303, 304, 305, 306, 307, 308, 309, 310, 314, 315, 319, 325, 337. *See also* Knabe, Helene Elise Hermine
Duden, Alice 166
dumbwaiter 103, 104, 180
Dunn, J.P. 11
Durham, Charles O. 97, 99, 102, 112, 113, 115, 119, 121, 122, 125, 128, 146, 150, 158, 161, 163, 164, 272, 323
Durham, Charles O. Coroner 113, 114
  Durham 113, 114

E

education 11, 34, 35, 47, 49, 62, 78, 91, 225, 238, 262, 279
Ehmke, Clara 19, 94, 297, 323
Ehmke, Daniel. *See* Ehmke, Daniel Friedrich Wilhelm
Ehmke, Daniel Friedrich Wilhelm 19
Ellison, William 154
engaged 64, 152, 154, 190, 197, 198, 206, 207, 218
engagement 138, 139, 156, 197, 198, 199, 206
Engelke, John F. 157
entertainment 58, 160
estate 83, 112, 113, 121, 123, 163, 170, 173, 174, 175, 202, 221, 223, 235, 268, 270, 271
estate. 173, 223, 270
Estates of Serenity 231, 236

excising 54

F

Fake 158
Ferguson, Charles Dr. 99, 107, 166
  Ferguson, Charles E. 99, 107, 166
  Ferguson, Dr. 99, 107, 166
finances
  collateral 12, 25, 59, 60, 64, 82, 87, 91, 111, 113, 125, 128, 139, 141, 142, 143, 146, 150, 154, 155, 159, 160, 171, 172, 177, 178, 183, 188, 199, 202, 203, 206, 225, 240, 244, 245, 246, 270, 273
  money 12, 25, 59, 60, 64, 82, 87, 91, 111, 113, 125, 128, 139, 141, 142, 143, 146, 150, 154, 155, 159, 160, 171, 172, 177, 178, 183, 188, 199, 202, 203, 206, 225, 240, 244, 245, 246, 270, 273
  paid 12, 25, 59, 60, 64, 82, 87, 91, 111, 113, 125, 128, 139, 141, 142, 143, 146, 150, 154, 155, 159, 160, 171, 172, 177, 178, 183, 188, 199, 202, 203, 206, 225, 240, 244, 245, 246, 270, 273
  pay 12, 25, 59, 60, 64, 82, 87, 91, 111, 113, 125, 128, 139, 141, 142, 143, 146, 150, 154, 155, 159, 160, 171, 172, 177, 178, 183, 188, 199, 202, 203, 206, 225, 240, 244, 245, 246, 270, 273
Flanner, Frank W. 131
  Flanner 131
  Flanner, Frank 131
Flanner Guild 92, 132, 306
  Flanner House 92, 132, 306
Flanner, Janet 131, 132, 133, 237, 291
Fleming, Katherine Agnes 163, 206, 229, 275, 298
Florida
  Sarasota 241
footsteps 103, 104, 138, 208
Forest Hill Cemetery 241
Frank Flanner. *See* Flanner, Frank W.
Franklin. *See* Franklin, Oscar
Franklin, Oscar 150
Frasier, Ian 131
Freeland, John L. Dr. 286, 304
funeral 64, 83, 123, 124, 131, 144, 170, 172, 199, 214, 225, 228, 234, 237

G

garbage 104, 152, 180, 215
Garrison, Winfred Ernest Dr. 47
Geis, John F. Dr. 67
  Geis, Dr. 67
German 11, 15, 16, 19, 24, 45, 77, 78, 95, 104, 112, 140, 144, 152, 157, 160, 178, 197, 225, 237, 239, 267, 270, 273, 314
German Evangelical Zion Church. 144

Germany 11, 15, 16, 19, 24, 33, 48, 64, 76, 94, 104, 128, 137, 138, 140, 152, 216, 225, 234, 235, 236, 239, 262, 267, 279, 293, 296, 297, 304, 321
Ghouls 47, 263, 306
Gott, W.T. Dr. 137
  Gott 137
Governor Marshall 141
Grace, John 108, 151
graduation. *See* commencement
Graham, Hannah Dr. 63, 93, 127, 136, 285, 291
  Graham 63, 93, 127, 136, 285, 291
grand jury 104, 127, 146, 161, 163, 164, 165, 170, 171, 182, 188, 189, 205, 214, 220, 221, 223, 249, 251, 252
  second
    Blaker, Louis J. 163
    Broden, James E. 163
    Jonas, Joseph 163
    Kane, Thomas P. 163
    McCloskey, John C. 163
    Reister, J.F. 163
grave robbers 47
Greene County 233
Greenham, Arthur F. 57
  Greenham 57
Gregory, Carrie Dr. 158
Greiner, Louis Adolph 84
Guthrie, J.E. 156

H

Hack, Charles 185
Hack, Oren 185, 244
Hagan, Alma 158
Haines. *See* Haynes, Jefferson
Hall, Elmer F. 121, 149, 283, 323
Hancock County Medical Society 127, 272
Haskett, Harry W. 105, 170, 292, 314
  Haskett, Harry 105, 166, 170, 179, 203, 230, 250, 292, 314
Hauser, J. A. Dr. 146
Haynes, Jefferson 95, 97, 102, 104, 122, 133, 138, 150, 196, 208, 226, 311
  Haines 166
Health Officer 49, 272, 289, 321
Heine, everend Johannes W.C. 16
Hildebrand, John 157
Hitt, Ella 122, 150, 285, 296

Hitt, Thomas Dr. 122, 150, 170
Holtz, William A. 147, 150, 282
Holy Cross Cemetery 242, 243, 244, 245
Holy Sepulchre 240
Holzman, John W.
  Holzman 185
  Holzmann 185
hookworm 53, 264
Hooten, Elliot R. 171, 185, 218
Hooton & Hack 185
Horace Wood Transfer Barn 170
  Horace Wood Livery 170
Hughes, J.E. Dr. 76
Hulen, Florence 167, 208
Hurlstone, Albert Reverend 48
Hurty, John N.
  Hurty, J. N. Dr. 67, 266, 312
Hurty, John N. Dr. 49, 125, 137, 284
  Hurty, Dr. 49, 125, 137, 284
Hygiene 40, 49, 50, 51, 56, 59, 60, 65, 66, 67, 78, 82, 90, 93, 176, 266, 289, 302
Hyland, Martin J. 123, 147, 242, 243
  Hyland 123, 147, 242, 243

I

Illinois
  Charleston 234
  Chicago 57, 63, 131, 154, 155, 195, 231, 233, 234, 239, 240, 244, 261, 262, 270, 271, 275, 285, 286, 289, 297, 299, 300, 325, 328
Indiana
  Alexandria 233
  Anderson 10, 233, 236, 263, 285, 286, 295, 319
  Avon 206
  Belleville 59
  Bridgeport 58
  Cambridge City 53
  Coatesville 59
  Darlington 244
  Evansville 56, 228
  Fort Wayne 10, 229
  Franklin 150, 228, 283, 327
  Indianapolis 50
  Liberty 50
  Marion 9, 11, 47, 50, 60, 65, 83, 84, 139, 141, 163, 177, 179, 182, 183, 185, 188, 190, 191, 196, 198,

    211, 212, 214, 216, 218, 220, 228, 231, 236, 238, 240, 241, 243, 246, 252, 270, 275, 276, 279, 280, 283, 288, 290, 291, 292, 294, 295, 300, 317, 318, 322, 323, 324, 326
  Mulberry 58
  Newark 233
  Noblesville 204, 230
  Plainfield 58
  Puro Water Company 57
  Shelbyville 10, 185, 190, 191, 195, 196, 206, 213, 219, 220, 221, 241, 277, 278, 292, 296, 299, 310, 322, 323
  West Newton 57
Indiana Association of Nurses 62
Indiana National Soldiers Home 50
Indianapolis 9, 11, 12, 19, 24, 25, 36, 41, 44, 47, 48, 49, 52, 54, 56, 58, 61, 64, 66, 70, 76, 84, 87, 91, 92, 93, 94, 97, 108, 112, 113, 116, 117, 118, 120, 121, 123, 124, 128, 129, 131, 134, 136, 139, 141, 142, 143, 144, 146, 151, 154, 155, 157, 158, 159, 160, 163, 167, 170, 171, 172, 178, 179, 180, 182, 183, 184, 185, 188, 189, 191, 195, 197, 198, 199, 202, 205, 206, 210, 213, 220, 224, 225, 226, 227, 228, 229, 230, 231, 232, 233, 234, 235, 236, 237, 238, 239, 240, 241, 242, 243, 244, 245, 246, 249, 261, 262, 263, 264, 265, 266, 267, 268, 269, 270, 271, 272, 273, 274, 275, 276, 277, 278, 279, 280, 281, 282, 283, 284, 285, 286, 287, 288, 289, 290, 291, 292, 293, 294, 295, 296, 297, 299, 300, 301, 302, 303, 304, 305, 306, 307, 308, 309, 310, 311, 312, 313, 314, 315, 316, 317, 318, 320, 321, 323, 324, 325, 326, 328
Indianapolis Hebrew Congregation Cemetery South 240
Indianapolis Sanitary Company 163, 170
Indianapolis Traction and Terminal Company 76
Indiana State Laboratory of Hygiene 50
Indiana State Medical Association 62, 66, 268, 301, 312, 313
Indiana State Medical Society 64, 66, 313
Indiana University 10, 61, 120, 198, 228, 229, 230, 234, 235, 267, 289, 290, 296, 300, 316, 327, 328
Indiana Veterinary College 62, 66, 83, 84, 85, 86, 156, 163, 167, 168, 170, 176, 178, 208, 210, 215, 218, 220, 227, 269, 290, 316, 317, 318, 328
  IVC 62, 66, 83, 84, 85, 86, 156, 163, 167, 168, 170, 176, 178, 208, 210, 215, 218, 220, 227, 269, 290, 316, 317, 318, 328
Indictment 170, 292, 322, 323
Inglewood Park Cemetery 236
Inman, Ephraim
  Inman 185, 288, 312
  Inman, Eph 185
investigation 102, 103, 105, 111, 116, 127, 128, 130, 139, 147, 153, 160, 161, 170, 171, 179, 205, 217, 220, 243, 244, 273
IU School of Medicine 34, 67, 68, 124, 229, 232
  Indiana University School of Medicine 61, 120, 198, 230, 234, 235, 267, 289, 290, 316

J

Jaeger, Alfred Dr. 88
Jameson, Henry Dr. 33, 48
Johns Hopkins 54, 61, 262, 267, 296, 321
Johnson County 228
journal 68, 120
Jury
  Arnold, Alfred 185, 190
  Barnes, Kimball E. 185, 190
  Good, Martin 185, 190
  Harrell, Ollie 185, 190
  Hurste, Perry 185, 190
  Lemasters, William 185, 190
  Swinford, Ralph 185, 190
  Weinantz, Louis 185, 190
  Wickler, Elbert 185, 190
  Willard, Elbert D. 185, 190
  Wright, Walter V. 185, 190
  Young, Marcus 185, 190

K

Kahn, Leo 105
Keene, T. Victor Dr. 53
  Keene, Dr. 53
Keller, Amelia Dr. 142, 160, 164, 188, 234, 286
Keller, Martha B. Dr. 127
Kell, J.S. Dr. 52
Ketcham, William A.
  Ketcham 185
Keys 121
Kiefer, L. A. 167
kimono 136, 161, 163, 164, 166, 172, 190, 208, 210, 212, 214, 215, 220, 221, 223, 251, 258, 319
Kinney, Jerry 149, 150, 243
  Kinney 149, 150, 243
Kirkpatrick, James Batey Dr. 35
Knabe, Augusta B. 16, 19, 101, 225
  Augusta Knabe 24, 95, 97, 99, 101, 102, 104, 108, 109, 111, 112, 116, 121, 123, 124, 127, 128, 129, 130, 135, 136, 138, 139, 140, 141, 144, 146, 157, 160, 170, 172, 173, 174, 175, 176, 179, 180, 184, 196, 199, 200, 201, 202, 204, 212, 213, 214, 215, 217, 218, 219, 221, 224, 226, 261, 262, 273, 278, 279, 297, 307, 313, 314, 315, 323
Knabe, Augusta (Krolow) 16
Knabe, Helene. *See* Knabe, Helene Elise Hermine Knabe Dr.
Knabe, Helene Elise Hermine. *See* Knabe, Helene Elise Hermine Dr.
Knabe, Helene Elise Hermine Dr. 1, 11, 48, 87, 95, 225, 249
knife 99, 102, 111, 117, 119, 120, 121, 124, 125, 146, 150, 152, 155, 158, 180, 201, 204, 208, 212
Knights and Ladies of Honor 66, 67
Kolmer, John Dr. 142, 144, 163, 166, 173, 213, 235, 286, 298, 301, 305

Krolow 16, 141
Kropp, Karoline C. 19
Kyle, John J. Dr. 67, 144, 236, 284, 285, 293
  Kyle, Dr. 67, 99, 144, 236, 284, 285, 293
  Kyle, John Dr. 67, 144, 236, 284, 285, 293

L

laboratory 35, 39, 45, 52, 54, 56, 61, 62, 64, 87, 94, 95, 121
Lawler, Ernest E. Dr.
  Lawler, E. E. 167
learner 12, 47, 65
Leeth, M. C. Dr. 167
lesbian 117, 131, 132, 133
Lindley, Blanche 128, 139, 176, 177, 178, 183, 287
Local Council of Women 142, 143, 161, 175, 188, 223, 273

M

Madstones 54
Marion County 9, 11, 47, 65, 163, 185, 188, 190, 191, 212, 214, 220, 238, 240, 241, 246, 252, 270, 275, 276, 279, 291, 292, 300, 317, 318, 322, 323, 324
Markey, Joseph T. Judge 185, 287
  Markey, Judge 185, 287
marriage 16, 179, 197, 199, 206, 218, 226, 228, 230, 237, 249, 250
Marshall, George D. 189
Marshall, Samuel T. 166
Maxwell, John M. 163, 166, 198, 208, 212, 281
Mayor 141, 150, 151, 153, 160, 243, 245, 263, 282, 283, 284, 300, 303, 312
McAfee, Loy Dr. 111
  Inghram 111
McCallister, Fred 146, 161, 170, 185, 212, 220, 244
McGreger, Maud
  McGregor, Maude 167
McLeay, J.D. Dr. 166
McPherson, Ila 166, 213
McPherson, Katherine 64, 95, 97, 98, 101, 102, 104, 116, 124, 127, 129, 130, 134, 135, 144, 146, 151, 155, 166, 170, 176, 182, 184, 196, 213, 214, 215, 216, 219, 221, 225
medical associations
  American Medical Association 64, 66, 313
  Indiana Association of Nurses 64, 66, 313
  Indiana State Medical Association 64, 66, 313
  Indiana State Medical Society 64, 66, 313
  Nu Sigma Phi 66, 188, 233
  Sydenham Society 40, 43, 45, 325
Medical College of Indiana 33, 34, 35, 44, 46, 48, 50, 60, 61, 66, 67, 85, 110, 159, 197, 229, 232, 236, 238, 239, 263, 267, 268, 289, 290, 301, 318, 325, 328
medical practice 64, 113, 177, 235
Meiks, George H. 185

Meiks & Hack 185
Memorial Park Cemetery 242, 246
Meyer, Harry Dr. 140
Meyers, Henry 167
Michigan
  Buchanan 131, 237, 242
  Troy 95, 108, 122, 150, 151, 167, 210, 213, 226, 236, 239, 242, 244
microtome 109, 121, 143, 250
Miyamoto, Richard Dr. 120
Miyamoto, Richard T. Dr. 10
money 12, 25, 59, 60, 64, 82, 87, 91, 111, 113, 125, 128, 139, 141, 142, 143, 146, 150, 154, 155, 159, 160, 171, 172, 177, 178, 183, 188, 199, 202, 203, 206, 225, 240, 244, 245, 246, 270, 273
Montgomery County 244
Moore, Arnold 213
Morgan, John W. 148, 245, 283, 324
Morgan, William 121, 149, 184, 324
Mound Cemetery 234
Mount Pleasant Cemetery 228
Mueller, Ferdinand Adolph 86, 89, 163, 166, 201
  Adolph Muller 86, 89, 163, 201
Mueller, Margrette 166
Mullin, John 148, 163, 170, 243, 246, 282, 312, 324
murder 11, 101, 103, 104, 105, 106, 107, 108, 109, 111, 112, 113, 115, 116, 117, 118, 121, 122, 123, 124, 128, 130, 131, 132, 136, 139, 140, 142, 143, 146, 147, 150, 151, 154, 155, 157, 159, 160, 161, 163, 164, 166, 167, 170, 175, 179, 180, 182, 188, 189, 195, 197, 203, 208, 210, 213, 215, 216, 218, 227, 243, 244, 251, 273, 287, 322
museum 39, 45, 62, 240

N

Neilan, Thomas H. 163
Neil, Maude
  McGregor, Maude 163
Newark Cemetery 233
Nichols, Seth
  Nichols, Seth T. 154, 155, 287, 294, 295
nightdress 98, 119, 155, 250
night gown. *See* nightdress
Noble, R.P. Dr. 163, 166, 170, 172, 210, 221
North American Gymnastic Association 62
  NAGU 62
not guilty 196, 217, 218
Nu Sigma Phi 66, 188, 233

O

Oak Dale Cemetery 230
Oak Ridge Cemetery 242
Ohio

Urbana 188, 230

P

pallbearers 144
paranormal 157, 247, 255
Pasteur 57, 64, 128, 177, 183
Patten, Blaine 167
pay 19, 34, 49, 59, 60, 64, 92, 98, 125, 137, 141, 143, 145, 162, 173, 177, 178, 182, 196, 203, 245, 252, 263
  paid 19, 34, 49, 59, 60, 64, 92, 98, 125, 137, 141, 143, 145, 162, 173, 177, 178, 182, 196, 203, 245, 252, 263
  paying 19, 34, 49, 59, 60, 64, 92, 98, 125, 137, 141, 143, 145, 162, 173, 177, 178, 182, 196, 203, 245, 252, 263
Peters, J. Christopher Reverend 144
Pfafflin, Charles Abraham
  Pfafflin 163
philosophy 165, 236
Philputt, A.B. Reverend 144
Physicians' Protective Association 59
pie 167, 212
Pierson, James W. 167
pillow 97, 98, 102, 106, 109, 164, 190, 204, 212, 216
Plater, Walter E. 167, 210
Poland 9, 11, 15, 247
police 10, 97, 99, 102, 104, 105, 108, 109, 111, 112, 113, 114, 116, 117, 118, 119, 121, 123, 124, 128, 129, 130, 131, 134, 136, 137, 139, 141, 143, 146, 147, 150, 151, 152, 154, 155, 158, 159, 160, 164, 179, 180, 181, 184, 188, 201, 204, 210, 215, 219, 221, 240, 242, 243, 244, 245, 246, 249, 270, 282, 283, 296, 300
Pott's fracture 76
Powell, Andrew 122
Powell, M.E. 167
Powell, Nettie Bainbridge Dr. 65, 95, 96, 141, 236, 286
Power, Taylor 167
preceptor 43, 45, 46, 144, 177
Prince 154, 314
prismatic glass 70, 76
Pritchard, James A. 185, 190
Pritchard & Pritchard 185
Professor 10, 67, 78, 87, 88, 89, 94, 97, 120, 124, 146, 229, 234, 235
Promotion 56
Prosecution
  Baker, Frank P. 5, 186, 218, 310, 315
  Campbell, Thomas H. 5, 186, 218, 310, 315
  Cheney, John C. 5, 186, 218, 310, 315
  Holzman, John W. 5, 186, 218, 310, 315
  Inman, Ephraim 5, 186, 218, 310, 315
  Ketcham, William A. 5, 186, 218, 310, 315

   McAllister, Frank 5, 186, 218, 310, 315
   Wray, A.F. 5, 186, 218, 310, 315
Protestant Deaconess 44, 62
Psychopathia Sexualis 131
Purdue Special, 46
Purdue University 61, 87, 228, 238, 284, 300, 321
Puro Water Company 57
Putnam County 237

Q

Quarantine 59

R

rabies 54, 56, 57, 58, 60, 61, 64, 66, 171, 176, 177, 276
Ragsdale, Alonzo M. 112, 121, 123, 168, 170, 279
   Ragsdale 112, 121, 123, 168, 170, 279
Regret 165
Resignation 56, 269, 302
reward 12, 141, 142, 203, 214, 233
Reyer, Ernest C. 99, 144, 166, 201, 229, 285, 301
   Reyer, Dr. 99, 144, 166, 201, 229, 285, 301
Riley, L.B. 163, 170
   Riley, Lauzenia B. 167
Rimmelin, Marie Dr. 127, 285
   Rimmelin 127, 285
ring 55, 65, 122, 139, 173, 268
Robert Nix 140, 160
Roberts, George H. Dr. 84, 89, 167
Roberts Park Methodist Episcopal Church 48
Rügenwalder 15, 17, 26. *See also* Rügenwaldermünde
Rügenwaldermünde 11, 15, 27, 29, 30, 140, 202, 227, 317
Rush County, 210

S

Salvation Army 100, 225
Schweitzer, Ada Dr. 66
scream 103, 105, 122, 150, 151, 198, 208
Shannondale Cemetery 244
Shea, Alice T. 163
Shelby County 9, 190, 192, 195, 216, 322
Shiloh Colored Baptist Church 102
Simmonds, J.P. Dr. 60, 61
Simon, Otto
   Simon 148, 170, 283, 299, 312
Sluss, John Dr. 67, 69
   Sluss, Dr. 67, 69
Smith, J.W. 108

Smith 108
snake 95, 99, 178
Solano, Solito 131
Sondermann, Froeda
  Sondermann, Frieda 167
Spaan, Henry N.
  Spann 185, 288, 312
State Board of Health 49, 50, 51, 53, 54, 55, 56, 57, 60, 66, 68, 83, 92, 125, 137, 138, 176, 189, 214, 215, 229, 238, 264, 265, 266, 272, 289, 290, 300, 312, 321
Stewart, George M. 148, 246, 283, 324
St. Joseph Cemetery 234
Stout's Shoe Store 98
streptococci 58
St. Vincent's Hospital 44, 76
suicide 99, 104, 108, 109, 111, 112, 113, 116, 117, 118, 119, 120, 122, 123, 124, 125, 127, 128, 129, 130, 131, 134, 136, 138, 139, 143, 146, 147, 151, 152, 159, 163, 164, 175, 179, 180, 183, 198, 199, 201, 202, 203, 205, 213, 216, 245, 251, 271
Suicide and Women 118
superintendent 49, 61, 146, 160, 163, 180, 182, 210, 230, 237, 238, 243
Sydenham Society 40, 43, 45, 325

T

Tariton, Charles S. 157
teach 12, 35, 54, 61, 62, 77, 78, 83, 85, 87, 92, 93, 124, 128, 137, 138, 177, 178, 225, 227, 233, 235
  teaching 12, 35, 54, 61, 62, 77, 78, 83, 85, 87, 92, 93, 124, 128, 137, 138, 177, 178, 225, 227, 233, 235
Templeton, Eva B. Dr. 163, 167, 179
Tenant, Nancy 281, 293
  Nancy Tennant 281, 293
Tennant. *See* Tenant, Nancy
Tetley, Olga M. 138
Thayer, Laurel 141
The Normal College of the North American Gymnastic Union 66, 76
  North American Gymnastic Union 66, 76
Tiede, Major von 16
Time Lag 121
Tousey, Elois 167
Turners 76, 77, 78, 79
Tutewiler, Harry Dunn Dr. 238
  Tutewiler 238
Tutt, Edward M. 166
typhoid 50, 52, 70, 229, 238, 239

U

Umbrella 183
United States Veterinary Medical Association 85

V

Vaught, Jewel Dr. 166
Vaught, J. H. Dr. 163, 170
Vendome Flats 105, 163, 217
verdict 113, 114, 115, 116, 161, 217, 218, 219
Virginia
  Arlington 234

W

Waggaman, G.M. Dr. 182
  Waggaman, Dr. 182
Wagner, Otto Dr. 163, 166, 210
Wailther, J.E.
  Wailther, Joseph E. 210
  Walther 160
Washington Park East Cemetery 226, 246
Watson, Frances Lee 10
Weapon 121
Webster, Harry C. 128, 162, 170, 175, 226, 280
  Webster 128, 162, 170, 175, 226, 280
wedding 139, 197, 206, 230
White Chapel Cemetery 226
White, James Paul 166
Widal test 50
William A. Holtz 147, 150, 282
  Holtz 147, 150, 282
Williams, Anna Wessels Dr. 54
Windschild 15, 16, 24, 226, 293
Windschild, Otto 16, 24, 226, 293
Women 3, 12, 17, 19, 38, 40, 43, 66, 92, 96, 116, 118, 136, 139, 142, 143, 161, 175, 188, 198, 223, 233, 234, 262, 268, 272, 273, 276, 277, 278, 293, 297, 302, 303, 304, 306, 307, 309, 312, 313, 314, 315, 321
Women's Club 66
wound 97, 99, 109, 112, 113, 116, 117, 119, 120, 121, 122, 130, 146, 181, 199, 201, 204
Wray, Albert F. 185
Wray & Campbell 185
Wynn 43, 45, 46, 70, 99, 102, 109, 111, 128, 143, 144, 166, 167, 170, 177, 196, 201, 202, 214, 231, 232, 238, 263, 268, 284, 289, 301, 303, 311, 314, 327, 328. *See also* Wynn, Frank B.
Wynn, Frank B. Dr. 43, 45, 99, 128, 144, 201, 238, 284, 301, 327

X

X-Rays 35, 70, 237, 327

Y

Young Women's Christian Association 62, 66, 92, 93, 141, 269, 270, 302
  YWCA 62, 66, 92, 93, 141, 269, 270, 302

www.ingramcontent.com/pod-product-compliance
Lightning Source LLC
Chambersburg PA
CBHW080407230426
43662CB00016B/2339